Rabbi Abraham Isaac Kook
and Jewish Spirituality

REAPPRAISALS IN JEWISH SOCIAL AND INTELLECTUAL HISTORY

GENERAL EDITOR: ROBERT M. SELTZER

RABBI ABRAHAM ISAAC KOOK AND JEWISH SPIRITUALITY

Edited by Lawrence J. Kaplan
and David Shatz

NEW YORK UNIVERSITY PRESS
NEW YORK AND LONDON

NEW YORK UNIVERSITY PRESS
New York and London

"Poetry of Spirituality" by Jerome Gellman is reprinted by permission of *Daat: A Journal of Jewish Philosophy and Kabbalah* (Winter 1991).

"Tolerance and Its Theoretical Basis in the Teaching of Rav Kook" by Benjamin Ish-Shalom is reprinted in translation by permission of *Daat: A Journal of Jewish Philosophy and Kabbalah* (Winter 1988).

"Remarks on the Rabbinic Rulings of Rabbi Kook" by M. Z. Nehorai is reprinted in translation by permission of *Tarbiz* 59 (1990), 481–505.

"Zion and Jerusalem-The Jewish State in the Thought of Abraham Isaac Kook" by Jerome Gellman is reprinted by permission of the Ben Gurion Research Institute of Ben Gurion University, Beer Sheeva, Israel, where it was originally presented at the conference, "The Making of the Israeli Citizen."

"What Would HaRav Kuk Have to Say About the State of Israel Today?" by Tamar Ross is reprinted by permission of *Jewish Action* (Spring/Summer 1988).

Rabbi Abraham Isaac Kook and Jewish spirituality / edited by Lawrence
J. Kaplan and David Shatz.
p. cm. — (Reappraisals in Jewish social and intellectual
history)
Includes bibliographical references and index.
ISBN 0-8147-4652-7 (cloth) — ISBN 0-8147-4653-5 (pbk.)
1. Kook, Abraham Isaac, 1865–1935. 2. Orthodox Judaism—
History—20th century. 3. Religious Zionism. I. Kaplan, Lawrence.
II. Shatz, David. III. Series.
BM755.K66R285 1995
296.8'32'092—dc20 94-17494
CIP

New York University Press books are printed on acid-free paper, and
their binding materials are chosen for strength and durability.

Manufactured in the United States of America

10 9 8 7 6 5 4 3 2 1

Contents

Acknowledgments

Work on this book began several years ago, in the aftermath of two stimulating conferences held in 1985 and 1986 to mark the fiftieth anniversary of Rav Kook's passing. The conferences were held at Stern College for Women of Yeshiva University and the Graduate Center of the City University of New York. They were conceived and organized by Rabbi Zevulun Charlop, dean of the Rabbi Isaac Elchanan Theological Seminary and descendant of Rav Yaakov Moshe Ḥarlap, one of Rav Kook's closest associates. Rabbi Charlop headed the international Rav Kook Memorial Committee, whose co-chair was Hermann Merkin. The late Jacob Hartstein, of blessed memory, formerly president of Kingsborough Community College, served as chair of the conference committee.

Shortly after the conferences, Robert M. Seltzer, Professor of History at Hunter College and the Graduate Center of the City University of New York and editor of the New York University Press series to which this book belongs, suggested that we build on some of the conference materials, invite other contributions, and produce ultimately a collection of essays that would bring the thought of Rav Kook to a wider segment of the academic community. While most of the essays that appear here were solicited especially for the anthology, the contributions of Lawrence Fine, Marvin Fox, Lawrence Kaplan, and Norman Lamm originated as papers delivered at one or the other of the conferences.

We also gratefully acknowledge the assistance and advice of our editors at New York University Press, first Kitty Moore and later Niko Pfund, Jennifer Hammer, Despina Papazoglou Gimbel, and David Updike. Rochelle Graubard, Sylvia Gross, and Andrew Ng provided typing assistance.

viii ACKNOWLEDGMENTS

Bella Hass Weinberg, professor of library and information science at St. John's University, New York, graciously clarified some issues pertaining to the index.

Some of the essays included here have been published or delivered elsewhere as well. We gratefully acknowledge the following sources for granting permission to utilize materials: the Ben Gurion Research Institute of Ben Gurion University, Beer Sheva, Israel, for permission to publish Jerome Gellman's "Zion and Jerusalem," delivered at a conference on "The Making of the Israeli Citizen"; *Daat: A Journal of Jewish Philosophy and Kabbalah*, for permission to reprint Jerome Gellman's article, "Poetry of Spirituality," from its winter 1991 issue and also to publish an English version of an article by Benjamin Ish-Shalom on tolerance that appeared in its winter 1988 issue; *Jewish Action*, for permission to reprint Tamar Ross's article, "What Would Rav Kook Have to Say about the State of Israel Today?," from its spring/summer 1988 issue; and *Tarbiz*, for permission to publish an English version of Michael Nehorai's "Remarks on the Rabbinic Rulings of Rabbi Kook," from volume 59 (1990). The format of the notes has been altered. Some notes have been abridged in the essays by Benjamin Ish-Shalom and Michael Z. Nehorai.

L. J. K.
D. S.

Note on Transliterations and Citations

Rav Avraham Yitzhak ha-Kohen Kook is often referred to by his acronym, ha-R-'-Y-H. Pronunciations of the acronym differ, however, and this poses a problem for anyone undertaking a transliteration. Rather than seek to impose consistency, we have let our authors follow their own preferred transliterations ("ha-Reiyah," "ha-Rayah," or "ha-Reayah").

Most of Rav Kook's works have been printed several times, and some (such as *Arpelei Tohar*) have appeared in different editions under different editors. Consequently, one author may cite a given work differently from another for example, by giving a different year of publication. We have preserved the references as originally submitted by our authors, rather than seek uniformity of citation. In the bibliography, only the most recent editions are cited.

In transliterations of book and article titles, we have used the spelling "Kook" rather than "Kuk" because of the familiarity of the former.

Contributors

ELLA BELFER is Associate Professor and Head of the Department of Political Studies at Bar-Ilan University. She is editor of *Spiritual Leadership in Israel* and author of *Malkhut Shamayim and the State of Israel: The Political Dimension of Judaism*. A Fellow of the Israel Academy for Advanced Studies (1980–81), she has worked extensively in general and Jewish political thought and culture.

SHALOM CARMY teaches Jewish studies and philosophy at Yeshiva University. A consulting editor of *Tradition*, he is a translator of the anthology *The World of Rav Kook's Thought* as well as of *Shevivim*, a selection of Rav Kook's writings. He is coauthor, with Norman Lamm, of a reader on Ḥasidism and editor of *Modern Scholarship in Talmud Torah: Contributions and Limitations*. His numerous articles focus on biblical studies and on such topics in Jewish thought as prayer, repentance, and Zionism.

ROBERT CARROLL holds a master's degree in Jewish philosophy from the Bernard Revel Graduate School of Yeshiva University and has studied Jewish mysticism as a doctoral candidate in Jewish Studies at New York University. He received ordination from the Rabbi Isaac Elchanan Theological Seminary.

LAWRENCE FINE is the Irene Kaplan Leiwant Professor of Jewish Studies at Mount Holyoke College. He taught for many years at Indiana University and served as the Padnos Visiting Professor of Judaic Studies at the University of Michigan. His work in the field of Jewish mysticism has been especially concerned with understanding the experiential and devotional aspects of kabbalistic life.

He has published *Safed Spirituality, Essential Papers on Kabbalah,* and numerous articles on the history of Jewish mysticism.

MARVIN FOX is Professor Emeritus of Jewish Philosophy at Brandeis University. His numerous works include *Interpreting Maimonides: Studies in Methodology, Metaphysics and Moral Philosophy.* He is a founder and former president of the Association for Jewish Studies and a member of the Governing Council of the World Union of Jewish Studies. He is currently writing a book on the philosophical foundations of Jewish ethics.

JEROME I. GELLMAN is Associate Professor of Philosophy at Ben-Gurion University of the Negev. He is the author of *Fear, Trembling, and The Fire: Kierkegaard and Ḥasidic Masters on the Binding of Isaac.* He has published numerous articles on the philosophy of religion and on Jewish thought, including several on Rav Kook.

WARREN ZEV HARVEY is Associate Professor of Jewish Thought at the Hebrew University. He has published many articles on medieval and modern Jewish thought, with special emphasis on Maimonides, Crescas, and Spinoza. He is also a coeditor of the journal *Tarbiz.*

BENJAMIN ISH-SHALOM is a Lecturer in Jewish Thought at the Hebrew University and, in addition, Founder and Rector of Beit Morasha of Jerusalem-Center for Advanced Jewish Studies. He has also held the Andrew N. and Rose Miller Chair in Zionism and Modern Israel at Yeshiva University. A specialist in modern Jewish philosophy, his numerous works include both Hebrew and English editions of *The World of Rav Kook's Thought* (coedited with Shalom Rosenberg) and *Rav Avraham Itzḥak HaCohen Kook: Between Rationalism and Mysticism.*

LAWRENCE J. KAPLAN is Associate Professor of Rabbinics and Jewish Philosophy in the Department of Jewish Studies at McGill University. He specializes in both medieval and modern Jewish thought and has published numerous articles in popular and scholarly journals. He is coeditor of *The Thought of Moses Maimonides* and received a special commendation from the National Jewish Book Council for his translation from the Hebrew of Rabbi Joseph B. Soloveitchik's *Halakhic Man*.

NORMAN LAMM is President of Yeshiva University and Jakob and Erna Michael Professor of Jewish Philosophy. His many books include *Faith and Doubt, Torah Lishmah: Torah for Torah's Sake in the Works of Rabbi Ḥayyim of Volozhin and His Contemporaries, Torah U-Madda: The Encounter of Religious Learning and Worldly Knowledge in the Jewish Tradition*, and a forthcoming reader on Ḥasidism (with Shalom Carmy). His scholarly articles focus on medieval Jewish thought, Jewish mysticism, and contemporary problems in Jewish thought and law. Dr. Lamm is the founding editor of *Tradition*, editor of Ktav's *Library of Jewish Law and Ethics*, and a member of New York State's Ethics Commission.

MICHAEL Z. NEHORAI is a member of the department of philosophy at Bar-Ilan University. He has published numerous articles on medieval and modern Jewish thought. He was ordained by the Yeshivah Merkaz Ha-Rav, founded by Rav Kook.

TAMAR ROSS is Senior Lecturer in the department of philosophy at Bar-Ilan University and also teaches Jewish Thought at Midreshet Lindenbaum in Jerusalem. Her many scholarly articles focus on traditional Jewish thought from the sixteenth century through the present, with emphasis on the tensions between rationalism and mysticism and on the repercussions of post-Kantian thought. Her doctoral dissertation at the Hebrew University was a philosophical examination of the Musar movement.

DAVID SHATZ is Professor of Philosophy at Yeshiva University. He has published numerous articles on both general and Jewish philosophy. His papers in general philosophy focus on epistemology, ethics, and the problem of free will, while those in Jewish philosophy focus on Maimonides and on twentieth-century rabbinic figures. He is coeditor of *Contemporary Philosophy of Religion* and *Definitions and Definability*.

Introduction

David Shatz and Lawrence J. Kaplan

While the legacy of Rabbi Abraham Isaac Kook (1865–1935), first Ashkenazic chief rabbi of mandatory Palestine, has been, in the words of one observer, "a ubiquitous, sometimes subterranean, sometimes explosive force in Israeli intellectual life,"[1] intellectuals in North America are only now beginning to evince appreciation of Rav Kook's profundity as a thinker and to take stock of his extraordinary impact and importance. Attractive English translations of Rav Kook's essays, letters, poems, and parts of his books have appeared over the past decade, and articles on Rav Kook are becoming more frequent and conspicuous in popular and scholarly journals.[2] But readers—especially when a thinker's writings are as difficult, allusive, and ambiguous as Rav Kook's—need more clarity than primary texts alone can convey, and require more scope, comprehensiveness, and interpretive diversity than an occasional journal article or even a good introductory essay can provide. What is needed are collections that bring to English-speaking audiences, in a systematic, organized, accessible fashion, a range of analyses and interpretations of the central issues in Rav Kook's thought.

In an attempt to help fill this gap, we bring together in these pages some of the leading interpreters of Rav Kook in the academic worlds of Israel, Canada, and the United States, and thereby open for discussion a wide spectrum of aspects of the Kook legacy. Our emphasis is on essays that have not been previously published and that are accessible and interesting to the general reader.[3]

I

Fascination with Rav Kook can be traced to several sources. The first is sheer admiration for the man. Kook's incredible combination of talents—talmudist, halakhist, kabbalist, mystic, moralist, poet, and communal leader—is itself cause for attention, though it was a natural expression of Kook's world outlook, which extolled breadth and derided narrow specialization. More striking still is the quality of his mind and work, attested to by an unusual gamut of admirers. In a study of the talmudic methodologies of such rabbinic luminaries as Rabbi Ḥayyim Soloveitchik, Rabbi Meir Simḥah Ha-kohen, the Ḥazon Ish (Rabbi Avraham Yeshayahu Karelitz), and others, the late talmudic scholar Rabbi Shlomo Yosef Zevin penned the following encomium in his chapter on Rav Kook:

> It would be no exaggeration to state that the great luminary, Rav Kook, of blessed memory, was the one person among the leading Torah scholars of our generation who possessed complete and equal mastery of both Halakhah [Jewish law] and Aggadah [nonlegal portions of Judaism, encompassing Jewish thought, literature, and the like]. What does mastery signify? When a person would ask him a question about some halakhic matter, Rav Kook did not have to research the issue before responding. Rather, he would on the spot present all the relevant Talmudic texts and then proceed to move from the Talmud to the Rambam [Maimonides] and from the Rambam to other halakhic giants; and in the course of his presentation he would illuminate obscure issues and clarify difficult texts, would make acute observations and engage in penetrating analysis, as if he had just been studying the matter under discussion. And if the questioner was himself a Torah scholar who had thoroughly researched the subject before presenting his question to Rav Kook, he would be astounded to see how Rav Kook, without any prior preparation, would, in the course of his response, come up with a multitude of new and original insights into the entire issue.
>
> But this was not only true for halakhic matters. The world of Aggadah was equally under his control. Vision and poetry, thought and speculation, theological reflections and observations—all would pour forth from him in an unending stream. . . .
>
> Indeed, Rav Kook was unique in his towering stature in both the realms of Halakhah and Aggadah, in both the exoteric and the esoteric teachings of Judaism. But what was even more wondrous was that in his person both worlds blended together to form a single splendid entity.[4]

Rabbi Zevin's words testify to the stature Rav Kook earned as rabbinic scholar in the eyes of a man who himself was one of the great rabbinic scholars of recent decades. For an assessment of Rav Kook the mystic, it suffices to quote the preeminent scholar of Jewish mysticism, the late Gershom Scholem. Rav Kook's *Orot ha-Kodesh*, Scholem writes, is "a veritable *theologia mystica* of Judaism equally distinguished by its originality and the richness of the author's mind. It is the last example of productive kabbalistic thought of which I know."[5] Here, in the quotations from Zevin and Scholem, are two tributes to Rav Kook, focused on two different spheres of his activity, from two scholars of diametrically opposed religious orientations. Their evaluations are hardly idiosyncratic. During his lifetime Rav Kook was revered by great traditionalist rabbinic scholars, critically trained orthodox historians, and secularly inclined modern Hebrew writers, all of whom, from their widely varying perspectives, looked to Rav Kook for inspiration and guidance.[6]

Scholem's remarks make clear that we have here a body of thought that displays exceptional richness and depth. But Rav Kook is also studied because of a persistent conviction that his teachings are of relevance to the contemporary setting. More than any other Orthodox thinker in modern times, he addressed, squarely and boldly, the confrontation between Judaism and the modern world. Responding to the rise of secular Jewish nationalism in the late nineteenth century, he produced the most eloquent, rich, and full-blown conception of religious Zionism yet articulated in modern times. His famous policy of tolerance, openness, and love for all, is invoked by many traditional Jews in the course of urging contact and cooperation between religious and secular Jews in Israel. Rav Kook also offered insight and perspective on modern thinkers, theories, and movements, from Spinoza and Schopenhauer to Kant, Darwin, and Bergson. The talmudic teaching, "A person ought not pray save in a place that has windows" (Berakhot 34b), was interpreted by Kook symbolically, as a call to awareness and receptivity to the world at large.[7] Judaism is a religion to be lived. Living means taking one's culture, technology, and social setting seriously, striving to understand them, and attempting to locate their significance within a broader spiritual vision.

Kook, then, engaged the modern world, and he serves as a natural model to those Jews who seek a religious understanding of and response to the culture and politics of the modern age. But it is precisely here, when we seek to grasp Rav Kook's thought and legacy, that our path becomes fraught with hermeneutical dangers.

II

Our problem is really threefold: determining what Kook taught; determining whether his teachings, even when disambiguated, apply to a changed set of political and social circumstances; and determining who is entitled to address the first two issues, that is, who is entitled to interpret him. Let us elaborate on the first and third of these difficulties; the second will be illuminated through the essays in the volume.

First, interpreting Kook. To begin with, much, perhaps the bulk, of what Rav Kook wrote has not been published, and access to manuscripts has been made difficult by disciples who zealously guard the master's heritage. We do not even know how much we do not have. A text found in newer published versions may be discrepant with that in manuscripts or earlier published articles; and while some of these discrepancies are well known to scholars, others may exist undetected. Assuming even that we had all Rav Kook's writings in pristine, original form, our problems would only just begin. Kook was not a systematic writer. His writings are the very antithesis of the carefully edited, checked and rechecked work. He presented his thoughts as "fresh warm bread on the day of its taking."[8] A prominent disciple described his work as "without a sense of composition, like the pronouncements of day-by-day visions."[9] Much of his writing is aphoristic and episodic; spontaneity is its hallmark. The result is a need for hesitation and uncertainty on the part of the interpreter when dealing with inconsistencies in the corpus. Are we dealing with two opposing thoughts that reflect different moods or moments? Did Kook's views perhaps evolve over time? Such questions become urgent when we deal with Rav Kook's views on such issues as education, imagination and intellect, the proper attitude toward sinners, and others. Compounding the problems, Kook, in concert with other mystics, protests that language is inadequate to the task of expression. "The world is sustained by the secret."[10]

We alluded earlier to the fact that Rav Kook's teachings may be applied in varying ways. A student attempting to extract a message from Rav Kook's writings for today may be tempted to highlight, underscore, or elaborate certain strands to the neglect of others. The problem has been elegantly formulated by Hillel Goldberg:

> Other than for purposes of hagiographic lip service, it is generally forgotten in Israel that the Kuk legacy is complex. . . . In contemporary times, Rabbi Kuk's multi-dimensional legacy is narrowed to suit a number of divergent, preconceived purposes. To traditional apologists for Gush Emunim, he is used to provide the intellectual foundations for establishing settlements in Judea and Samaria under any and all conditions. To anti-traditionalists he becomes the paradigm of restraint and leniency, far too sophisticated for his benighted constituency. To non-modern traditionalists, again he becomes a man of restraint and leniency, but thereby too unsophisticated for his constituency. To aspiring traditionalist scholars of contemporary Jewish thought, he is made the symbol of tradition in intellectual encounter with its age. . . . Name your policy—whatever it is—and you will find a sympathetic ear ready to call down Rabbi Kuk's name upon it and sanctify it. Further, to Zvi Yehudah Kuk, Rabbi Kuk's son, only direct disciples, raised in Rabbi Kuk's hearth, legitimately interpret Rabbi Kuk; while to Israeli scholars, only those who objectively analyze his writings legitimately interpret him. Now, elements of these widely divergent views can be reconciled, and multi-faceted influence can be a sign of profundity. But Rabbi Kuk's legacy is more manifold than any single one of his interpreters would have us believe. The tight compartmentalization of his legacy into essentially mutually exclusive concepts betrays exploitation of the legacy for polemical purposes.[11]

The state of affairs Goldberg portrays proves to be an especially unfortunate one when we call to mind a leitmotif of Rav Kook's thought: his insistence on never mistaking the part for the whole. To slice up Rav Kook's teachings, preserving some and ignoring others, not only flouts general standards of intellectual integrity, but in this case betrays the very principles Rav Kook urged. He, more than anyone else, cautioned against the dangers of parochialism and espoused balance and breadth.

Faced with these problems of interpretation and application, no

Kook scholar should proceed without a healthy measure of caution and modesty. And there is another serious methodological concern, noted by Goldberg. Many of Rav Kook's disciples in Israel would protest the very idea of an academic group approaching Kookian texts. Academics stand at too much of a distance; they lack first-hand, intimate contact with the man. Only disciples, who form part of a living chain of tradition, are in a position to grasp the true spirit of Rav Kook's teaching and determine its contemporary meaning and relevance. Or so many have argued.

We certainly make no claim to privileged access or exclusivity. We also would respond, however, that there is no such thing as "the academic" perspective on Rav Kook. Academics differ in their understanding of the man, as this collection should amply illustrate. What unites them is a concern for assembling all relevant texts, establishing their accuracy, reading them carefully, inquiring into their historical contexts, finding interrelationships, and constructing, on the basis of such reasoned reflection, the most coherent and convincing interpretation possible. It is hard to see how a methodology of this sort can mislead and obfuscate. Any misapplications of the methodology, moreover, are likely to be brought to public notice by other scholars.

We recognize full well that an anthology produced under other auspices would reflect not only a different set of substantive claims but a different style of discourse and even a different agenda of problems. Yet Rav Kook himself stressed that all views and perspectives contain value and kernels of truth as long as they do not pretend to exclusivity; he, so we believe, would be the last to deny the legitimacy of this or any other project of its kind. In his view, the more encompassing a perspective is, the more valuable it is. The best anyone can do is to confront Kook's work honestly, strive for objectivity, and keep an eye on the broader framework, all the while retaining humility and standing open to reasoned argumentation on behalf of other approaches.

III

Since our anthology is meant to appeal not only to Rav Kook specialists but also to that elusive creature, "the intelligent general reader," we have chosen to concentrate on three core areas: Rav Kook's relationship to the various streams of the Jewish tradition; his approach to faith, culture, and their interrelationship; and his political thought. In following this order we move from the sources of Rav Kook's thought to its major theoretical perspectives and principles to its more practical side. By organizing the essays around these topics, we of necessity scant more specialized topics such as evil, aesthetics, repentance, and Kook's relationship to particular thinkers or literary figures. Robert Carroll's bibliography will lead readers to works on these more specialized topics. It is the fullest bibliography on Rav Kook available in English.

Part one sets out to characterize the relationship between Kook and Jewish tradition, taking into account the multifaceted nature of that tradition: philosophy, mysticism, halakhah, and poetry.

Characterizing Rav Kook as "without question, the greatest Jewish mystical thinker of the twentieth century," Lawrence Fine's essay attempts to pinpoint the original, distinctive aspects of Kook's mysticism. At the same time, it serves as a lucid introduction to basic principles and themes of his thought. Fine stresses that Kook's mystical thought follows the Ḥasidic, as distinct from the Lurianic, tradition, by focusing on the psychological dimensions of mysticism while downplaying its speculative/theosophical aspect. Not the internal processes of the divine, but rather the subjective state of human beings, is Kook's concern. Again like Ḥasidut, Kook resists dualistic and ascetic tendencies of the sort we find in early and sixteenth-century kabbalah. He has a positive evaluation of the material world. As Fine observes, Kook's emphasis on finding the divine *within* the material provides him with a conceptual basis for his religious Zionism. For Kook, Fine writes, "Israel's spiritual life will only flourish when its body is rejuvenated." It is interesting to note that already in Fine's essay the three areas we have chosen to treat intermesh. Fine moves from the mystic sources of Rav Kook's thought to its fundamental principles to some practical implications. This blend may be found in many of the essays in this volume, though not necessarily in equal measures.

Lawrence Kaplan examines Rav Kook's creative use and transformation of the Jewish philosophical tradition in developing his worldview. In particular, Kaplan focuses upon Rav Kook's highly complex and dialectical relationship with the thought of Maimonides. Both Maimonides and Rav Kook believed that a human being's highest achievement is to unite intellectual knowledge of God with passionate love for God. However, Kaplan argues, while for Maimonides that union expresses itself as the pathos of intellect, for Rav Kook it gives rise to an intellectualized passion. This observation leads Kaplan to suggest that, for Rav Kook, the primary function of the Jewish philosophical tradition within the *totality* of Jewish thought is precisely to guarantee the intellectual purity of the Jew's burning passion and desire for God's closeness. At the same time, Rav Kook felt that Jewish philosophy, taken *by itself*, can only issue forth in a cold, abstract, pallid, and lifeless religious rationalism. Kaplan's analysis leads him to conclude that Rav Kook, in terms of his *substantive* views, was closer to the kabbalists than to the philosophers. He counterbalances this conclusion, however, by arguing that it was not the kabbalistic tradition, but the Jewish philosophical tradition—in particular the writings of Maimonides—that served Rav Kook as the model for how one could and should confront external cultural and intellectual challenges: "critically, seriously, honestly, openly, and, above all, unafraid."

Reacting to both Fine and Kaplan, Marvin Fox prefers to regard Rav Kook as "neither a systematic philosopher nor a systematic kabbalist." Kook's style and approach is not systematic, Fox says. He does not trade in evidence and arguments as philosophers do; he is not seeking "demonstrative truth." For these reasons he is not a systematic philosopher. Fox also believes that Kook's deemphasis of theosophy (the classical outer-directed kabbalistic study of the nature of the divine) in exchange for a concern with inwardness (the tendency stressed by Fine) sets him apart from kabbalists, who, like the philosophers, albeit in their own special modes, sought to give general accounts of reality. As an alternative, Fox views Rav Kook as "poet rather than as philosopher."

"Poetry of Spirituality," by Jerome Gellman, is an intriguing counterpoint to Fox's paper. Gellman analyzes two poems of Rav Kook: one representative of "introvertive" mystical experience, in which the divine is revealed internally, within one's human soul, the second of "extrovertive" mysticism, in which the divine is per-

ceived via contemplation of the external world of nature. Through
his analysis, Gellman portrays the spiritual world of Rav Kook
while linking his motifs and ideas to sources in Jewish tradition,
particularly midrash and kabbalah. Gellman shows that words used
to evoke emotion in these poems are not just poetic metaphors, but
refer as well, in a strikingly precise fashion, to metaphysical concepts. If, for Fox, Rav Kook's kabbalah can better be seen as a form
of poetry, for Gellman, Kook's poetry, if not kabbalistic theosophy
in a strict sense, certainly is grounded in a well-defined kabbalistic
worldview. And if, for Fine, Rav Kook's kabbalah is fundamentally
psychological, Gellman's analysis suggests a correlation between
the language of inwardness and theosophical doctrines. Gellman's
essay is the closest reading of Kook's poetry to appear in English—
indeed, in any language—and it well documents both the richness
of Kook's language and allusions and the complexity of his thought.

If there is one moral that emerges from these explorations of Rav
Kook's relationship to the varying streams of Jewish tradition, it is
that Rav Kook defies easy labelling.

While one may quarrel to what extent Rav Kook was either a
kabbalist, philosopher, or poet of mysticism, no one can gainsay
Rav Kook's preeminent role as a talmudist. No collection devoted
to Rav Kook, therefore, can be balanced and rounded without representing him as rabbinic scholar and decisor and in particular
without addressing the question of the relationship between Rav
Kook's more strictly halakhic activity and scholarship and his general religious worldview. Kook's responsa and talmudic commentaries occupy numerous volumes. Because Rav Kook so clearly valued
certain modern developments and stood open to nontraditional
views and movements, one might presume that his practical decisions would tend toward leniency, particularly in matters possessing national significance. Indeed, based on a highly selective
sample of his rulings, some have maintained that Rav Kook in fact
took a liberal approach when ruling on such matters. Challenging
such depictions, Michael Nehorai insists that precisely regarding
such national questions Kook adopted a conservative halakhic
stance. On such vital issues as milking animals on the Sabbath,
voting rights for women, and autopsies, Nehorai shows that Kook
displayed a striking tendency toward strictness. Even his celebrated

ruling setting forth a halakhic device that would permit Jews to work the land during a sabbatical year is, in Nehorai's view, hedged with many qualifications and not as permissive as often painted. How can this be, asks Nehorai, given Kook's passionate attachment to the national revival and to the furthering of Zionist goals? Nehorai suggests that Rav Kook was convinced that his age was "a short, transient episode whose task was only to prepare the way for the real and ideal state of Israel." His halakhic rulings are geared to this ideal messianic age. That is, to decide leniently on national issues is to give normative status to contemporary outlooks that in truth are but part of a dialectical preparation for the ideal Jewish society of the future. While Nehorai's portrayal of Rav Kook is surely controversial, inasmuch as it goes against common conceptions, it stands as the only major study in English to date of Rav Kook as halakhist; and at the very least, it serves as a much needed and healthy corrective for the misleading and rather simplistic picture of Rav Kook as a religious or halakhic "liberal."

IV

For all its breadth and diversity, Rav Kook's philosophy is remarkably unified. Much of his thought is an application of a single fundamental principle: that all reality has its source in the divine. Since all things derive from one divine source, all opposition, discord, and conflict are illusory; in the profoundest vision of things, all reality is one and unified.

Rav Kook's principle of unity is not without its ambiguities. Quite clearly we experience the world as one of fragmentation and pluralism. Why is this so? It is tempting to suppose that the fragmented character of our experience is due solely to our subjective failings or limitations; the problem lies solely in our perception—reality itself is unified and harmonious. Yet Rav Kook also affirms that an ideal, preexistent unity has been ruptured by sin. Such an assertion lends a more objective character to the fragmentation we experience—we encounter a reality that is indeed, in some sense, torn, and our human task is to mend it, restoring the ideal unity of old. The question as to whether fragmentation is objective or subjective affects another issue, namely, what Rav Kook means when he speaks of progressing toward unity. Are we merely progressing toward a more accurate perception of the unity that is already there? Or is the cosmos itself progressing toward unity? These alternatives are perhaps not even exclusive. Rav Kook on occasion suggests that our perception itself restores unity to the cosmos, while on the other hand, the evolution toward ever higher levels of unity in the cosmos impacts on our perceptions. These problems of interpretation deserve serious attention. But ambiguities aside, we may say that just as in Rav Kook's view, the divine is the root of all things, so, too, the principle of unity is the root of all else in Rav Kook's thought. However—to extend the analogy—just as one can only appreciate the divine unity as it reveals itself in the manifold, concrete workings of historical, empirical reality, so too one can appreciate Rav Kook's principle of unity only as it is brought to bear on an incredible variety of issues—metaphysical, social, political, and cultural.

Cognizant of the centrality of this theme of unity, the essays in Part Two all develop consequences and implications of the monistic principle, while at the same time attempting to define its limitations.

Norman Lamm's essay both examines Rav Kook's monism, or as Lamm prefers to term it, harmonism, and shows it at work. Lamm's essay, as the title indicates, treats three apparently distinct themes in the thought of Rav Kook: harmonism, the new, and the sacred. Lamm, however, demonstrates that these three themes are, as one might expect, interrelated. And it is precisely harmonism, that is, the principle of unity, that serves as the essay's unifying principle. Thus, after an analysis of the principle of harmonism as embodied in both Rav Kook's thought and life, Lamm proceeds to show how Rav Kook's commitment to harmonism and his critical and discriminating esteem for the novel are deeply bound together. On the one hand, "the successful perception of the underlying unity of existence . . . lead[s] to holy novelty." On the other hand, the radical novelty of the situation created by the Zionist experiment, by the renaissance of Eretz Israel redeemed by its own children, made it clear to Rav Kook that "the foundation of spirituality must no longer be that of the individual in his relation to his Maker, but that of the people . . . and that . . . in turn, must be based on the . . . integration . . . of the sacred and the profane."

It is precisely this theme of the integration of the sacred and the profane in Rav Kook's thought that, very naturally then, forms the concluding part of Lamm's essay. Here, Lamm's analysis of the roots of Rav Kook's view on this question in Ḥasidic sources neatly dovetails with and complements the issues treated in Fine's essay. Lamm shows how Rav Kook's position builds upon but goes further than Ḥasidism. For Ḥasidism—Lamm argues—the raw power of the sacred annihilates the profane, while for Rav Kook, the profane is not annihilated by the sacred, but rather both sacred and profane are included together in the comprehensive embrace of the holy of holies. This conclusion of Rav Kook, so Lamm believes, gives power-ful expression to his deep appreciation of the religious credibility and enduring significance of the secular world.

Whereas Lamm elegantly articulates the drive of Rav Kook to-ward integration, David Shatz, in an essay titled "The Integration of Religion and Culture: Its Scope and Limits in the Thought of Rav Kook," highlights the limits of that integrative impulse.[12] Shatz points to a disparity between Rav Kook's frequent exhortations to Jews to open themselves to the full range of secular culture, and a certain conservatism and absence of integration with respect to specific issues, such as, the conflict between evolution and Torah. Shatz argues that Rav Kook's willingness to integrate secular cul-ture with religious teachings was inhibited by certain facets of his epistemology. First, Rav Kook stressed the innate character of religious knowledge and at times seems to see religious knowledge as independent of general science and culture. Second, for Rav Kook, truth is not fixed or static but rather evolves over the course of history. If no particular representation of truth in a particular period can lay claim to finality, then the pressure to accommodate any particular scientific or cultural teaching or body of theory within one's prior religious worldview is correspondingly lightened. Shatz also seeks to explain the fact that Rav Kook did not person-ally cultivate the study of secular disciplines to the degree one would expect given his theoretical pronouncements.

Benjamin Ish-Shalom shows the workings of Rav Kook's monism in a central motif of his writings: tolerance. As Ish-Shalom points out, religion, because it seemingly attempts to give expression to absolute truth, is prima facie not congenial to pluralism and does not rank tolerance high on its scale of values. Yet Rav Kook's monism entails pluralism and a policy of tolerance. Arousing the ire of many traditionalist Jews of his time who vehemently denied any positive value to secular Zionism, Rav Kook accorded at least partial legitimacy even to secular, atheistic nationalism: "We know that no thought in the world is vain." All dimensions of reality reveal divinity. Even atheism has its source in holiness; even secular nationalism has positive aspects. This general approach governs Rav Kook's attitude to the whole gamut of cultural expression, including philosophy, science, other religions, and moral systems. The truth is too great, too rich, and too multifaceted to be grasped or exhausted by any one particular theory. In every theory inheres a grain of truth. To be sure, Rav Kook affirms distinctions in level and value—the more embracing a theory and the less fanatical and exclusionary, the more valuable it is. Not surprisingly, Judaism ranks highest on this scale. But no view should be rejected totally.

Yet Rav Kook set limits to freedom of inquiry, a point elaborated in differing ways by both Ish-Shalom and Shalom Carmy. Ish Shalom distinguishes between theoretical tolerance (to which Rav Kook was committed) and practical tolerance. On concrete public issues, Rav Kook adopted "extremist and uncompromising positions." This, Ish-Shalom suggests, is because he appreciated the value of the war of ideas in maintaining "a healthy balance among disparate views." Carmy reminds us that Rav Kook had to develop an "ethics of belief" within a halakhic framework and to that extent had to impose bounds on thought and inquiry. In this context Carmy isolates several philosophical principles that determine when one ought to assent to the propositional beliefs affirmed by one's national or faith community. He then subjects these to a rigorous philosophical critique. This highly analytical approach to Kook's theory of belief tacitly presupposes that this theory rests on an underlying, if not completely articulated, structure of argument that would make such a method appropriate. In this respect Carmy's approach forms a striking contrast to that of Fox, which, as we may recall, depreciates the role of evidence and argument in Rav Kook's writings.

Common to these essays is an awareness of frequent tensions between theory and practice in Rav Kook. On the level of theory all views have value and need to be integrated into a harmonious and all-embracing totality. On the level of practice Rav Kook accepts some propositions and rejects others, often doing so with vehemence, confidence, and assertiveness.

A final essay in this section, by Tamar Ross, deals with another aspect of interaction between religion and culture. Earlier we broached the possibility that, for Rav Kook, enhanced spiritual perception can effect the restoration of unity to the cosmos, while, reciprocally, social, cultural and technological changes may give rise to expanded spiritual consciousness. As understood by Ross, Rav Kook indeed maintains that enhancement of our spiritual vision can improve material existence and heighten our ability to control our physical environment. Advances in medicine and technology are made possible by modifications of controlling images that symbolize how humanity relates to its environment. Our greater sense of connectedness, integrity, and freedom of movement creates new modes of interaction with our surroundings. In turn, each new improvement, by enlarging the definition of natural possibility, opens new vistas of cognition and understanding. This sort of reciprocal spiral will ultimately enable human beings to conquer even death itself. The monistic vision in which one transcends the limits of natural consciousness, complemented by a positive attitude to culture and technological activism, reaches its climax in this remarkable triumph.

V

The aspect of Rav Kook's thought that has captured the greatest public attention, and at the same time has been the greatest source of controversy, is his views on politics—in particular, Zionism and messianism and the relationship between the two. Rav Kook saw the return to Zion, the upbuilding of the land of Israel, and the renaissance of the Jewish people in that land as an integral part of a broader historical process invested with messianic significance. To be sure, all these developments were seen by him not only as messianic events but as realizations of the monistic vision, in which the soul of the Jewish people is reunited with its body—he compared the return to the land with the resurrection of the dead—and in which the full richness of Judaism, the integration of religion with culture, holy with profane, is made manifest in historical reality.[13] It is interesting to inquire whether the return to Zion as a realization of Rav Kook's monistic ideal can be divorced from seeing the return within messianic categories. Of course, for Rav Kook, the monistic vision and the messianic vision are two sides of one coin; still, one can ask whether they can be detached from each other through a process of delicate conceptual surgery. This is a much debated issue among interpreters of Rav Kook today.

Elsewhere, Aviezer Ravitsky has set Rav Kook's Zionism within the broader context of late nineteenth- and early twentieth-century approaches to Jewish nationalism—its relationship to Jewish tradition on the one hand, and to the messianic vision on the other.[14] Ravitsky focuses on the fact that, within classical Jewish thought, the messianic redemption will be whole, complete, total. How could the Zionist enterprise, which was clearly partial in nature and, with the passage of time, growing increasingly secular, cohere with this traditional messianic vision? Ravitsky delineates three pre-Kookian responses to this problem. The first, endorsed by the bulk of traditional orthodoxy, rejected the Zionist program precisely because of its deviation from the messianic vision, viewing it instead as an illegitimate exploitation of the traditional halo associated with messianism. Zionist activism, in this view, inevitably leads to secularism; redemption is taken out of the hands of God and given over to the hands of man. Traditional orthodoxy, it was claimed, would never accept this ersatz version of redemption. The second view discussed by Ravitsky, that of the "forerunners" of religious Zionism, based itself on a minority stream within traditional Jewish messianism. These "forerunners" gave a more activistic cast to messianic redemption, seeing it more as an ongoing process in which human beings could play a role than as a one-time divine supernatural event. Within this perspective the Zionist return to and upbuilding of the land could be seen as the initial stage of this redemptive process. This second position, espoused by religious thinkers of the mid-nineteenth century, became, however, more difficult to maintain as the Zionist movement grew increasingly secular. In response to this problem, those religious thinkers who wished to maintain a positive attitude toward Zionism adopted still a third view. They distinguished sharply between political Zionism and religious messianism—denying any redemptive significance to the former. Precisely because of this sharp distinction, there could not be any competition between the two. The function of political Zionism is to ensure the physical well-being of the dispersed and persecuted Jewish people. As Rabbi Jacob Reines, founder of the religious Zionist Mizrachi movement, stated: "If my family is trapped in a burning house, it matters not to me whether the person who rushes to their rescue is religious or secular."

Such a neat division between Zionism and messianism proved hard to maintain, given the traditional religious and messianic significance associated with the return to and upbuilding of the land. It is against this background that the position of Rav Kook must be seen. Rav Kook's view constitutes a return to the second position, that of the forerunners, but set within a far broader metaphysical frame. He had before his eyes the vision of an ideal State of Israel, a state that would be "the foundation of the throne of God in the world and would unite earthly and heavenly realms." This raises the question of how Rav Kook came to terms with the dilemma of the ever-growing secularity of the Zionist enterprise. For a treatment of this issue we turn to the paper by Ella Belfer.

As Belfer notes, the traditional messianic vision was composed of two elements: the realistic-historical and the spiritual-metaphysical. Throughout history different approaches to messianism have emphasized one or the other of these elements. Rav Kook's approach stands out, for Belfer, in that it maintains that both elements must be realized to their fullest. We have here a maximalist messianic approach: "the completely spiritual, the completely material." It is in the light of this maximalist vision, coupled with his dialectical approach to the providential messianic process, that Rav Kook grapples with the secularity and physicality of the Zionist enterprise. For Rav Kook, precisely this secular, profane, and physical character of the Zionist movement is itself part of this messianic process. The secular rebellion against the holy will lead, in the final dialectical turn of the messianic drama, to the ultimate redemptive reintegration of holy and profane.

What would Rav Kook say about the State of Israel today? Israel has not become—at least not yet—"the foundation of the throne of God in the world," nor has the hoped-for reintegration of the sacred and profane occurred. Two specific questions are often raised: what would he say about Jewish settlements in the territories, and how would he address the ever-widening gap between religious and secular Jews? Or is all this just a pointless guessing game? The final three essays of the book all pose these questions in different ways.

Jerome Gellman does not seek to answer these questions with finality, but he does suggest that in Rav Kook's writings we may find certain guidelines that aid us in our own attempts to address them. Gellman opposes a common reading of Rav Kook promulgated by the religious nationalist movement Gush Emunim (Bloc of the Faithful), according to which Rav Kook, because of his messianic vision, would undoubtedly have protested the surrender of even one inch of Israeli soil. The state, in this view, exists only as an instrument for religious ends. Gellman rejects this instrumentalist reading. Based on an analysis of certain kabbalistic motifs in Rav Kook's writings, as well as certain of his publicistic statements, Gellman argues that "the purpose of [the Jewish] state is essentially to make manifest that very holiness immanent within the state itself." For Rav Kook this means that the primary goal of the Jewish state has to be the attainment of peace and the avoidance of even justified bloodshed. Territoriality must, therefore, be subordinated to morality.

Warren Zev Harvey highlights Rav Kook's thesis, expressed in a homily, that "the contemporary return to Zion is no less than a return to Mount Sinai." Harvey interprets this in two senses. First, the ideal Torah was intended to govern the entire life of the Jewish people. However, during the exile it became restricted to the ritual and "spiritual" aspects of Jewish existence. With the return to the land, once again the opportunity for the Torah to be realized in its fullness presents itself. Second, when the Torah was received, the original divine plan was for the Jewish people to be settled in their land peacefully. The biblical war of conquest led by Joshua was, for Rav Kook, the result of the sin of the golden calf. The return to the land now, however, gives us a second chance, an opportunity to realize the original ideal and to achieve the reinstitution of Jewish sovereignty in a peaceful manner. For Rav Kook, Harvey claims, these two propositions are intertwined: if "the Jews will receive the Torah in holiness, [they] will enter the Land in peace, build it up in peace, and govern it in peace." This leads to Harvey's postscript, in which he raises the question of how Rav Kook would respond today, in a situation in which neither of these hopes has been realized. The Jewish people in the Land and State of Israel have not accepted the Torah in its entirety. Certainly this is true of secular Jews. Even religious Jews continue to limit the Torah to its more ritual aspects, as was the case in exile. As for peace, after Israel's having fought six wars and with the continuing presence of the *intifada*, it remains as elusive a goal for Israel as ever. (See, however, the "post-postscript" added by Harvey after the historic peace agreement of September 1993.)

Whereas Gellman's primary focus is the issue of territories, Tamar Ross subordinates that question to that of the polarity between religious and secular Jews, and in particular to the problem posed by the secular nature of the state of Israel today. Rav Kook's optimism regarding the religious potential of secular Jewish nationalism seems to have been refuted. For Rav Kook, the national and ethical idealism underlying secular Zionism could be seen as expressions of a fundamentally religious urge. What are we to say today, however, when this idealism has largely evaporated, its place taken by an often crass materialism? Ross suggests, however, that this ideological cul-de-sac of secular Zionism may force the more thoughtful among the secularists to reexamine the religious option. She makes the further observation that just as Rav Kook in his day, while appreciative of the nationalist revival, criticized it for its one-sidedness, so in our day, while he would certainly be appreciative of the current religious revival, he might level a parallel critique at it for its equal and opposite one-sidedness.

For all the rich variety of the perspectives represented in this book, no single collection could do more than serve as an invitation to the reader to embark upon the enormously demanding yet greatly rewarding task of mining the thought of Rav Kook and exploring its application to contemporary life. It is our hope that this volume will contribute to the ever-broadening and ever-fructifying encounter with this rich and remarkable legacy.

Notes

1. Hillel Goldberg, "Review of Israeli Intellectual Life," *Tradition* 18, 1 (Summer 1979): 122.
2. See the Bibliography by Robert Carroll.
3. Two volumes of English essays on the thought of Rav Kook have appeared in recent years. *Essays on the Thought and Philosophy of Rabbi Kook*, edited by Rabbi Ezra Gellman, consists of sixteen previously published contributions on Rav Kook, together with two brief selections by him. *The World of Rav Kook's Thought*, edited by Binyamin Ish-Shalom and Shalom Rosenberg, consists, as a publisher's note indicates, of "presentations [on Rav Kook] from an Avi Chai-sponsored conference held in Jerusalem, August 19–22, 1985, on the occasion of the fiftieth anniversary of Rav Kook's death." (This collection originally appeared in Hebrew under the title *Yovel Orot*.) Both volumes are of high quality and we warmly recommend them. Our volume differs from Gellman's, however, in that most of the essays have not previously been published, and from the Ish-Shalom and Rosenberg collection in that it is less specialized, exploring the main areas of Rav Kook's thought. Still, the anthologies complement one another, and the interested reader is strongly encouraged to examine all three collections.
4. Rabbi Shlomo Yosef Zevin, *Ishim ve-Shittot* (Tel Aviv, 1958), 232.
5. Gershom Scholem, *Major Trends in Jewish Mysticism* (New York, 1941), 354 n.17. Rivka Schatz-Uffenheimer, another eminent scholar in the field of mysticism, stresses, like Scholem, Rav Kook's originality: "The perspective of his vision is not a continuation of the Jewish mystical writing he had read. He is not the continuation of the Zohar or the Cabbalah of the Ari (Rabbi Isaac Luria) or of any other Cabbalistic work. His mysticism is not only new in its answers but also in its questions." See Schatz-Uffenheimer, "Preface II," in *Abraham Isaac Kook*, trans. Ben-Zion Bokser (New York, 1978), xxii.
6. Examples of great traditionalist scholars are Rabbi Yaakov Moshe Harlap (1883–1951), head of Yeshivat Merkaz ha-Rav (the yeshiva founded by Rav Kook) and author of the multivolume works *Bet Zevul* and *Mei Marom*; and Rabbi Tzvi Pesaḥ Frank (1873–1960), chief rabbi of Jerusalem and author of the multivolume *Har Tzvi*. Critically trained Orthodox historians include Rabbi Dr. Binyamin Menashe Lewin (1879–1944), a leading authority on Geonic literature and editor of *Otzar ha-Geonim*, and Rabbi Dr. Moshe Seidel (1886–1971), Professor

of Bible at Yeshiva University and author of *Hikrei Mikra*. Examples of modern Hebrew writers are Hayyim Nahman Bialik (1873–1934), the greatest Hebrew poet of modern times, and Shmuel Yosef Agnon (1888–1970), Nobel laureate in literature and the leading writer of modern Hebrew fiction in the twentieth century.

7. *Olat Reiyah* (Jerusalem, 1985), I, 259–60.
8. *Iggerot ha-Reiyah* (Jerusalem, 1984; first published 1962), II, #687, p. 293 (referring to the work *Arpelei Tohar*).
9. Rabbi David Cohen, editorial statement in *Orot ha-Kodesh* (Jerusalem, 1938; reprint, 1955), I.
10. *Iggerot ha-Reiyah*, I, #216; see *Zohar, Idra Rabba*, Naso, III, 128a.
11. Goldberg, 123.
12. Originally Shatz's essay was to appear in this collection, but he chose to withdraw it when it became necessary to shorten our manuscript. We have retained our original summary in this introduction in order to balance our discussion of Rav Kook's views on culture.
13. *Orot* (Jerusalem, 1989), 80.
14. Ravitsky's ideas may be found in his *Ha-ketz ha-Meguleh u-Medinat ha-Yehudim* (Tel Aviv, 1993). Some years before the appearance of his Hebrew book, Professor Ravitsky kindly provided us with an English article based on the book's early chapters. However, Professor Ravitsky later revised this material for the English edition of his book, *Messianism, Zionism, and Jewish Religious Radicalism*, to be published by the University of Chicago Press. Since the later, revised version would be available in the Chicago edition, and we needed to shorten our manuscript, we and Professor Ravitsky jointly decided not to publish the earlier version. At the same time, because of the importance of Ravitsky's analysis, we have kept the summary of his essay in our introduction.

Rav Kook and the Many Streams of Jewish Tradition

CHAPTER I

Rav Abraham Isaac Kook and the Jewish Mystical Tradition

Lawrence Fine

Abraham Isaac Kook is, without question, the greatest Jewish mystical thinker of the twentieth century, and leaving aside comparison with the masters of Ḥasidic tradition, Kook is the most influential mystical figure since the dawn of the modern period. Assessing Rav Kook's work, Gershom Scholem wrote in 1941: "[It] is a veritable *theologia mystica* of Judaism equally distinguished by its originality and the richness of the author's mind. It is the last example of productive Kabbalistic thought of which I know."[1]

It is thus more than a little curious that, until rather recently, contemporary students of Jewish mysticism have, by and large, ignored Kook's contribution to the mystical tradition. For example, despite Scholem's admiration for Kook's writing, one searches in vain in the exceedingly lengthy *Bibliography of the Writings of Gershom Scholem* for any article devoted to Kook. Indeed, the bibliography on Rav Kook yields few articles, much less books, by major scholars of Jewish mysticism. The most widely known essays on Kook's religious thought have, in fact, been written not by scholars of Jewish mysticism, but by students of contemporary Jewish religious thought, most notably the discussions by Samuel Hugo Bergman and Nathan Rotenstreich.[2] As valuable as these thoughtful essays are, neither of them pretends to explore in any depth Kook's relationship to Jewish mysticism. Happily, this situation is beginning to change, as several important papers have recently appeared.[3] My goal in this paper is to make a modest contribution to this subject by asking about the kind of mystical approach taken by Rav Kook, and by painting with fairly broad strokes a picture of how it might be situated within the broader context of Jewish mysticism.

I

I want to begin by making three general observations about Rav Kook and his work in order to suggest some of the obstacles confronting the scholarly evaluation of his mystical point of view. These observations bear upon the question of why the scholarly state of affairs to which I referred exists.

To begin with a patently obvious point, Kook is a contemporary figure, in terms of the questions he asked, as well as in many of the intellectual categories he employed. His thinking has to be situated within the late 19th- and early 20th-century milieu in which he lived. Historians of Jewish mysticism are, by the very nature of their enterprise, more interested in the past than the present. They tend, for perfectly understandable reasons, to gravitate to classical periods and texts. The tendency is to regard figures such as Rav Kook, if even unconsciously, as presenting little need for the same kind of careful and systematic analysis brought to bear upon more classical authors. The inclination is to consider them as being too much contemporaries, too modern in their idiom and intellectual framework, to require or even deserve the attention of scholars who are likely to believe that their training is better suited for the complexities of premodern Judaism. The initial obstacle, then, that must be overcome, is the proclivity to take less seriously a figure such as Rav Kook simply because he is a post-traditional thinker.

Second, Kook's mystical writing is notoriously unsystematic; much of it was produced in a relatively spontaneous and inspired fashion. This is particularly true of *Orot ha-Kodesh* (The Lights of Holiness), which best represents his mystical thinking.[4] Composed over a period of fifteen years, between 1904 and 1919, *Orot ha-Kodesh* is constituted of rather brief passages that Kook recorded as they occurred to him, that is, as inspirations or illuminations. Analysis and assessment of Kook's mystical work has to take into account the fact that we do not have a systematic presentation, laid out along clearly defined lines.[5] In Rav Kook, the medium, that is, the fragmented, poetic, and ethereal quality of his language, and the message itself are inextricably linked to one another.

Third, Rav Kook was eclectic in the extreme; he was prepared to draw upon ideas and insights from the most diverse and wide range of sources. This can easily be illustrated by reference to the array of mystical sources whose influence can be discerned in *Orot ha-Kodesh*. From the period of early Kabbalah, for example, we find the influence of *Sefer ha-Bahir*, *Sha'arei Tzedek* and *Sha'arei Orah* by Joseph Gikatilla, the whole range of Zoharic literature, the commentaries on the Torah by Naḥmanides, Baḥya ben Asher, and Menachem Recanati, commentaries on *Sefer Yetzirah*, as well as *Sefer ha-Kanah* and *Ma'arekhet ha-Elohut*. From the sixteenth century Rav Kook draws on the writings of Moses Cordovero, Ḥayyim Vital's version of Lurianic Kabbalah, *Shemonah She'arim*, as well as the arrangement of Lurianic materials by Meir Poppers, *Etz Ḥayyim* and *Pri Etz Ḥayyim*. Later kabbalistic sources to which we can point include, among others, *Shenei Luḥot ha-Brit* by Isaiah Horowitz, the writings of the Maharal of Prague, *Emek ha-Melekh* by Naftali Bacharach, *Shefa' Tal* of Shabbetai Sheftel Horowitz, *Ḥesed le-Avraham* by Abraham Azulai, Joseph Ergas's *Shomer Emunim*, *Sha'ar ha-Shamayim* of Abraham Herrera, the writings of Moshe Ḥayyim Luzatto, and various Ḥasidic authors. The study of Kook's mystical thought obviously must have at its center careful analysis of the ways in which he appropriated a wide variety of mystical ideas and language.

At the same time the task of analyzing Kook's use of earlier sources has to take seriously the fact that Rav Kook's thinking was *original* in a range of fundamental ways. Some thinkers are, needless to say, more original than others. In Kook's case we are presented with a mind of unusual inventiveness, one that fashioned from the many influences upon him a highly distinctive point of view.

II

Turning our attention to Rav Kook's mystical viewpoint itself, it is possible to identify three critical aspects of his thinking. These include what I shall call his epistemology, his theological meta-physics, and his teleology. The point of departure for Rav Kook's religious thinking is epistemology, or the question of human cogni-tion, its nature, its potential, and its function. Virtually every-where one turns in Kook's writings one encounters a preoccupation with the problem of how we go about perceiving the world. Ac-cording to Kook, individuals are afflicted by the tendency to focus selectively on discrete aspects of reality to the exclusion of others. That is, our view of reality is fragmented, partial, myopic. The diversity of the world arrests our attention, freezes our perception, so that we see the world only in its diversity, its multiplicity:

> All the defects of the world, the material and the spiritual, all derive from the fact that every individual sees only the one aspect of exis-tence that pleases him, and all other aspects that are uncompre-hended by him seem to deserve purging from the world. And the thought leaves its imprint in individuals and groups, on generations and epochs, that whatever is outside one's own is destructive and disturbing. The result is the multiplication of conflict.[6]

Human cognition in its ordinary state, then, is mired in a narcis-sistic isolation, a narrow parochialism that perceives the world in a fragmentary way, as disunified and chaotic. Indeed, for most individuals the world *is* disunified and beset by chaos. This problem is directly tied to another one, namely the tendency that human beings have for focusing upon the outer appearance of all things. The senses gravitate toward the surfaces of reality which, in Rav Kook's view, comprise the outer "shell" or "garment" that conceals the true essence, an inner reality: "Only the limitations of our mental capacities impede us from glimpsing those dimensions of the spiritual domain that are immanent in every part of it. When one rises in his spiritual development his eyes will see properly."[7]

The central task of all human beings is to see the world afresh, to see it as it truly is. To discover the world in its true nature is to perceive the essential unity that underlies and inheres in all appar-ently diverse things, rather than the partial and surface realities that make up our ordinary perception. Human life ought to be nothing less than a continuous striving for expanding our con-sciousness, for widening our perception, for the ever-increasing of our awareness and perspective. It is in these terms that it is possible to understand Rav Kook's view that the philosophic mode of cognition is inadequate to the needs of enlightenment. Philosophy, he argues, by its nature concerns itself with analyzing particulars, with dissecting the world and understanding its component parts.[8] Moreover, it only concerns itself with certain aspects of the world:

> Philosophy embraces only a given part of the spiritual world. By nature it is detached from whatever is outside its sphere. By this itself it is fragmented in its being. The grace of perceiving how all thoughts, all feelings and tendencies, from the small to the large, are interdependent, how they act on each other, how separate worlds are organically related—this it cannot portray. For this reason it must always remain an aristocratic discipline, set apart for special individuals.[9]

Superior to the philosophical enterprise is the mystical perspective *(ha-Sodiyut)*, by virtue of the fact that it alone enables us to recognize "the inner unity of all existence":

> Greater than this is the mystical quest, which by its nature penetrates to the depth of all thought, all feelings, all tendencies, all aspirations, and all worlds, from beginning to end. It recognizes the inner unity of all existence, the physical and the spiritual, the great and the small, and for this reason there is, from its perspective, no bigness or smallness. Everything is important, and everything is invested with marked value. There is no lost gesture, there is no vain imagining. . . . Because of this advantage, mystical vision, in being able to embrace within itself all thoughts and all sparks of the spiritual, is alone fit to chart for us the way to go. Therefore, the mystical dimension alone is the soul of faith, the soul of the Torah. From its substance derives all that is revealed, all that is circumscribed, all that can be conceived by logic, and all that can be carried out in actions. The far reaching unity of the mystical dimension embraces all creatures, all conditions of thought and feeling, all forms of poetry and exposition, all expressions of life, all aspirations and hopes, all objectives and ideals, from the lowest depths to the loftiest heights.[10]

Elsewhere, he puts it in these terms:

> It is in the nature of a spiritual perception to embrace everything in a harmonious way. This is its distinctive characteristic, which differentiates it from an ordinary perception, which is always concerned with particulars, and which brings them together with difficulty into general categories. Those souls which are especially drawn to see things in their inwardness are attached to universality with all their strength.[11]

There *is* an important place for the analytical or rational faculty of the individual; but it exercises a preparatory role in relationship to the spiritual or mystical intuition. Thus, for example, in speaking of the unity of the domains of *halakhah* (Jewish law) and *aggadah* (theology and ethics), Kook wrote:

> After the analytical disposition has done its work of analysis in order to clarify each discipline according to its category, it must make room for the synthesizing disposition to be activated in the soul, which has been illuminated by the concept of unification. On that account will all knowledge, all the spiritual disciplines in their respective categories, be revealed as different organs in one enduring, multifaceted body that is illumined by one enduring, multifaceted living soul.[12]

The emphasis that Rav Kook placed on the role of human perception contrasts strikingly with the dominant forms of theosophical Kabbalah, that of the Zohar in the thirteenth century and Lurianic Kabbalah in the sixteenth. In these two systems contemplative imagination may be said to be outwardly directed to the theosophical plane. The focus of attention is primarily on the means by which divine emanation occurs, that is, the processes of cosmogony and theogony, be it the ten *Sefirot* in the case of earlier Kabbalah, or the more complex Lurianic pleroma with its multileveled hierarchies of divine light. It is true that both of these systems have a great deal to say about the human soul, as well as the influence upon the world of divinity exerted by human action and contemplation. But neither focuses much on the nature of psychological processes per se and their role in the mystical life.

Kook's stress on the "psychological" at the expense of the mythical and theosophical can be illustrated by reference to one aspect of Kook's interpretation of the event known in Lurianic Kabbalah as the "breaking of the vessels," *Shevirat ha-Kelim*. In Lurianic myth the "breaking of the vessels" refers to the turbulent process in which vessels or shells containing divine light shattered under the impact of the emanation of that light. That is, the vessels whose task it was to contain divine light in a structured and orderly fashion as it emanated from within the deepest recesses of God proved insufficiently strong. The result was the emergence of a material world comprised of shards of broken vessels to which there are attached sparks of the holy light that they originally contained. In the Lurianic schema, this process took place within God, and divinity itself may be said to have suffered a rupture.

Rav Kook appropriates some of the Lurianic language of *shevirah*, but understands it as something that happens to human beings rather than to God. According to him, God bestows His boundless goodness upon human beings (and the world of creation as a whole) in accordance with His infinite nature. But human beings, being finite, cannot absorb such limitless love without becoming "broken." The broken recipient longs to return to God, and to perfect himself in a way that would not have been possible had he not received the overflowing love of God in the first place.[13] Thus it is humanity that is broken, not God. It is human beings who are the vessels that "shattered" by virtue of their incapacity to withstand the fullness of God's light.

This shift from the mythic categories of Lurianic Kabbalah to psychological ones is, of course, an essential feature of Ḥasidic theology. In Ḥasidism too we encounter a fundamental demythologization of both the sefirotic universe of Zoharic Kabbalah and the mythological drama of Lurianic Kabbalah. In Ḥasidism the *Sefirot* are construed less as dimensions of divine being projected onto the cosmic realm and more as stages in the human psyche itself. This point has been made as clearly as anyone by Arthur Green:

> Though the *sefirot* [in Kabbalah] no doubt to some extent represent stages in the unfolding of human consciousness, and particularly of the reemergence of consciousness as one returns from the mystical heights, almost all discussion of them takes place on the theosophical, rather than the psychological plane. First and foremost the *sefirot* were said to exist in the mind and person, as it were, of God. The Kabbalist, characteristically shy about speaking of his own inner life, felt more free when discussing the realms above than those within. Indeed, it is only by attempting to translate back from theosophical projection, or by peering behind the speculative language of the Kabbalists, that we can hope to gain some of that inner experience which motivated their speculative life.
>
> All this has changed in Hasidism. Here, in a world where true worship and attachment to God are the only valid goals, talk of the stages of the *human* inner life has become essential. Claims of experience and assertions of experience in the cultivation of inwardness that

many an earlier Kabbalist would have found audacious have become commonplace in Hasidism. So too the *sefirot:* Their value as cosmology has given way to their psychological use; rather than realms within God, they now describe stages and qualities of human personality that are essential to the religious life.[14]

This process of the psychologization and allegorization of kabbalistic categories had begun as early as the seventeenth century and reached its fullest development in Ḥasidic theology. Ḥasidism, with its notions of transforming ordinary consciousness *(katnut)* into expanded consciousness *(gadlut)*, and of purifying and elevating that which appears to be fallen by perceiving the holy within it, is endlessly concerned with the proper discernment of the true nature of reality. There is no question that Rav Kook was heir to such a Ḥasidic legacy, although the language he uses is distinctively his own.

III

What is the *nature* of true reality which the mystical vision seeks to reveal? When we look beneath the facade that covers all things, what is that we find? Rav Kook's answer to this question is, on one level, disarmingly simple. It is God whom we discover. The world in its infinite manifestations bears nothing less than the manifold refractions of divinity. Wherever we turn, proper seeing permits us to discern the infinite lights of God's existence:

> If you will it, man, observe the light of the divine presence that pervades all existence. Observe the harmony of the heavenly realm, how it pervades every aspect of life, the spiritual and the material, which are before your eyes of flesh and your eyes of the spirit. Contemplate the wonders of creation, the divine dimension of their being, not as a dim configuration that is presented to you from the distance but as the reality in which you live. . . . Look at the lights, in their inwardness. Let not the names, words, the idiom and the letters confine your soul.[15]

Knowledge of God can be derived as an "inference from the world, that is, the faith based on contemplating natural existence," as well as through "the faith communicated by the Torah."[16] But the source for knowledge of God that is closest to an individual is internal, the soul itself, "the faith that is rooted in the inner life of the person and communicated from the depths of the soul." [17] "The uniqueness of the inner soul, in its own authenticity—this is the highest expression of the seed of divine light, the light planted for the righteous, from which will bud and blossom the fruit of the tree of life." [18]

Individuals must be able to recognize and confront the true identity of their souls, for it is upon this that the spiritual life rests:

> As long as a person is constrained to wait for a time when the creative spirit will inspire him, and then he will create, meditate, sing—this is a sign that his soul has not yet been illuminated. Surely, the soul always sings. It is robed in might and joy, it is surrounded by a noble delight, and the person must raise himself to the height of confronting his soul, of recognizing its spiritual imprints, the rushing of its wings that abound in the majesty of the holy of holies, and he will always be ready to listen to the secret of its holy discourse. . . . At all times, in every hour, it [the soul] releases streams of its precious gifts. . . . On contemplating inwardly in the depths of the soul, one realizes that the activating thrust of the truly higher life does not cease even for a moment. [19]

Moreover, the inner light of every human being shares an identity and a kinship with *Ein Sof*, the infinite, hidden transcendent light from which all particular, immanent lights are derived, and through which they are endlessly nourished: "Waves from the higher realm act on our souls ceaselessly. The stirrings of our inner spiritual sensibilities are the result of the sounds released by the violin of our souls, as it listens to the echo of the sound emanating from the [transcendent] divine realm." [20]

Self-awareness, such as described in these passages, is for the purpose of leading an individual to the recognition of the divine beyond the self. Kook never tires of repeating his conviction that divinity discloses itself in *all* manner of existence: "The realm of mystery tells us, you live in a world full of light and life. Know the great reality, the richness of existence that you always encounter. Contemplate its grandeur, its beauty, its precision and its harmony. . . . In everything you do you encounter sparks full of life and light." [21]

One of the essential and enduring problems of kabbalistic theology was the question of the relationship between *Ein Sof*, the transcendent source of all reality, and the world. What is the ontological status of the world? If it is invested with the vitality of divinity, as all kabbalists believed, is it *one* with transcendent divinity, or is it separate from divinity? The answer to this and related problems depends, according to various theories about these issues, on whether one has in mind God's point of view or the human point of view.

Rav Kook's response to this question appears to be the following: From God's perspective there is no separation or difference whatsoever between divinity and the world. The cosmos is a perfect unity. According to this acosmic view—expressed in elaborate and radical ways by the mystical theology of Ḥabad Ḥasidism—the world has no substantial reality, no real existence of its own independent of God.[22] Everything that appears to exist apart from God possesses no real substance, for all true substance is rooted in divinity. However, from the perspective of human perception, the *illusion* exists that the world is separated from its divine source. This separation exists only within the consciousness of human beings.[23] The apparent separateness or disunity of the cosmos, then, is epistemological in nature, not ontological. It exists only by virtue of the cognitive and conceptual limitations that characterize the human mind. The consequences of this conclusion are considerable. For it implies, from Rav Kook's point of view, that individuals cannot attain the uttermost concealed realm of divinity, the core of *Ein Sof*, by knowledge of this world. Instead, one generally comes to know divinity through its "finite" aspects as they disclose themselves to us in the world. Due to the constraints upon our cognitive abilities, we know God from our finite, limited point of view, rather than from His infinite, unlimited point of view:

> It is necessary to show how one may enter the palace: by the way of the gate. *The gate is the divine dimension disclosed in the world*, in all its phenomena of beauty and grandeur, as manifested in every living thing, in every insect, in every blooming plant and flower, in every nation and state, in the sea with its turbulent waves, in the panorama of the skies, in the talents of all creatures, in the thoughts of writers, the imagination of poets and the ideas of thinkers, in the feelings of every sensitive poet, and in the heroic deeds of every person of valor. The highest domain of divinity toward which we aspire—to be absorbed in it, to be included in its radiance—but

which eludes all our longing, descends for us into the world, and we encounter it and delight in its love, and find peace in its tranquility.[24]

Not only is God revealed in and through these immanent "phenomena of beauty." The holy is also embedded within the realm of physicality. Divine immanence extends to every region of the material and, in Kook's expression, to all "worldly pursuits." Here Rav Kook betrays once again his close affinity with Ḥasidic theology and its classic doctrines of *Avodah be-Gashmiyut* ("service of God through the material"), and *Yeridah le-Tzorekh Aliyah* ("descent for the sake of ascent"). This affinity can be readily exemplified by reference to Rav Kook's discussion of a subject common in Ḥasidic literature, namely, the act of eating.

> As there are holy sparks in the food we eat, so are they in all human activities, and similarly so in everything we hear and read. At times worldly pursuits from the most remote order of being become associated with the profound principles of the Torah, and everything serves a divine purpose, in the perspective of the holy. . . . The holy sparks embedded in the food we eat rise together with the holy sparks that ascend from all movements, all speech, all actions and acquisitions. To the extent that there is good and uprightness in all expressions of life is there an ascent of the holy sparks in food and drink and in all things that yield keenly felt pleasures.[25]

The "evil" dimension of the material, according to Kook, falls away into complete lifelessness when an action is performed with the proper intention:

> Excessive eating and drinking certainly induces pride, and likewise so if these take place without any holy intention. The extent to which proper intention is needed depends on the level of the person involved. The holy sparks in food and drink, by their nature, seek to ascend. When one eats with the proper motivation one paves a way for them to ascend in holiness. The evil admixture in them descends, while the good rises for enduring benefit and holy and noble delight. In the soul of the one who eats there is automatically stirred an elevation of the good and a lowering of the evil.[26]

This distinctly Ḥasidic perspective contrasts strikingly with the ascetically oriented attitudes that characterized sixteenth-century Kabbalah in Safed, of which Lurianic Kabbalah was the most vivid expression. Lurianic myth taught that the material world is fundamentally tainted. The broken vessels that brought the material realm into being became active demonic forces with which human beings are engaged in constant striving. Given this, the pious are advised to distance themselves from the material as far as possible so as to separate the holy from the material. From one point of view holiness consists in utterly divesting oneself of this world and its pleasures, enjoying instead the pleasures of the supernal realm.[27]

But in Rav Kook's view, as in Ḥasidism, the material has no genuine ontological reality of its own. One engages the material world precisely for the purpose of discovering the sacred within it. Materiality and world are, to a significant degree, purposeful, positive. The world is an intentionally constructed vehicle through which the divine has delimited itself. Only by virtue of such delimitation are human beings able to come near to God's presence.[28] Kook thus seeks to avoid the dualism implicit in earlier Kabbalah and explicit in sixteenth-century Kabbalah, in favor of a radically more positive appreciation of the world.

This, it should be pointed out, is the basis upon which Kook's positive regard for Zionism's processes of rebuilding the Land of Israel, the physical people of Israel, and a Jewish nation stands. The spiritual and the physical must be properly balanced. Israel's spiritual life will only flourish when its body is rejuvenated:

> Inestimably beautiful is the ideal of establishing a chosen people, a kingdom of priests and a holy nation, out of a people sunk in frightful servitude, the brilliance of whose patriarchal origins shall illumine the darkness. In the divine heights this ideal abides in the secret hiding place of its purity. But it must be materialized, set within a particular boundary, among people with good and evil passions, in communities in need of sustenance, of gaining a foothold on the land, of governmental authority.[29]

IV

Finally, we turn to the question of the goals of mystical life. What are the ultimate objectives of human existence in Rav Kook's view? In the first place Kook was preoccupied with the ethical life as the foundation for spiritual realization. A significant portion of his writing is devoted to issues of ethics and moral behavior, especially his *Orot ha-Teshuvah* (The lights of penitence) and *Midot ha-Rayah* (The moral principles). One of the categories Kook employs in these treatises is *tikkun*, which may be translated variously as "restitution" or "repair." This term is central to Lurianic myth, where it refers to the elaborate processes of redeeming the divine sparks attached to the broken vessels. For Isaac Luria, *tikkun* is primarily the repair of the world on high, the world of divinity, into which the souls of Israel are to be reintegrated. For Rav Kook, however, every moral act has the effect of improving or repairing the individual who performs the act, and at the same time, this world as a whole.[30]

It is well known that Rav Kook admired the Darwinian concept of evolution and that he interpreted it in spiritual terms. He believed that the world in which we live was progressing, evolving toward moral and spiritual perfection in every area of life: political, national, scientific, and religious. Kook identified the evolutionary process with Kabbalah in general, and frequently with the notion of *tikkun* in particular:

> The doctrine of evolution, which is presently gaining acceptance in the world, has a greater affinity with the secret teachings of the Kabbalah than all other philosophies. Evolution, which proceeds on a course of improvement, offers us the basis for optimism in the world. How can we despair when we realize that everything evolves and improves? In probing the inner meaning of evolution toward an improved state, we find here an explanation of the divine concepts with absolute clarity. It is precisely the *Ein Sof* in actuality that manages to bring to realization the potentiality of *Ein Sof*.[31]

One of the specific goals of mystical life, according to Rav Kook, was the cultivation of love for each and every living thing. This flowed from the attainment of a sense of the unity of all reality discussed earlier. Thus Kook wrote:

> The heart must be filled with love for all. The love of all creation comes first, then comes the love for all mankind, and then follows the love for the Jewish people, in which all other loves are included, since it is the destiny of the Jews to serve toward the perfection of all things. All these loves are to be expressed in practical action, by pursuing the welfare of those we are bidden to love, and to seek their advancement. But the highest love of all loves is the love of God, which is love in its fullest maturing. . . . The flame of the holy fire of the love of God is always burning in the heart. It is this that warms the human spirit and illumines life. The delights it yields are endless, there is no measure by which to assess it.[32]

The love of God and all creation that Kook describes here might be called a type of normal ecstasy, in the sense that it is within reach of every individual, although it is not achieved without great effort and continuous struggle. But at a level of intensity beyond this, Kook describes flashes of ecstasy in which a person experiences a fleeting glimpse of the transcendent. Here Kook appears to contradict himself. Earlier we asserted that Kook seemed to limit the experience of divinity to the manifestations of the holy in the world. But he also suggests in various places that it is sometimes possible to transcend momentarily this world:

> The highest domain of divinity toward which we aspire—to be absorbed in it, to be included in its radiance—but which eludes all our longing, descends for us into the world, and we encounter it and delight in its love, and find peace in its tranquility. At times, however, we are privileged with a flash emanating from the higher radiance, from that higher light which transcends all thought. The heavens open for us and we see a vision of God. But we know that this is only a temporary state, the flash will pass and will descend once again not inside the palace, but only in the courts of the Lord.[33]

This type of experience, which is alluded to frequently in Kook's poetry, may be called an ecstasy of transcendence, available only to the few, and even to them only rarely. Neither of these types of experience requires the highly developed symbolic language of theosophical/theurgical Kabbalah. While it is true that references to the *Sefirot* are scattered throughout his writing, along with other technical terms and expressions from the kabbalistic tradition, the fact is that such language is essentially dispensable for Kook. Kook, as we have seen, did not think of God in terms of discrete stages of being, each of which corresponds to some highly defined symbolism. Reminiscent of Ḥasidism, Kook locates his God in the transcendent heights on the one hand, and in the closer quarters of our world on the other. As such, there is little need for a highly structured set of symbols to identify a divine pleroma that occupies the realm between the world and *Ein Sof.* The demythologization to which Kook subjected Kabbalah, as discussed above, is strikingly evident in the nonsymbolic character of his language.

It should also be clear that Kook had little use for the theurgy typical of earlier Kabbalah. With respect to Jewish mysticism, theurgy refers to the practice of seeking to manipulate the constituent elements of divine being through contemplation and ritual piety. Just as his goal is not, as we have seen, theosophical speculation, that is, sustained reflection on the *Sefirot*, so too he is not concerned with their unification in the sense that one encounters in theurgical mysticism. In place of theurgical manipulation of divinity, Kook posits the more general notion of raising the holy toward the heights and improving and perfecting all reality.

Conclusions

If I were to categorize this remarkable individual who sought to breakdown conventional categories, I would characterize his mysticism as both neo-Kabbalistic and neo-Hasidic. He is neo-Kabbalistic in that he was thoroughly immersed in kabbalistic literature and ideas and used much of its language, but he subjected all of it to a fresh and sometimes radical reinterpretation. Kook thoroughly demythologized and dehypostasized the theosophical traditions of Kabbalah. In this regard he followed the path of earlier kabbalists of the post-Lurianic period, such as Joseph Ergas and Moshe Hayyim Luzatto, who were instrumental in initiating a revisionist understanding of Lurianic mysticism that reached mature expression in Hasidism.

It would be a mistake to regard Rav Kook, however, merely as a Hasidic master dressed in a more contemporary garb. Kook's thinking differed from Hasidic perspective in a great many ways, not least in his talent for pushing the implications of certain Hasidic notions to their logical extreme, and in applying such ideas in practical, even political ways. This is demonstrated, for example, by his passionately felt love for all humanity, his genuine respect for all political and national points of view, his love of secular Jews, and his willingness to engage secular knowledge in all its variety. Kook himself, of course, consciously distanced himself from those aspects of Eastern European traditionalism he regarded as too narrow, parochial, and rigid in style and outlook.

Finally, a variety of his ideas, such as his Darwinian-inspired belief in the evolutionary processes at work in the world, and his enthusiasm for all those aspects of modernity that bear "lights of holiness," mark Abraham Isaac Kook as a genuinely original religious personality. In his own life Kook fulfilled his existential conviction that each person must allow her or his autonomous and unique self to flower:

> The inner essence of the soul, which reflects, which lives the true spiritual life, must have absolute inner freedom. It experiences its freedom, which is life, through its originality in thought, which is its inner spark that can be fanned to a flame through study and concentration. But the inner spark is the basis of imagination and thought. If the autonomous spark should not be given scope to express itself, then whatever may be acquired from the outside will be of no avail. . . . The uniqueness of the inner soul, in its own authenticity—this is the highest expression of the seed of divine light, the light planted for the righteous, from which will bud and blossom the fruit of the tree of life.[34]

Notes

1. G. Scholem, *Major Trends in Jewish Mysticism* (New York, 1941), 354 n.17.
2. See S. H. Bergman, *Faith and Reason: An Introduction to Modern Jewish Thought*, ed. and trans. A. Jospe (Washington, D.C., 1961), 121–141; N. Rotenstreich, *Jewish Philosophy in Modern Times* (New York, 1968), 219–38. For additional bibliography on Rav Kook, see Ben-Zion Bokser, *Abraham Isaac Kook* (New York, 1978), 389–90.
3. See, for example, T. Ross, "Musag ha-Elohut shel ha-Rav Kook," *Daat* 8 (1982): 109–28 and *Daat* 9 (1982): 39–70; J. Ben-Shlomo, "Shelemut ve-Hishtalmut be-Torat ha-Elohut shel ha-Rav Kook," *Iyyun* 33, 1–2 (1984): 289–309; Y. Dison, "Arba'ah Motivim be-Orot ha-Kodesh ke-Basis la-Arikhah Ḥadashah," *Daat* 24 (1990): 41–86. See as well the recent full-length book by Benjamin Ish-Shalom, *Harav Kook: Bein Ratsiyonalism le-mistikah* (Tel Aviv, 1990). This important volume also contains a comprehensive bibliography on our subject. The current paper, prepared as a lecture for a conference on Rav Kook sponsored by the Graduate Center of the City College of New York, was written before the appearance of Ish-Shalom's book and thus does not make use of it. Increased interest in Rav Kook's thought has been stimulated, in part, by the appearance of some of his writings in English translation, most especially *Abraham Isaac Kook: The Lights of Penitence, Lights of Holiness, The Moral Principles, Essays, Letters, and Poems* (New York, 1978), ed. and trans. Ben-Zion Bokser. See also Bokser, *The Essential Writings of Abraham Isaac Kook* (New York, 1988);

T. Feldman, ed. and trans., *Rav A. Y. Kook: Selected Letters* (Jerusalem, 1986).

4. *Orot ha-Kodesh* was published by Mosad ha-Rav Kook in three volumes in Jerusalem. Volume I was published in 1963, volumes II and III in 1964.
5. On the subject of the ways in which Rav Kook's works were edited, see the article by Y. Dison referred to in note 3.
6. *Orot ha-Kodesh* I, 120. Many of the translations in this paper are drawn or adapted from Bokser's *Kook*.
7. *Orot ha-Kodesh*, I, 22.
8. Ish-Shalom's book, referred to in note 3, is centrally concerned with the relationship between philosophical and mystical thinking in Rav Kook.
9. *Orot ha-Kodesh*, I, 9.
10. Ibid. 9–10.
11. Ibid. 41.
12. Ibid. 25.
13. See, for example, ibid. II, 526–27. Cf. ibid. III, 76.
14. A. Green, ed. *Menahem Nahum of Chernobyl* (New York, 1982), 10.
15. *Orot ha-Kodesh* I, 83.
16. *Maamarei ha-Rayah*, 70.
17. Ibid.
18. *Orot ha-Kodesh* I, 175.
19. Ibid. 172.
20. Ibid. II, 334.
21. Ibid. 343.
22. For important discussions of acosmism in Hasidic thought, see A. Green, "Hasidism: Discovery and Retreat," in *The Other Side of God*, ed. P. Berger (New York, 1981), 104–30, and R. Elior, *The Paradoxical Ascent to God* (New York, 1993), especially part 2.
23. For a more detailed discussion of this question in Rav Kook's theology, see Ross, "Musag ha-Elohut", *passim*.
24. *Orot*, 119–20. *Orot*, a collection of essays, not to be confused with *Orot ha-Kodesh*, some of which appeared separately in journals or in booklet form. The essay from which this passage was taken is found in a group of such essays which appeared in 1914 under the title "Zir'onim" (A row of plants) in a periodical entitled *Ha-tarbut ha-Yisraelit*. They were reprinted under the same title in *Orot*, published in 1963 by Mosad ha-Rav Kook.
25. *Midot ha-Rayah* (Moral principles), published as part of a volume entitled *Musar Avikha* (The admonitions of the father) by Mosad ha-Rav Kook (Jerusalem, 1971). The format of these reflections imitates the style of a treatise on moral behavior by the Hasidic master Nahman of Bratslav, entitled *Sefer ha-Midot*. Cf. *Orot ha-Kodesh* III, 125.
26. Bokser, *Kook*, 159–60.
27. This problem in Lurianism is more complicated than presented here

insofar as the world is constituted of a *mingling* of divine sparks and materiality. Concerning this subject, see L. Fine, *Safed Spirituality* (New York, 1984), 11–16; Fine, "Purifying the Body in the Name of the Soul: The Problem of the Body in Sixteenth-Century Kabbalah," in *People of the Body*, ed. H. Eilberg-Schwartz (New York, 1992), 117–42.

28. Such is the allegorical interpretation given to the Lurianic doctrine of *tzimtzum* in Kook's thought. Following the lead of earlier post-Lurianic thinkers, *tzimtzum* is no longer conceived as divine withdrawal or contraction in the literal sense, but as the process by which God invests Himself in the world in "finite" ways. Such an interpretation stresses that God does not actually experience any change or transformation as a result of this process. See Ross, "Musag ha-Elohut," part 1.

29. *Orot*, 133. The translation is by Bokser, *Kook*, 278.

30. See, for example, Bokser, *Kook*, 185. Concerning Kook's notion of *tikkun*, see also *Orot ha-Kodesh* III, 125, 180–82, 237.

31. *Orot ha-Kodesh* II, 537. Cf. II, 543.

32. Beginning of *Midot ha-Rayah* on "Love."

33. *Orot*, 120.

34. *Orot ha-Kodesh* I, 175.

CHAPTER 2

Rav Kook and the Jewish Philosophical Tradition

Lawrence J. Kaplan

Rav Kook's thought, as is well known, is both holistic and organic. He sought to reconcile such ostensibly opposing values as body and spirit, individual and community, order and spontaneity, means and ends, ethics and piety, and the like by showing how these apparently conflicting values can be brought together and synthesized into a harmonious, higher unity. This holistic, organic approach also determined Rav Kook's attitude toward the Jewish tradition. He sought to encompass the tradition in its totality, not ignoring its diversity, but viewing its diverse aspects as different and complementary facets of an overarching whole. Consequently, he opposed any split between the realms of *halakhah* and *aggadah* and, certainly, any split *within* these realms. Thus, he sought in his writings and, even more so, in his lectures to integrate halakhic analysis and interpretation with aggadic insights and concepts.[1] Within the field of *halakhah* itself, his synthesizing approach expressed itself in his bringing together texts that were often viewed in isolation from one another, such as the Babylonian and Palestinian Talmuds,[2] or in his integrating methodologies that had grown apart from each other, such as *gemara*—the process of argumentation and dialectic—with *pesak*—the normative ruling.[3] Similarly, within the field of *aggadah*—our present concern—he sought to encompass and harmonize seemingly competing theological and philosophical positions and points of view. It was a mistake, he argued, to oppose, for example, Maimonides to Halevi; rather, both emphasize different aspects of a larger whole, and their true worth is perceived only when they are viewed together, seen not as antithetical but as complementary.[4] Even more broadly, he argued against setting the various streams of Jewish thought—Jewish philosophy, Kabbalah, ethics, piety, and the like—against each other. Rather, one must weave together the various strands, must integrate these differing approaches, perspectives, schools, and styles, and fashion thereby the *whole* that is Jewish thought.[5] Indeed, we may suggest that since Rav Kook's holism is evolutionary in character, that is, he believed that the world, both nature and society, was evolving and reaching ever greater levels of unity, Rav Kook may have viewed his *own* attempt at synthesizing the various streams of Jewish thought as precisely one more example of this move, this drive toward unity unfolding itself in history.

In order to truly understand and appreciate Rav Kook's worldview, then, we need to see how he sought to develop that worldview by means of a creative synthesis of the various streams of Jewish thought, and we need, further, to determine how he used, interpreted (or, perhaps, creatively misinterpreted), and transformed these various streams in the process. Now, Rav Kook's thought clearly bears the imprint of his mastery of Kabbalah and reflects, in equal measure, the impact of nineteenth-century Jewish thought. The influence of these streams of Jewish thought on Rav Kook and his use and transformation of them have been, therefore, the subject of much recent scholarly examination and are beyond the scope of this present study.[6] I would like, in this paper, to focus my attention on Rav Kook's attitude toward the Jewish philosophic tradition and his use and transformation of that tradition in developing his own evolutionary and holistic religious worldview. Obviously, even this delimited topic is a large one and one that has been largely unexplored. This paper, then, will only present preliminary reflections and observations on the subject and will offer a few illustrative examples that, I trust, will shed some light on Rav Kook's synthesizing approach. In particular, I want to concentrate on Rav Kook's attitude toward Maimonides and his use of Maimonidean thought. First, however, let me offer at least one example, not related to Maimonides, to illustrate Rav Kook's attitude toward and use of the Jewish philosophic tradition. This example is particularly instructive because it serves as a paradigm of how Rav Kook takes a view that in his opinion was, in its original form, clearly wrong, perhaps even heretical, and shows how that view reflects an admittedly fragmentary and one-sided perception of the truth. Thus, this view can be "reclaimed," "redeemed," as it were, its true worth displayed, if it is integrated into the broader, more encompassing whole in which it belongs and of which it constitutes an important building block.

One of the classic disagreements between the philosophical and the religious traditions, Rav Kook notes, revolves about the issue of providence. The classical and the medieval philosophical traditions affirm general providence, but deemphasize or even deny individual providence. For traditional religion, however, individual providence is central, indeed, crucial.[7] Now, even some Jewish philosophers, Gersonides, for example, were not immune from this philosophic predilection and denied or, at the very least, severely limited God's providence over human individuals while upholding His providence over the human species as a whole.[8] Certainly, for Rav Kook, the denial of divine providence over individual human beings is a denial of a fundamental principle of Judaism. Nevertheless, for Rav Kook, in taking this position, the philosophic tradition and Gersonides in particular were pointing the way to a deep truth. For Rav Kook claims—and here we see his organic philosophy coming to the fore—there are no individuals, taken in isolation.[9] Everything exists only as part of a whole. The "world of fragmentation" is a lie, a deception; the only true world, the only true reality is "the world of unity."[10] Thus providence, for Rav Kook, is extended to human individuals only insofar as they are part of a larger whole. All divine providence, then, is general providence, but this general, divine providence watches over the individual as part of this whole. Indeed, Rav Kook states, "This general providence penetrates more thoroughly to all the particulars, which only appear as particulars on account of our own darkness [i.e., our limited perception], than any type of individual providence [which would watch over particulars as particulars] that we could imagine."[11] The mistake of philosophy was to believe that human individuals do exist as individuals, and that these existing, discrete, human individuals are not subject to divine providence. Once, however, we adopt the true organic picture of reality, the true significance of the philosophic view reveals itself. On the other hand—we would argue—the philosophic view with its emphasis on general providence, on the order, structure, and harmony of the whole that reflects divine providence, represents, for Rav Kook, a move in the direction of the organic viewpoint.[12] We have here, I repeat, a classic example of how, for Rav Kook, progress takes place in a dialectical fashion through the emergence and clash of one-sided views, each one of which sees one part of the whole, sees it truly, but mistakes it for the whole. These one-sided views are destined, over the course of history, to reach their higher synthesis, but they can only reach that synthesis via dialectical opposition and reconciliation.

I now turn to Rav Kook's attitude toward Maimonides and his use and transformation of Maimonidean thought. This topic is very rich and complex. Certainly, Maimonides, in Rav Kook's eyes, is a heroic figure, one of the towering spiritual giants of Judaism.[13] In 1935, the last year of his life, Rav Kook wrote two major essays in praise of Maimonides. When the historian Zev Yawetz, in the posthumously published twelfth volume of his *History of Israel*, criticized Maimonides' philosophic views as expressed in the *Guide*, and contrasted those views with Maimonides' "authentically" Jewish views as expressed in the *Mishneh Torah*,[14] Rav Kook in reply wrote an essay, "Le-Aḥduto shel ha-Rambam," in defense of Maimonides, in which he argued that Maimonides' thought, both in the *Guide* and the *Mishneh Torah*, forms a unified whole and that all of it is authentically Jewish.[15] Shortly thereafter, Rav Kook, a few months before his death, wrote another essay, "Ha-Maor ha-Eḥad," in which he lauded Maimonides for embracing within himself both the light of the world-intellectual rigor and purity—and the strength of the world-religious longing and passion—both light and strength blended together in a consummate, splendid unity.[16] This essay, written in honor of the 800th anniversary of Maimonides' birth,[17] was the very last essay of Rav Kook published in his lifetime.

Of course, for Rav Kook, Maimonides is so central, so "heroic" a figure, precisely because of his multifacetedness, because he was both a great halakhic scholar and an outstanding philosopher. And, given Rav Kook's holistic approach to the Jewish tradition, it comes as no surprise that Rav Kook views Maimonides' life and work as constituting an organic and unified whole.[18] Yet when we examine Rav Kook's attitude toward Maimonidean thought the picture becomes much more ambiguous. Thus, Rav Kook's "defense" of Maimonides in his reply to Yawetz is not so much a defense of the truth of Maimonides' views but rather, of their legitimacy as authentically Jewish views, something quite different. Indeed, precisely in the course of examining this defense, the difference between Rav Kook's religious views and those of Maimonides will, paradoxically or not so paradoxically, become clear.

Rav Kook's defense of Maimonides in this essay may be divided into three parts. I would like to examine these three parts in reverse order of presentation, moving from less ambiguous to more ambiguous.

First, Rav Kook sharply differentiates between Maimonides' views on creation, prophecy, and providence, and the classical, philosophical, Aristotelian views on these issues. He argues that Maimonides' position on these matters is separated from the philosophic position by an "infinite abyss," and that, consequently, for Maimonides, the stance of Torah on these questions and the stance of the Greek and Arabic philosophers are completely and absolutely opposed.[19] In this connection, Rav Kook, basing himself on the conclusion of the *Guide*, further argues that, for Maimonides, the highest human perfection is not intellectual perfection divorced from moral qualities and actions, but, rather, intellectual perfection combined with moral qualities and actions.[20]

Rav Kook's general approach to Maimonides, as manifested in his contentions as set forth above, places him within the line of "conservative" interpreters of Maimonides, beginning with Isaac Abarbanel and Mordecai Jaffe and extending down to Rabbis Y. M. Harlap and J. B. Soloveitchik. These scholars, in their commentaries or essays on Maimonides, tone down the "radical" edges of Maimonidean thought by differentiating his oftentimes ambiguous positions on central theological issues from the naturalistic and intellectualistic philosophical positions and assimilating them, to the extent possible, to more traditional rabbinic doctrines. Such an approach ought to be contrasted with the approach of "radical" interpreters of the *Guide*, starting with Samuel ibn Tibbon, Joseph Kaspi, and Moses Narboni and extending down to Leo Strauss and Shlomo Pines, who see Maimonides' theological views as essentially naturalistic and intellectualistic and assimilate his ambiguous positions on central issues to those of the philosophers; they argue that Maimonides' ambiguity was a device, a "ruse" intended to conceal the true radical and philosophical nature of his positions from the multitude.[21]

Our saying that Rav Kook adopted a "conservative" interpretation of Maimonides' positions on central theological issues, that he differentiated Maimonides' views on those issues from those of the philosophers and sought to assimilate them, to the extent possible, to traditional rabbinic doctrine, does not mean, however, that Rav Kook was a Maimonidean, or, more to the point, that he agreed with Maimonides' positions on these issues, even in the form in which he understood them. Though "conservative" commentators on Maimonides offer interpretations of Maimonidean doctrines designed to make such doctrines more acceptable and palatable from a traditional rabbinic point of view, they oftentimes immediately proceed to state or, indeed, preface their interpretations by stating that they personally do not agree with these Maimonidean doctrines, even in their "conservative" version. Thus, to take only the most prominent example: Isaac Abarbanel's commentary on the *Guide* is probably the most important "conservative" commentary on the *Guide* ever written. In the commentary, Abarbanel, the staunch spokesman of tradition, sets out to "defend" Maimonides, the Master, against such unworthy disciples as Kaspi and Narboni (and, to a lesser extent, Shem Tov and Efodi) who, so he argues, falsely attempted to attribute their corrupt doctrines to him. Time and again, he attacks their radical interpretations as distortions of Maimonides' true views that he sees as having a more conservative and traditional cast. But, at the same time, Abarbanel, after his "defense" of the Master, after his reconstruction of the Master's true doctrine, proceeds, more often than not, to engage in a stringent and rigorous critique of Maimonides' views. For Abarbanel, even if central Maimonidean doctrines are not as radical and philosophical as Kaspi, Narboni, et al. claim, they are still much too radical and philosophical for his own taste.[22] To come back to Rav Kook, then, the conservative interpretation that Rav Kook offers of Maimonides only means that, for Rav Kook, Maimonides' doctrines are certainly acceptable from a traditional rabbinic point of view and are not to be equated with the doctrines of the philosophers. It does not mean that Rav Kook necessarily agrees with these doctrines.

Our examination of the "first" part of Rav Kook's "defense" of Maimonides (the last in order of presentation) tells us, then, less than might appear to be the case, at first glance, about Rav Kook's agreement or disagreement with Maimonidean views.

Second, Rav Kook, following along the lines set down by Naḥmanides in his open letter to the Sages of northern France,[23] praises Maimonides for destroying, once and for all, the belief in a corporeal God. "How can we not give thanks to our Master, the Rambam, for the great task he carried out in the *Guide*, by establishing the foundation of the holiness of faith in its purity and by expelling from the borders of Israel that frightful folly of ascribing to God corporeal attributes."[24] Maimonides here plays a crucial, critical, heroic role for Rav Kook in the purification of the faith. And yet, despite the lavish and deeply felt praise, it should be noted-and precisely at this point we begin to see Rav Kook's views diverging from those of Maimonides-that, though both Maimonides and Rav Kook stress the importance of believing in God's incorporeality, though both reject any anthropomorphic concept of God, Rav Kook differs from Maimonides on the fundamental issue of the function and meaning of the anthropomorphic imagery used by the Bible and the Sages.

I speak of both function and meaning, for we may differentiate between the question of the function of anthropomorphic images, that is, "What purpose do they serve?" and "Why are they used?" and the question of the meaning of these images, that is, "How are we to understand and interpret them?"

Let us first turn to the question of function.

Maimonides follows an already venerable Geonic tradition in understanding the rabbinic statement, "The Torah speaketh in the language of the sons of man,"[25] as referring to, among other things, the Torah's use of anthropomorphic imagery.[26] However, Maimonides gives a radical twist to this statement by equating "the language of the sons of man" with the "imagination of the multitude."[27] As Maimonides explains, "The meaning of 'The Torah speaketh in the language of the sons of man' is that everything that all men are capable of understanding and representing to themselves *at first thought* have been ascribed to God. . . . Hence attributes indicating corporeality has been predicated of Him, in order to indicate that He . . . exists, inasmuch as the multitude cannot *at first* conceive of any existence save that of a body alone" (*Guide* I:26:56; emphasis mine). Thus, for Maimonides, the Torah allows the multitude to use corporeal images ascribed to God in order that they may establish more clearly and firmly in their minds the truth of His existence; however, immediately after this truth has been clearly and firmly established in their minds, they should proceed to unequivocally negate any belief in His corporeality. Corporeal images are thus part of an early stage of education and are destined to be transcended and negated. We might almost say that these images are designed to be self-liquidating.[28]

For Rav Kook, the reason why "The Torah speaketh in the language of the sons of man," the reason for its use of anthropomorphic imagery flows not from its desire to accommodate itself to the imagination of the multitude but rather from the intrinsic limitations of human language when speaking of divine matters. For him, then, the use of anthropomorphic imagery is not limited to some preliminary stage in the education of the multitude, but rather constitutes an ineluctable, inescapable, and *permanent* necessity when speaking of God. Moreover, with respect to the multitude who do not understand the inner content alluded to by the anthropomorphic imagery, the function of this imagery is not pedagogical or educational, but, rather, inspirational. The use of this language is never, not even for a single moment, to be understood literally by the multitude. Rather, the multitude must understand that these images do allude to profound divine secrets, secrets that are otherwise inexpressible and that can only be hinted at via these images, even if they have no idea what these secrets may be. These images, then, precisely by virtue of their allusive, suggestive, almost numinous quality, induce in the multitude a spirit of fear, awe, trembling, and piety.[29]

Two significant differences between Maimonides and Rav Kook emerge here. First, Maimonides stresses the function of these images in teaching the multitude the *truth*; Rav Kook stresses the function of these images in arousing in the multitude a spirit of *piety*. (We will return to this issue of truth vis-à-vis piety later when speaking of the third part of Rav Kook's "defense" of Maimonides.) Second, for Maimonides, these images are intended to be taken literally, then transcended and negated; for Rav Kook these images are intended to be taken, at all levels of understanding, by multitude and sage alike, as symbolic. This second difference leads us to the difference between Maimonides and Rav Kook concerning the meaning of anthropomorphic imagery.

For Maimonides, corporeal images, when applied to man and God, are, once truly understood, homonyms, that is, they have one corporeal meaning when applied to man, and another, totally different meaning, when referring to God, expressible in abstract conceptual categories. To take two examples: the term "standing," when applied to man, has the physical meaning of "to rise and stand"; the term when applied to God means "stable and enduring" (*Guide* I:13: 39–40). Or the term "eye" when applied to man generally refers to his seeing eye, but when applied to God refers to His providence and purpose or to His intellectual apprehension (*Guide* I:44:95). We may say that the multitude, to begin with, should take these corporeal terms when applied to God literally, in order to establish thereby the truth of God's existence in their minds (*Guide* I:26:56). Once this truth is established, they should be taught, on the basis of traditional authority, to negate the literal meaning of these terms. If they are still unable to understand the true equivocal or figurative sense of the terms, they should be told, clearly and authoritatively, that these terms possess a figurative or equivocal sense, albeit a hidden one (*Guide* I:35:79–81). Eventually some select few may be elevated to the level of understanding the true figurative or equivocal sense of these terms when applied to God (*Guide* I:33:71–72).

For Rav Kook, as we have seen, these corporeal terms were never intended, not even for a moment, to be taken literally when referring to God. Nevertheless, these terms are not simple homonyms. Rather, they serve a symbolic function; they point to a truth about divine existence that is inexpressible in abstract, conceptual categories, but may only be brought to light by use of these symbols. To state the matter more sharply, the very corporeal referents of these corporeal terms—the physical eye or ear, maleness or femaleness, place and location, and the like—are symbols of supernal, purely spiritual, noncorporeal realities existing in God. This difference between Maimonides and Rav Kook regarding the meaning of anthropomorphic images calls to mind the distinction between philosophical allegory and kabbalistic symbolism that Gershom Scholem has stressed, though I do not believe that one can really speak of Maimonides' interpretation of these images as allegorical.[30]

Interestingly enough, Rav Kook, in a letter upholding the truth and holiness of the Kabbalah, uses a Maimonidean text as a basis for viewing anthropomorphic imagery symbolically. Rav Kook cites Maimonides' statement (*Yesodei Ha-Torah* 2:9), "All existents, aside from God . . . exist by virtue of the truth of His existence . . . and because He knows Himself . . . He knows everything." Rav Kook comments, "It follows that all existents, down to the slightest and most insignificant, and, consequently, all movements, down to the slightest and most insignificant, derive their existence from the truth of God's existence, so that God by knowing Himself knows them all. However, in God's supernal holiness, as it were, everything exists in a state of extreme purity and holiness without any impropriety or unseemliness, heaven forbid."[31] It is this truth, in Rav Kook's view, to which the anthropomorphic imagery of the Bible, the Rabbis, and particularly the Kabbalah points.

Can such a symbolic interpretation of anthropomorphic imagery be attributed to Maimonides? What *is* the meaning of Maimonides' statement in *Yesodei Ha-Torah* cited by Rav Kook? Certainly, it is true that, for Maimonides, to cite Professor Alfred Ivry, "the forms of the world . . . are one in God, though the mode of the existence of these forms in God is beyond our comprehension."[32] Note though that Ivry is referring specifically to the existence of the *forms* in God. God, for Maimonides, is the efficient, formal, and final cause of the world, *not*, in any sense, its material cause (*Guide* I:69:167–70). Matter, for Maimonides, is always "a concomitant of privation" (*Guide* III:10:440), while God's being consists of true existence (*Guide* I:69:169; *Laws of the Foundations of The Torah* 1:1–4). As Ivry notes, "Matter, unlike form, is neither with God from all eternity, nor close to Him after its creation."[33] We may confidently conclude, then, that Maimonides, *contra* Rav Kook, did not believe that the anthropomorphic imagery of the Bible or the Sages served in any way as a symbolic expression of the truth that "the forms of the world . . . are one in God."[34]

To sum up our discussion of the second part of Rav Kook's defense of Maimonides: while Rav Kook was deeply grateful to Maimonides for destroying any anthropomorphic conception of God, our analysis has shown that the differences between Rav Kook and Maimonides regarding both the function and meaning of the anthropomorphic images ascribed to God that do exist in the sacred texts of Judaism are clear and go very deep. Paradoxically, we might speculate that Rav Kook believed—though he never made any statement to this effect—that precisely because Maimonides destroyed the hold of anthropomorphism on the Jewish community, the Kabbalah could be so free in developing its own luxuriant anthropomorphic descriptions of God, since there was no longer any danger that they would be taken literally.[35]

Our analysis has also brought to light an important, far reaching, and fundamental speculative difference between Maimonides and Rav Kook. As we have seen, for Maimonides only the forms of the world exist in perfect oneness in God, while for Rav Kook, "all existents . . . and all movements . . . [exist] in God's supernal holiness . . . in a state of extreme purity." We have here expressed, at its deepest and most conceptual level, the difference between Maimonides' radical philosophical monotheism and Rav Kook's— to use his own self-description—mystical "monotheistic outlook tending toward a pantheistic explication, but purified of [pantheism's] dross."[36] As we shall see, this fundamental speculative difference between Maimonides and Rav Kook gives rise, in turn, to other important differences between them.

Third, and most ambiguous of all, Rav Kook seeks at the beginning of his essay to defend Maimonides on the basis of what appears, to me at least, to be clearly non-Maimonidean premises. Rav Kook argues that what is ultimately significant about religious views, about spiritual conceptions, is whether "they bind the hearts of people to holiness, purity, faith, and observance of the Torah and commandments." Some people may be inspired to holiness and faith by one set of views and conceptions; other people may be inspired by another set. If Maimonides, "that great giant, that holy luminary," could be inspired by his own views to attain almost unparalleled heights of holiness, faith, and divine service, that in itself is proof of the legitimacy of those views[37]—their legitimacy, not their truth. Indeed, the issue of truth becomes secondary.

As I just stated, Rav Kook's "defense" of Maimonides on this point rests upon a strikingly non-Maimonidean premise. For in Maimonides' view truth is all important.[38] Here we see the gap between Rav Kook and Maimonides on the issue of truth vis-à-vis piety emerging even more clearly than we had seen before when discussing their differing views regarding the function of anthropomorphic imagery.

Why does Rav Kook believe that what is significant about religious views is their capacity to induce in a person a spirit of faith and piety? The answer, I believe, lies in Rav Kook's view as to what constitutes man's ultimate perfection. For Rav Kook, the highest human perfection, that "supernal well" from whence all other perfections derive, is "ha-tom ha-penimi," the inner wholeness of faith.[39] For Maimonides, however, the ultimate human perfection is intellectual perfection, the acquisition of the rational virtues, that is, knowledge of the truth (Guide I:1–2; III:27, 51, 54). To state the point more sharply: For Maimonides, it is the intellect "that . . . is the bond between us and [God]" (Guide III:51:621). For Rav Kook, the bond between man and God is fundamentally nonintellectual in nature; it is created by the deep faith in God that wells up from within, by the love of the soul for God as the absolutely good. The intellect, to be sure, plays an important role for Rav Kook in purifying this faith, but it is faith, not intellect, which is the bond.[40]

We arrive here at the heart of the difference between Maimonides and Rav Kook. As already noted, Rav Kook, in his other essay on Maimonides, "Ha-Maor ha-Eḥad," lauded Maimonides for embracing within himself both the light of the world (intellectual rigor and purity) and the strength of the world (religious passion and love), both light and strength blended together in a consummate, splendid unity. And, no doubt, Rav Kook sought to achieve a similar synthesis in his own thought—and person. Their views, however, as to how this synthesis or union is to be achieved move in opposite directions; they therefore arrive at diametrically opposed conclusions that one might say are reverse mirror images of each other.

For Maimonides, the true love of God is the intellectual love of God, that is, one begins with the intellectual knowledge of God, but then imbues that intellectual knowledge with drive, passion, and desire that are themselves cognitive in nature, thereby transforming intellectual knowledge of God into intellectual love of God.[41] For Rav Kook, the true love of God is the intellectually and morally refined desire for God's closeness, that is, one begins with a passionate, intuitive, noninferential, and nonintellectual love of God, but then subjects that intuitive and passionate love to moral and intellectual refinement and purification, so that the love of God is no longer dark and turbid, but clear and luminous, so that the love of God also becomes knowledge of God.[42] Rav Kook, in "Ha-Maor ha-Ehad," views the raw, passionate desire for God's closeness as a principle of affirmation, and moral and intellectual refinement as a principle of negation.[43] To use these categories of affirmation and negation, we may say, then, that for Rav Kook, a person in achieving the union of intellect and love starts with the affirmation and concludes with the negation, while for Maimonides, the direction of movement is reversed. In a word, for Maimonides man binds himself to God through the pathos of intellect, for Rav Kook, through intellectualized passion.[44]

This view of Rav Kook emerges with particular clarity and force in a letter to Rabbi Samuel Alexandrov:

> The true characteristic of the Israelite, fixed firmly in the depths of the Hebrew soul, is the blessing of Abraham our father, may he rest in peace, concerning whom Scripture testified, "the seed of Abraham, My lover" (Isaiah 41:8). The essence of Jewish life is contained only in the love of God, may He be blessed, a love for His name . . . as designated specifically in the name of "the Lord, God of Israel." All the other, many and broad, detailed and general, conditions of life are only effects of or supplements to this foundation of fundamental life. This is our principal characteristic that prevailed within us in the first dewy days of our childhood and which accompanies us forever. . . . This characteristic has not changed and will not change. The procession of life and its external forms may, at times, undergo some change, but not its inward content. . . . This . . . fixed and

everlasting characteristic needs no research or philosophy, nor any preservative in the world for its maintenance or essential existence. We broaden and perfect our knowledge and cognition only in order to give broader scope for this divine, essential characteristic to expand and reveal itself more fully. . . . These external manifestations [however] do not resemble at all nor may their value be compared to the exalted rank of strength and clarity possessed by this inward characteristic of the love of the Lord, God of Israel, hidden within us.[45]

We would suggest that this root difference between Maimonides and Rav Kook as to whether the fundamental bond between man and God is essentially intellectual or nonintellectual in nature derives, at least in part, from the root difference between them that we had brought to light earlier, namely, whether or not "all existents . . . and all movements . . . [exist] in God's supernal holiness"—Rav Kook's view—or only the forms do—the position taken by Maimonides. For Maimonides, since it is the forms that exist in a mysterious oneness in God, man binds himself to God through the cognition of the forms. But it is only the intellect—itself a form[46]— that, for Maimonides, is able to cognize the forms,[47] and therefore only the intellect is able to serve as a bond between man and God. For Rav Kook, since all existents and all movements exist in God, one perceives this indwelling of the world—in its wholeness, in its oneness, in all of its facets—in God's supernal unity via a mystical, intuitive, nonintellectual perception, and thereby binds oneself to God. To state matters even more sharply: for Rav Kook, via this mystical, intuitive, nonintellectual perception, a person first integrates himself into the world's wholeness and oneness, and then, as part of that wholeness and oneness, incorporates himself together with the world in the divine supernal unity.[48]

If this difference between Rav Kook and Maimonides regarding the issue of truth vis-à-vis piety, intellect vis-à-vis faith, derives at least in part from an earlier difference we discussed, it, in turn, gives rise to yet another difference. Maimonides's view of the way to ultimate human perfection is monistic in character. There is only one truth, and only knowledge of that one truth confers perfection upon man. Rav Kook's view of the way is pluralistic; there may be, indeed are, many and various conceptual paths leading man to faith. In line with this, Maimonides has a very exclusive view as to what constitutes authentic Jewish doctrine, Rav Kook, a much more inclusive view. For Maimonides, there is and ultimately can be only one school of authentic Jewish thought, namely, his own. Only one school can possess the one truth. For Rav Kook, there can be many such schools. Different schools can, in different ways, lead different persons to a life of faith, piety, and observance.[49] It need not be emphasized that Rav Kook's approach on this point is more in accord with the modern temper than that of Maimonides. We also have here the closing of a circle, as Rav Kook arrives via this particular route at the pluralism and harmonism, the holism and organism, that constitute the fundamental and constantly recurring leitmotifs of his worldview.

Our analysis of Rav Kook's "defense" of Maimonides has gradually brought to light many and profound differences dividing them. And this ought not be surprising. For, despite Rav Kook's great admiration for Maimonides as a person, their religious worldviews differed fundamentally. No doubt Rav Kook was well aware of this. In addition to all the various major disagreements between Maimonides and Rav Kook that we have seen until now, we may take note of two others. First, Maimonides' metaphysics was primarily Aristotelian in nature;[50] Rav Kook's metaphysics, influenced as it was by Kabbalah and nineteenth-century Jewish thought, was primarily neo-Platonic in character.[51] Second, and more relevant for our purpose, Maimonides is the great proponent of the fixed, stable, unchanging, eternal *a parte post* structures of nature[52] and Torah[53]. Rav Kook's thought, by contrast, is deeply evolutionary in character and he foresees the possibility—indeed, the certainty—of nature[54] and even Torah[55] undergoing fundamental changes as the world progresses to ever higher levels of goodness, unity, and perfection.

And yet I would argue that Rav Kook, in line with his general approach to traditional Jewish sources, including Jewish philosophic sources, believed that many Maimonidean concepts and theories, if suitably transformed, could serve as building blocks for his own worldview. Thus, Rav Kook's own organicism, his very emphasis on unity, is certainly profoundly influenced by Maimonides' famous description of the world as one individual (*Guide* I:72), though, of course, the world, "this whole of being," this "one individual," is an evolving organism for Rav Kook, an unchanging organism for Maimonides. As another example, Eliezer Goldman, in "Rav Kook on the Secular," has shown that Rav Kook's claim that "there is an immanent drive of the created being toward perfection"[56] is reminiscent, in many respects, of Maimonides' view that each level of creation aspires, in its own fashion, to the divine perfection,[57] although again, as Goldman hastens to note, "Unlike Maimonides, Rav Kook regards this process as dynamic rather than static and possessing an evolutionary character." I would like at this point, then, to focus on one key issue where Rav Kook appears to disagree fundamentally with Maimonides, but where, upon closer examination, it turns out that Rav Kook's position is more a modification of the Maimonidean position, a modification, again, resulting from the shift from Maimonides' more static to Rav Kook's more dynamic approach to reality. I refer to the issue of intellect and imagination.

As is well known, the issue of intellect and imagination is a central, recurring theme in the *Guide*, appearing in such diverse contexts as Maimonides' discussion of man's knowledge of God, prophecy, divine providence, the law, and many other issues as well. For Maimonides, to state matters briefly, the act of intellect is contrary to the act of imagination. The intellect can analyze, abstract, conceptualize, and differentiate the universal from the individual. It is the intellect, then, which gives us a true representation of reality. Imagination "apprehends only that which is individual and composite as a whole, as it is apprehended by the senses." Indeed, "in its apprehension, imagination is in no way able to hold itself aloof from matter." The imagination, then, gives us a distorted picture of the world.[58] Moreover, Maimonides states that "the impossible has a stable nature . . . [and] the power over the maker of the impossible is not attributed to the deity" (*Guide* III:15:459). And, for Maimonides, it is the intellect, not the imagination, that determines the possible and the impossible (*Guide* I:73:211). Hence, Maimonides sharply criticizes the Mutakallimun, who believed that whatever imagination can imagine as possible is possible (*Guide* I:71:179–80; I:73:206–12; I:76:230–31).

Rav Kook, in a number of different places in *Orot Ha-Kodesh*, appears to side with the Mutakallimun on this crucial issue. He states: "In the realm of the holy there can be no exaggeration in existence. Whatever may be imagined—exists in truth. And this was the supernal kernel [of truth] in the view of Kalam, rejected by the scholastics."[59] "Rejected by the scholastics," and, we may add— though Rav Kook does not—by Maimonides, as well.

Rav Kook goes even further in another passage and argues that Maimonides' view regarding the stable nature of the impossible, as well as his assertion, flowing from that view, that there must necessarily be different levels of existence, are experienced by the soul as perilous limitations on God's power.[60] Here Rav Kook might seem to come close to the views of Rav Naḥman of Bratslav, who exalted the function of the imagination and revelled in God's ability to perform the impossible.[61] Of course, for Rav Naḥman, as opposed to Rav Kook, Maimonides was not a great hero, but, on the contrary, a great heretic, and the *Guide* was a dangerous, indeed un-Jewish book.[62] What, then, is the relationship between Rav Kook's views on intellect, imagination, and the nature of the impossible and those of Maimonides? Are Rav Kook's views on these issues so totally opposed to those of Maimonides as might appear at first glance?

I shall not attempt a definitive answer to such difficult questions. Maimonides' discussion in the *Guide* concerning intellect, imagination, and the nature of the impossible is, at one and the same time, both highly technical and exceptionally subtle, forbidding in both its complexity and profundity.[63] Rav Kook's reflections on these matters in *Orot ha-Kodesh* are, oftentimes, more suggestive than explicit, alluding to profound, mystical depths in a poetic and elusive language. Moreover, *Orot Ha-Kodesh* was originally written by Rav Kook as a mystical diary over the course of many years and was only edited and organized topically by his disciple R. David Ha-Kohen, who, unfortunately, did not inform us as to the date of each passage.[64] Perhaps, then, one ought not expect in *Orot ha-Kodesh* a completely consistent and systematic view on any particular subject. I do not, therefore, pretend to fully comprehend either Maimonides' or Rav Kook's views on these issues. However, to the extent that I do comprehend them, let me offer the following tentative suggestions as to how we might view the relationship between Rav Kook's and Maimonides' positions on this question.

For Maimonides, as noted, the structures of nature and Torah are permanent and unchanging.[65] These structures, being consequent upon divine wisdom, are intelligible structures and therefore can be apprehended through the intellect and only through the intellect.[66] The Mutakallimun, on the other hand, abolish the nature of existence (*Guide* I:71, 73, 76). For them, both the works of God (Nature) and the laws of God (Torah) are consequent upon the divine will and can be entirely other than they are if so willed by God (ibid.; also III:25, 26). Thus "no consideration is due to how that which exists is, for it is merely a custom" (*Guide* I:71:179). Consequently, having abolished the nature of existence, having reduced it to mere custom, solely dependent on the arbitrary will of God, the Mutakallimun affirm "that that which can be imagined is . . . something possible, whether something existing corresponds to it or not. On the other hand, everything that cannot be imagined is impossible" (*Guide* I:73:207). Rav Kook, unlike the Mutakallimun, does not abolish the nature of existence. He agrees with Maimonides that there is a nature to existence. However, for Rav Kook, that nature is an evolving nature, not a stable and permanent nature. Thus, for Rav Kook, at any particular moment in time there are intelligible structures underlying both nature and Torah. But since nature and Torah are evolving to ever higher levels of perfection, new and different intelligible structures will emerge, superseding current intelligible structures. To give just two famous examples: death is gradually being conquered and will eventually be conquered entirely;[67] the spirit of knowledge will, one day, come to rest over animals and not be limited only to men.[68] We may then say as follows: Rav Kook would agree with Maimonides that the structure of reality, of both nature and Torah as they exist at any particular moment, may be apprehended by the intellect and only by the intellect. And, in terms of *that* moment, it is the intellect that determines what is possible and what is impossible. But this holds true only for the present. Insofar as both nature and Torah are evolving, insofar as new intelligible structures will, one day, emerge, superseding current intelligible structures, what is impossible today in the present, in light of the current structures, may be possible tomorrow in the future, in light of the new structures.

But how can we grasp these future possibilities? Only through the imagination. In a word, for Rav Kook, intellect grasps the present; imagination grasps an open future, radically different from the present. It is this truth, I believe, to which Rav Kook refers when he states that the imagination casts its glance afar, while the intellect reveals the richness of the here-and-now.[69]

If, however, as the world evolves toward ever-higher levels of perfection, radically new intelligible structures, and, consequently, radically new possibilities are constantly emerging, it follows, then, that it is only from the vantage point of the present moment that these structures and possibilities still lie in the future, and it is, consequently, only from that vantage point that these structures and possibilities need to be grasped by the imagination. When, however, the future moment arrives and these structures and, in their wake, these possibilities, finally do emerge, they will then be current structures and present possibilities, and they will then, at that point in time, be able to be grasped by the intellect. The cosmic evolutionary process, then, corresponds to an epistemological evolutionary process. As Rav Kook states: "And, in the course of time, matters that can now be only imagined will be able to be conjectured, and those matters that can now be only conjectured will be clarified through clear knowledge and cognition."[70] The imagination, in Kook's view, is thus always seeking to anticipate the future, always chafing against the limitations and restrictions of present reality. And this drive, this desire on the part of imagination to outstrip the limits of present reality is what, for Rav Kook, endows it with greatness. "Let us ascribe greatness to the life-giving power of our supernal imagination which rises above all boundaries and limitations pertaining to the conditions of our arid and impoverished reality.[71] . . . Only the free dream that rebels against reality and its limits is, in truth, the most existential truth of reality."[72]

Rav Kook believes, together with Maimonides, that reality as we perceive it does have limits and boundaries. And he believes, together with Maimonides, that it is only the intellect that can know reality as it is within those limits and boundaries. However, for Maimonides these limits are fixed and unchanging and any attempt on the part of the imagination to go beyond or to deny those limits, is naught but folly and vanity. For Rav Kook, those limits are temporary and ever changing, and the superiority of imagination over intellect lies precisely in the fact that imagination, unlike intellect, can pass beyond them.

Until this point we have discussed the issue of intellect and imagination in Rav Kook from the perspective of his evolutionary theory, from a historical and chronological vantage point. But this horizontal approach needs to be complemented by a vertical approach. Rav Kook's evolutionary, historical theory must be set and understood within the broader framework of his ontological, emanationist outlook. For Rav Kook, as for many modern philosophically inclined thinkers of a historicist bent, the evolution or dialectical progression of reality over the course of time toward ever higher levels of perfection is just a projection onto a horizontal plane of a vertical, dynamic emanationist stance where the overflow of the divine source results in different levels of reality, in a hierarchical chain of being, in a dialectical movement of alienation and return. Emanation, in the modern view, is seen not as a timeless but as a preeminently historical process. Thus, as one moves further along the horizontal axis, progressively higher levels of being are projected thereon.[73]

To return to Rav Kook, the new intelligible structures that will emerge in the future already exist in the present—except that in the present they exist in a remote supernal realm, inaccessible to man's intellect, in a realm that may be reached only by the imagination. The imagination grasps not only future possibilities but that hidden supernal realm, lying beyond the bounds of intelligible reality.[74] As one moves, however, from the present to the future, this hidden realm will become clear and manifest as it is projected onto the horizontal axis, as it emanates "downward" in time. And, following from the above, this realm, which now may be grasped only by the imagination, will in the future be knowable by the intellect. The evolution of the cosmos upward toward ever higher levels of perfection is thus a mirror image of a historical emanation downwards of ever higher levels of divine reality.

This matter is also presented by Rav Kook using somewhat different terminology.[75] In the divine reality, there is no potentiality, only actuality; there are no nonexistent future possibilities, for everything in God is pure being. Potentiality, nonexistence, future possibilities—all these categories have meaning and "reality" only from man's point of view. And these—from our point of view—nonexistent future possibilities may be grasped only by man's imagination.[76] However, from God's point of view, these—from our point of view—nonexistent future possibilities are actual present existents, supernal realities, and as such are the objects of the infinite divine intellect. When, through the process of emanation over the course of history, these nonexistent future possibilities from our point of view—but actual present existents from God's point of view—will become actual present existents from our point of view as well, and will become transformed from supernal realities into empirical realities, they will then become the objects of our human intellects as they are now the objects of the infinite divine intellect. For the realm of possibility is grasped by the imagination, the realm of actuality by the intellect. In God's true existence, from God's point of view, all is actuality and all, therefore, is known by His infinite divine intellect. However, in our empirical world, looking at things from our point of view, the movement from possibility to actuality on the ontological plane is paralleled by a movement from imagination to intellect on the epistemological plane.[77]

To return, then, to our starting point: for Rav Kook, "in the realm of the holy there can be no exaggeration in existence [and] whatever may be imagined, exists in truth"[78]—in concealed form, from God's point of view, in the present; in revealed form, from man's point of view, in the future. For the holy is the cosmic drive to reach greater and greater levels of perfection. And as these levels are reached, what is hidden today, concealed in God's inner being, will become visible tomorrow; what from man's point of view is only a bare possibility today will be actualized and certain tomorrow. Consequently, that hidden, future possibility that may only be grasped by man's imagination today will, in its visible actuality, be known to man's intellect tomorrow, as indeed it is already today, as an actual existent in God's true being, known to the infinite divine intellect.[79]

Rav Kook's position is thus both less and more radical than that of the Mutakallimun. For the Mutakallimun, that which can be imagined is already a present possibility, but only a possibility. For Rav Kook, that which can be imagined is, from our point of view, only a nonexistent future possibility, while, from God's point of view, it already possesses actuality in the truth of the divine existence. At the same time, Rav Kook's apparent break with Maimonides on this central issue of intellect versus imagination is upon closer examination not quite the total break it appeared to be at first. Rather Rav Kook's position ought to be seen—at least from his perspective—as being a profound modification and radical expansion of Maimonides' views. Rav Kook keeps the Maimonidean role of intellect as the instrument whereby one knows the intelligible structures of reality. However, he allows the imagination to grasp a supernal hidden present and an open future radically different from the visible present, an open future when the supernal hidden present will no longer be hidden but will itself become visible. Of course, for Maimonides such notions of a supernal hidden present and an open future are mere fantasies of the imagination! This profound disagreement, however, should not obscure the significant area of agreement.[80] And, once again, the root cause of the disagreement derives from the clash between Maimonides' vision of a stable cosmos and Rav Kook's vision of an evolving cosmos.

I have sought to show here how Rav Kook used Maimonidean concepts and views, creatively transforming them in the light of his own evolutionary, holistic approach. And yet, if truth be told—and it must be told!—there can be no doubt that, as we have already noted, Rav Kook, in terms of his metaphysics and theology, was much closer to kabbalistic theories and approaches than to Maimonidean or philosophic positions. Indeed, if we may use Rav Kook's categories of the principle of affirmation, of religious passion, and the principle of negation, of intellectual purity, we may suggest that despite what he wrote about Maimonides uniting in his person and thought both principles, Jewish philosophy for Rav Kook primarily functioned as the principle of negation within the totality of Jewish thought. Within that totality, then, as part of that whole, Jewish philosophy served an important purpose by guaranteeing the intellectual purity of the Jew's passion for God, by refining his intense, burning desire for divine closeness. At the same time, Jewish philosophy, taken by itself, could only issue forth in a cold, abstract, pallid, and lifeless religious rationalism, lacking vitality, drive, and depth of experience.

Yes, the truth must be told. Rav Kook, in terms of his substantive views, was closer to the kabbalists than to the philosophers. But there is another, equally important, counterbalancing truth, and this truth must also be told. For, I would argue, with respect to one crucial, fundamental, methodological issue, Rav Kook performed a turnabout and drew his inspiration from the Jewish philosophic tradition—in particular, from Maimonides—and *not* from the kabbalistic tradition. With this turnabout I should like to conclude.

The Jewish philosophers as a group, and specifically Maimonides, developed their philosophic positions in close dialogue and interaction with the intellectual, scientific, and philosophic culture and currents of thought surrounding them. Maimonides, as Rav Kook himself notes,[81] did not simply reject or ignore the various philosophic systems of his own days despite their variance with Judaism, but examined and confronted them seriously, rigorously, honestly, and critically, rejecting those elements that could be shown to be clearly contradictory to Judaism, but maintaining an open mind to the rest, and indeed claiming and showing how the truths uncovered by philosophy could deepen and enrich one's understanding of Judaism.

This was the very model that Rav Kook avowedly adopted in developing his own thought. He, too, confronted the various intellectual movements, philosophic schools, and scientific theories of his own day. Sifting carefully, he took over and adopted those elements in modern western culture that he considered to be true, valuable, and precious and utilized them in the course of working out his own conception of Judaism.[82] In this respect, his own very clear interaction with and response to the broader general culture of his day, its challenges and stimuli, place him in the philosophic camp. The development of the kabbalistic tradition, while certainly not free from outside influences, took place in a more internal, insulated, and isolated fashion. It is ironic, then, that today, many would-be disciples of Rav Kook take his system as a closed one, developing it solely from within, and seeking to isolate it—and themselves—from the intellectual and cultural challenges of our day.

The Jewish philosophic tradition as a whole, and the writings of Maimonides in particular, served Rav Kook as a model how one could and should confront external challenges: critically, seriously, honestly, openly, creatively, and, above all, unafraid. Rav Kook stated that one must never confuse *yir'at shamayim*, fear of heaven or piety, with *yir'at mahshavah*, fear of thought. And he went on to state: "For if a person is afraid to think he will progressively sink deeper into the mire of ignorance that will deprive him of his soul, sap his strength, and darken his spirit."[83]

Perhaps it was this truth, more than any other, that Rav Kook, the man and the thinker, learned from Maimonides, the man and the thinker.

Notes

1. See *Orot ha-Kodesh* (Jerusalem, 1963), I, 25–27; *Iggerot ha-Re'iyah* (Jerusalem, 1961), I, 123–26 and 187 (letters 103 and 146 to R. Isaac Halevi); and "Ha-Yeshivah ha-Merkazit ha-'Olamit bi-Yerushalayim," in *Ma'amarei ha-Re'iyah* (Jerusalem, 1984), 63–64. Cf. R. Shlomo Zevin, "R. Avraham Yitzhak ha-Kohen Kook," in *Ishim ve-Shitot* (Tel Aviv, 1958), 231–37; and R. Moshe Zuriel, "Ha-Kodesh, ha-Nistar, ve-ha-Aggadah be-Haguto shel Ha-Re'iyah zt"l," in *Be-Oro*, ed. Haim Hamiel (Jerusalem, 1986), 172–255.

2. See *Iggerot ha-Re'iyah*, letter 146 and "Ha-Yeshivah ha-Merkazit"; and *Orot ha-Torah* (Jerusalem, 1961), 73–84.

3. See *Hartza'at ha-Rav* (Jerusalem, 1921) (reprinted as an appendix to *Orot ha-Torah*). In this lecture Rav Kook suggested a two part project to fill the gap: *Halakhah Berurah* and *Birur Halakhah*. While Rav Kook finished writing *Halakah Berurah* in his lifetime, he left the completion of the project to his students. This massive undertaking is only now in the process of being finished. For an evaluation, see Eliav Schochetman, "Talmud Bavli im 'Halakhah Berurah' u-'Birur Halakah': Masekhet Sukkah," *Shenaton Mishpat ha-Ivri* 3–4 (1976–77): 409–30. Cf. Schochetman, "Al Shittat ha-Limud shel ha-Talmud be-Ikkevot Hazono shel Maran ha-Rav Kook Ztz"l," in *Be-Oro*, ed. Haim Hamiel, 87–120.

4. See "Keytzad Mevakkerim," in *Ma'amarei ha-Re'iyah*, 13.

5. See *Iggerot ha-Re'iyah* I, 84 (letter 79 to R. Abraham Neuwirth), 187 (letter 146 to R. Isaac Halevi), and 192–93 (letter 149 to R. Isaac Halevi); II, 173 (letter 541 to R. Noah Gottlieb); IV, 65 (letter 1044 to R. Shneur Z. Slonim).

6. For Rav Kook and the Kabbalah, see Tamar Ross, "Musag ha-Elohut shel ha-Rav Kook," *Daat* 8 (Winter 1982): 109–28, and 9 (Summer 1983): 39–74; Yosef Ben-Shlomo, "Shelemut ve-Hishtalmut be-Torat ha-

Elohut shel ha-Rav Kook," *Iyyun* 33 (1984): 289–309; Rabbi M. Z. Neriyah, *Mo'adei ha-Re'iyah* (Jerusalem, 1980), 435–60; Shmuel Livneh, "Perakim mi-Torat ha-Musar," in *Zikhron Re-iyah*, ed. Y. Rafael (Jerusalem, 1986), 77–90; and Leon Ashkenazi, "Shimush be-Musagim Kabbaliyim be-Mishnato shel ha-Rav Kook," in *Yovel Orot*, ed. B. Ish-Shalom and S. Rosenberg (Jerusalem, 1986), 123–28. For Rav Kook and nineteenth-century Jewish thought, see Eliezer Goldman, "Responses to Modernity in Orthodox Jewish Thought," *Studies in Contemporary Jewry*, vol. 2, ed. P. Medding (Bloomington, Ind., 1986), 63–65; and *idem*, "Tziyyonut Hilonit, Te'udat Yisrael, ve-Takhlit ha-Torah: Ma'amarei ha-Rav Kook be-*Peles* 5661–64 (1901–4)," *Daat* 11 (Summer 1983): 103–26.

7. See *Orot ha-Kodesh* (Jerusalem, 1964), II, 549. Cf. R. Joseph B. Soloveitchik, "Ish ha-Halakhah," in *Be-Sod ha-Yahid Ve-ha-Yahad*, ed. P. Peli (Jerusalem, 1976), 172–77; in English, *Halakhic Man*, trans. Lawrence J. Kaplan (Philadelphia, 1983), 123–28.

8. See Gersonides, *Milhamot Adonai*, Books 3 (Divine Knowledge) and 4 (Divine Providence), and his *Commentary on Job*.

9. *Orot ha-Kodesh* II, 549.

10. See *Orot ha-Teshuvah*, 5th ed. (Jerusalem, 1970), 72–73; *Orot ha-Kodesh* II, 395–401.

11. *Orot ha-Kodesh* II, 549.

12. Ibid., 550.

13. On the emergence of an "heroic image" of Maimonides, see Bernard Septimus, *Hispano-Jewish Culture in Transition: The Career and Controversies of Ramah* (Cambridge, Mass., 1982), 45–46. For varying perceptions of Maimonides in the modern period, see James Lehmann, "Maimonides, Mendelssohn, and the Me'asfim," in *Leo Baeck Institute Yearbook* 20 (1975): 87–108; and Jay Harris, "The Image of Maimonides in Nineteenth-Century Jewish Historiography," in *Proceedings of the American Academy for Jewish Research* 54 (1987): 117–39.

14. Zev Yawetz, *Toledot Yisrael* (Tel Aviv, 1935), 12: 1–54.

15. "Le-Ahduto shel ha-Rambam: Ma'amar Meyuhad," printed in Zev Yawetz, *Toledot Yisrael* 12: 211–19; reprinted in *Ma'amarei ha-Re'iyah*, 105–12. All citations are to *Ma'amarei ha-Re'iyah*. (Rav Kook's disciple, Rabbi Benjamin Menashe Lewin, the editor of vol. 12 of Yawetz's *Toledot Yisrael*, gave Rav Kook access to Yawetz's manuscript before it was published, and he incorporated Rav Kook's response as a special appendix to the volume.) Cf., however, "Tallelei Orot: Hashkafah 'al Ta'amei ha-Mitzvot," in *Ma'amarei ha-Re'iyah* 19 ("Fragments of Light: A View as to the Reasons for the Commandments," in *Abraham Isaac Kook*, trans. B. Z. Bokser [New York, 1978], 304–5), where Rav Kook distinguishes between the "logical form of the *Guide of the Perplexed*" and "the form of holiness and divine wholeness of the *Mishneh Torah* which is suffused with a refined feeling that with a strong hand

(be-yad ḥazakah) transcends the bounds of logical reasoning," as well as between the "focus on the past" found in the *Guide* and the "merger of past with present and future" found in the *Mishneh Torah.*

16. "Ha-Ma'or ha-Eḥad," Passover Eve, 1935, reprinted several times, most recently in *Ma'amarei ha-Re'iyah*, 113–17; and *Zikhron Re'iyah*, 1–4 (all page references are to *Ma'amarei ha-Re'iyah*). I discuss this essay of Rav Kook at great length in an as yet unpublished essay, "The Light and the Strength: The Unity of Intellectual Purity and Religious Passion in the Thought of Rav Kook."

17. In truth, however, Maimonides was born in 1138, not 1135. See S. Z. Havlin, "Le-Toledot ha-Rambam," *Daat* 15 (Summer 1985): 70–79.

18. See "Le-Aḥduto shel ha-Rambam," 112; "Ha-Maor ha-Eḥad," 115–17; and "Ha-yesodot ha-Kozvim shel Mevakrei ha-Mikra," in *Ma'amarei ha-Re'iyah*, 470.

19. "Le-Aḥduto shel ha-Rambam," 107–8.

20. Ibid., 108–10. Rav Kook's approach here corresponds with the neo-Kantian interpretation of Maimonides set forth by Hermann Cohen in his classic essay, "Characterstik der Ethik Maimunis," *Jüdische Schriften*, 3 (1924): 227–89 ("Ofyah shel Torat ha-Middot le-ha-Rambam," in *Iyyunim be-Yahadut U-ve-Ba'ayot ha-Dor* [Jerusalem, 1977], 17–59) and Julius Guttman in his standard work, *Ha-Philosophia shel ha-Yahadut* (Jerusalem, 1951), 164 (*Philosophies of Judaism* [New York, 1964], 200). For a thorough, up-to-date, scholarly discussion and critique of the neo-Kantian approach, particularly as applied to the conclusion of the *Guide*, with full bibliographical guidance, see Menahem Kellner, *Maimonides on Human Perfection*, Brown Judaica Studies 202 (Atlanta, 1990).

21. I set out and analyze the differences between "conservative" and "radical" interpreters at great length and with full documentation (particularly for the medieval period) in chapter 3 of my doctoral dissertation, *Rationalism and Rabbinic Culture in Sixteenth-Century Eastern Europe: Rabbi Mordecai Jaffe's Levush Pinat Yikrat*, Harvard University, 1975. An abbreviated discussion of this topic, based upon my thesis, may be found in my essay, "Rabbi Mordekhai Jaffe and the Evolution of Jewish Culture in Poland in the Sixteenth Century," in *Jewish Thought in the Sixteenth Century*, ed. B. D. Cooperman (Cambridge, Mass., 1983), 277–79. See, as well, the important article by Aviezer Ravitsky, "The Secrets of the Guide to the Perplexed: Between the Thirteenth and the Twentieth Centuries," in *Studies in Maimonides*, ed. Isadore Twersky (Cambridge, Mass., 1990), 159–207.

22. See chapter 3 of my dissertation for a thorough discussion of Abarbanel. See, as well, Alvin J. Reines, *Maimonides and Abrabanel on Prophecy* (Cincinnati, 1970).

23. See *Kittevei ha-Ramban*, vol. 1, ed. Rabbi C. D. Chavel (Jerusalem, 1963), 336–51 (in particular 345–48).

24. "Le-Aḥduto shel ha-Rambam," 106.
25. See, for example, *Yevamot* 71a and *Bava Metzia* 31b. For further references and full discussion, see "Dibrah Torah bi-Leshon Benei Adam," in *Entzyklopedia Talmudit,* vol. 7, ed. Rabbi S. J. Zevin (Jerusalem, 1979), 77–82.
26. For earlier authorities who employed the phrase, "The Torah speaketh in the language of the sons of man," to refer to the Bible's use of anthropomorphisms, see *Shenei Perushei R. Avraham ibn Ezra li-Terei Asar,* ed. Uriel Simon, vol. 1, *Hosea, Yoel, Amos* (Ramat Gan, 1989), 110 n.8; and *Ha-Risalah shel Yehuda ben Quraysh,* ed. Dan Bakar (Tel Aviv, 1984), 180 n.4. The list includes rabbinic scholars such as Hai Gaon, philologists such as Menaḥem, Dunash, ibn Quraysh, and ibn Janaḥ, exegetes such as ibn Balaam and ibn Ezra, and philosophical moralists such as Baḥya ibn Pakudah.
27. *Guide of the Perplexed,* trans. S. Pines (Chicago, 1963), I:26: 56. References to the Guide will be given in the following format: part:chapter(s); or else part:chapter:page number. All the page references are to this edition of the *Guide.* Cf. *Guide* I:14:40 on the identification of the "sons of man" *("benei adam")* with the multitude. For other citations by Maimonides of the statement "The Torah speaketh in the language of the sons of man," see *Guide* I:29:62, I:33:71, I:46:100, I:59:140, III:13:453; and *Laws of the Foundations of the Torah* 1:9.
28. This interpretation of Maimonides' position constitutes an attempt on my part to reconcile the apparent contradiction between the *Guide* I:26 and I:46 (where it would seem that, according to Maimonides, the multitude are to conceive of God as being a body) and I:35 (where Maimonides insists that the multitude "should be made to accept on traditional authority the belief that God is not a body"). In my reconciliation, I place great stress on Maimonides' use of the term "at first" in I:26. (See my italicization of the citation in the text.) For a different approach to this apparent contradiction, see the fourteenth-century commentator on the *Guide,* Joseph ibn Kaspi, *Amudei Kesef,* ed. S. Werbluner (Frankfort, 1848; reprinted in *Sheloshah Kadmonei Meforshei ha-Moreh,* Jerusalem, 1961), 38–39 (on *Guide* I:26) and 45–46 (on *Guide* I:35); Lawrence Berman in *Ibn Bajja and Maimonides* (unpublished Ph.D. dissertation, Hebrew University, 1959), xiv–xvi, 106–10; and Zev Harvey, "She'elat I-Gashmiyut ha-El etzel ha-Rambam, ha-Rabad, Kreskas, ve-Spinoza," in *Meḥkarim be-Hagut Yehudit,* ed. S. Heller-Wilensky and M. Idel (Jerusalem, 1989), 68–69.
29. My analysis of Rav Kook's view is based primarily on his "Letter on the Truth and Holiness of the Wisdom of the Kabbalah" (henceforth "Letter on the Kabbalah"), in *Ma'amarei ha-Re'iyah,* 518–21. Cf. *Iggerot ha-Re'iyah* II, 247–48 (letter 626, an open letter on the holiness of the Zohar), and *Orot ha-Kodesh* I, 110 and II, 402. One should note that Rav Kook is critical of certain, in his view, extreme instances of kab-

balistic anthropomorphic imagery. See "Letter on the Kabbalah," 520; and *Iggerot Re'iyah* I, 162 (letter 133 to J. D. Eisenstein).

30. See Gershom Scholem, *Major Trends in Jewish Mysticism* (New York, 1961), 27. For critical discussions of Scholem's distinction and the use he makes of it, see Frank Talmage, "Apples of Gold: The Inner Meaning of Sacred Texts in Medieval Judaism," in *Jewish Spirituality*, ed. Arthur Green (New York, 1986), I, 337–44; and Moshe Idel, *Kabbalah: New Perspectives* (New Haven, 1988), 200–234.

31. "Letter on the Kabbalah," 520.

32. Alfred Ivry, "Providence, Divine Omniscience, and Possibility: The Case of Maimonides," in *Divine Omniscience and Omnipotence in Medieval Philosophy*, ed. T. Rudavsky (Boston, 1985), 148–49.

33. Ibid., 146.

34. It is worth noting, however, that precisely the symbolic approach taken by Rav Kook was anticipated by Moses Narboni in his "Epistle on *Shiur Qomah*." For Narboni "All existents . . . are in [God] in the most noble [way of] existence . . . in perfect and simply unity." And it is precisely this notion which, as Professor Alexander Altmann has observed, "struck Narboni as offering a key to the understanding of . . . *Shiur Qomah*." See Alexander Altmann, "Moses Narboni's 'Epistle on *Shiur Qomah*,' " *Jewish Medieval and Renaissance Studies*, ed. by A. Altmann (Cambridge, Mass., 1967), 246–47.

35. After I wrote this, I came across an account by Yeshayahu Leibowitz of an extended conversation he had with Rav Kook during Sukkot in 1928, in which Rav Kook related to him that Maimonides' doctrine of the unity and incorporeality of God served as a brake against the danger of the deterioration of the Kabbalah into idolatry. See Y. Leibowitz, *The Faith of Maimonides* (New York, 1987), 37–38; and *'Al Olam u-Melo'o: Sihot im Michael Shashar* (Jerusalem, 1989), 93–95. Cf. *Orot ha-Kodesh*, I, 231 (*Osher ha-Dimyon*).

36. *Orot ha-Kodesh* II, 399; cf. II, 395–396. It is also worth noting that Rav Kook, in this passage, attributes this outlook to the "intellectual wing of the new Hassidic movement," i.e., Habad Hassidism. See David ha-Kohen's appendix to *Orot ha-Kodesh*, listing Rav Kook's sources, 606:6; and cf. 606:4 for earlier adumbrations of this view in classical Jewish texts. For analyses of Rav Kook's rootedness in and creative use and development of Hassidic sources, see the essays of Lawrence Fine and Norman Lamm in this volume. See, as well, Ella Belfer's essay in this volume for an analysis of this passage in *Orot ha-Kodesh* from a somewhat different vantage point than my own. Finally, note how in this passage this "monotheistic outlook tending toward a pantheistic explication" is contrasted with the standard, more strictly theistic position—as represented perhaps by Maimonides?

37. "Le-Ahduto shel ha-Rambam," 105–6; Cf. *Orot ha-Emunah*, ed. Moshe Gurwitz (Jerusalem, 1985), 38–39.

38. *Guide* II:47:409: "For only truth pleases Him, may He be exalted, and only that which is false angers Him."

39. *Orot ha-Kodesh* (Jerusalem, 1950), III, 144. See Shmuel Livneh, "Perakim mi-Torat ha-Nistar" (above, note 6), 87–88, for a discussion of Rav Kook's concept of "Ha-Tom ha-Penimi" and for a comparison of Rav Kook's views with those of Maimonides.

40. This point is discussed at length with full documentation in my essay, "The Light and the Strength: The Unity of Intellectual Purity and Religious Passion in the Thought of Rav Kook" (see above, note 16). For the meanwhile, see the following essays in *Ma'amerei ha-Re'iyah*: "Derekh ha-Teḥiyah" (1–9); "Ha-Maor ha-Eḥad" (113–15); and "Al Gerei ha-Zedek" (200–202); as well as *Iggerot ha-Re'iyah* II, 43 (letter 379 to Dr. Moshe Seidel); and *Orot ha-Emunah*, 72–88.

41. This is the theme of the *Guide* III:51, that great chapter which is not only one of the peaks of medieval—nay, of all—Jewish philosophy, but also one of the clearest, purest, and most intense expressions in all Jewish—and world—literature of the knowledge and love of God. Cf. *Laws of Repentance*, chap. 10.

42. See the references in note 40.

43. "Ha-Maor ha-Eḥad," 114: "The spirit of affirmation is the desire for divine closeness, [while] the spirit of negation [is] the desire that the spirit of this [divine] closeness be pure."

44. The terms are drawn from R. Joseph Soloveitchik, "U-Bikkashtem mi-Sham," in *Ish ha-Halakhah: Galui ve-Nistar* (Jerusalem, 1979), 123 n. 2: "Maimonides, instead of concerning himself with intellectualized passion *(hegyon ha-lev)*, focused upon the pathos of intellect *(levaviyut ha-higgayon)*." The application of Rav Soloveitchik's contrast to Maimonides and Rav Kook is, of course, my own.

45. *Iggerot ha-Re'iyah* I, 43 (letter 44). (In a few places, I have drawn upon the translation of this letter in Tzvi Feldman, *Rav A. Y. Kook: Selected Letters* [Ma'aleh Adumim, 1986], 82–83.) Cf. *Arpelei Tohar* (Jerusalem, 1983), 46–47, for a somewhat different approach.

46. I am not referring here to a person's rational faculty that is his or her natural form (*Guide* I:1:22, I:41:91; *Laws of the Foundation of the Torah* 4:8), but to his or her intellect which, as Maimonides states in one place, is the form of the "person perfect in knowledge" (*Laws of the Foundations of the Torah* 4:8) or, as he states in another place, "the form of the soul" (*Laws of Repentance* 8:3), i.e., the form of the rational faculty.

47. *Guide*, I:3:27, I:68:163–65, I:73:209 ("A Call Upon the Reader's Attention"); III:8:431–32, III:27:511, III:54:635.

48. See "Ha-Hayyut ha-'Olamit," in *Orot ha-Kodesh* II, "Ha-Hayyut ha-'Olamit" (329–70); and "Ha-Aḥdut ha-Kollelet," in ibid., 391–447. See, as well, Rav Kook's famous poem, "Laḥashei ha-Havayah" (Whispers of Existence), in *Sinai* 17 (1945): 15. (An English translation of this

poem with an extensive and penetrating commentary may be found in
Jerome Gellman's essay in this volume.) Note that in the body of my
text, I state that the "difference between Maimonides and Rav Kook as
to whether the fundamental bond between man and God is essentially
intellectual or nonintellectual in nature derives, *at least in part*, from
the root difference between them that we brought to light earlier,
namely, whether or not 'all existents . . . and all movements . . .
[exist] in God's supernal holiness'—Rav Kook's view—or only the
forms do—the position taken by Maimonides." I state "at least in
part," for the difference between Maimonides and Rav Kook as to
whether the fundamental bond between man and God is essentially
intellectual or nonintellectual cuts even deeper than indicated in the
body of my text. The two experiences of, or approaches to, God that are
set forth by Maimonides and Rav Kook, which I discuss and contrast in
my text, are both extrovertive in nature. That is, in both cases a person
approaches God or experiences God via the cosmos or external reality—
except that for Maimonides, the approach is via the intellectual cognition of the forms, while for Rav Kook, it is via a mystical perception of
reality in its totality. Both approaches, however—even that of Rav
Kook—being extrovertive in nature, are consequently *mediated* experiences of God, are, to some extent, *inferential* approaches, that is,
one infers from the cosmos to God, whether rationally or mystically.
However—and this is the deepest difference between Rav Kook and
Maimonides—while for Maimonides, the only possible approach to
God is extrovertive or mediated and indirect, for Rav Kook this extrovertive approach, for all its grandeur and significance, its power and
profundity, is secondary; the primary approach to God, in his view, is
introvertive—direct and unmediated. Thus, Rav Kook, in a famous
passage in *Olat Re'iyah* (Jerusalem, 1962), II, 3, states: "There is a love
for God . . . that derives from creation and its splendor, [from] the
loving tenderness of God that fills the world and the good He bestows
upon His creatures. And there is a love that is felt within the soul, that
derives from the very exalted rank of the soul to love the wholly good.
This latter love is fundamental and is more precious than any love that
arises out of considerations of [external] reality." By contrast, see *Guide*
I:34:74: "There [is] nothing in what exists besides God . . . and the
totality of things He has made. . . . There is, moreover, no way to
apprehend Him except it be through the things He has made." For
further analysis of these two approaches in Rav Kook's thought and the
differences between them, see Gellman's essay in this volume.

49. Contrast, for example, Maimonides' sharp and unequivocal condemnation, in *Laws of Repentance* 3:7 and *Guide* I:36:84–85 of inadvertent
heresy, that is, a person's adherence to heretical views because-"in
good faith!"—he mistakenly believes that these views are taught by
the Torah, with Rav Kook's exculpation of such heresy in "Perek be-

Hilkhot Tzibbur," in *Ma'amarei ha-Re'iyah*, 55–56. For a discussion of the conflicting medieval views on this issue, see Warren Zev Harvey, "She'elat I-Gashmiyut ha-El etzel ha-Rambam, ha-Rabad, Kreskas, ve-Spinoza" (above, note 28), 63–78; and Menaḥem Kellner in his many articles and books, in particular "What is Heresy?," *Studies in Jewish Philosophy* 3 (1983): 55–70; "Kefirah be-Shogeg be-Hagut Yehudit bi-Yemei ha-Beinayim," *Meḥkerei Yerushalayim be-Maḥshevet Yisrael* 3 (1984): 393–403; and *Dogma in Medieval Jewish Thought* (Oxford, 1986). For a complete listing of Kellner's articles and books, see *Dogma*, viii-ix. Interestingly enough, though Kellner in "What is Heresy?," 214, argues that one should "allow . . . for unintentional exculpable sin with respect to beliefs," he does not cite Rav Kook in support of his position and appears to be unaware of his essay on the subject. In general, given the importance and the live nature of this issue today and given Rav Kook's towering rabbinic standing, his authoritative pronouncement on this question deserves to be better known than it is.

For the theoretical basis of Rav Kook's "higher inclusiveness," see "Le-Milḥemet ha-De'ot ve-ha-Emunot," in *Orot*, (Jerusalem, 1961), 129–31. If we may, somewhat speculatively and tentatively, combine what Rav Kook says in this article both with his general dialectical evolutionary approach and with his various statements about Maimonides that we have examined until now, we may suggest the following. For Rav Kook, just as Maimonides' radical monotheism was a necessary transition stage between paganism and Rav Kook's own "monotheistic outlook tending toward a pantheistic explication," so too Maimonides' intolerance flowing from that radical monotheism was a necessary transition stage between the "perverse kind of tolerance" associated with paganism and the "higher inclusiveness" that stems from Rav Kook's own theological "monotheistic cum pantheistic" outlook. Rav Kook, in speaking of the tolerance of the "higher inclusiveness," states: "This [higher inclusiveness] is aware that there is a spark of light in all things, the inner spark of divine light that shines in all the different beliefs, as so many different educational systems for human culture . . . but they exist on different levels. . . . The spark of divine light appears in the more advanced religions and beliefs in a rich and exalted form and in the inferior religions and beliefs in a blurred, poor, and lowly form" ("Le Milḥemet ha-De'ot ve-ha-Emunot," 131). Of course, as Rav Kook goes on to emphasize, "Breadth and depth, inclusiveness and eternity are immanent in the light of Israel . . . , and every spark of what is manifest in the world stems from its source and is linked with it in a natural bond" (ibid.). For further discussion of Rav Kook's views on pluralism and tolerance, see the essay of Benjamin Ish-Shalom in this volume.

50. Recently, however, Alfred Ivry has emphasized the neo-Platonic elements in Maimonides' thought. On many issues, as Ivry picturesquely

states, "Maimonides comes perilously close to abandoning his Aristotelian anchors and setting off on a Neo-Platonic sea." See his essay,
"Providence, Divine Omniscience, and Possibility" (above, note 32),
143–49 (the picturesque comment cited immediately above is this essay's concluding sentence); "Islamic and Greek Influence on Maimonides' Philosophy," *Maimonides and Philosophy*, ed. S. Pines and Y.
Yovel (Dordrecht, 1986), 139–56; and, most recently and centrally,
"Neoplatonic Currents in Maimonides' Thought," in *Perspectives on
Maimonides*, ed. by Joel Kraemer (Oxford, 1991), 115–40.

51. See above, note 6. The profound influence of neo-Platonism on the
Kabbalah, particularly on the more conceptually and philosophically
oriented Kabbalah, is a commonplace, and has been the subject of
extensive research and discussion by Scholem, Tishbi, Altmann, Idel,
and others. For the connection between neo-Platonism and nineteenth-
century Jewish thought, particularly of the idealist variety, see Jacob
Taubes, "Naḥman Krochmal and Modern Historicism," *Judaism* 12
(1963): 150–64; and Eli Schweid, "Beyn 'Ḥokhmat ha-Torah al ha-
Emet' ve-'Sod Yiḥud ha-Emunah' le-'Philosophiah shel ha-Dat,' " *Iyyun*
20 (1969): 29–60.

52. See *Guide* II:28–29; *Mishneh Torah, Laws of Kings and Their Wars* 12:1;
and *Eight Chapters*, chap. 8.

53. See *Guide* II:39; III:34; III:41:562–63; *Laws of the Foundations of the
Torah*, chap. 9; *Laws of Kings and Their Wars* 11:3; "Introduction to
the Commentary on the Mishnah"; and "Introduction to Ḥelek," the
Ninth of the "Thirteen Principles of Faith."

54. See *Orot ha-Kodesh*, II, *Hit'alut ha-'Olam*, 515–74; and see below notes
67 and 68.

55. See *Iggerot ha-Re'iyah* I, 173 (letter 140 to R. Samuel Alexandrov); and
Orot ha-Kodesh (Jerusalem, 1990), IV, 516–17.

56. See "Kirvat Elohim," in *Ma'amerei Re'iyah*, 32–39; and *Orot ha-Kodesh*
II, 529–34. Cf. Y. Ben-Shlomo, "Shelemut ve-Hishtalmut be-Torat ha-
Elohut shel ha-Rav Kook" (above, note 6); and B. Ish-Shalom, *Ha-
Rav Kook: Beyn Ratziyonalism ve-Mystikah* (Tel Aviv, 1990), 158–70.
Goldman's essay is not yet published.

57. *Guide* I:72; II:4–6; III:8, III:10, III:12, III:25. See Ivry, "Providence,
Divine Omniscience, and Possibility: The Case of Maimonides" (above,
note 32); and E. Goldman, "Al Takhlit ha-Metziut be-Moreh Nevuk-
him," in *Sefer Yeshayahu Leibowitz* (Tel Aviv, 1977), 164–90.

58. *Guide* I:73:209–12 ("A Call Upon the Reader's Attention"). Cf.
II:12:280; "[The] imagination . . . is also in true reality the evil impulse. For every deficiency of reason or character is due to the action of
the imagination or consequent upon its action." See above, note 47, for
further references in the *Guide* concerning the action and nobility of
the intellect.

59. *Orot ha-Kodesh* I, 212 (*Arpelei Tohar 5*).

60. Ibid., II, 461. Cf.I, 213 (paragraph 44, "Beyond Possibility and Impossibility").

61. See Arthur Green, *Tormented Master: A Life of Rabbi Nahman of Bratslav* (Tuscaloosa, Ala., 1979), "Excursus I: Faith, Doubt and Reason," 285–336, and "Excursus II: The Tales," 341–44.

62. A convenient collection of statements of Rabbi Naḥman sharply condemning philosophy in general and Maimonides' *Guide* in particular may be found in Joseph Dan, *The Teachings of Hasidism* (New York, 1983), 142–45. For further bibliographical references and discussion, see Green, 331, n. 8. Rabbi Naḥman's statement that "anyone who studies the *Guide* loses the image of God" is particularly striking, inasmuch as the purpose of the *Guide* is to open the gates of wisdom so that the righteous person may enter therein (*Guide*, Introduction to the First Part: 20; introductory verse to I:1:21)—the righteous person being one who gives all his time to seeking knowledge and who does justice thereby to his rational soul (*Guide* I:34:76, III:53:631)—and, once inside, actualizes his intellect which is his image of God (*Guide* I:1:22; III:8:431–32)!

63. See Ivry, "Maimonides on Possibility," in *Mystics, Philosophers, Politicians: Essays in Honor of Alexander Altmann*, ed. J. Reinharz and D. Swetchinski (Durham, N.C., 1982), 67–84.

64. For some of the problems involved in editing *Orot ha-Kodesh*, see Yoninah Dison, "Arba'ah Motivim be-*Orot ha-Kodesh* ke-Basis le-'Arikhah Ḥadashah," in *Daat* 24 (Winter 1990): 41–86; and Dov Schwartz " 'Arikhah mul Yetzirah," in the same issue of *Daat*, 87–92. As both Dison and Schwartz note, the systematic conceptual framework that R. David ha-Kohen (the Nazir) used in order to organize Rav Kook's mystical diaries may very well have been the Nazir's own and not that of Rav Kook.

65. See above, notes 52 and 53.

66. As Professor Yehudah Gellman, independently of me, has stated: "[There are] two foundational assertions [in the *Guide*]. The first foundational view is that the world and Torah have intelligible, rational structures, due to their being in accordance with Divine Wisdom, rather than the Divine Will (*Guide* III:25, 26); or, more precisely, due to the Divine Will being subservient to the Divine Wisdom. The second foundational view is that human cognitive endowment, though limited in scope, is validly capable of knowing the rational structures of the world and of Torah" (*Guide* I:1, 2 and *passim*). See Yehudah Gellman, "Radical Responsibility in Maimonides' Thought," in *The Thought of Moses Maimonides*, ed. I. Robinson, L. Kaplan, and J. Bauer (Lewiston, N.Y. 1990), 250.

67. *Orot ha-Kodesh* II, 373–86. See S. H. Bergman, "Mavet ve-'almavet be-Maḥashavto shel ha-Rav Kook," in *Hogim u-Ma'aminim* (Tel Aviv, 1959), 101–11 (translated as "Death and Immortality in the Teachings

of Rav Kook," *Judaism* 7, no. 3 [1958]: 242–47); and the essay by Tamar Ross in chapter 9 of this volume.

68. *Olat Re'iyah* I, 292, s.v. *ve-'arvah la-Adonai*. Cf. "Tallelei Orot" (above, note 15), 26–28 ("Fragments of Light," 317–21).

69. *Orot ha-Kodesh* I, 238.

70. Ibid., 219. But see below, note 79.

71. *Orot ha-Kodesh* I, 223.

72. Ibid., 226. Cf. 230.

73. My analysis here is deeply indebted to Jacob Taubes's essay, "Nahman Krochmal and Modern Historicism" (see above, note 51), 156–57. I am essentially arguing that Taubes's claim that the dynamic emanationist scheme of neo-Platonism provided both Hegel and Krochmal with "an ontological context for their historiosophic concept of spirit" holds true for Rav Kook as well. Rav Kook's indebtedness to nineteenth-century idealism in general has been demonstrated in several essays of Goldman (above, note 6). The question of the specific influence of Krochmal on Rav Kook, however, has been alluded to in the literature on Rav Kook but never has been the subject of sustained analysis. Certainly, to take one example, Rav Kook's essay, "Le-Mahalakh ha-Ideot be-Yisrael," *Orot*, 102–18, bears the deep imprint of Krochmal. To my knowledge, however, Rav Kook only mentions Krochmal once in all his writings and then very critically. See the passage from the manuscript of *Orot ha-Emunah* that was not included in the published version of the book, but was published separately by Moshe Zuriel in *Otzerot ha-Re'iyah* (Ma'aleh 'Adumim, 1988), 635. In private conversation, Professor Eliezer Goldman expressed the opinion that Rav Kook would no doubt have felt a deep affinity with Krochmal's philosophy of history, but, at the same time, would have been strongly opposed to his spirit of historical criticism.

74. The notion that the imagination, building upon and purified by the intellect, can go beyond it and penetrate into supernal realms inaccessible to the intellect, may be found in *Orot ha-Kodesh* I, 218, 231, 234, 240. On the other hand, in the unit, "Aḥdut ha-Regesh, ha-Sekhel, ve-ha-Ratzon," in ibid., 247–63, intellect appears to be higher than imagination, and the hierarchy, in ascending order, is action, imagination, feeling, intellect, and supernal spiritual awareness (see 235, 247–49). We might, of course, argue that since the texts forming *Orot ha-Kodesh* were originally entries over many years in a sort of mystical journal, we ought not to be surprised by contradictions or inconsistencies. But see ibid., 237, where Rav Kook argues that imagination as a spontaneous act is a mere shadow of intellect, whereas imagination as a receptive faculty is fit to receive an exalted illumination and *as such* is higher than intellect.

75. I am basing myself here primarily on *Orot ha-Kodesh* I, 214 (section 46), as well as section 45 on 213.

76. Rav Kook in this key text (214) states without qualification that that which does not exist from our point of view cannot be known by us. However, in light of Rav Kook's other statements and our analysis of his general viewpoint, I assume he means that it cannot be known by our intellect but that it may be grasped by our imagination.

77. R. David ha-Kohen in his notes (2: 592) suggests the *Guide* I:57 and its commentaries as a possible source for *Orot ha-Kodesh* I, 214 (section 46). To this we should also add the *Guide* I:68. At the same time, Rav Kook's use in this passage of the terminology "from God's point of view" *(le-gabei ha-Elohut)* and "from our point of view" *(le-gabei didan)* suggests that a very different and equally important source is the thought of the famous nineteenth-century Ḥabad theoretician, R. Aharon ha-Levi of Starosselje. Cf. *Orot ha-Emunah*, 23–24. (For the reference to *Orot ha-Emunah* and the observation that the phrase *"le-gabei ha-Elohut"* and *"le-gabei didan"* derives from R. Aharon ha-Levi of Starroselje, I am indebted to Bezalel Naor, "Rav Kook and Emmanuel Levinas on the Non-Existence of God," *Orot* [New York, 1991]). We have, then, in this critical passage in *Orot ha-Kodesh* both a striking blend of Maimonidean motifs and Hassidic motifs of the Habad school and a transformation of these motifs in the light of Rav Kook's evolutionary holism.

78. In light of our analysis, we may suggest that there is a double meaning to the phrase "exists in truth" *("be-emet matzui")*. It may of course simply mean "to truly exist." It may, however, also mean "to exist in the truth of God's existence." Thus, in this paragraph, Rav Kook is arguing that whatever may be imagined exists in holiness in the truth of God's existence, that is, from God's point of view, though from our point of view, this imagined entity is only a nonexistent future possibility lacking concrete empirical reality, which is precisely why it may only be imagined and not intellected by us. On the other hand, when in section 45, 213, Rav Kook states "whatever derives from the intellection of the intellect possesses concrete reality" *(metziut mamash)*, he is referring to existents both when they possess reality from God's point of view, insofar as they are the objects of His infinite divine intellect even though they do not as yet possess reality from our point of view, and when they acquire their reality from our point of view as well and become objects of our human intellect. See notes 79 and 80.

79. At the same time, leaving to the side Rav Kook's belief in the general evolution of the cosmos to higher levels of perfection, he also certainly believed that a person, through his own efforts, could spiritually progress and reach greater degrees of *devekut* and higher levels of perfection and insight, so that what was once only accessible to his imagination would become accessible to his intellect, and new levels of reality that were entirely beyond his grasp would become accessible to his imagination. This is then another meaning of the statement from *Orot*

ha-Kodesh I, 219, cited above, 59. We have, then, in Rav Kook's thought, an interplay between a cosmic evolutionary process and a process of individual human spiritual ascension. In the cosmic evolutionary process, nonexistent future possibilities that exist only from God's point of view and can be grasped only by a person's imagination emanate downward over the course of history, acquire reality from man's point of view, and become known to his intellect. Similarly, in the course of human spiritual ascension to greater levels of perfection and *devekut*, supernal levels of reality that existed only from God's point of view, and that therefore could previously be only imagined, can now be intellected, and are *endowed*, through that intellection, with concrete reality, from man's point of view as well as from God's. We see here a creative role for the human intellect, whereby that intellect, in a manner similar to the divine intellect, not only intellectually cognizes that which already possesses reality, but also, through intellectual cognition, *endows* beings with reality. See the statement of Rav Kook in *Orot ha-Kodesh* I, 213, cited in the previous note, "whatever derives from the intellection of the intellect possesses concrete reality." On the creative role Rav Kook ascribes to human knowledge, see *Orot ha-Kodesh* I, 165–200; and see Tamar Ross's essay in chapter 9 of this volume. For the possible Maimonidean roots of the creative role of intellect, see the *Guide* III:21; and *Laws of the Foundations of the Torah* 2:10.

80. For a different approach to intellect and imagination in Rav Kook, see B. Ish-Shalom, *Ha-Rav Kook* (above, note 56), 64–76. Ish-Shalom's first chapter, "Metzi'ut ve-Emet", 47–97, is a profound and thorough analysis of many of the issues—and many of the texts—I have treated in this section of this paper, and the reader is urged to compare—and contrast!—his approach with mine, such as my analysis in note 78 of the relationship between *Orot ha-Kodesh* I, 212 (section 43) and 213 (section 45) and that of Ish-Shalom, 58–59.

81. "Le-Aḥduto shel ha-Rambam" (above, note 15), 106–107.

82. Of course, for Rav Kook, those true, valuable, and precious elements in modern western culture, those elements that constitute the "beauty of Yefet," are already present, in an even truer, more valuable, and more precious form, in the sources of Judaism, in the "tents of Shem." Thus, Jerome Gellman argues that "Rav Kook was a singular figure in the history of Jewish thought who was able to perceive and then successfully elaborate a broad parallel between an optimistic theology based upon rabbinic, kabbalistic, and Ḥassidic sources, on the one hand, and a current mood in nineteenth-century philosophy, influenced by Hegel and Darwin, on the other. He genuinely believed that the broad strokes of the nineteenth century philosophy of optimism were to be found fully in the tents of Shem" ("Between Rationalism and Mysticism: Review Essay [of Ish-Shalom, *Ha-Rav Kook*]," *Jewish Action* 51, 3 [Sum-

mer, 1991]: 74–76). Gellman's view is certainly correct. I would just add that it was Rav Kook's exposure to nineteenth-century philosophy, to the beauty of Yefet, that, at least in part, contributed to his working out that optimistic theology drawn from sources found in the tents of Shem and thereby helped him successfully elaborate the broad parallel to which Gellman refers.

83. *Orot ha-Kodesh* (Jerusalem, 1950), III, 26; and cf. *Iggerot ha-Re'iyah* II, 19–21 (letter 355 to R. Meir Berlin). "We can not deny that there are many fine things even in severely flawed works [of Jewish history by non-Orthodox historians], and that [the Orthodox historians Zev Yawetz and Isaac ha-Levi] were not always justified in their tendentious criticisms [of these works]. *And the truth is more beloved than anything; and precisely in it will the exalted God, may He be blessed, be praised* (emphasis mine)." See as well Ish-Shalom's essay in this volume.

CHAPTER 3

Rav Kook: Neither Philosopher
nor Kabbalist

Marvin Fox

My purpose in the seemingly provocative title of this essay is not to cast any doubt on the eminence of Rabbi Abraham Isaac Kook. He was, by the most rigorous standards, one of the most interesting and creative Jewish thinkers of this century. Unlike certain other modern Jewish thinkers whose knowledge of the primary sources of Judaism was limited, Kook was a great rabbinic figure who had superb mastery of the entire classical literature. There was no area of classical Jewish learning that he did not control. Bible, Talmud and its associated literatures, philosophy, kabbalah, hasidism— he was equally at home in all of them. He spoke always with an authentic voice that reflected his deep roots in Jewish learning and in Jewish faith. There was a dimension of originality, even a touch of genius, about everything that he wrote, whether it was a halakhic treatise, an essay on a contemporary issue, reflections on basic questions of Jewish thought, or his mystical soul giving expression to its loftiest visions. This makes him a figure worth our most careful attention, one who should be studied, despite the difficulties of his style, far more seriously than has been the case until now.

It is therefore no derogation of his stature or eminence to say that he was neither a systematic philosopher nor a systematic kabbalist. It is not a service to his thought to try to force it into artificially constructed systematic forms since this is certain to distort its inner meaning and to rob it of its force.[1] Kook was fully

conscious of the unsystematic character of his thought, a point
evident in his open struggle with the problem of expressing his
vision in language that can communicate adequately. In his private
diary he recorded the following statement: "My thoughts are
broader than the very sea; I cannot express them in prose. Although
it is not what I most prefer, I am forced to be a poet, but a poet who
composes in free verse. I cannot be chained by consideration of
meter and rhyme."[2] In a poem that is frequently quoted, Kook gives
vent to the frustration and anguish he suffers because he cannot
give full and adequate expression to his unique vision.

> Expanses, expanses,
> Expanses divine my soul craves.
> Confine me not in cages,
> Of substance or of spirit.
> My soul soars the expanses of the heavens,
>
> Who will voice my bitterness,
> The pain of seeking utterance?
> I thirst for truth, not for a conception of truth,
> For I ride on its heights,
> I am wholly absorbed by the truth,
> I am wholly pained by the anguish of expression.
> How can I utter the great truth
> That fills my whole heart?
>
> Whatever I say
> Only covers my vision.
> Dulls my light.[3]

This incapacity to give satisfactory expression to a mystical vision
is typical of the greatest mystics of all religious traditions. It is one
of the ironies of this phenomenon that the very mystics who com-
plain most bitterly about the ineffability of their vision produce
some of the most magnificent literary expressions of that vision. In
this respect, Kook is no exception. What lies behind their bitter
complaint is not their lack of language, but their intense awareness
that no language, however sensitive and beautiful, can ever be a
satisfactory vehicle for their subject.

Philosophers may sometimes have difficulty in conveying their
insights to their readers. Yet in the very nature of their work,

philosophers, who are explicators of the *logos*, are comfortable with the language that is the product of their very existence as rational (i.e., *logos*—bearing) beings. Since their entire enterprise is to give systematic form to a rational apprehension of ultimate things, it is natural that they should consider it possible to achieve that goal. The same can be said, *mutatis mutandis*, of the systematic kabbalists, those who attempt to give expression, in however esoteric a form, to a structured account of the world of the divine. In the case of the Zohar, to take the most familiar example, the system of the *sefirot* is not evident on the surface and the terminology is anything but fixed. Nevertheless, the system is there, and a diligent student can uncover it and even recast it in a less obscure form.

For Kook, unlike the philosophers and kabbalists of the type we have been discussing, the lack of system is inherent in his subject matter and in his method. The episodic aphoristic style is not just a matter of taste or of a preference for a particular rhetorical form. It is certainly not due to any inability on his part to write extended systematic essays. The corpus of his writings gives the lie to any such claim, since there are numerous extended essays that are clear and systematic in structure. This is the case not only with his halakhic works, but also with his publicistic works and with much of his extended correspondence. However, when he comes to give expression to his vision of the ultimate, he can only adopt a poetic or quasi-poetic mode of expression. Perhaps this is because the infinite, by its very nature, cannot be confined by definitions or captured in any linguistic formulation. Plato is explicit in saying this about his own vision of ultimate being, namely, the Form of the Good. Socrates refuses to talk about it directly just because it cannot be captured adequately by human reason, nor can it be expressed in the discursive language which the philosopher ordinarily uses. He must therefore satisfy himself with giving a systematic philosophical account of the nature and structure of reality up to the point where reason breaks down. It appears, however, that this is precisely the point at which Kook wants to begin his thinking. He feels deeply the frustration of not being able to express his vision in language which is adequate to it, but he is wise enough to know that to reduce the indefinable to definitions is a gross distortion of truth.

This is what is meant by the statement that Kook was not a philosopher. In his work we find hardly any argument or marshalling of evidence in a way that is characteristic of the work of the philosopher. He shares his insights, but we can exercise no control over the truth claims of those insights. If he succeeds in helping us to experience his vision, argument and evidence become irrelevant. What one experiences directly is verified by the experience itself and does not require arguments to establish its reality. In fact, arguments alone cannot convince one that he experiences what he does not, nor are arguments needed to convince him that he experiences what he actually does. Thus, if he fails to help us share his vision, then nothing he can add will be of any use. This amounts to saying that Kook does not do philosophy in any normal sense of the term because his subject matter and his goals are not those of the philosopher.

In his essay in this volume, Lawrence Kaplan points out correctly that Kook had a deep and reverent regard for Maimonides. Kaplan goes on to note that Kook put great emphasis on the Jewish legitimacy of the thought of Maimonides, and he wisely distinguished between legitimacy and truth. As Kaplan puts it, "Rav Kook's . . . reply to Yawetz is not so much a defense of the truth of Maimonides' views but rather of their legitimacy as authentically Jewish views." Again Kaplan makes the point that Rav Kook takes the position that "if Maimonides . . . could be inspired by his own views to attain almost unparalleled heights of holiness, faith, and divine service, that in itself is proof of the legitimacy of those views—their legitimacy, not their truth. Indeed, the issue of truth becomes secondary." This position of Rav Kook, as Kaplan immediately goes on to observe, "rests upon a strikingly non-Maimonidean premise. For in Maimonides' view truth is all important."[4] Kaplan's point is so obviously correct that it hardly needs any corroboration. Yet it might be useful simply to remember Maimonides' own statement on the subject. He says that with careful reflection on his teachings concerning prophecy, one may be saved from serious error. "And then only intelligible beliefs will remain with you, beliefs that are well ordered and that are pleasing to God. For only truth pleases Him, may He be exalted, and only that which is false angers Him. Your opinions and thoughts should not become confused so that you believe in incorrect opinions that are very remote from the truth and you regard them as Law. For the Laws are absolute truth if they are understood in the way they ought to be."[5]

As a philosopher, Maimonides is necessarily concerned with the truth of his doctrines, not simply their legitimacy within the Jewish tradition. This is why he regularly presents carefully constructed arguments that are aimed at establishing the truth of his views. In considering, for example, the question whether the world is eternal or created, he gives us a meticulous analysis of the arguments on both sides of the question. In this case he concludes that there are no demonstrative arguments on either side, and that there is no satisfactory way even to establish relative probabilities. However, when he admittedly takes his stand on purely religious rather than philosophic grounds, he makes it clear that if a demonstration could be provided for the eternity of the world, he would be constrained to affirm that doctrine since truth is for him a controlling consideration.[6] Kook, not being constrained by considerations of philosophic rigor and demonstrative truth, can properly put the stress on the "legitimacy" of Maimonides' doctrines. For him their Jewish authenticity is what matters, not their independently established claims to truth. For Maimonides, in contrast, it is demonstrated truth that becomes the determinant of correct Jewish doctrine.

Kook praises Maimonides for having finally and definitively purified the Jewish idea of God of all vestiges of corporeality. What he fails to note, however, is that Maimonides first demonstrates that God must be absolutely incorporeal, and then argues that therefore all anthropomorphic references to God in Scripture should be read nonliterally. For the philosopher, it is the truth of his doctrine that is the controlling consideration, and it is truth alone that determines legitimacy in every case where demonstration can be called upon to establish the truth. It is easy to see in this regard why we should not consider Kook to be a philosopher.

Lawrence Fine, in his paper in this volume, presents us with another striking instance of a problem that concerns Kook and the philosophers, a case in which we can again see how different are their methods and their aims. Kook often takes up the problem of human cognition, what Fine labels "the problem of epistemology." What is most instructive in this case is just the fact that while Kook has much to say about human cognition, he is, in fact, not dealing with the problem of epistemology as philosophers understand it. The epistemologist is concerned not only with the nature and contents of human knowledge, but no less with the grounds of human knowledge. The question "How do we know?" is for him as important, perhaps more important, than the question "What do we know?" The former question appears not really to have concerned Kook at all, and with respect to the latter question he makes his case by way of assertions, not arguments based on a careful examination and analysis of the evidence.

Kook holds that all reality is organically interconnected and that all true knowledge must, therefore, also be organismic in character.[7] This is a view that has also been held by some philosophers. To see the nonphilosophic way in which Kook deals with this topic, one need simply contrast his bald and undefended assertions with the elaborate arguments and explications to be found in Hegel and the late Hegelians. The very ambience of Kook's treatment of such a subject makes one feel that it is pointless, not to say improper, to raise the question "How do you know?" A philosopher must be prepared to answer such a question or his work is of no serious philosophical interest. A mystical visionary can allow himself to assert without offering any further evidence.

Fine also points out that Kook was convinced that the problem of human cognition is aggravated by the fact that we tend to be satisfied with a knowledge of the outer reality of things while we fail to penetrate into their inner reality that is their true essence. One hears echoes here of Kant's distinction between phenomenal and noumenal knowledge. However, when Kant claims that we can know only phenomena and never noumena, he bases himself on a most elaborate analysis of the knowledge situation and on a set of philosophic arguments that are exquisite in their detail and in their thoroughness. Kook, in effect, challenges the basic thesis of the Kantian theory of knowledge (consciously or not), but his challenge is unsupported by anything that even remotely resembles the philosophic work that Kant did in order to arrive at his position.

A striking instance of Kook's nonphilosophic stance is brought to our attention in Kaplan's comments on his preference for the imagination over the intellect. The major philosophic tradition of the West has rested for the most part on the conviction that there is a parallelism between the order of reason and the order of reality, that, as Hegel expressed it, the real is the rational and the rational is the real. This doctrine goes back at least as far as Parmenides. It receives its classical formulation in the divided-line image in Book 6 of Plato's *Republic*, in which the order of knowing and the order of being are exactly parallel, with true knowledge culminating in rational apprehension of the forms. Knowing and being are conceived here as fixed and stable, permanent rather than passing, unchanging rather than changing. It is the character of reason that its objects are just these fixed and universal aspects of being as over against the changing and particular objects of sense experience.

For this kind of philosophy, which is the dominant rationalism of our tradition, imagination poses a special problem. Since imagination is not in any way confined by the fixed order of reason or nature, we need to ask if the objects of imagination are reflective of reality. Maimonides fought against the doctrine of the Kalam that affirmed that whatever is present in imagination may be the case in reality. This is applied to the order of nature itself, all of whose fixed patterns are now treated as contingent rather than necessary. Thus, since we can imagine, for example, the sun rising in the west, it follows that this is as likely as that it should rise in the east. The net effect of this is to make all of nature dependent on God's will at each moment not only for its very existence but for each detail of its structure. In this case, it follows that no science is possible, since all facts are contingent rather than necessary.

It is possible to go even further in this direction and to assert that even that which may not be accessible to our imagination at this moment, may yet be possible because it may be grasped by a more highly developed imagination. Thus, there are even those who go so far as to hold that logical truths are not necessarily the case and that they too are contingent. In this case one could then even assert that the principle of noncontradiction is not a necessary description of the real world, but that it is possible that a thing should be both p and not-p in the same sense and at the same time. This, of course, represents the final destruction not only of all philosophy but of all intelligible discourse. It is not clear just how far Rav Kook would go in his defense of imagination against the claims of the intellect. However, any move in this direction must be construed as an attempt to destabilize the very foundations on which philosophy and science rest. Even David Hume was ready to admit, after all of his attacks on the rationalist claims about the world, that the rejection of their views runs counter to our own natural needs. If Rav Kook could say, as cited by Kaplan, "Whatever may be imagined exists in truth," then he certainly could not claim to have cast his lot with the philosophers of the great tradition.

Even in his mysticism, Rav Kook goes against the line that is concerned with providing the kabbalistic alternative to philosophical metaphysics. As Fine points out, Kook's mysticism focuses on the internal psychology of man, rather than on theosophy. Zoharic and Lurianic kabbalah are both concerned to provide us with an account of the processes within the divine being out of which the world emerges. Like the metaphysicians, although in their own special mode, they seek to make available to us an understanding of the ultimate nature of reality and of the way in which the chain of being extends from the Creator to the world of our experience. However esoteric their expositions may be, and however much they employ arcane symbolism, they nevertheless offer a genuine alternative to philosophic accounts of the world. When Kook abandons theosophy for concern with human inwardness, he reflects again his basically nonphilosophical stance.

In this regard he is, of course, influenced by certain types of Ḥasidism, but he tends in other regards to go even further than almost any usual Ḥasidic doctrine would take him. It is well known that many kabbalistic systems flirt with pantheism. In fact, this flirtation is itself part of the kabbalistic response to philosophy. As Scholem puts it,

> Authoritative Jewish theology, both mediaeval and modern, in representatives like Saadia, Maimonides and Hermann Cohen, has taken upon itself the task of formulating an antithesis to pantheism and mythical theology, i.e.,: to prove them wrong. . . . What is really required, however, is an understanding of these phenomena which yet does not lead away from monotheism; and once their significance is grasped, that elusive something in them which may be of value must be clearly defined. To have posed this problem is the historic achievement of Kabbalism.[8]

Yet Scholem teaches us how cautious most works of kabbalah are never to overstep the line and affirm pantheism openly and directly. "The author of the Zohar inclines towards pantheism, a fact made clearer by the Hebrew writings of Moses de Leon, but one would look in vain for confession of his faith beyond some vague formulae and hints at a fundamental unity of all things, stages and worlds."[9] A similar restraint with respect to pantheism is evident in most works of kabbalah. It is revealing to see how far Rav Kook goes in the direction of pantheism, and more remarkably, the openness with which he affirms his views. He is not restrained by any of the concerns that animate the philosophic writers who see pantheism as the ultimate defeat of Jewish teaching concerning God. Neither is he as cautious as the kabbalistic writers usually are.

Kook in some passages of his writings seems openly to avow pantheism, and, what is more, he uses the very term itself without hesitation or apology. Thus he writes that the human heart "takes special delight in the notion that all existence in its entirety is nothing but a matter of divinity and nothing else exists outside of God."[10] He goes on to argue that the only antidote to the feeling of worthlessness and inconsequentiality that often besets man is a purified pantheism (he actually uses the term) that makes it possible for man to perceive himself as an element in the divine reality. The pantheistic doctrine that teaches that there is nothing outside of the absoluteness of the divine is affirmed and defended openly by Rav Kook.[11] One is reluctant to think that he was prepared to take this doctrine in its full literalness, yet there is no question that he not only follows in the line of much kabbalistic and Hasidic teaching, but does so in a straightforward way that is not typical of these movements. It may well be that Kook's concern for the individual person was so great that he welcomed any doctrine that he felt could elevate man and bring him closer to redemption. In this case, the fact that the doctrine was anathema to the philosophers and a source of some anxiety to the kabbalists did not seem to disturb him.

It should now be clear, even from this brief discussion, why we took the position that Rav Kook was neither philosopher nor kabbalist. This is not meant to detract from his greatness, but rather to call attention to his unique qualities as a thinker and an expounder of Judaism. It may well be that he can speak to the quest for Jewish spirituality in our time more effectively than those thinkers who follow a classical model. His vision of the supernal reality, his burning love of God, and his equal love for man are the animating forces in his thought. They may give us more than we can hope for from the great system builders, but this remains to be seen. What is clear, however, is that we must learn how to read Kook perceptively and sensitively. If we come to him looking for a twentieth-century Maimonides, we are bound to be sorely disappointed. If we allow him to engage our imagination and our intellect, to speak to us as poet rather than as philosopher, we may discover through him new visions and new worlds.

Notes

1. Both Lawrence Kaplan and Lawrence Fine, in their contributions to this volume, are fully aware of the unsystematic nature of Kook's thought as is clearly evident from their papers. I seek in this discussion only to expand the point and to explore more fully its significance.
2. Cited in A. Haberman, "Shirat HaRav," *Zikkaron*, ed. J. L. Fishman (Jerusalem, 1945), 10.
3. Ibid., 17–19. Translation is taken from Ben Zion Bokser, *Abraham Isaac Kook*, (New York, 1978), 379–80.
4. Kaplan, 52 in this volume.
5. *Guide of the Perplexed*, trans. Shlomo Pines (Chicago, 1963), II: 47, 409. (Fox's essay was based on an earlier version of Kaplan's paper that did not include notes. The version published here cites this passage in note 38.–eds.)
6. Ibid. II: 25: 327–28.
7. Kook's view about the world as an organic whole is also noted and discussed by Professor Kaplan in his essay.
8. Gershom G. Scholem, *Major Trends in Jewish Mysticism* (New York, 1941), 38.
9. Ibid., 222.
10. *Orot Hakodesh* (Jerusalem, 1964), II:396.
11. Ibid., 399–400.

CHAPTER 4

Poetry of Spirituality

Jerome I. Gellman

Rabbi Abraham Isaac Kook lived a life of rich spirituality. He knew of the desire to reach "transcendent Divinity, to be swallowed up within it, to be added to its light." But he also knew that "the heavens open" only rarely, and we are left to dwell "outside the sanctuary." This, however, is not cause for despair; for the transcendent holiness "descends for our sake to the world and within it, and we discover it and take pleasure in its love, finding calm and peace in its rest."[1]

Rav Kook's writings record two kinds of spiritual consciousness that dwell in his soul. The first is the experience of leaving the world behind to ascend to higher realities, to attain a disclosure of the Divine in its transcendent glory. This is "from below upward." We may call this an "introvertive experience," in that it reveals the Divine within the confines of one's own soul. The second is the consciousness of the Divine within our experience of the world. Here the world is the object of our consciousness, and the Divine is seen *through* it. If you were to ask of me, when in this mode of understanding, what I am *looking at*, I might reply: the world around me. If you were to ask me what it is I *see*, I might very well reply: God. The second mode of spiritual cognition may be called "extrovertive"—one sees Divinity in looking out on the world. It is an experience of "from above downward."[2]

I have chosen here two poems of Rav Kook, respectively portraying the introvertive and extrovertive spiritual experiences. The first, "The First One Drew Me," written around the years 1924–25, records the intensity of the introvertive ascent to transcendence. The second, "The Whispers of Existence," concerns the second, extrovertive experience and was written in all probability around the years 1912–13.[3] These poems have been chosen both for their clarity in presenting their respective experiences, as well as for their great richness of imagery and suggestions of biblical and kabbalistic images and concepts. My aim in commenting on these poems is threefold: first, to portray the spiritual world of Rav Kook through his poetry, an especially deep and rich source of discovery; second, to make explicit their intricate and subtle hints and references to the treasures of Jewish tradition; third, to illustrate that Rav Kook's poetry is not only an aesthetic expression of poetic images, but also a source for understanding his metaphysical world. Words that seem to be no more than evocations of poetic emotion are in truth intended to refer, with precision, to ideas laden with metaphysical meaning.

The reader should not get the impression, however, that Rav Kook necessarily labored hard and long to squeeze kabbalistic references, and the like, into his poetry. Particularly instructive, in this regard, is this observation of the poet H. N. Bialik: "What I write is more stylized that what Rav Kook writes. However, how do I accomplish that? I write once, correct, cross out, and write again, until it comes out right. Not so Rav Kook. I know that everything of his that has been published is the way he wrote it the first time. And to write like that the first time—only Rav Kook can do!"[4]

Bialik's words may be an exaggeration, but, in any event, we are to think of Rav Kook's poetry as flowing easily from the thought-world of which he was a part. The reader in reconstructing the soul of the poet from the external marks of the poet's hand discovers a poetry of spirituality.

I

The First One Drew Me

The first one drew me with his rope,
Into the sanctuary of his Holy of Holies.
And from the strings of his harp,
my soul does hear his song.

And the sea of knowledge roars,
Its waves beating within me.
Thought upon thought, like a wall,
"and behold, God stands upon it."

And a mute thought sails,
like a swift cloud on high.
Were I to ask, here below,
amongst the gates of desolation:

Where goes
this captive of the heavens?
There is no one who can reveal to me the book,
or explain to me the chapter.

This poem describes an ascent on the ladder of spiritual experience to the level of transcendent unity—a unity above the multiplicity of our usual experience. The central image is from the dream of Jacob in Gen. 28:12–17, from which line 4 of the second stanza is a direct quotation. The ladder of Jacob's dream is the ladder of Rav Kook's ascent and the poem employs various biblical and kabbalistic references to Jacob's dream. To understand the poem, we must realize that the spiritual ascent it portrays is in accordance with the structure of the sefirot and culminates at the sefirah Ḥokhmah (Wisdom). We therefore turn first to a brief exposition of the nature and role of Ḥokhmah in the sefirotic scheme.

In the structure of the sefirot, Ḥokhmah appears as either the first, highest sefirah or the second, next highest sefirah. In one scheme, Ḥokhmah is the first sefirah, followed by Binah (Understanding) and then Da'at (Knowledge). (These constitute Ḥabad: the three highest sefirot, which possess a supernal, lofty status amongst the ten sefirot.) In a second scheme, Keter (Crown) is the first sefirah, followed by Ḥokhmah and then Binah, with Da'at either not appearing at all or identified with the lower sefirah, Tiferet (Beauty).[5] In either case, Ḥokhmah is named "the first" ("reishit"). For even in the scheme where Keter appears as the highest sefirah, Keter is beyond thought and therefore "Nothing" ("Ayin").[6] Ḥokhmah is "Something" ("Yesh"), the first instantiation of being in the sefirotic realm that approaches the possibility of comprehension.

What, then, is Ḥokhmah? It is undifferentiated, bare unity, with no multiplicity. It is the ground out of which multiplicity emerges, in the lower level of Binah. (Binah, "Understanding"—as in "understanding one thing from out of another"—is the emergence of multiplicity from out of bare unity.) Ḥokhmah is the simplicity of the *thought*, which is then transformed into the components of *speech*. According to a kabbalistic interpretation of Jacob's dream, Jacob in his dream ascends the "ladder" of the sefirot to the heights of Ḥokhmah, there to glimpse the transcendent ground of all multiplicity. Thus, upon awakening, Jacob declares, "Surely, there is [yesh] God in this place" (Gen. 28:16). "Yesh" is the designation of Ḥokhmah as "Something."[7]

In adopting the imagery of Jacob's dream in his poem, then, Rav Kook conveys to the reader the sense of spiritual ascent the poet has made—an ascent to the unity above multiplicity. It is a spiritual adventure that pulls the poet out of the world to a higher reality. In what follows we will trace the richness of imagery of this poem, centering around Jacob's dream and the revelation of Ḥokhmah.

Stanza 1

> The first one drew me with his rope,
> Into the sanctuary of his Holy of Holies,
> And from the strings of his harp,
> my soul does hear his song.

The "first one" ("rishon") is Ḥokhmah, the sefirah of transcendent unity. Rav Kook is *being drawn* toward this higher realm of being. The experience seizes him, as though he is forced beyond his own choice to something above him. The "rope" is the instrument of ascent, the "ladder" that carries him higher and higher. The Hebrew word used here for "rope" is "ḥevel." This is a play on words, based on the verse, "Jacob is the lot of his inheritance" (Deut. 32:9). The word for "lot" is "ḥevel," also meaning "rope." Jacob is compared to a rope, "the upper end of which is tied above, and its lower end below."[8] Why is Jacob like a rope? Jacob is identified with the third letter of the Divine Name "Y-H-V-H," that is, the letter "V."[9] This letter is written as a straight line, a "rope," and joins the first "H" to the second "H". The first "H" designates the sefirah of Binah (Understanding), which belongs to the supernal realm of sefirot, while the second "H" designates the sefirah of Malkhut (Kingship), the lowest of the sefirot, also called "eretz" or "ground." The "rope" of Jacob thus corresponds to the ladder of Jacob's dream, which "stands on the ground with its top reaching to the heavens" (Gen. 28:12). The "rope" is the means of going from the "ground," Malkhut, first to "the heavens," Binah, and then to Ḥokhmah, corresponding to the first letter of the Divine Name, "Y." The rope image is used by Rav Kook in the opening lines, suggesting immediately the association with Jacob and his dream.

The Zohar notes that the verse "Ki Ya'akov baḥar lo Yah" (Ps. 135:4) is ambiguous and can mean either that Jacob chose God or that God chose Jacob.[10] The latter reading is supported by the verse of Deuteronomy that Jacob is the lot of His inheritance (Zohar I, 161b). God chooses Jacob. The term for "God" here is "Yah," which means Ḥokhmah in Kabbalah (Zohar III, 10a). Jacob is *pulled* up by the "lot" = "ḥevel" = "rope," to Ḥokhmah. Moreover, Jacob, in being chosen, in being pulled up to Ḥokhmah, is granted Ḥokhmah as an inheritance. "To bestow [literally: to give as an inheritance] Being [Yesh] upon those who love Me" (Prov. 8:21). The "inheritance" bestowed upon Jacob, the lover of God, is "Being," "Yesh" = Ḥokhmah.[11]

Rav Kook is thus singled out, chosen, and pulled upward on the rope of Jacob, to a realm beyond.[12]

That realm, in the poem, is identified as "the sanctuary of the Holy of Holies."[13] Upon awaking from his dream, Jacob declares: "This is none other than the House of God" (Gen. 18:17), hence the "sanctuary." The word of God flows ultimately from the sefirah of Ḥokhmah, and the "sanctuary" as the place from which God's Word is communicated is the source of Ḥokhmah for the world.[14] The "Holy of Holies" is *one* Holiness, containing within it, in a uniformity of oneness, all the "Holies" that emerge from it. Hence, Ḥokhmah is the transcendent ground of the multiple Holies. But Ḥokhmah is not only the ground of what appears to us as *holy*, but also the ground of what appears to us as *profane*. As Rav Kook writes:

> There is a world of the profane and a world of the holy, worlds of the profane and worlds of the holy. These worlds stand in opposition to one another. Of course, the opposition is subjective. A person with

his limited understanding cannot mediate between the holy and the profane, and cannot resolve their oppositions. But these oppositions are resolved in the highest reaches of reality, in the ground of the Holy of Holies.[15]

This passage is striking for its implied interpretation of the "Holy of Holies." The Holy of Holies reveals the profane as well as the holy to be holy. The true ontological ground of the profane is revealed to be holy by its source—Ḥokhmah. The term "Holies," therefore, refers to what appears to us as holy *and* to what appears to us as profane. Hence the two, the holy and the profane, are really "Holies," two "Holies."

The ascent to Ḥokhmah is therefore an ascent above our ordinary subjective consciousness that contains the categories of the holy and profane; it thereby involves a radical break with the normal human mode of cognition of the world. Hence, the world is left behind not only in the sense that it is not the object of the experience of the poem, but also in the sense that worldly epistemic awareness is abandoned for a form of awareness that negates it and expose it for its lack of truth.

And from the strings of his harp,
my soul does hear his song.

The second half of this stanza borrows its imagery from a highly mystical passage in the *Tikkunei Zohar*, Tikkun 13. The Hebrew word for song is "shir," and the *Tikkunei Zohar* divides the latter into the components "Y shar," meaning that the letter "Y" sings. We have already noted that "Y" corresponds to Ḥokhmah. Why does Ḥokhmah sing? Rav Kook says "song" is "the supreme expression of the 'intellect,' which arises from the wide and deep gazing into the light of the supreme God."[16] The word for intellect is "sekhel," which often refers to Ḥokhmah in Rav Kook's writings. The supreme God is "El Elyon," which refers to an aspect of Keter, the sefirah above Ḥokhmah.[17] Rav Kook's meaning, therefore, is that "song" is the level of Ḥokhmah, which draws from the level above, that is, the level of "Ayin" or Keter.

The "song" of Ḥokhmah, continues the *Tikkunei Zohar*, is played on "the five strings of the violin." The "five strings" are the five major levels of the sefirot reflected in the unity of Ḥokhmah.[18] All the *sefirot* find their unitary ground in the song of the letter "Y." This violin becomes Rav Kook's "harp."

The *Tikkunei Zohar* then goes on to comment that the ladder described in Jacob's dream—"And behold a ladder standing on the ground and its top reaching to the heaven" (Gen. 28:12)—is itself comprised of a progression of six notes, reaching from the lowest Sefirah, to the highest realms. The number six denotes the central complex of six sefirot, the "Ze'ir Anpin," associated with Jacob, hence "Jacob's ladder." This corresponds to "V," with the numerical value of six. It is worthwhile noting here that the numerical value of the word "sulam" (ladder) is the same as that of the word "kol," meaning voice or sound. Hence, in the Kabbalah, the verse "The voice [kol] is the voice of Jacob" (Gen. 27:22) means the voice/sound of *Jacob* is the *ladder* of Jacob. The *means of ascent*, the ladder, is a progression of notes/sounds, which lead up to, and are absorbed into, the total unity of Ḥokhmah. The ladder (a progression of six notes/sounds) connects the lower to the higher.

Rav Kook's soul "hear[s] his song," hears the strings of the harp (in the *Tikkunei Zohar*: "violin"). The Midrash records a dispute between Rabbi Ḥiyya and Rabbi Yannai. The former says the angels of Jacob's dream were ascending and descending upon the Biblical ladder. The latter maintains that the angels ascended and descended within Jacob himself (*Genesis Rabbah* 68:12). The world of angels is the world of "yetzirah," corresponding to the six-fold complex of "Ze'ir Anpin"—again representing Jacob. The angels ascend and descend *within* Jacob, and they correspond to the progression of six notes that Rav Kook's *soul* hears.

To summarize, the first stanza establishes the transcendent nature of the experience Rav Kook is called to, as well as its mystical intensity. There is a sense of abandoning both the world—as in a dream—and worldly modes of cognition. There is the sense of a passage, an ascent, to the unitary ground of all multiplicity, to a song that is not heard by the ear, but only by the soul: "My soul does hear his song."

Stanza 2

> And the sea of knowledge roars,
> Its waves beating within me.

Thought upon thought, like a wall,
"and behold, God stands upon it."

At this point, the experience grows in intensity and spiritual import. There is a "roaring" or "swelling" of the sea, the waves carrying Rav Kook to the height of the experience, to the revelation of "God," who is here the sefirah of Ḥokhmah. "Knowledge" (Daʿat) is below Binah and Ḥokhmah, at the threshold of the supernal realm of the sefirot. The image is of the ascent through Daʿat to the higher reaches of Ḥokhmah. The "sea" of knowledge is "yam," with the numerical value of fifty; this "sea" holds the forty-nine gates of Understanding (Binah), which originate in Binah. A total of seven sefirot emanate from Binah and comprise the lower realm of the sefirotic structure,[19] and each of these is a complex of all seven, so that there are a total of forty-nine facets of sefirot in the lower realm.[20] Daʿat is thus the "pool" or "sea" of multiplicity, holding the forty-nine gates of Binah.

The reference to "sea" is derivative upon the image of "waves," in the continuation of the above cited passage of the *Tikkunei Zohar*. The *Tikkunei Zohar* notes that the verse "Cry out with a shrill voice, daughter of the waves" (Isa. 10:30) refers to the infusion of the "essence" of Ḥokhmah into the lowest sefirah, Malkhut, also called the "daughter."[21] Malkhut ascends as in "waves" to receive the higher essence. The "waves" are a "song" of mystical "progression" of the Divine Name, as follows:

Y
YH
YHV
YHVH

This progression constitutes ten letters, the number 10 being the numerical value of "Y," the letter of the Divine name denoting Ḥokhmah, the goal of the progression. The whole image, then, is of an ascent by "waves" to a realm where one experiences profound infusion into oneself of the higher spirituality. This infusion then changes the earlier image of "hearing the song." Previously, in the first stanza, the soul only *heard* the song, but now Rav Kook himself becomes the *instrument* upon which/within which the song is played. For, in the *Tikkunei Zohar* (Tikkun 13), the song of ten notes is "beaten" out by the "ten fingers" of the ascent, from the lowest to the highest of the ten sefirot. Hence, when Rav Kook says the waves are "beating within me," he means that *he* is the instrument upon which the fingers "beat," playing the song. And indeed the image of *his* being the instrument occurs elsewhere in Rav Kook's writings: "The higher waves work upon our souls without stop. Our inner spiritual movements are the results of those swellings that our *soul-violin* swells, from her listening to the echo of the sound of the supreme emanation" (*OHK* II, 334; my emphasis).

The violin of the soul resonates to the echo of the song the soul hears. Rav Kook now has passed from listening to the song of Ḥokhmah to being infused with the song. He himself becomes a harp, becomes the source of song.

This imagery bears a close resemblance to a passage by the great Christian mystic, Jacob Boehme: "The voice of God continually and eternally brings forth its joys through the creature, as through an instrument; the creature is the manifestation of the voice of God: What God is in the eternal word out of the great mystery of the Father's property, that the creature is in the image as a joyful harmony, wherewith the Eternal Spirit plays our melodies." [22]

> Thought upon thought like a wall:
> "and behold, God stands upon it."

These lines rely upon plays on words. The word for wave is "gal," which can also mean a pile of stones. Hence, wave upon wave equals "pile upon pile" of stones. The waves or thoughts in the sea of Da'at are indeed, then, at the same time, a pile of stones like a wall. They bring one to the higher level of Ḥokhmah: "and behold, God stands upon it." The latter is quoted from the Genesis account of Jacob's dream, but together with the line preceding it suggests Amos 7:7: "And behold God stands upon a wall of a plumb line with a plumb line in his hand." The "plumb line" suggests the rope of the poem's opening line and brings the reader full circle—reminding him that the ascent began with a feeling of being pulled upward beyond one's own capacities.

A further play on words is in the Hebrew "ke-ḥomah," meaning "like a wall." The letters of "ke-ḥomah" divide into two words "koaḥ mah," meaning "potentiality for what." This is sometimes cited as the inner meaning of the term "Ḥokhmah," composed of the same letters.[23] Ḥokhmah is the transcendent unity that contains individual beings only implicitly but not in actuality. There is in Ḥokhmah only the possibility of individuation, hence "koaḥ mah"—"potentiality for what." If this is correct, these two lines contain unusual literary intricacy: connecting the waves to the wall, the wall to the rope, and the whole lot to Ḥokhmah, via the wall and the verses in Genesis.

In the second stanza, the ascent has been accomplished; Rav Kook has been infused with the power of transcendent unity and stands with God upon high.

Stanza 3

> And a mute thought sails
> like a swift cloud on high.
> Were I to ask, here below,
> amongst the gates of desolation:

Here the poem turns. In the first two lines the result of the ascent is described, while in the last two a certain dissatisfaction with the experience of the first two stanzas begins to be expressed.

The level of Ḥokhmah is the level of a "mute thought." When a *thought* first occurs to us, it does so as a unit, not divided into parts, into words. The division into words is a second stage in which the thought "descends" from its original seamless oneness. At the moment of the thought's creation it is at the level of the transcendent unity of Ḥokhmah. It is *mute* because it is prior to "speech" that divides the aboriginal thought into a multiplicity of concepts. Thus, as Rav Kook writes elsewhere (*OHK* II, 334), when we hear the song of Ḥokhmah, "we hear no enunciation of letters or separation of words."

The thought sails like a "swift cloud" (literally "light cloud"). This latter phrase is borrowed from Isa. 19:1, "Behold God rides upon a swift cloud." This verse, in turn, seems to have been suggested by association with the last line of the previous stanza: "and behold God. . . ."

But the term used here for cloud, "av," is also, in Kabbalah, a reference to Ḥokhmah. This is shown as follows. The Divine Name, "YHVH," has various so-called "fill-ins." A fill-in of the Divine Name consists in spelling out each of the letters of the Name the way it is pronounced. Thus, for example, the fill-in of the English letter "b" is "b-e-e," and the fill-in of the letter "l," "e-l." The Divine Name can be filled in in more than one way, and one method uses the letter "Y" as the fill-in, in honor—yes—of Ḥokhmah, since, as we have already seen, Ḥokhmah corresponds to the "Y" of the Divine Name. Now, the particular fill-in using "Y" yields a numerical value of seventy-two.[24] This is called "the name of seventy-two," and denotes the level of Ḥokhmah. The numerical value of "av," cloud, is seventy-two, and hence is a reference to the level of Ḥokhmah! The "name of seventy-two" is in fact called "the name 'av.' " Rav Kook sails in the realm of Ḥokhmah, beyond speech.

The cloud is *swift* (literally: "light"). Here too there is a meaningful numerology. The term for "swift" is "kal," with the numerical value of 130. Now recall the progressive waves of mystical ascent via the letters of the Divine Name:

Y
YH
YHV
YHVH

These waves bring one from the lowest sefirah, Malkhut, to the heights of Ḥokhmah. Now the ascent is via the "rope," the center sefirah of Tiferet, the sefirah of Jacob. If we fill in all the letters of this progression in the manner appropriate to Tiferet (which uses the letter "aleph" prominently in the fill-in, instead of "Y" in the fill-in appropriate to Ḥokhmah) we get a series of letters with the total numerical value of 130 = "kal" = swift.[25] "Kal" is therefore an oblique reference to the progression that brings one to Ḥokhmah. The "av" (cloud) of "kal" (swift) is the cloud *of* the swift, the "av" *of* the "kal"—that which emerges from the progression.

At this point the poem makes its critical turn to more than a hint of dissatisfaction, of being troubled, in spite of the glory of the experience itself. The next line of this stanza, "Were I to ask here below," is ambiguous, and may either mean (1) "Were I to be below, and ask," or (2) "Were I, who am above, to direct a question below." In either case, though more clearly so in sense (1), there suddenly intrudes into Rav Kook's consciousness a new perspective, not seen before in this poem: a perspective outside his experience, looking at it from the outside—the perspective of the "below," as opposed to the "on high" from within the experience itself. Rav Kook senses, is concerned with, how he looks from the outside. He steps outside of himself to test how he might look from there. In so doing he envisages the "gates of desolation." Now, when Jacob awakes from his dream he declares, "This is none other than the house of God, and this the gate of heaven" (Gen. 28:17). "Heaven" is "ha-shamayim." Rav Kook takes this word and turns it into "ha-shomeimim," based on Lam. 1:4, "All her gates are desolate," ("shomeimim"), hence his "gates of desolation." Here Rav Kook is, as it were, like Jacob, stepping out of the dream, looking at his experience from the outside, not from the "gates of heaven," but from the gates of "desolation," a play, as we have just seen, on "gates of heaven." He indeed stands at the gates of heaven, but feels he must know how he is perceived from the gates of desolation.

Stanza 4

> Where goes
> this captive of the heavens?
> There is no one who can reveal to me the book,
> or explain to me the chapter.

Here is the question from below. And it has no answer.

The Jerusalem Talmud in Megillah uses the phrase "those who sail on the seas, and those who go through deserts." One sails on the sea, in deserts one only goes. In the third stanza, Rav Kook sails on the waves of the sea of the second stanza. Those below are in the gates of desolation, are in a desert. They can only think in terms of "going." They know nothing of "sailing." So the question down below must be, "Where goes this captive of the heavens?" and not "Where sails this captive of the heavens?"

Those below cannot reveal the book. The word for reveal is "yigaleh," a play on the word "gal," meaning "wave," and used in the second stanza with that meaning. Those in the desert cannot conceive of the "waves" of the sea carrying one upward. Neither can they "explain" the chapter. The term for "explain" used is "yifaresh," which has a second meaning: to sail. They do not sail, they can only go. The word here for chapter, "perakim," can also refer to a "crossroads." Hence, a second meaning for the last line of the poem would be: no one below knows how to navigate, to sail, the roads above.

In this stanza, Rav Kook uses the word "shehakim" for "heavens," apparently drawing on Deut. 33:26: "He rides upon the heavens . . . , and in His excellency in the skies" ("shehakim"), surely associated, in the context of the poem, with 2 Sam. 22:12: "Clouds of heaven" ("shehakim"). But the term "shehakim," translated as "heavens," can also be translated as "tattered clothing" (see Mishnah *Ketubot* 5:8). Similarly, the term for "book," "masekhet," can be translated as a weaving, as in Judg. 16:13–14. A second reading of this stanza is therefore possible, namely, that what has happened to Rav Kook cannot be mended, cannot be put back together, to be made whole and intelligible down below. Rav Kook is not so much a captive of the heavens as he is a captive of the tattered, broken, and unintelligible, to those below.

There is a sense of solitude, of being cut off, in this final stanza of the poem. And why? Because the experience cannot be communicated, it cannot be broken down to "books" and "chapters." From below it is at an epistemic distance. And the captive of above is himself distant from those below. He leaves them behind, for he leaves behind their precious books and chapters. "For the man who studies to gain insight," wrote Schopenhauer, "books and studies are merely rungs of a ladder on which he climbs to the summit of knowledge. As soon as a rung has raised him one stage, he leaves it behind."[26] Substitute "Hokhmah" for "knowledge" in this quotation, and you have the final stanza of this poem based on the dream of Jacob's ladder.

The lament of this stanza is expressed most sharply in a passage of *Orot ha-Kodesh* (II, 297): "If the person possessed of holiness of the silence lowers himself to restricted service: in prayer, in Torah study, in the restriction of morality, and in the minutiae of particulars, he will suffer and be depressed. He will feel that a soul full of all reality is being pressed tight by pincers."

Summary

"The First One Drew Me" is an account of a powerful introvertive spiritual experience. In the first stanza, we learn that it is an experience of transcendent unity, reached by an ascent seemingly imposed upon one, not of one's choice. The second stanza describes the full intensity of the experience, when the ascent is complete. The first two lines of the third stanza tell us of the silent inwardness of the experience, while the stanza's last two lines, together with the last stanza, communicate the sense of the resulting estrangement from others. The "heavens open" only rarely, but when they do we are transformed forever after (see *Orot* 120).

II

The Whispers of Existence

The whole of Existence whispers to me a secret:
I have life, take please, take,
If you have a heart, and in your heart there is blood,
not poisoned by the poison of despair.

And if your heart is uncircumcised
And my beauty does not enchant you—
Existence whispers to me—
Turn away from me, turn away,
I am forbidden to you.

If every delicate chirp,
every living beauty, does not arouse within you
the splendor of a song of holiness,
but instead an alien fire,
Then turn away from me, turn away,
I am forbidden to you.

And a generation will arise and live,
And will sing to beauty and to life,
And will draw pleasure without end,
from the dew of heaven.

And from the vistas of Carmel and Sharon,
the ear of the living nation shall hear

the abundance of the secrets of life,
And from the pleasure of song and beauty,
It will be filled with the light of holiness.
And the whole of Existence will whisper to it:
My chosen, I am permitted to you.

This poem describes a spiritual experience different from that of the earlier poem in at least three respects: (1) The spiritual experience here is *extrovertive*, rather than *introvertive*. The Divine descends into the world, for us and to us. It is "from above downward"; (2) it does not involve being drawn, pulled beyond one's own choice, but requires the movement and choice of the subject; (3) it is in principle available to everyone, and can even be a collective, even a national experience. Within this spiritual state, the solitude of the introvertive experience can be overcome in a sense of fellowship.

In this poem the spiritual force flows downward from Ḥokhmah. As noted earlier, Ḥokhmah is the principle of unity above all multiplicity, a transcendent oneness with no trace of individuation. Multiplicity does emanate from Ḥokhmah at lower levels of being, but that potentiality for multiplicity is a mere potentiality—the multiplicity itself from the vantage point of Ḥokhmah is unknown. Ḥokhmah, as we have seen, is "koaḥ mah," a potentiality for "I know not what." From Ḥokhmah there emanates Binah, Understanding. If Ḥokhmah is like a "thought" in its pristine simplicity, then Binah is the principle that draws out the implicit complexity of that thought. Binah is the principle of multiplicity. As such, the lower realm of being exists within Binah, not as comprised of separated, scattered particulars, but as constituting an organic unity.

Ḥokhmah is the father, the source, the "seed." That seed, while a simple unity undifferentiated into parts, is, at the same time, the potential source of life (Zohar III, 290a, 256b). Binah is the mother, within whose womb the seed undergoes differentiation into an organic whole, a multiplicity of organs and limbs (Zohar III, 84a). In Binah there is life. She herself is the "bundle of life." Both Ḥokhmah and Binah are unities: Binah a unity of particulars, Ḥokhmah a unity transcending the particulars.

In the extrovertive experience herein portrayed, Ḥokhmah descends into the world, first through the medium of Binah, and then through the lower sefirot as they emerge, from out of the womb of Binah, in separated form. To look at the world in the way here described is, first, to see through the scattered multiplicity to the organic unity in which it inheres, and, then, to see beyond that to the ground of the world in a transcendent unity. To experience Ḥokhmah, one need not ascend a ladder; for Ḥokhmah descends and is discernible here, deep within the world. To perceive the organic unity of reality is to perceive its Binah-like nature. To perceive it ground in transcendence, through perceiving reality, is to perceive its Ḥokhmah-like ground.

Stanza 1

> The whole of Existence whispers to me a secret:
> I have life, take please, take,
> If you have a heart, and in your heart there is blood,
> not poisoned by the poison of despair.

The speaker in this poem is "the whole of Existence," a term used generally by Rav Kook to refer to the whole of the created order. For example, Rav Kook writes: "The final end of *the whole of Existence* is the revelation of the light of the Divine, in the height of its spiritual pleasure, in such unity that there will not be any spark of life whose self-being does not ascend to the heights" (*OHK* II, 394, my emphasis; see also 288, 565).

The whole of the created order invites us to experience, through her, the higher spirituality. The invitation, however, is only whispered. No roar here, no song, no voice, only a whisper. That soft voice is barely audible. You might miss it. You have to strain to pick it up. Whether you hear it or not depends on you. It whispers a *secret*. At the start, the secret is of the spirituality of Binah, of the sense of the organic wholeness of the created order (hence: "the *whole* of Existence"), but soon enough, it is deepened to the level of transcendent unity.

The secret is "sod." (In the last stanza, the word for "secret" changes to "raz.") The numerical value of "sod" is seventy, equalling the numerical value of "yayin," meaning "wine." The two are linked in the Talmudic dictum: "When wine enters, the secret is out" (Erubin 53b). The imbibing of wine causes the secret to surface. Now the Zohar (III, 127a) offers a mystical identification of wine with Binah.[27] Thus, when Binah enters, the secret comes out. And the secret of Existence is precisely that she has within her the possibility of seeing the organic unity of the whole created order, that is, of seeing, Binah within her.

Each person must listen carefully to hear the whisper and learn the secret: "I have life, take please, take." The "life" offered by Existence is the life that follows from Binah, the Mother of organic unity. Here is how Rav Kook writes of the "life" of existence in *Orot ha-Kodesh* (II, 403): "The unity that gives life to the multiplicity, that absorbs the multiplicity into itself, and rises above all reality and all content, cannot diminish the vigor of life, but can only increase it by the abundance of the power and greatness of the unity within multiplicity."

The words "take please" ("kaḥ na") occur in Gen. 33:11, when Jacob urges Esau to accept his gifts. But they also occur in the Divine command to Abraham to sacrifice his son: "Take please, your son, your only son, whom you love, Isaac, and go to the land of Moriah, and offer him there for a burnt offering" (Gen. 22:2). On the face of it, Rav Kook's words have nothing to do with this biblical source. After all, their point in the poem is to *offer* "life," but in regard to Abraham they ask the opposite. There they denote the destruction of life, the request to *kill* Isaac. Life is to be lost, not gained! Are we to conclude, then, that the use of the phrase "take please" bears no relation to the binding of Isaac? I suggest the opposite is the case, that Rav Kook intends to draw the reader's attention to these words as addressed to Abraham. For although in their immediate purport they ask for the loss of life, in Rav Kook's eyes the overall understanding of the binding of Isaac reveals them to be offering life.

I propose that Rav Kook chooses the words "take please" from the Abraham story, and does so to intimate that its meaning is to be sought—paradoxically—in the *giving* of life. To appreciate this we must digress to present Rav Kook's interpretation of the Akedah—the binding of Isaac.[28] But first we must pause to see the image of Abraham in Rav Kook's writings.

Before coming to the true faith, Abraham had been a worshipper of idols. Idolatry, says Rav Kook, has a certain passion and zeal that deserve to be purified and retained in the true worship: "In the contamination of idolatry, great is the spirit of faith in all its wildness and coarseness, in its boiling and horselike power, [to the point of] burning sons and daughters."[29] Now Abraham, in the Jewish tradition, is portrayed as coming to belief in God via a kind of philosophical contemplation.[30] His history of idol worship, for Rav Kook, then, was a valuable corrective to the cold, detached manner of philosophical speculation.[31]

At the same time, idol worship contains a central evil that must not be carried through to the true worship.[32] To be sure, idolatry sees, albeit darkly, the great truth that "the Divine is the most precious thing of all, and everything else precious and beloved is *as nothing in comparison*" (my emphasis). But idolatry derives from this inner perception the conclusion that everything is to be rejected and denied in the name of the Divine. This is expressed in the extreme by the burning of sons and daughters. This practice is rooted in the recognition of the ultimacy of the Divine, but at the same time it is corrupted by a holy—or is it an unholy?—passion that negates and destroys life. The truth is that the passion for the holy should include within it the love for all. The love for the Divine encompasses all reality within its embrace.

This was Abraham's dilemma. He had to negate the negating aspect of idolatry, and was thereby in danger of rejecting its passionate nature. The Akedah was intended to combine the passion and frenzy he knew from idolatry with the affirmation of life and of love from within the true religion. In the Akedah, Abraham is transformed. And, had it not been for this transformation, the worship of the holy would have remained either "ugly and wildly emotional" or else cold in spirit, "devoid of deep life."

The Akedah accomplishes this transformation by bestirring Abraham to the height of passion in the service of God. He is told to kill his son *for God*, and, with his history of idol worship, Abraham is well suited for the passionate nature of the act. He undertakes to perform the deed, feeling that "all private and general matters of nature and reality are *as nothing in comparison*."[33] These are the exact words used by Rav Kook (and quoted above) to characterize idolatry! Abraham is deliberately aroused to the idolatry-like rejection of life and human values. At the height of that impassioned zeal, when about to slaughter his son, God commands him to hold on to that deep, deep passion, but not to do *anything* against his son. The passion for God, God informs Abraham, encompasses within it a deep passion for life—the life of your son, of your family, of the world around you, of all reality. The passion is not denied, it is cherished. It is not to be diminished or cooled, but encouraged. Abraham learns to be a passionate lover of God, yet also to love his son. Abraham, the passionate one, has had his son given to him. He has received life. In retrospect, God's command to Abraham, "Take, please, your son" assumes new meaning. God was really telling him: "Take your son, Abraham. Take him to yourself and for yourself. For the fervent love of God does not require the rejection of all other loves." "I have life," God says, "take please, take."

> If you have a heart, and in your heart there is blood,
> not poisoned by the poison of despair.

The "life" is available to you if you have life within you, if you have a "heart." The heart, "lev," represents the thirty-two "paths of Ḥokhmah." ("Lev" is numerically equivalent to thirty-two.) They serve as the conduits for conveying Ḥokhmah's influence to the worlds below.[34] But in order to have life you must also have blood, the basis of life, in your heart. The blood in the heart is first cleansed of its impurities in the liver, from which it is then sent to the heart (Zohar I, 138a). If the blood is not poisoned, and has reached the heart cleansed, without despair, then Existence has life to give.

Despair is the first of the reasons offered in the poem why a person may be precluded from the invitation of Existence. Elsewhere, Rav Kook writes of the despair, the "yeush," which comes from being overwhelmed by the world's evil. And we may assume that this is his intention here as well. It is "the full recognition of evil" that leads a person to "absolutely despair of the whole of reality." The attitude of Israel is "to save everything, . . . the very evil itself, just as the good. And even more, to transform the evil into complete good" (*OHK* II, 488).

The way to overcome despair over evil is to come to see that evil itself has an organic nature, that it is not chaotic or accidental. It is part of the structure of the world and its plan. When we survey the evil in the world, writes Rav Kook, "we discover in it organic order and structure, and cannot attribute it to chance." We come to know that it was created "to raise up the existence of the good . . . in such a way that without the evil the good would not be so complete." In the end, we come to recognize that "the inner basis of the evil is a content of good, a very exalted content of good" (*OHK* II, 479).

Here we have a process that leads from the perception of discrete aspects of reality to their perception within an organized structure, and beyond, to their source above, in undifferentiated unity. This, then, is the way out of despair. Paradoxically, for Rav Kook, the despair of pessimism, that sees evil at the heart of existence, may itself be the way to its own negation. For such pessimism does not deem the evil to be chance or accident. Thus, this point of view is open to an organic understanding of evil, leading to the truth.

Despair, then, is the first reason in the poem for not being able to heed the call of Existence.

Stanza 2

> And if your heart is uncircumcised
> And my beauty does not enchant you—
> Existence whispers to me—
> Turn away from me, turn away,
> I am forbidden to you.

These lines, as well as others in the poem (in the third and fifth stanzas), contain a clear sexual metaphor that brings a new understanding to the poem. Existence is whispering her sexual availability. But if you are not "circumcised," she is forbidden to you. Only to her "chosen" one is she permitted.

In order to understand better the purpose of the sexual metaphor, we turn to Rav Kook's views on sexuality and circumcision.

For Rav Kook, the sexual drive is the "eternal, infinite aspect, hidden in the essence of a person . . . and is therefore the cornerstone of all moral values of human culture" (*OHK* III, 296). He rejects the "new science" that recognizes the sexual drive from birth and therefore wishes to free it from moral constraints, an apparent reference to Freudian psychoanalysis (*OHK* III, 297).

Sexuality gains its depth, and is the strongest of all our physical drives, because it contains in itself the source of new life, the "continuation of the generations" (*OHK* III, 298). In saying this, Rav Kook seems to be echoing Schopenhauer's view of sexuality. For Schopenhauer, the sexual drive is impelled by the power of the Will, the *noumenon*, to bring new individuals into existence in the realm of *phenomena*. This explains, for Schopenhauer, the power and irrationality of sexuality: "It is the future generation in the whole of its individual definiteness which is pressing into divinity. . . . The passion of two lovers is just as inexplicable as is the quite special individuality of any person."[35]

But Rav Kook's view of sexuality differs in an important way from Schopenhauer's. For the latter, the very creation of a new person suffices to explain the power and centrality of the sexual drive. The Will is "satisfied" to be expressed in a new person. It has no further aim. But for Rav Kook, the forward-directed nature of sexuality is the source of its energy and focus in our lives. Reality, for him, evolves to higher and higher levels of spirituality. The sexual drive is thus rooted in the metaphysical drive in all reality, not only for continuity, as in Schopenhauer's philosophy of despair, but for evolution to higher spiritual states: "The sexual drive flows toward the future, to the improvement of life that time will bring, to the World to Come in this world. And since future life is so full of glory and spiritual pleasure, thus so great is the desire and strength of will of this world-drive" (*OHK* III, 299).

In Rav Kook's optimistic view of world history, the sexual drive is teleological and an expression of the purpose of all creation: the successive evolution of higher spiritual levels. Of course this is a metaphysical, not a psychological, explanation, and it does not assume that people are actually aware of this motive. Schopenhauer anticipated Freud in declaring the all-pervasiveness of the sexual drive in human affairs. Rav Kook agrees: "The sexual drive includes in its nature . . . the foundation of all human drives" (*OHK* III, 300). Rav Kook could assert this because for him sexual desire is but an expression of a metaphysical principle of change pervading all reality. Freud's insights on sexuality may be correct in themselves, but they are mistaken in seeing the sexual drive as *ultimate* and not as the expression of something more fundamental.

Precisely because of its power and pervasiveness, the sexual drive can become diffuse and destructive. It can become functionally disconnected from its metaphysical teleology and turn into sheer power and desire. Circumcision removes the foreskin that covers and thus distorts the true nature of sexuality. Circumcision consecrates sexuality, on the conscious plane, to the furthering of the world's spiritual evolution: "Behold, man shall pave his sublime path through perfecting the Holy *Brit* [covenant/circumcision], through circumcision. And then he shall find all his powers directed to a general and ideal holy purpose" (*OHK* III, 301).

Since sexuality so dominates all other drives and is their ground, circumcision, by directing our sexuality, can unify the entire human personality into the supreme holy task of furthering spiritual growth: " 'From his own flesh a person shall see God' [cf. Job 19:26]. If a man possesses the power to unite all his inner powers and all his drives, [directing them] to one intellectual and moral goal, he experiences unity in his internal world, and the unity of the world in general becomes increasingly clear to him" (*OHK* III, 300).

Circumcision allows us to experience ourselves as organic unities, and from our reflective self-knowledge we are enabled to see the world that way as well. The organic unity of multiplicity is, thereby, revealed to us.

We are now able to explain the appropriateness of the sexual metaphor for Rav Kook in this poem. If your heart is "uncircumcised," then I am forbidden to you, Existence whispers. You cannot experience the organic unity of reality if you are "uncircumcised." You will project onto the world in general that separateness and opposition you yourself experience within. I am forbidden to you, for your sexuality is unredeemed and destructive.

In sum, the metaphysical ground of sexuality and the ground of the experience of organic unity are one.

The first stanza contains the first reason for not hearkening to the whisper of Existence: your despair at the world's evil. The second stanza contains a second reason: your inner life is itself so fragmented and aimless that it does not allow you to see the wholeness and direction in the world at large.

Stanza 3

> If every delicate chirp,
> every living beauty, does not arouse within you
> the splendor of a song of holiness,
> but instead an alien fire,
> Then turn away from me, turn away,
> I am forbidden to you.

The first two stanzas depict the inability to see any unity in the created order. This stanza speaks of a different, opposite danger, the danger of seeing only the organic unity of all multiplicity. A full spiritual life includes relating the organic unity to its ground in the unity above all multiplicity. An arrested spirituality that sees the unity of the world but denies the more fundamental ground of transcendence is a kind of pantheism to which Existence forbids herself.

In kabbalistic terms, the stanza speaks of a revealing of Binah in the world that does not proceed further to Ḥokhmah. The "song of holiness" is a reference to Ḥokhmah, as we saw in the first stanza of the first poem. The term for "gentle" is "'adin," related to "'eden," which denotes Ḥokhmah (Zohar II, 90a). The "chirp" and the "beauty" have the power to invoke Ḥokhmah. But instead an "alien fire" is aroused within one. What is this "alien fire"? The term occurs in the biblical account of the sin of the sons of Aaron, Nadav and Avihu, who "offered alien fire before God" (Lev. 10:1). Rav Kook's interpretation of their sin will shed light on the term "alien fire" and on this stanza as a whole.

In Rav Kook's understanding, the sin of Nadav and Avihu consisted in a spiritual consciousness that arrested at Binah and did not reach Ḥokhmah. The ideal source of Jewish spirituality is Ḥokhmah: "From the source of life, which is higher than life, Israel draws its spirit. . . . In order that the light of life shine on all souls and all reality, the light of holiness of the content of absolute being appears in its fullness, and rivers of pleasantness flow in the spirit of Binah" (*OHK* II, 284).

Binah is life, and Ḥokhmah the source of life, higher than life. The light of Ḥokhmah appears in its fullness, and rivers of "pleasantness," " 'eden," are discovered within Binah, within life. The "absolute being" is "yesh," Hokhmah, and appears in its fullness below.

If one thinks that "the enjoyment is the source of Existence . . . and aims only toward it," then "the foundations of life crumble because of the forsaking of the transcendent light" (OHK II, 284). "The enjoyment," "no'am," refers to Binah. "Life" cannot be sustained if one forsakes the transcendent light, Hokhmah. The result will be a "scattering" of the content of life: "In descent after descent in the flow of generations, the contents can become scattered to the point of total darkness" (OHK II, 284–85).

The word for "scattered" used by Rav Kook has the same root as the word for "alien" in "alien fire," "zar." The root occurs in the sense of scattered in Exod. 32:20 and Ezek. 36:19. The sin of Nadav and Avihu was in the offering of a scattered or scattering fire—a fire rooted in the principle of multiplicity.[36] Their devotion was to Binah and not to Hokhmah. The Zohar (I, 192a) says the sons of Aaron were drunk from "wine." They were so impressed by the unity within the world (= Binah = wine) that they forsook the unity beyond the world. Intoxicated by the spiritual joy of the world itself, they died. The life (spoken in the secret = wine) of the world was forbidden to them (see OHK II, 286).

This stanza speaks of a person whose appreciation of the world turns into a kind of pantheistic worship of its "scattered" unity, failing to ground it properly in its transcendent source. Such an individual does not sing a song of holiness, but instead offers a scattered fire and worships the beauty and majesty of the world in all its splendor.

The scattered fire was a real spiritual danger in Rav Kook's time. A striking example is the poem by Shaul Tschernichovsky, "Before the Statue of Apollo," which, along with his other poems with similar themes, greatly influenced the circles of the nascent Zionist movement. In this poem, Tschernichovsky contrasts the life and vitality of ancient Greece with what he considers the constricted, lifeless spirituality of the Judaism he knew. Standing before Apollo's statue, the poet declares:

I am a Jew: your adversary of old!
I am the first to return to you,
in a moment when I loathed death-throes for ever,

my vital soul, to earth cleaving,
burst the chains that bound it.[37]

Standing before Apollo, the Jew proclaims:

And I come to you, to your statue I will kneel,
I will kneel, I will bow, to the good and the sublime,
to that which is exalted throughout the world,
to all things splendid throughout creation
and elevated among secret-mysteries of the Cosmos.
I will bow to life, to valour, and to beauty,
I will bow to all precious things.[38]

The poet expresses worship of all things splendid and beautiful in the world. (Compare the following from the *Mah Tovu* prayer in the morning prayers: "I will prostrate myself, I will bow, I will bend the knee before God my Maker.") Written at the turn of the century, during Tschernichovsky's student years, the poem had a profound effect on Hebrew literature. Rav Kook's poem was written around 1912, and in it can be heard a reply to the themes of Tschernichovsky's poetry. If beauty arouses within you a "scattered fire" only, then the secret of Existence is forbidden to you.

In another poem, "The Statue," Tschernichovsky depicts the dedication of a statue at which the gathered shout "kalos! kalos! kalos!"—"beauty! beauty! beauty!"[39] These words replace and defy the affirmation of Jewish prayer: "kadosh! kadosh! kadosh!—"holy! holy! holy!" "If . . . beauty does not arouse within you the splendor of a song of holiness, but instead an alien fire," if you replace "kadosh" with "kalos," "I am forbidden to you," Existence declares.

This stanza also contains a hint of the nationalist theme to be made explicit in the next stanza. The word for "chirp," "tziftzuf," also means a gradual rising of light in the morning darkness. This word is used to describe the process of national redemption in the following midrash: "R. Ḥiyya Rabbah said to R. Shimon Ḥalafta: Thus shall be the redemption of Israel—gradually rising. As it is written, 'For when I sit in darkness, God is my light' [Mic. 7:8]. At first little by little, afterwards shining more, then increasing and multiplying, and then continually expanding" (*Cant. Rabbah*, 10).

The word for "gradually rising" is the same root as "tziftzuf" (chirp). The redemption comes slowly, at first only glimmering out from the dark, a gentle, delicate glimmering of light. If this second meaning is intended by Rav Kook, then he is suggesting that the first ray of the redemption, the Jewish nationalist movement, is to be seen as a spiritual event, carrying within it the promise of the highest holiness. It is possible to discern in it, if only you listen closely, a song of holiness. It is not merely a movement of national unification, bringing back the scattered children of Israel into organic nationhood. It is also to be a vehicle for mediating transcendent holiness.

Stanza 4

> And a generation will arise and live,
> And will sing to beauty and to life,
> And will draw pleasure without end,
> from the dew of heaven.

In this stanza, the poem takes an explicitly nationalistic turn. Until now Rav Kook spoke of the individual. Here, he speaks of a perception of reality shared by an entire nation. For him, the Zionist movement was deeply spiritual at its core, and it was destined to bring in its wake a renewal of Jewish engagement with the practical aspects of life. Jewish exile was an unnatural life of ephemeral piety, to which the return to Zion is a corrective (see *Orot*, 52, 159). A nation will sing to beauty and to life.

Life in the Diaspora is detached from the fullness of Jewish experience. Rav Kook can thus sympathize with Tschernichovsky's charge that "the God of men who conquered Canaan in a whirlwind/ then bound Him with the straps of their phylacteries."[40] But he cannot accept Tschernichovsky's worship of beauty and life as the solution. Rather, these are to mediate holiness, pulling down, as by a rope, the higher into the lower. The descent into the world is indicated by the progression from "pleasure" to "heaven" to "dew." "Pleasure" is "'eden," which, as we have seen, is a reference to Ḥokhmah. The Talmud speaks of " 'eden," the rewards of the righteous, as without measure (Ta'anit 10a). The pleasure is thus "without end." "Heaven" commonly denotes Binah or the lower sefirah, Tiferet (Zohar I, 50b), and "dew" is either the lowest sefirah, Malkhut, or that which flows down to the lowest sefirah from the sefirah just above, Yesod (Foundation) (Zohar I, 232a).

Malkhut, as we have seen, is also called "land," "eretz," and is associated with the nation of Israel. The stanza thus portrays the progressive descent of transcendent unity into the nation and into the land. For Rav Kook, the Zionist dream is well expressed in the biblical blessing: "May God give you of the dew of heaven, and of the fat of the earth, and a plenitude of corn and wine" (Gen. 27:28).

Stanza 5

> And from the vistas of Carmel and Sharon,
> the ear of the living nation shall hear
> the abundance of the secrets of life,
> And from the pleasure of song and beauty,
> It will be filled with the light of holiness.
> And the whole of Existence will whisper to it:
> My chosen, I am permitted to you.

The nation shall settle the mountain, the Carmel, and the valley, the Sharon, and the secrets of life will flow down as from a mountain to the valley. Then Existence will permit the chosen people to approach her.

The Carmel and the Sharon figure in the imagery of the prophet Isaiah, when he envisions the national redemption: "The wilderness and the parched land shall celebrate, and the desert shall rejoice and blossom as a rose. It shall blossom and rejoice with joy and song. The glory of Lebanon shall be given it, the vistas of Carmel and Sharon. They shall see the glory of God, the vistas of our Lord" (Isa. 35:1–2). But I believe there may be a deeper meaning in the reference to Carmel. And it is related to the "scattered fire" previously discussed. Mount Carmel is where Elijah the prophet confronted the worshippers of Ba'al and brought down the fire from heaven (1 Kings 18:30). Now Elijah was the reincarnation of the soul of Pinhas, son of Aaron, and Pinhas reincarnated the souls of Nadav and Avihu (Zohar III, 57b). Successive reincarnations are for purposes of Tikkun, of correcting the damage caused by previous sins. The sin of Nadav and Avihu was the bringing of a "scattered fire" into the Tabernacle. This sin is repaired by Elijah, who brings down a fire from above, in an act of sacrifice that takes place, paradoxically, outside the Temple. The fire that "falls" is a fire with a transcendent source. It is the corrective to the offering of

Nadav and Avihu, that did not reach transcendence, but remained instead within the realm of multiplicity.

Continuing with the symbolism of this stanza, the "ear" of the living nation stands in contrast to the "uncircumcised heart" of the first stanza. The prophet Jeremiah laments: "To whom shall I speak and give warning, that they hear? Behold their ear is uncircumcised, they cannot hear" (Jer. 6:10). In contrast with the uncircumcised heart, Rav Kook says the ear of the nation shall be circumcised, and they shall hear. What does it mean for the ear to be "uncircumcised"? It means the ear does not *hear* the unity in what it hears. In contrast, the uncircumcised heart lacks the inner unity enabling it to *see* the unity of all creation. The uncircumcised ear hears words, but does not hear the thought; it hears the sounds, but not the meaning.

In Kabbalah, parts of the human body are mystically associated with the sefirot. In one such scheme, the ear is Binah (see Zohar III, 138b). The medium of hearing is intrinsically different from seeing. That which is heard must be expressed serially, and the ear must catch the successive words, which are then united into one thought. Intrinsically, hearing is the building of a unity out of discrete parts. The sense of sight can see in a total unity, not necessarily serially. Hence, the eyes pertain to the aspect of Hokhmah.[41] The secrets of Existence flow down from Hokhmah through Binah and are heard by the "ear."

The term for "secrets" in this stanza changes from the word for "secret" of the first stanza. There the term was "sod," here the term is "razei." Its singular form, "raz," has the numerical value of "or," "light." "Secrets" here, therefore, points ahead to the "light of holiness" of line 5 of this stanza. This "light of holiness" is the light that emanates from Hokhmah, the Holy of Holies. Again, the secrets of Binah must be referred upward to Hokhmah. In addition, "raz" is the transposition of "zar," the word for the "alien" or "scattered" fire of the third stanza. The "raz" of this stanza is the corrective of "zar," the scattered fire of the third stanza, just as Carmel was the corrective of the sin of Nadav and Avihu. The negation of "zar" yields "raz," the light of transcendent unity.

There is likewise a shift in the word for "whispers" from the first to the last stanza. In the first stanza, the word is "tilhash," meaning to speak softly. Here the word is "tedovev," which has the additional meaning of "pouring down," especially a pouring down of wine, as in the verse: "And the roof of your mouth [is like] the good wine that goes down smoothly for my beloved, pouring down to the lips of those that sleep" (*Song of Songs* 7:10). And so the end returns to the beginning. Existence will pour down wine, Binah, and thus the "sod," the "secret," of the opening stanza.

Perhaps we may conjecture that the poem means to suggest that the dispersal of the Jewish people in exile corresponds to the fragmented inner life of the uncircumcised. Just as the latter projects his own chaotic inner state onto external reality, and so cannot apprehend its organic unity, so the disjointed Jewish existence of Galut prevents the Jewish nation from apprehending the organic unity of all reality. It is only when the ear of the nation is circumcised, only when the nation returns to Zion and experiences its own oneness, that its soul is opened to the possibilities of existence. When the exiles begin to be ingathered, in the first ray of light in the morning darkness, the unity is not yet apparent. But its driving force can be discerned, and its metaphysical source appreciated, even then. The Jewish exile has been long and hard, filled with troubles and pain. Are we to succumb to despair, a despair that poisons our very blood? Are we to die away from the stage of history? A generation will arise that will overcome its despair, that will settle the mountain and the valley, and drink wine from the vineyards of the desert. The nation will not die, but live. And it is to this living nation that Existence whispers: "My chosen, I am permitted to you."

Summary

The experience of this poem is one of transcendence that descends into the world and makes itself available to us. But we must move toward it, we are not pulled. We must overcome despair, we must unify our inner life, and we must be capable of seeing beyond multiplicity. The experience is not confined to individuals in the solitude of their spiritual inwardness. It is available to a nation, the Jewish nation, and is realizable in the national redemption of Zionism.

III

In these two poems I have tried to uncover some of the profundity, intensity, and complexity of Rav Kook's spiritual life. Rav Kook knew of both the introvertive experience of the Divine, which tended to isolate him from the masses, as well as the extrovertive experience he thought was available in and through the Jewish nation. The two complement one another, but they also reflect a certain tension between Rav Kook, the poet and mystic, and Rav Kook, the Chief Rabbi of Palestine.

Rav Kook once wrote: "There will surely arise a poet of Return, who will be a poet of life, a poet of revival, the poet of the national soul that is being redeemed."[42] We might add: And a poet of spirituality.

Notes

1. All quotations in this paragraph are from *Orot* (Jerusalem, 1975), 120.
2. The terms "introvertive" and "extrovertive" are borrowed in this context from W. T. Stace, *Mysticism and Philosophy* (London, 1961). I do not intend, however, to thereby imply agreement with Stace's thesis regarding these two types of experiences.
3. See A. M. Haberman, "Poetry of the Rav" (in Hebrew), *Sinai* 17, 1 (1945): 17–18 and 15, respectively, for the text of the two poems I treat along with a discussion of their respective dates of composition. "The Whispers of Existence" also appears with slight changes in *Orot ha-Ra'ayah* (Jerusalem, 1982), 69.
4. Quoted by Rabbi M. Z. Neriah in *Moreshet*, 1973, as cited in Zvi Yaron, *The Philosophy of Rav Kook* (Jerusalem, 1974), 27.
5. The difference between the two schemes is sometimes explained by saying that Keter is "hidden" until the eschatological redemption, whereas Da'at is "revealed" in the here-and-now. The scheme including Keter is therefore the hidden truth, and that including Da'at, the revealed truth. See Rabbi Moshe Haim Luzatto, *Klah Pithei Hokhmah*, sections 92 and 93.
6. See Joseph Gikatila, *Sha'arei Orah* ed. Joseph Ben Shlomo (Jerusalem, 1981), 2; 118–19. See also Zohar III, 288b.
7. See Gikatila, *Sha'arei Orah* 2: 84.
8. Rabbi Shneur Zalman of Lyady, *Iggeret ha-Teshuvah*, chap. 5, in *Likkutei Amarim, Tanya*.
9. For convenience I shall use single letters of the alphabet to represent

Hebrew letters as follows: "Y" = "Yod"; "H" = "Heh"; "V" = "Vav"; "H" = "Heh."

10. While English syntax requires that the transitive verb of a sentence follow the subject, this is not the case with Hebrew, where it can either follow or precede the subject.

11. See Gikatila, *Sha'arei Orah* 2: 84.

12. The symbol of the rope reaching to the sky as a means of ascent to a different order is well entrenched in the folklore and religions of many people. For a study of rope symbolism, see Mircea Eliade, "Ropes and Puppets," in *The Two and the One* (Chicago, 1962), 160–87.

13. The poem contains the word "devir," which I have translated as "Holy of Holies." See 1 Kings 8:6 and 2 Chron. 5:7.

14. See Rav Kook, *Orot ha-Kodesh* (Jerusalem, 1964) [henceforth abbreviated *OHK*], II, 285.

15. Ibid. II, 311. This passage occurs with minor changes (e.g., "relative" in place of "subjective") in "Ne'edar ba-Kodesh," in *Ma'amarei ha-Ra'ayah* (Jerusalem, 1984), 400.

16. *'Olat Re'iyah* (Jerusalem, 1962), I, 200.

17. See Ḥayyim Vital, *Peri Etz Ḥayyim*, "Sha'ar ha-'Amidah," chap. 14.

18. For more on this, see the commentary of Rabbi Y. Ashlag to *Tikkunei Zohar* (Tel Aviv, 1960), 284. The five levels are: Ḥokhmah, Binah, Da'at, Tiferet, and Malkhut.

19. These are in order of descent: Ḥesed, Gevurah, Tiferet, Netzaḥ, Hod, Yesod, and Malkhut.

20. It is not unusual for numbers to be rounded off in kabbalistic exposition, hence the discrepancy between forty-nine and fifty.

21. This is in accordance with Zohar III, 258b, that the "Father gives the 'basis' for the daughter." The "Father" is Ḥokhmah.

22. Jacob Boehme, *The Signature of All Things*, ed. Ernest Rhys (London, 1912), 213. Note parallels in the "voice" of God, the "Father" (see n. 28), and "instrument." For the possible influence of Kabbalah on Boehme, see Jurgen Habermas, "Der deutsche Idealismus der judrachen Philosophen," in Habermas, *Philosophisch-politische Profile* (Frankfurt, 1981).

23. See Ḥayyim Vital, *Etz Ḥayyim*, "Sha'ar ha-Kellalim," chap. 2. Also *Tikkunei Zohar*, Tikkun 18.

24. The fill-in is:

Y:YVD = 20
H:HY = 15
V:VYV = 22
H:HY = 15
     ──
     72

where "D" is the letter "dalet."

25. The fill-in is in accordance with the following key:

Y:YVD = 20	YVD	= 20
H:HA = 6	YVD+HA	= 26
V:VAV = 13	YVD+HA+VAV	= 39
H:HA = 6	YVD+HA+VAV+HA	= 45
45		130

where "A" is the letter "aleph."

26. Arthur Schopenhauer, *The World as Will and Representation*, trans. E. F. J. Payne (New York, 1966), 2: 72.

27. The reasons for this are many, including: (1) wine is *red*, representing the side of "Din" (judgment), to which Binah belongs; (2) Binah is "contained" within Malkhut, the lowest sefirah, which is compared to the vineyard or the grapes; and (3) the numerical value of "yayin" is seventy, there being seventy facets in all in the lower sefirot that emanate from Binah.

28. This interpretation appears in the main as a commentary on the Genesis story in Rav Kook's *'Olat Re'iyah*, 82–97.

29. Rav Kook, *Orot ha-Emunah* (Jerusalem, 1985), 3.

30. See Maimonides, *Laws of Idolatry* 1:3.

31. *Orot ha-Emunah*, 77.

32. The account that follows is drawn from Rav Kook *Iggerot ha-Ra'ayah* (Jerusalem, 1962), II, 43, with the exception of one quotation whose source is indicated in the next note.

33. *'Olat Re'iyah* I, 87 (my emphasis).

34. See *Sefer Yetzirah* I:1 and 2. The thirty-two paths are the ten sefirot and the twenty-two letters of the alphabet, the mystical building blocks of reality.

35. Schopenhauer, *The World as Will and Representation* 2, 536.

36. Fire is associated with "Din," the principle of severity and individuation, which, in turn, is associated with Binah.

37. With minor changes from *Saul Tschernichovsky: Poet of Revolt*, by Eisig Silberschlag, trans. Sholom J. Kahn et al. (Ithaca, 1968), 97.

38. Ibid., 98.

39. In *Kol Shirei Shaul Tschernichovsky* (Jerusalem, 1937), 213.

40. Silberschlag, *Tschernichovsky*, 98.

41. The symbolic differences between hearing and seeing are the theme of Rabbi David Cohen's work, *Kol ha-Nevuah: Ha-Higgayon ha-'Ivri ha-Shim'i* (Jerusalem, 1970).

42. Rav Kook, *Orot ha-Teshuvah* (Jerusalem, 1970), 124.

CHAPTER 5

Halakhah, Metahalakhah, and the Redemption of Israel: Reflections on the Rabbinic Rulings of Rav Kook

Michael Z. Nehorai

It is widely believed that present-day rabbis are very strict in their halakhic rulings pertaining to practical, contemporary problems, and were Rav Avraham Yitzḥak Kook alive, he would surely have tended toward more lenient rulings.[1] In fact, however, an examination of Rav Kook's halakhic rulings reveals that, in general, he was wont to be quite strict in his decisions, particularly when the issue related to fundamental national questions, such as those that arose at the beginning of the Zionist enterprise in the land of Israel.[2]

If we begin with the self-evident assumption that different halakhic rulings on the same issue testify to the fact that the halakhic decisors (*posekim*) possess different world outlooks, then the strictness of Rav Kook causes even greater surprise; for his deep and passionate attachment to the national revival is well known and

[This essay was translated by Joshua Levisohn from a Hebrew version that appeared in *Tarbiz* 59 (1990):481–505. Notes have been abridged. In references to *Iggerot ha-Re'iyah* (abbreviated as *Iggerot* in some references), the Arabic numerals denote page numbers rather than the numbers of the letters that are contained in the volume. —Eds.]

Special thanks go to my good friend, Mr. Yehudah Neuman, a member of Kibbutz Ein Tzurim, who helped me greatly in collecting and examining the primary sources upon which this article is based. I would also like to thank Dr. Yeḥezkel Cohen, Dr. Yonah Ben-Sasson, and Rabbi Simḥah Friedman (of blessed memory) for their fruitful comments.

we would not have expected that his rulings would pose difficulties for the attainment of Zionist goals, particularly when other rabbis, including some who were not Zionists or who were even anti-Zionists, ruled more leniently. This essay will be dedicated to demonstrating Rav Kook's halakhic strictness and to suggesting a possible explanation for it.

Since *pesak halakhah*, the process of ruling on questions of halakhah, especially regarding national questions, is, as already stated, a function also of theory, we must preface this essay with a few comments about the place and nature of two central components of the philosophy of Rav Kook: Zionism and the Jewish people. We will begin with Zionism.

In Rav Kook's opinion, the sole reason the Zionist movement arose was in order to restore religion to its central place in the social and cultural life of the Jewish people. More, the Jewish nationalist tendency is only one of the manifestations of religion in its broad and true sense. This restorative task, in which mystical and metaphysical motivations are intertwined, possesses cosmic significance, and its realization pertains directly not only to the Jewish people but to all humankind. The First World War was seen by Rav Kook as an apocalyptic event that would ultimately result in the destruction of European culture, "its foundations, its literature, its theater, all its institutions, and all its laws whose foundations are but vanity and sin."[3] Parallel to this, the war would bestir the power of the Messiah that, in turn, would bring about the complete revival of the Jewish people as a result of which redemption would come to the whole world.[4]

> The rebuilding of the world, which is collapsing now on the heels of the terrible storms caused by the bloody sword, demands the building of the Jewish people. The building of the nation and the revelation of its spirit is a single matter, and it is entirely united with the rebuilding of the world, which is crumbling and is awaiting a unifying and exalted force; and all of this exists in the soul of the community of Israel. . . . All the cultures of the world will be renewed through the renewal of our spirit, all opinions will correct themselves, all life, with our revival, will shine in the joy of its new birth, all beliefs will wear new clothes, they will remove all the filthy clothes from upon them, and will put on precious garments, they will abandon all the filth, all the impurities, all the abominations that are in their midst,

and will join together to suck from the dew of the holy lights which were set aside in the wellspring of Israel from the beginning of time for every nation and every person. The blessing of Abraham to all the nations will begin its activity, forcefully and openly, and on this basis, our rebuilding in the land of Israel will begin anew.[5]

However, the great Messianic expectations raised by the World War and the Zionist awakening were accompanied by the concern that perhaps the Jewish people would not be aware of the importance of the moment; perhaps it would lack the power and will to fulfill its designated task. This concern took on particular force in light of the fact that those who participated in the Zionist enterprise were "weak in spirit and d[id] not dare to raise the flag of Israel with a mighty hand, but rather [were] only paint[ing] a foreign flag with a Hebrew color."[6] The danger of the separation of religion and peoplehood—or, to use Rav Kook's terminology, the "divine idea" and the "national" idea—was viewed by him as a physical and metaphysical crisis of unimaginable consequences. "When the spirit of the nation awakens to the revival, unaccompanied by any return to observing the Torah and to cherishing the faith, this constitutes a public proclamation that the spirit of Israel does not require the Torah and faith." Thus, together with his yearning and hope, the fateful possibility occurred to him that a religious revival would not accompany the tempestuous spirit of the national revival. "And this could, heaven forbid, cause the terrible downfall of the spirit of faith and religious feeling; and we know that as a result of this downfall the spirit of the nation will consequently fall to the dust, and in the aftermath there will not remain any position upon which the national spirit could base itself."[7] There is no doubt, then, that these views of Rav Kook would necessarily find their expression in his halakhic writings.

From here we move to his outlook on the second component: the Jewish people. In a letter responding to those who criticized him for his practice of befriending Jewish sinners, Rav Kook wrote:

There are two main elements that together forge the sanctity of Israel and the divine bond with them. The first is a special inner quality [segulah]. . . . And this segulah is an internal holy force placed in the nature of the soul by the will of God, like the nature of every existing thing that cannot change at all. The second is the issue of choice (behirah); this depends upon good deeds and the study of the

Torah. The *segulah* element is immeasurably greater and more holy than the element that depends on choice. . . . And in the period of the footsteps of the Messiah the force of the *segulah* gains in strength. It is this *segulah* that is referred to in the phrase, "He Who remembers the kindnesses of the fathers and Who lovingly will bring a redeemer to their children's children for the sake of His Name," that is to say, [God will bring a redeemer] not because of the aspect of choice that results from the good deeds of the sons and from repentance, but for the sake of His Name that reveals itself through the remembrance of the kindnesses of the fathers.[8]

It is difficult to exaggerate the importance of this text in clarifying the significance of the concept of "Israel" in the view of Rav Kook. The *segulah* about which Rav Kook speaks in this passage is the essence of Jewish existence. Thus, the extent to which an individual relates to this existence is measured according to the extent to which an individual partakes of the *segulah*. The fortuitous existence of a particular individual in the formal framework of the Jewish people does not automatically mean that he belongs to the people in an essential way. Rav Kook makes his position very clear in the continuation of the aforementioned letter. He claims that there are many in our generation "who are tainted with evil deeds and evil opinions, God spare us, yet the light of the *segulah* still shines in them." There are also those, however, who "have lost all of the *segulah*." And even though he excludes the generation of the footsteps of the Messiah from this principle, and says "that in any case there is an aspect of holiness within them,"[9] this statement refers only to the generation as a whole and not to this or that individual. "God knows that I do not try to draw all the sinners closer, only those whom I sense possess a *segulah* force in their inner being; and there any many ways toward this knowledge, and many books need to be written in order to explain this."[10]

These views of Rav Kook concerning these two components—Zionism and the Jewish people—are expressed in varying ways in almost every page of his writings; our concern here, however, is not to analyze these views in detail. We engage in this brief discussion only in order to clarify the possible background of his rulings regarding questions pertaining to the emerging cultural character of the new *yishuv* (settlement) in the land of Israel. In his inner spiritual perception, Rav Kook discerned that "the ideal State of Israel—the base of the throne of God in the world"[11] is the sole legitimate expression of the *segulah* of Israel and, thereby, includes within itself the totality of normative perfections which in the future will be included in this *segulah*.

> In order to fulfill this aspiration, it is particularly necessary that this community possess a political and social state and national sovereignty at the acme of human culture—"a wise and intelligent people is this great nation" [Deut. 4:6]. The absolute divine idea reigns in the State and enlivens the nation and the land in the light of its own vitality. All this in order to know that not only outstanding sages, pietists, Nazarites, and holy individuals live in the light of this divine idea, but so do entire nations, perfected and adorned with all of the fixtures of culture and of political civilization.[12]

All the above statements clearly make manifest the vast distance separating the historical reality of the Jewish people in the beginning of the twentieth century from the reality that—in Rav Kook's view—was to unfold in the future. The question, of course, is: to which of the two realities did Rav Kook relate in his own halakhic rulings? It would seem that those rulings related more to the future reality, whereas the contemporary reality was perceived by him as a brief, transient episode, whose function was only to prepare the way for the ideal State of Israel. Rav Kook speaks about this quite openly when he sets forth the distinction between the Torah of the Land of Israel and the Torah of the diaspora. In his opinion, in the Land of Israel the Torah relies on the "roots of prophecy," and the *halakhot* (laws) unite with the *aggadot* (nonlegal teachings). "But the [talmudic] learning in the diaspora is not worthy of prophecy, and, consequently, the branches of the 'holy spirit' do not intertwine with the halakhah and its analytic components. Therefore, as regards its method of learning, the only [valid] opinions are those one can derive through rational logic, and aggadic issues have no connection whatsoever with halakhah."[13] Whatever the precise meaning may be of these words of Rav Kook, for our purpose their importance lies in making evident his opinion that prophetic considerations are legitimate components in the formation of the halakhah in the land of Israel. In the light of what was said previously, it seems clear that everything connected to the revival of Israel would be included in these considerations. The main aspect of the revival of Israel is its connection to prophecy, and this connection, of necessity, is forged, in the opinion of Rav Kook, by means of the halakhah.

According to this view, the halakhah cannot respond to the external side of life, that is, to "rational logic," by establishing criteria on the basis of what is required by the difficult and abnormal conditions of the present situation. For these criteria are liable to become permanently entrenched and will thereby thwart the actualization of the ideal political entity. Thus, the halakhah, for Rav Kook, is not supposed to "adjust" itself to the existing reality, but, rather, to bring reality toward it by setting the parameters for the crystallization of the ideal state. And, indeed, on fundamental questions of a national character, one recognizes in Rav Kook a clear and systematic halakhic tendency to rise above the demands deriving from the lifestyle of European culture through a far-reaching and farsighted vision of the yearned-for era of redemption. This tendency, then, follows Rav Kook's premise that the goal of halakhah is not to provide easy solutions to current problems, but, rather, to point the way to the formation of the permanent and enduring future. The vision of Rav Kook transcended the given reality to encompass the desired reality.

The halakhic problems on the national plane that confronted Rav Kook arose from two constants that characterized the pioneer movement at its inception: secular ideology and economic hardship. Rav Kook totally negated the legitimacy of secular ideology and in this connection applied the law excluding from the community of Israel anyone whose actions demonstrate that he has no part in the *segulah* of Israel. We do not know exactly what is the criterion for this determination, but it becomes apparent that the utmost devotion and sacrifice to the Zionist cause cannot serve as a source of merit for a person included in this category. Though Rav Kook both displayed and demanded from others great love toward *Klal Yisrael*, the community of Israel, even if its outward actions are corrupt, he also exhibited the stringent visage of the zealous and uncompromising law toward any particular individual who brazenly transgresses the words of the Torah. "Therefore, one who, through his opinions and, all the more so, through his actions, causes a weakening of the spirit that vivifies the nation is a national transgressor; forgiveness to [him] would be folly."[14] With uncommon and courageous candor, Rav Kook emphasized that what seems to many a show of patience and even love on his part toward violators of the Torah was naught but a cover for a completely different inner attitude.

> It is difficult, very difficult to love a Jew who contemptuously transgresses the laws of our holy Torah. . . . Only the few who are endowed with an extra amount of tolerance, only they can continue to treat them with external politeness, which others grasp as a type of sycophancy; but the majority cannot in any way suppress their disgust, and their bitterness toward every transgressor and shameless profaner of the holy is as strong as death. There is a great inner awareness within our nation as a whole that the transgression of the Torah and her commandments is the main cause toward sapping our national spiritual vigor which has severe consequences both for our general and particular lives.[15]

It is worth taking note here of two instances where Rav Kook gave practical expression to this view. The first instance was Rav Kook's great hesitancy in eulogizing two martyrs who died in defense of the Galilee. Rav Kook did not personally know either of the two murdered youths, but since he knew that they were members of "Hapoel Ha-tza'ir," he could assume that they had a negative attitude toward religion. Because of this, Rav Kook expressed his opinion that he was prevented from eulogizing them on the basis of the law that declares, "One who separates himself from the ways of the community, their brothers and relatives wear white and wrap themselves in white, and they eat and drink and rejoice that those who hate God have perished, as it is said, 'For I will hate those that despise thee, God.'"[16] Only with great difficulty did he finally rely upon another law as providing sufficient grounds for a permissive ruling that could serve as a basis for him to mourn them: "Some say that we do mourn an apostate who was killed by gentiles."[17]

The second instance concerns the well-known writer, the father of modern Hebrew, Eliezer Ben-Yehudah, who, in the heat of a polemic against the opponents of the Uganda plan, wrote: "We have all turned our backs on the past, and that is our pride and our glory."[18] The virtues of Ben-Yehudah and his contributions to the Zionist movement did not stand him in his stead, and Rav Kook spoke out against him in very strong terms: "I give the benefit of the doubt to this atrophied limb of ours. . . . Perhaps his Jewish name, as far as he is concerned, is completely decayed and rotten; it is possible that he himself no longer feels any attachment to our past, and can comfortably say that he has turned his back upon it. And, in truth, when desiccated leaves such as these fall from trees, they do not result in a great loss to the vineyard of the House of Israel."[19]

These two expressions of Torah opinions are just a very small sample of the sharp reactions found in Rav Kook's writings against the proponents of the ideology of secular nationalist Zionism. Of course, all rabbis felt responsible for ensuring that Jewish peoplehood preserve a clearly religious character, but in contrast to other rabbis, Rav Kook, as a result of his world outlook, saw himself as obliged to deal with and oppose all deviant manifestations. Apparently, because of a concern regarding *yayin nesekh*, Rav Kook attempted to have two workers in the winery at Rishon Le-Tziyyon who were suspected of violating the Sabbath dismissed, though most *posekim*, including the great nonzionist rabbinic authority, the Ḥazon Ish, permit one to drink wine handled by a Sabbath violator.[20] This one particular incident was seen by Rav Kook as possessing general national significance, inasmuch as it might set a negative precedent that would delay the advent of the anticipated redemption. Such types of halakhic considerations did not enter into the analyses of the other decisors.

> If we miss the moment of opportunity at the beginning of the development of the yishuv . . . and the arrogant hand that is armed with lawlessness and the ways of the gentiles . . . [the arrogant hand] that outwardly clothes life with an Israelite form whereas the inside is completely non-Jewish, [the arrogant hand] that stands ready to turn into a destroyer and a monster and in the end also to hatred of the people of Israel and the Land of Israel, as we already have seen to be the case on the basis of experience—if that impure hand will prove triumphant, then the magnitude of the tragedy is beyond conception. But in God I trust, that He will not let us stumble. . . . We will begin to establish in Zion the precious cornerstone and to instill life in the yishuv on the basis of the purity of faith.[21]

In what will follow we will deal with the central nationalist problems that arose with the beginning of the yishuv. These problems were critical, and the halakhic rulings accepted in practice to resolve them have determined the socioeconomic and cultural image of Israeli society until today. Many extensive studies have analyzed these topics from different angles: our purpose here is only to examine the halakhic principles of Rav Kook and, in keeping with the subject of this essay, to compare them with those of other rabbis.

The Commandment of Shemittah

The social and economic problems connected with the prohibition of work during the sabbatical year (*shemittah*) were brought to the great halakhists in the generation preceding Rav Kook for deliberation.[22] Among those rabbinic scholars, there were those who absolutely forbade any work of the land during the sabbatical year,[23] and those who permitted it. Among those who permitted the work, there were those who claimed that the laws of the sabbatical year are not in force at the present time,[24] and those who made the permission to work subject to two conditions: (1) that the land be sold to a non-Jew by way of circumvention, as we are accustomed to do with unleavened bread on Passover; and (2) that all manner of agricultural work—to begin with—be done by non-Jews, and that even in a situation of duress all modes of work that are biblically prohibited should not be done by Jews.[25] Rav Shmuel Mohliver made his permissive ruling issued in 1896, allowing the land to be worked on the sabbatical year, subject to the first condition, namely, that the land be sold to non-Jews; but he did not insist on the second condition, and allowed the colonies of the *Hovevei Tziyyon* movement to use Jews in working the land. "I staunchly maintain my position, as set forth in my monograph, that all manner of work may be performed by Jews."[26] These varying rulings reflect, in general, the different views of the decisors concerning the question as to whether or not the sabbatical year is in force nowadays.

In 1910, six years after he moved to the Land of Israel, Rav Kook addressed this question. At that time, he already found the *heter mekhirah*, the legal device of the sale of the land on the basis of which people were acting, in place. As he said, "I was not the first one to rule permissively" (*Iggerot* I, 334). Rav Kook criticized those who raised doubts about the halakhic validity of the *heter mekh-*

irah, because its nullification was both likely "to inflict deprivation upon many families from among our Jewish brethren, who look forward to living from the fruits of their labor" and to result in disrespect for the earlier rabbis who ruled permissively. "And besides all this, the matter borders on slander of the earlier rabbis, for those who ruled permissively, whom the halakhah and the practice actually follow, were great Torah scholars; and heaven forbid that we belittle their honor and publicly indicate that they caused large numbers of our holy people to act in a forbidden manner."[27] And yet, even though Rav Kook stood fast against the unbridled attacks launched by those who questioned the halakhic validity of the basic notion of the *heter mekhirah*, he, too, was not completely satisfied with many of the details of this permissive ruling. In contrast with Rav Mohliver, Rav Kook ruled that the categories of work that are biblically forbidden can be permitted only if done by Gentiles.

> Now, as to what people say in my name, that I permitted Jews to do all categories of work following the sale of the land, this is not true, and, moreover, contradicts what is well known. For I have already explicitly explained in a letter that was appended to the *heter* that the four categories of work which are biblically forbidden should be done by gentiles. . . . And if the matter comes to the point where it would be necessary to find some modification, then we would have to rule that the act of sowing should necessarily be done by non-Jews . . . ; and with reference to it, there is no way at all to issue a lenient ruling [and allow sowing to be done by Jews].[28]

The limitations that Rav Kook placed on the *heter mekhirah* on the strength of his personal authority shifted the given halakhic situation in a more stringent direction.[29] Moreover, had these limitations been accepted, they might have endangered the very existence of the new settlements. Indeed, there were those who accused the rabbis who ruled more stringently of attempting to use a biblical prohibition in order to nullify the whole Zionist enterprise.[30] It is clear that this stance of Rav Kook has no explanation unless we assume the existence of principled metahalakhic considerations. The issue of the sabbatical year holds a very central place in the kabbalistic theories of messianic redemption:

> The God-fearing individual will both seek to carry out in practice all the details of the sanctity of the sabbatical year, even in these times,

as much as possible, and will also seek, through his actions and his influence, to hasten the flourishing of our salvation and the revelation of the light of the Messiah. For the lights will be effective in the abundance of their holiness even if, Heaven forbid, his actions, in practice, were unsuccessful (*Iggerot* II, 196).

Similarly, the commandment of the sabbatical year was deemed to have a special impact on the realization of the spiritual *segulah* personality of the Jewish people. "The interruption of the social order, in certain respects, at regular intervals [through the observance of the sabbatical year] results in the nation's ascending, when it is properly ordered, to the heights of the most inward qualities of the spiritual and moral life.[31] Those rabbis who were more permissive than Rav Kook viewed the *heter mekhirah* only as an emergency measure, as a temporary concession necessitated by desperate circumstances, "until God will enlarge the boundaries of people and we will be able to observe all the commandments that depend on the Land of Israel, without having to resort to circumventions or nullifications."[32] However, for Rav Kook, those events bound up with the success of the Zionist enterprise already possessed a redemptive quality. These events, then, lent both immediacy and actuality to the biblical view concerning the sensitivity of the land of Israel to *mitzvah* performances and, conversely, to transgressions, as well as to the kabbalistic view concerning the relationship between the terrestrial land of Israel and the supernal land of Israel. Thus, "in order that the permissive ruling not be too well ingrained" (*Iggerot* I, 349) even in a temporary emergency situation, it was impossible for him to compromise, as did his predecessors, and to permit those categories of work that were expressly forbidden by the Torah during the sabbatical year. In a manner similar to R. Judah Halevi (*Kuzari* 2:8) and the Ramban (commentary to Lev. 8:25), Rav Kook believed that the entire phenomenon of the return to the Land of Israel is dependent on the renewal of the bond between Israel and its God through the performance of the commandments in general and the commandments dependent on the land in particular. This ruling of Rav Kook, then, clearly echoes the penetrating comment of Rabbi Naftali Tzvi Yehudah Berlin (the Netziv) who was adamant about forbidding work during the sabbatical year: "The resettlement of the Land of Israel was not in order to restore a Palestinian haven, but to reinstate the holiness of the Land of Israel, the land in which we are commanded to perform all the commandments, more so than in the Diaspora."[33]

The Permission to Use Sesame Oil on Passover

Around the time of the *shemittah* controversy, there also arose the controversy about the use of sesame oil on Passover.[34] It is worth mentioning this incident here for it clearly highlights the difference between the attitude of Rav Kook toward halakhic questions possessing a national character and his attitude toward questions lacking such a character. The question of the permissibility of using sesame oil was already the subject of a dispute between the *posekim* even before it was ever brought to Rav Kook in his capacity as Chief Rabbi of Jaffa.[35] At the head of those rabbis who forbade its use was the Supreme Judicial Court of the Hassidic Community of Jerusalem, while among those who permitted its use were the Chief Rabbi of Jerusalem, Rabbi Shmuel Salant, Rabbi Yitzhak Elhanan, and others.[36] Rav Kook joined the ranks of those permitting the use of this oil, and on this issue he demonstrated not only his halakhic genius, but also the full measure of his stature as a public leader. Against those who disagreed with him he stated:

> Heaven forbid that one should think that because we permit that which is permitted, we are giving license to those intent on breaking all barriers [and will thereby encourage the performance of forbidden acts]. On the contrary, when the people will see that we permit that which is permitted, they will then certainly believe that when we forbid something, it is because it is in fact forbidden by the law of the Torah or by the custom of Israel which is also like the Torah. But if we forbid those things that arise as a result of completely new creations, they will say that the rabbis want to be strict because they feel like it and do not care at all about the community; and in this there is inadvertent support for great breaches in the law, may God spare us.[37]

As we will see, this statement of Rav Kook against those who prohibited the use of sesame oil contains the principal arguments leveled against Rav Kook himself by those who objected to his rulings. It would seem that the explanation of this is to be found in the distinction between what we may term formal halakhic rulings

and halakhic rulings in which prophetic, ideological, and metahalakhic components are critical. The question of the status of sesame
oil belongs to a completely different category than the great national questions such as the sabbatical year, milking cows on the
Sabbath, suffrage for women, and autopsies. We will now proceed
to discuss these last three issues.

Milking on the Sabbath

The halakhic question as to whether it is permissible to milk on the
Sabbath was brought to Rav Kook for deliberation in his later years
(1933). From a chronological point of view, then, the question as to
whether women are allowed to vote arose earlier (1919). Nevertheless, we will move directly from our discussion of the question of
the sabbatical year to a discussion of the problem of milking on the
Sabbath, because the two issues have one thing in common: the
question of the possibility of maintaining a financially profitable
agricultural economy within the framework of halakhah. The problem of milking on the Sabbath arose in all its acuteness when many
farms that made a living from dairy products could not survive by
following the halakhah that permitted such milking only if done by
non-Jews (*Shulkhan Arukh, Orah Hayyim* 305:2). This was because: (1) there were places and situations where no gentile could
be found for such a purpose; (2) there was a reluctance to bring an
Arab into a Jewish settlement, both because of security reasons and
the possibility of transmitting cattle diseases; (3) the milking of
cows on a regular basis by a gentile contravened the pioneering
Zionist principle that work be done primarily by Jews; (4) refraining from milking cows one day a week was enough to cause
severe and irreversible damage to the health of the cows; and (5)
the difficult economic situation did not allow for sacrificing one-
seventh of the dairy produce by milking on the ground.

Despite these above-mentioned hardships, Rav Kook found no
room for leniency. He issued a restrictive halakhic ruling, formulated in apodictic terms and lacking any supportive argumentation,
which did not even permit, before the fact, milking cows so that
the milk would fall to the ground. If his ruling would have been
followed it would have meant that the farmers would have had to

abandon all dairy farming. This ruling thereby violated one of the principles of the religious Zionist faith, according to which it must be possible to observe all the commandments and at the same time maintain a modern agricultural economy. The farmers, therefore, turned to other rabbis—most prominently Rav Ḥayyim Hirschensohn and Rav Ben Tziyyon Uziel—and these rabbis issued permissive rulings that allowed the farmers to milk on the Sabbath.[38]

Rav Hirschensohn[39] dealt with the problem following an appeal by an American Jewish farmer. This farmer used to hire a gentile to milk his cows on the Sabbath, but the gentile quit and the farmer was unable to hire another gentile in place of the first, despite his readiness to pay a handsome salary. The farmer claimed that if the cows were not milked on the Sabbath, they would undoubtedly be harmed and would stop their production of milk, as a result of which his family would find itself in dire straits. The responsum of Rav Hirschensohn clearly indicates that he approached the halakhic deliberation from the start with the recognition that it would be necessary to find a permissive solution to the problem. "We must now search for a way to permit it." He therefore examined the opinion of the Talmudic sages who are permissive, and contended that although the halakhah was not decided in accordance with their views, they are still worthy of being relied upon in such dire circumstances.[40] Rav Hirschensohn anticipated that this problem "would undoubtedly soon be one of the pressing questions confronting the new settlements [in the land of Israel] . . . for the Arabs are not at peace with them."[41] In fact, very shortly after he issued his first responsum, another question on this matter reached him from the "Committee for the Settlement of Bnei-Brak." We will cite the question in full, inasmuch as it appears to contain an indirect criticism of Rav Kook, the Chief Rabbi.

> Bnei Brak, built according to pure Torah principles, hired an Arab for milking on the Sabbath. . . . But there was an outbreak of cattle disease in the area and the government imposed a quarantine preventing people from walking from one town to another because of the fear of contagion. We are in a state of great confusion about what to do concerning milking on the Sabbath, and there is no one to teach us the halakhah. I, myself, am astounded, surprised, and dumbfounded, for can it be the case that if we will merit the expansion of our settlements, we will have to increase the number of Arabs in our

midst for the purpose of milking on the Sabbath. This is something reason cannot accept, for have we not been commanded, "Do not do all work"—neither he nor others—"so that the sons of your handmaid and the stranger may be refreshed" [Exod. 23:12]? And can we legislate against the raising of sheep and cattle? So what are we to do with the prohibition of milking? We have no choice but to conclude that a halakhah was forgotten, and there is a halakhic *heter* regarding this matter that was used during the era of the original settlement of Israel, and the prohibition has developed by virtue of our being in the diaspora, uprooted and separated from agriculture. We have thus grown accustomed to the prohibition. Now, however, the matter should return to its original *heter*, on the strength of the promise that the land of Israel "flows with milk and honey" [Exod.3:8]. . . . And inasmuch as it is the opinion of experts that there is a danger to the animal both in the delay in milking and in any change in the milking, and the agricultural economy will suffer from neglecting this issue, we have the responsibility to find a *heter*, while still following the Torah and the commandments.[42]

The conclusion of the halakhic deliberation of Rav Hirschensohn was that it is permissible to milk into a dish, in some abnormal manner, very slowly, all the while being careful to consider the milk *muketzah*, that is to say, forbidden for use until after the Sabbath, and even after the Sabbath the milk would be permitted only for purposes of eating, not drinking.[43]

Rav Uziel[44] also saw himself as obliged to find some way to permit milking on the Sabbath. He appended four limiting conditions to the permission of milking: that it be done (1) by a pressure utensil, (2) in private, (3) only when it is impossible to find a gentile to do it, and (4) very slowly, just to the extent necessary to relieve the pain of the animal. We can determine Rav Uziel's conception of Torah and of life, at the root of his halakhic deliberations, from the following statement:

Inasmuch as the dairy industry is one of the bases of the economy of the yishuv from which hundreds or perhaps thousands of families make their living or supplement their living; and inasmuch as refraining from milking on the Sabbath would inflict great pain on the animals, as it causes them to stop producing milk and sometimes even shortens the lives of the milking cows, resulting in the destruction of entire families whose sole source of income is from the dairy industry, as well as in the destruction of settlement areas whose conditions for existence include the dairy industry; and inasmuch as throwing out the milk or milking into food would not by themselves be sufficient cause to permit milking and the only permissible recourse remaining is using a non-Jew, which itself is somewhat dubious if we rule that milking is biblically prohibited; and inasmuch as not everyone always has a non-Jewish worker in his employ—for all these reasons I am inclined to rule permissively on the basis of the rabbinic saying, "It is fitting to rely on Rabbi Shimon in an emergency situation." And inasmuch as there is an issue here of causing pain to an animal, for the animal suffers on account of the milk in her teats, and we consider causing pain to an animal to be biblically prohibited, the biblical law overrides the rabbinic ordinance. . . . In addition, we find that certain rabbinically forbidden types of work on the Sabbath [shevut] are permitted on account of the settling of the land of Israel [yishuv eretz Yisrael]. . . . Moreover, in our case, where all these [mitigating] factors are present—the bodily pain of the animal, great loss of money, settlement of the land of Israel—there is room to permit milking on the Sabbath according to the opinion of the Ramban and those like him who think that the prohibition of milking on the Sabbath is a rabbinically forbidden type of labor [shevut]; and the Ramban is of sufficient stature that he may be relied upon in case of dire need.[45]

As we stated previously, our concern here is not to evaluate the cogency of the various halakhic deliberations from a formal halakhic viewpoint but to examine the nature of the motivations that stand behind them. In this context, the fact that Rav Kook creates such a wide chasm between the Torah and real life is at first glance quite surprising. It is as if the matter in question were some purely theoretical learned issue raised in the beit midrash and not the very real danger of bankrupting the entire agricultural economy and perhaps even endangering the entire revival of religious settlement in the Land of Israel. In a letter to Rav Uziel, Rav Kook writes:

I saw [Rav Uziel's] faithful effort on behalf of our brethren, the milkers; but, after all is said and done, it is very difficult to construct any basis for a permissive ruling [heter] in a matter considered by most of the medieval authorities [rishonim] to be a [biblical] prohibition that carries with it the penalty of stoning. . . . It is enough that we avert our eyes from those who act leniently by milking on the ground [as a way of circumventing the prohibition], and even this [mode of circumvention] should not be articulated as an explicit ruling by a rabbinic scholar who is respected for his halakhic rulings,[46] but, heaven forbid, that we further broaden the scope of the heter. I hope, with the help of God, that if we band together to strengthen the hand of those who take the sanctity of the Sabbath seriously, non-Jews will be found even now who are able to milk the animals and who will enter the settlements with the express permission of the government.[47]

In my view, special significance should be attached to the conclusion of this statement, where Rav Kook expresses his hope that by virtue of the merit of observing the Sabbath, "non-Jews will be found even now who are able to milk the animals and who will enter the settlements with the express permission of the government." The existence of the "Shabbos goy," in Rav Kook's opinion, is not just a matter of necessity but rather an integral element of the ideal society. We will return to this issue later.

In another place, Rav Kook bitingly expresses his sharply negative evaluation of the cogency of the halakhic rulings of the rabbis who permit milking.

There are those who devised strained *heterim* that have no basis in practical halakhah and go counter to the ruling that was accepted by the Jewish people from early on, that one who milks violates the Sabbath by doing biblically prohibited work, for which one is obligated to bring a sin-offering if the work was done by accident, or is subject to excision or stoning if the work was done intentionally. And if those rabbis who inclined in the direction of leniency were to see the terrible harm that results from such permissive rulings, they themselves would certainly have cried out against it and would have prevented this tremendous breach of the law with all their might. I do not want to enter here into detailed legal casuistic analysis regarding the *heterim* that are almost laughable, for they are not more than illusions, like milking into food . . . or like milking with the left hand. . . . And even though the rabbis who attempted to set forth their opinions [justifying] these *heterim* are great scholars, whom I honor and revere, one must not, Heaven forbid, pass over in silence things that lead to such harm and anarchy with regard to the sanctity of the holy Sabbath.[48]

As stated previously, though Rav Kook was well aware of the dairy industry's difficult economic situation and the fact that its very survival hung in the balance, he staunchly maintained his restrictive view and forcefully opposed any attempt at compromise. Indeed, in a responsum he addressed to the members of a kibbutz, he wrote "that they should not buy a single cow if they have not already hired a gentile to milk on the Sabbath."[49] In another responsum, he stated: "Concerning milking on the Sabbath, I have not permitted it in the past, Heaven forbid, and I will not permit it in the future; and in a responsum that I wrote to a rabbi who wanted to rule leniently on this question, I explained that there is no basis for this *heter*, and that this ought not to be the practice in Israel."[50] At the same time, Rav Hirschensohn, in contrast, wrote: "At a time when the conditions of life demand it, for the very purpose of guarding the laws of God, [one should] employ the principle that the power of *heter* is preferable [to the power of prohibition] in circumstances where strict rulings will not contribute to the improvement of religion and life."[51]

It is, of course, superfluous to cite all the evidence that proves that Rav Kook's concern for the physical plight of the farmers in Israel—"whose eyes are directed toward supporting themselves and their household from the bounty of their land" (*Iggerot* I, 348) — was not less than that of Rav Hirschensohn, who lived in New Jersey. It is therefore impossible to explain and understand Rav Kook's unbending stand on this issue without assuming that it was motivated by his total commitment to a fundamental concept: Rav Kook saw himself as the community's representative, appointed by divine providence, who would lead his people in the formation of the ideal state,[52] a state possessing a Torah framework that determines the mentality of its citizens. It would only be proper, then, that the economic demands of the citizens of that state would conform to the laws of the Torah regulating the permitted and the forbidden. "The commandments will mold human nature until they themselves will become part of the fixed nature of mankind."[53] In this ideal state, given its fundamental character, there would be no need to seek *heterim* under the influence of norms derived from foreign cultures. If we extend this line of thought to the matter of the sabbatical year discussed earlier, we may suggest that perhaps in the ideal Jewish state Rav Kook envisioned there would no longer be any need for the *prozbol* (a technical circumvention of the prohibition of collecting debts after the sabbatical year), since in this state Jews would not hesitate to lend money before the sabbatical year, and would be prepared to forgo the money after the year was over.[54] The following letter testifies to this line of thought:

In response to his question, I answer that milking on the holy Sabbath by a Jew is completely forbidden and constitutes a terrible violation of the Sabbath, and Heaven forbid that one should rule leniently on this matter. There is no way to milk other than by a gentile, as our fathers always did in the past; and, in general, it is impossible that a Jewish settlement not have a few non-Jews in it, deriving from the necessity that certain things need to be done [on the Sabbath and holidays in the settlement] that may be done on these days only by non-Jews. The laws of the holy Torah are certainly incomparably stronger than all the concocted practices people have devised for themselves,[55] for "they are our life and the length of our days" and the basis of our revival upon this land.[56]

Beyond the fleeting present, Rav Kook saw the ideal model of the traditional halakhah, on the basis of which the permanent features of the kingdom of Israel slowly emerging into reality would be forged. The laws of the Torah contain within themselves the norms of the ideal state, and only these laws faithfully reflect the values and attitudes characterizing the Jewish *segulah*. The very fact that the Torah prohibited the milking of an animal on the Sabbath by Jews makes it incumbent upon subsequent generations to observe this halakhah in the same manner our fathers have always done, that is, by having the milking done only by a gentile. The messianic era, which for Rav Kook's generation was just an abstract hope, was for Rav Kook himself a reality, and his contemporaries, so he believed, were obliged to lay its foundation. According to this conception, it is clear that the new structure being built cannot in any way be different than the original one. It can be concluded, therefore, that the halakhic rulings of Rav Kook on national questions were decided on the basis of his future-oriented messianic vision and not on the basis of the present empirical situation.

Women's Suffrage

The question of the granting of political rights to women—to vote for and to be elected to the representative council—raised a storm in the yishuv for a period of about eight years (1918–26). Rav Kook was asked about this issue almost immediately after he had been appointed Chief Rabbi of Jerusalem in 1919, and he ruled against the women's right to vote as did other rabbis,[57] even though these other rabbis were accused by the new yishuv of conspiring to undermine the realization of Zionism.[58] Rav Kook based his prohibition on the halakhah, on moral values, and on concern for the well-being of family life. In his open letter to the Mizraḥi organization, which struggled with this question,[59] he ruled in an absolute fashion that the halakhah is very clear on this topic, and that there was no room for doubt or debate. "Regarding the law in this matter, I have nothing to add to the words of the earlier rabbis. In the Tanakh, in the Halakhah, and in the Aggadah we hear one unified pronouncement, namely, that the obligation of public service devolves only upon males."[60] Therefore, Rav Kook limited himself just to offering an extended explanation of the moral outlook contained within this prohibition. In his opinion, the Balfour Declaration regarding the rights of the Jewish people to the Land of Israel would never have been issued were it not for the British people's recognition of the holiness of the Tanakh. This fact, thereby, obligates the Jewish people to be worthy of its name, that is, to behave according to the moral standards of the Tanakh. If the Jewish people will exchange the moral values of the Torah for those of European culture, the enemies of Israel will be able to claim that the Jews have already lost their rights to the Land of Israel, inasmuch as they have severed their ties to the Tanakh.

> We now must stand guard to show to the whole world that the soul of Israel lives according to its true character, and the biblical land belongs to the biblical people, for the people live, with its entire soul, in the spirit of the Holy Land and this holy book. . . . It is worthwhile stressing that we are marching toward redemption, not in order to be particularly disciples of European culture—which regarding at least morality and ethical purity has completely failed. We can be certain that this strength will bring us more honor in the world than would be conferred upon us by an imitation of external fashions, an imitation that generally derives from an internal weakness. . . . Every rash step we take in the course of our public affairs without considering our own outlook concerning the value of the woman in the present and the future, a value etched deep in our spirit, just serves to hinder this ideal process. . . . Only the return of Israel to its land, to its foundation and its kingdom, to its holy spirit, its prophecy, and its sanctuary will bring to the world that very exalted illumination, for which all of the sublime souls of humanity yearn.[61]

In another letter,[62] Rav Kook explained that the whole idea of granting the vote to women is a product of the distressing situation in which women in European society found themselves. Giving rights to women in the public domain is, in his opinion, just a transparent attempt to conceal all the severe flaws that exist in the intimate sphere of family life. If the woman's familial situation were good, as it is among the Jewish people, women themselves would forgo this "right" to vote.

Rav Kook further claimed that the granting of suffrage to women would likely lead to disharmony in Jewish family life and from there to disharmony in Jewish national life. "It is liable to undermine *shalom bayit* [household peace], and this, in turn, will necessarily give rise ultimately to grave corruption in the general national and political life." This claim is justified by invoking the psychological coercion to which a woman would be subject in the event that her political outlook differed from that of her husband. This tension would likely lead to what he calls "sycophancy," where the woman would feel compelled, for the sake of *shalom bayit*, to suppress her opinions in favor of her husband's outlook.

> When we demand that a woman enter the public political arena and that she entangle herself in the matter of elections and general political matters, then we achieve one of two results: Either she learns how to be a sycophant, by falsely flattering her husband and voting in accordance with his wishes though it go contrary to her views—and this undermines both her ethical integrity and her inner freedom—or, as a result of the clash of views between husband and wife, *shalom bayit* is completely destroyed; and these slight cracks in the family will of necessity give rise to great breaches in the nation as a whole. And our honor will decline in the eyes of the nations when we show the world that we lack any original doctrine deriving from our essential spiritual being as that being manifests itself in our sacred teachings and traditions, teachings and traditions which we do not simply view as symbolic matters but rather as concrete, living values—that we lack such an original doctrine for a political program, but rather, in the very first steps we are taking in carrying out our political experiment, we feel it necessary to take upon ourselves the role of lowly disciples of the contemporary cultured nations of the world, nations which themselves are very confused in dealing with the difficult problems of their existence, and particularly in dealing with their spiritual and moral problems, and even more par-

ticularly in dealing with this exceptionally knotty problem of the relationship between family and state.[63]

Many rabbis, including Rabbis Hirschensohn and Uziel, came out against Rav Kook's ruling, opposing both the ethical and psychological rationales underlying the ruling, and the socioreligious implications arising from it. According to Rav Uziel, there is no halakhic basis for denying women the right both to vote and to stand for office. "All Israel, the men and the women, are holy and are not suspected of overstepping the boundaries of modesty and morality."[64] It is precisely ethical considerations—Rav Uziel claimed—that forbids one from obliging women to listen to the nations's elected representatives, while at the same time not allowing them any part in choosing these representatives. And if women are denied the right to vote on account of their "inferior intellect" (kallut da'at), something contradicted by reality, one would then have to deny the right to vote to anyone who appears to have an inferior intellect. And even the fear of possible breaches of the norms of modesty has no basis in reality. "What immodesty can there be with regard to this thing, where everyone just walks to the ballot box and hands in his own ballot?" And if the community were to become so fearful, then walking in the street or entering a store ought to be prohibited. Similarly, one should not deny women the right to vote for fear that, if her outlook differs from her husband's, it would undermine the harmony of the household, because, in that case, one would have to prohibit the suffrage of sons as well, or of anyone, for that matter, who is a dependent of the head of the household. Furthermore, the fact is, regardless of one's right to vote, one cannot simply suppress one's opinions on current political issues. With regard to the fear of "sycophancy" that Rav Kook mentioned, since the elections are by secret and not by open ballot, there is no need to worry.

> In conclusion, I saw some newly concocted reason for the prohibition against giving women the right to vote: the fear of sycophancy, lest the woman falsely flatter her husband by voting for the party or the person he supports. It is well stated in *Malki ba-Kodesh* [by Rav Hirschenson] that this is not sycophancy but the proper education of love, etc. And I would like to add: would that a woman give such honor to her husband to the point of suppressing her own will in

favor of her husband's will. This might thus constitute a positive reason for granting suffrage, so that a woman will thereby come to show endearment and high esteem for her husband, and, on account of this, there will be more harmony in the Jewish home. And were we to worry about sycophancy, the opposite conclusion would be more logical, that we should worry that the woman would disagree with the opinion of her husband and, for reasons of peace or fear, would flatter him and say that she agreed with him. But if this were a real concern, we would have to set up open and public elections because the same applies to children and other friends and loved ones. In truth, though, this is not considered sycophancy. Instead, it comes under the category of those things "which one is permitted to change [i.e., not to tell the truth] for the sake of peace" (Yebamot 65b).[65]

Particularly sharp was the response of Rav Hirschensohn, which set forth fundamental arguments of principle. First, he stated, there is no halakhic source upon which to base the denial of a woman's right to vote. Since this is so, the halakhic ruling that women may not vote involves forbidding something that is really permitted (see Rambam, *Hilkhot Mamrim* 2:9). Moreover, this ruling is the type of enactment which the community will surely not be able to uphold. Second, if we constantly attempt to impose upon the public halakhic rulings that are unacceptable, the public will eventually also reject even clear-cut halakhic prohibitions.[66] Regarding the crux of the matter, Rav Hirschensohn claimed that it is a woman's right to participate in elections, since "the Torah does not limit the rights of any human being and certainly not the rights of women who have served as mothers in Israel. God gave women added insight over men, and the Torah would not deprive them of something they deserve."[67] Additionally, the right to vote is a natural right in that it is a "general obligation devolving upon every member of human society."[68]

Let us remember that these two outstanding rabbinical scholars were among the circle of Rav Kook's admirers; yet they opposed his ruling, using very strong language ("Elections are not time-bound commandments from which women are exempt" or, even more sharply, "We do not derive halakhic conclusions from past conditions . . . just as we do not derive the conclusion that we are required to sit in tents from the fact that our forefathers sat in

tents").[69] Again, we must note that Rav Kook's motives derived
from the halakhah in its larger sense, from what is termed nowadays as *"da'at Torah"* (the authoritative Torah view on broad policy issues) or, to use his phrase, "the spirit of the Torah." As Rav
Kook states, "God forbid that we should think that any high rabbinical court would consider changing even one letter of the Torah
because of the freedom of life, if it not be in accordance with the
spirit of the Torah."[70] Even Rav Kook's staunchest opponents did
not doubt his phenomenal genius, though they did not identify with
or even disagreed with his overall philosophy. However, even his
admirers could not always fully comprehend the full implications of
his philosophy, of which his stand on the issue of women's suffrage
constitutes a prime example. We are speaking here about a principled worldview, according to "the spirit of the Torah," about the
very nature of male and female, and it is this worldview, in turn,
that gives rise to Rav Kook's position about the place of women in
the ideal Jewish state, and, by extension, in the perfected society of
the messianic era. Rav Kook gave forceful expression to this
worldview in his commentary on the blessing in the morning prayers, "that He has not made me a woman." In his commentary, he
claims that the woman was designated by her very nature to be led
by the conquering, creating man. It follows from this claim that
granting women the vote encourages the woman to be the con-
queror and the leader of the man, which constitutes a reversal of
the intention of creation.

> The souls in their individual fates are divided into active and the
> passive souls, into those that impress themselves upon life and upon
> their own existence . . . and those that are impressed. This is the
> essential difference between the soul of the man, which acts, fash-
> ions, conquers, and subdues, and the soul of the woman, which is
> impressed, acted upon, fashioned, conquered, and subdued by the
> behavior of the man. How many good and exalted virtues, and how
> much happiness and expansiveness are there in this good portion, in
> man's soul being active, creating, innovating, and developing activi-
> ties and thoughts, strivings and actions according to its inner self
> within its holy framework. [The soul of man is thereby] raised above
> the soul of the woman, which is considered as matter to form, as
> opposed to the soul of the man which is the form. Great, then, is the
> thanks owed to the Creator of the soul from each and every man—
> "that He has not made me a woman."[71]

It would appear that this text, in which Rav Kook sets forth a position that, in his opinion, gives expression to the metahalakhic dimension, that is to say, to the spirit of the Torah, obligates us to reevaluate both his considerations and those of his opponents regarding women's suffrage. It also sheds some light on an obscure passage cited earlier. We noted that, according to Rav Kook, granting the vote to women "is liable to undermine *shalom bayit* [household peace], and this, in turn, will necessarily give rise ultimately to grave corruption in the general national and political life." This idea dovetails nicely with the framework of Rav Kook's whole philosophy regarding the place of the woman in biblical society and in the future ideal society. His uncompromising stance on this issue constitutes a rejection of the analogy between the Jewish national rebirth and those of other peoples, for it is impossible that the special character of the ideal Jewish state not be clearly manifest already when its foundations are in the process of being laid. Now, of course, as one can see from his works *Orot ha-Kodesh* and *Mussar ha-Kodesh*, Rav Kook was very well aware of the humanistic and democratic tendencies pervasive in his time. Nevertheless, at the cost of the loss of his own popularity, he opposed the tendency, which pervaded even religious Zionist circles, to find all kinds of support in Jewish sources for "modern" norms of life and thought. In his opinion, which he expressed in many different ways, the morality of the ideal Jewish state will replace the morality of Europe, the bankruptcy of which—so he believed—is glaringly evident. "When the divine idea will fuse with the national idea and the two together will fuse with the moral and religious idea to form a coherent organic whole . . . then the vivifying spirits found in all the laws will rise up and be resurrected, those laws which those who look on them from afar dismiss as dry bones."[72]

Autopsies

At first glance, the question as to whether it is permissible to perform autopsies on Jewish corpses in order to study medicine is similar to the question as to whether it is permissible to use sesame oil on Passover. For, unlike the other questions we have discussed, the question of autopsies does not appear to raise national and social issues, and, therefore, would not seem to be relevant to our analysis. But this is not so.

Rav Kook's halakhic ruling on this issue clearly indicates that he viewed the question as critical, insofar as it is tied to the larger issue of the status of the Jewish people as a unique, special nation *('am segulah)* in the eyes of the nations of the world. We have already noted Rav Kook's attempt to determine the social norms of the present on the basis of the criteria of the envisioned future Jewish state. But this vision of Rav Kook rests, at least in part, on the contention that hidden in the subconscious of humanity is the anticipation of spiritual and cultural salvation through the instrumentality of the Jewish people when its unique *segulah* will become fully actualized. Rav Kook, furthermore, did not doubt that this recognition on the part of non-Jews of the collective *segulah* of the Jewish people also includes the—perhaps intuitive—acknowledgment of the exalted sanctity of the empirical physical body of an individual Jew, insofar as that body is a bearer of this *segulah*. The—not surprising—halakhic upshot of this view is Rav Kook's opposition to the performance of autopsies on Jews for the advancement of medicine. Thus, in 1931, Rav Kook ruled that autopsies done for the advancement of medicine may be carried out only on non-Jews. Moreover, he claimed that this prohibition against performing autopsies on Jews should be self-evident to both Jews and gentiles alike.

> In my opinion, desecration of the dead is one of the prohibitions unique to Israel, for God charged us concerning the sanctity of the body, just as we are prohibited from eating forbidden foods, which prohibition does not flow from the nature of the body . . . [i.e., because such foods would be deleterious to one's health] but from the sanctity unique to Israel, whom God has called "a holy nation." Now, just as gentiles are careful only about food [if the food be harmful] in a natural manner, so there is no reason for them to be so careful about not desecrating the human body, if such desecration will serve a natural goal such as medicine. We must, therefore, buy corpses from other nations for the purposes of science. And one need not worry about arousing the hatred of the gentiles, because the upright gentiles will understand that, in the final analysis, this nation, which was chosen to bring the holy light of the knowledge of the true God to the world, suffers immeasurable hardships on account of this, and, therefore, deserves a certain privilege of sanctity, while

the corrupt gentiles will not cease to libel us even if we perform autopsies on Jewish corpses.[73]

This view of Rav Kook was opposed by many rabbis whose views find their fullest expression in the following statement of Rav Uziel:

> The matter under discussion involves definite *pikuaḥ nefesh* [saving of a life], and anyone who knows even a little bit about medicine, about the development and advancement of this science and its utility will not doubt their [autopsies'] benefits for a second. And particularly in our time, when surgery to cure the sick has developed to a great degree, and in this way very many sick people who were close to the gates of death have become healthy, [autopsies are necessary]. For certainly autopsies help a great deal in recognizing and understanding the disease itself and its effect on other parts of the body and [therefore enable one to arrive at] the proper surgical procedure and medical treatment. And in circumstances of *pikuaḥ nefesh* and of benefit to the living, there is no disgrace and no desecration of the dead body, inasmuch as the dead corpse does not feel any shame or disgrace, while the living know that this is not a desecration, but an absolute necessity that is done with the proper respect and with returning the corpse to the grave with the proper respect after the autopsy has been completed. . . . Perhaps one may say that it is possible to carry out autopsies on non-Jewish corpses. But this surely should not be said and, even more so, should not be written. For the prohibition against desecration flows from the shame caused to every living person, that is to say, it is shameful to allow a dead person who was created in the image of God and endowed with intellect and understanding to subjugate and rule over the animals to remain uncared for and in a state of decomposition. Thus, the Tur and the Rambam are careful to write, "It is disgraceful to all living persons"; they do not say, "It is disgraceful to all Israel." Surely, in this matter there is no difference between a gentile and a Jew and between those deserving of the death penalty and those who are not. Nor does it depend on [any previously expressed] desire of the dead person himself nor on the consent of his heirs, because no one can permit the desecration and disgrace of his body and image.[74]

It is clear that this democratic equation of all of mankind in the matter of respect for the dead necessarily gives rise to Rav Uziel's ruling. However, in Rav Kook's consciousness, the Jewish people "constitutes a special unique entity . . . whose characteristic is that of an all-encompassing spiritual treasure including all talents and all higher spiritual strivings."[75] The halakhic ruling of Rav Kook on this issue is nourished, therefore, by his general worldview, which allots a central place to the Jewish people among the nations of the world and that posits an essential distinction between Jews and non-Jews. "The difference between the [individual] Israelite soul— its essence, its inner longings, its aspirations, its characteristics, and its status—and the soul of all gentiles, in all their levels, is greater and deeper than the difference between the soul of man and the soul of an animal, for between the latter two there is only a quantitative difference, whereas between the former two a qualitative difference prevails."[76]

It can be said, therefore, that Rav Kook's unique worldview is characterized by his perception of a future-oriented vision as the true reality. Rav Kook believed in shaping the future from out of the midst of the present through the medium of the halakhah; he sensed the implication of events taking place in his time for that future, and he thereby lived the present from the vantage-point of an inner future-oriented perception.

This essay constitutes an attempt to account for Rav Kook's stringent halakhic rulings by viewing them against the background of his unique vision of the ideal Jewish state. For this purpose, we have analyzed some examples of critical problems possessing a national dimension that arose at the beginning of the new yishuv in the land of Israel and were brought before posekim for halakhic rulings. Rav Kook's rulings on these questions were restrictive, and the general public did not follow them. In Rav Kook's day, religious Jews milked cows on the Sabbath, worked the land during the sabbatical year in the normal manner, and performed biblically forbidden types of work, following the permissive rulings of other rabbis. Women voted and were elected to the founding council of the national institutions, and in hospitals dissections were performed on Jewish corpses for the purpose of medical training.

The question arises then: How did Rav Kook achieve such an exalted position in the movement of national revival? From what has been stated earlier, it is clear that Rav Kook did not attain this position by virtue of his halakhic rulings. Nor, for that matter, can we attribute his status to his manifold public activities and projects, for example, his many representations before the British authorities, his founding of the Chief Rabbinate and the rabbinic courts, his inspiration of the *Entzyklopediyah Talmudit*, and the like. I would suggest, that the public esteem bestowed on Rav Kook derived from the fact that the Zionist movement, which, like him, was moved and driven by a vision of an ideal state, found in the person of Rav Kook what it was looking for. Despite the fact that the Zionist vision of the ideal state differed completely from that of Rav Kook, in the great and authoritative rabbinic personality of Rav Kook—the halakhic giant and philosopher, the saint and kabbalist, the thinker and poet—the movement of national rebirth sought and found its full justification as a legitimate and immanent chapter in the continuing flow of Jewish history. And in its search for and attainment of this justification, this national movement found support in the folk legend that drew a picture of an imaginary Rav Kook according to its fancy, a picture bearing no resemblance to the real Rav Kook who might have proved a disturbing presence indeed.

Notes

1. The literature on Rav Kook's halakhic methodology is exceptionally meager, in striking contrast to the rich literature on his general thought. See E. M. Lifshitz, "Ha-Rav," *Azkarah*, ed. Rav Y. L. Fishman-Maimon (Jerusalem, 1938), 168–78; Rav Shlomo Goren, "Halakhah Berurah u-Shelemut ha-Torah," *Ha-Tzofeh*, 1 Elul 5735 (1975); Rav Shlomo Zevin, "Mizug Halakhah ve-Aggadah," *Ha-Tzofeh*, 1 Elul 5735 (1975); idem, *Ishim ve-Shittot* (Tel Aviv, 1952), 203–51; idem, "Shittat ha-Rav [Kook] be-Halakhah," *Torah she-be-'al Peh*, ed. Rav Y. L. Maimon, (Jerusalem, 1961); Rav A. Hilvitz, "Le-Ba'ayat Da'at Makhra'at be-Halakhah ve-Shittat ha-Rav Kook," *Be-oro*, ed. Ḥ. Ḥamiel (Jerusalem, 1986), 121–52; M. Klein, " 'Ekronot Tefisato ha-Ra'ayonit shel ha-Rav Kook et ha-Halakhah," Be-oro, 153–66; and Z. Kaplan, "Le-Darko be-Halakhah," in *Ha-Re'iyah*, ed. Y. Rafael (Jerusalem, 1966), 70–77.
2. It is possible that the myth that Rav Kook was lenient in his halakhic rulings derives from the mistaken assumption that anyone who possesses great love for his fellow Jew surely tends to rule leniently. However, many rabbinic scholars have pointed out that not only does Rav Kook generally join forces with those who rule more strictly, but he even tends to rule strictly in cases where others rule leniently. Thus, for example, Rabbi Aharon Szelensky, in his book, *Likkutei Batar Likkutei* (Jerusalem, 1973), 6, states: "On the basis of my limited knowledge, I am unaware of almost any great rabbi in recent times who ruled more strictly that did our master, Rav Kook, z"l." Rabbi Szelensky proceeds

to discuss (6–11) a whole range of issues concerning which Rav Kook ruled more stringently than many other leading rabbinic scholars, even anti-Zionist rabbinic scholars! Among such issues are the acceptance of candidates for conversion who are not particularly religiously motivated, the fitness of hybrid *etrogim*, the granting of kosher certification to hotels that violate the Sabbath by accepting money, and certain problems surrounding the use of electricity on the Sabbath and holidays. See also M. Tzuriel, ed., *Otzerot ha-Re'iyah* (Tel Aviv, 1988), 1:24, which similarly provides a long list of halakhic issues concerning which Rav Kook ruled strictly.

3. Rav Kook, "Divrei Niḥumin", *Sinai*, ed. Y. L. Fishman-Maimon, Vols. 9–12 (1943), 328–29. It should be emphasized that Rav Kook did not deny the existence of a natural human morality that does not possess a religious foundation; on the contrary, he recognized "that the very striving for justice, whatever form it takes, is itself the most luminous divine influence" (*Iggerot ha-Re'iyah* I, 45). However, this type of natural, nonreligious, moral foundation is not sufficient to support "the general cosmological structure." The erection of the structure of society on the basis of natural morality alone, without the special revelation of morality the Torah provides, seemed to him "like a child's building, for it builds the outer shell of life before it knows how to build life itself" (ibid., 46). See, as well, *Ma'amarei ha-Re'iyah* (Jerusalem, 1980), 41; *Orot ha-Emunah* (Jerusalem, 1985), 21; and *'Arpalei Tohar* (Jerusalem, 1985), 15.

4. Rav Kook, *Orot*, 13: "When there is a great war in the world the power of the Messiah awakens. . . . And afterwards, at the close of the war, the world renews itself with a fresh spirit, and the footsteps of the Messiah openly reveal themselves . . . and the revealed end [of days] is indicated by the settling of the land of Israel."

5. Ibid., 16–17. See also *Iggerot ha-Re'iyah* III, 137: "As long as the situation of the [people of] Israel will not be rectified by having the land stolen from them returned back to them, this terrible war will not bear any fruits for the general peace of mankind." See, as well, ibid., 22, 113, 213. Rav Kook, in a manner similar to that of the students of the Gaon of Vilna, viewed political upheavals—even those not global in nature—as signs of the approaching redemption. See A. Morgenstern, "Tzippiyot Meshiḥiyot Likrat Shenat ha-Tor (1840)," *Meshiḥiyut ve-Eskatalogiyah*, ed. Zvi Baras (Jerusalem, 1986), 350.

6. *Iggerot ha-Re'iyah* II, 340. On the attempt to form a national religious movement under the name "*Degel Yerushalayim*" (Banner of Jerusalem), parallel to the Zionist Movement, see *Iggerot ha-Re'iyah* III, 169:IV, 83–84.

7. Rav Kook, *Afikim ba-Negev* (Jerusalem, 1972), 22; and *Iggerot ha-Re'iyah* II, 30. See also E. Goldman, "Hitgabbeshut Hashkafotav ha-Merkaziyot shel ha-Rav Kook," *Bar Ilan Annual*, 22–23 (1988), 66–78;

and my article "The Land of Israel in the Thought of Rav Kook," *Da'at*, 2–3 (1978):35–40.

8. *Iggerot ha-Re'iyah* II, 186–87.
9. On the analogy between our era and that of Ezra the Scribe, see *Iggerot ha-Re'iyah* I, 348.
10. Ibid. II, 188.
11. *Orot*, 160.
12. Ibid., 104; and cf. 14 section 3.
13. *Iggerot ha-Re'iyah* I, 124.
14. This criticism is directed against Eliezer Ben-Yehudah. See *Iggerot ha-Re'iyah* I, 20. In an essay on Rav Kook, Dov Sadan writes: "Not only did Rav Kook not make his peace with secular Judaism, but he didn't even admit that such a phenomenon was possible, particularly in the Holy Land. Rather, he saw the secular reality there as a type of attempt, albeit unconscious, to reach a holy end" (*Beyn Din le-Heshbon* [Tel Aviv, 1963], 327).
15. *Afikim ba-Negev*, 23.
16. See "'Al Bamoteynu Hallalim," *Ma'amarei ha-Re'iyah*, 89–93. The quotation from *Shulhan Arukh* is from *Yoreh De'ah* 346:5.
17. *Shulhan Arukh*, *Yoreh De'ah* 340:5, gloss of Remah. Cf. Shakh, ad. loc.; and Hatam Sofer, *Responsa*, *Yoreh De'ah* 333: "One who is killed by a murderer lying in ambush is endowed with the presumption of righteousness and fitness, and is considered a martyr." See Y. Avneri, "Rav Kook u-Maga'av 'im Anshei ha-Aliyah ha-Sheniyah be-Shanim 1904–1914," in *Bi-shevilei ha-Tehiyah* (Ramat Gan, 1983) 1:73–74.
18. E. Ben-Yehudah, "Bat-Kol mei-ha-'Ittonim," *Hashkafah* 6, no. 48 (1905):4.
19. *Iggerot ha-Re'iyah* I, 16 (letter 18). Ben-Yehudah printed Rav Kook's letter in his journal under the title, "Iggeret ha-Rav ha-Gaon Kook" and appended to it a brief preface and afterword. In his preface, he wrote, "I have no complaint against the great rabbinic scholar from Jaffa, for it is the [zeal for] the law that has aroused his wrath. And such a response is befitting a Rav. Therefore, I wish to cite here the entire letter verbatim and I will not omit even its rather coarse statements." In his afterword, Ben-Yehudah noted how impressed he was by the fact that Rav Kook, among other things, wrote, "I am far from demanding control of any person's views, [for such control] nowadays is unacceptable." In connection with this statement, Ben-Yehudah commented: "For such a statement to be uttered by a rabbi is exceptionally gratifying, and would that all rabbis feel as he does. . . . However, is not this [view of Rav Kook] a denial of our past? Did not the entire foundation of our past consist of the control of other people's views? Is it not on account of this that we are now waging battle against the fanatics?" (*Hashkafah* 11, no. 52 (1905):2).

20. *Iggerot ha-Re'iyah* I, 145; and cf. Ḥazon Ish, *Yoreh De'ah: Hilkhot Sheḥitah*, section 2, 7. The Ḥazon Ish explains that the principle involved in the prohibition against drinking wine that was touched by a non-Jew who is not an idol worshipper is "because of their daughters," i.e., the danger of intermarriage, and "since with reference to a Jewish apostate who violates the Sabbath, there is no problem of intermarriage nor a problem of idolatrous libations, there is no reason to prohibit drinking the wine [they handle]." See also R. Ya'akov Etlinger's collection of responsa, *Binyan Tziyyon ha-Ḥadashot* (Vilna, 1878), no. 23; R. Ḥayyim Hirschensohn, *Malki ba-Kodesh* (St. Louis, 1921) 2:160; and R. Ovadiah Yosef, *Yabi'a Omer: Yoreh De'ah* (Jerusalem, 1986), no. 11.

21. Another Torah-based opinion of Rav Kook worth mentioning is his stance regarding the murder of Ḥayyim Arlosoroff. Rav Kook, despite the heavy criticism leveled against him by the leaders of the yishuv, staunchly defended the accused, Avraham Stavsky. This matter is discussed at length by Zvi Yaron, *Mishnato shel ha-Rav Kook* (Jerusalem 1984), 360–62; and S. Daniel, "Harninu Goyyim 'Amo," in *Meor*, vol. 1 (Jerusalem, 1984). Judge Ḥayyim Cohen relates that Rav Kook told him, "It is not possible [that Stavsky should have been the murderer]. A Jew is not capable of murder; it is impossible. In the Jewish soul there is nothing like this." See Ḥayyim Cohen, *Siḥot 'im Michael Shashar* (Jerusalem, 1989), 63. As opposed to this widespread yet problematic explanation of the grounds of Rav Kook's defense, it seems to me that Rav Kook was only following his own theory that the halakhic rule of "*dina de-malkhuta dina*," the law of the kingdom is the law, does not apply when the secular law conflicts with a prohibition of the Torah (*Iggerot ha-Re'iyah* III, 136), and in a Jewish state only the Sanhedrin has the authority to judge capital crimes (see Rambam, *Hilkhot 'Edut*, chap. 1, and *Hilkhot Rotzeaḥ* 4:8). See also *Otzerot Re'iyah*, 871; Y. Hadari, "Ha-Halakhah be-Haguto shel ha-Rav Kook," *Hagut ve-Halakhah* (Jerusalem, 1968), 59.

22. See M. Friedman, "Le-Mashma'uto ha-Hevratit shel Pulmos ha-Shemittah," *Shalem*, vol. 1 (Jerusalem, 1974); Y. Gilat, "Le-Tokefan shel Ḥarishah u-Melakhot Aḥerot bi-Shevi'it," *Perakim be-Hishtalshelut ha-Halakhah* (Ramat Gan, 1992), 262–72.

23. Rav Naftali Tzvi Yehudah Berlin (1817–93) (one of the heads of the Volozhin Yeshiva), *Meishiv Davar* (Warsaw, 1894), 2:58–59.

24. Rav Mordecai Eliasberg (1817–1889), the rabbi of Bausk before Rav Kook, wrote: "My view, the view of the Torah, is inclined to leniency, and decides to completely permit our brethren the colonists to work in the present sabbatical year, so long as we have not merited that they can support themselves from the land's yield even in the years they do work! For how can it be that they should entirely cease working their fields and vineyards and require an even greater amount of support?

What would follow is that this ceasing [to work on the sabbatical year] would just prolong the time required for the redemption of the land" ("Mikhtav Galui," *Ha-Melitz* [1889], no. 268, 1–2).

25. Rav Yitzḥak Elḥanan Spector (1817–96), the rabbi of Kovno and the leading halakhic authority of his generation, wrote: "If we do not search for a solution and a permissive ruling, the result may be that the land of Israel will lie desolate, God forbid, and the colonies will be destroyed, and this relates to the saving of hundreds of lives" (*Ha-Melitz* [1889], no. 58, 3). See, also, Rav Avraham Borenstein, the Admor of Sokhochov (1839–1910), *Avnei Nezer* (Warsaw, 1914), *Yoreh De'ah*, no. 258.

26. Rav Shmuel Mohliver (1834–98), the Rabbi of Bialystok, "Bi-Devar ha-Shemittah," *Ha-Yehudi* 26 (21 Tammuz 1910): 3–4. In addition to maintaining the halakhic correctness of his position, Rav Mohliver noted: "Now that the number of Jewish workers in our land has greatly increased, and their entire livelihood is derived from the wages they receive from working the fields and vineyards of their brethren . . . if we forbid them to work we will be taking food out of their mouths and they will, Heaven forbid, die of starvation."

27. *Mishpat Kohen* (Jerusalem, 1966), 146.

28. Ibid., 132, 149; and *Iggerot ha-Re'iyah* I, letters 289 and 311. Rav Szelensky, in *Likkutei Batar Likkutei* (9) relates that M. Lilienblum, the administrator of the Odessa Council of the Lovers of Zion (*Hovevei Tziyyon*) at the time, expressed surprise at this limitation, because on the basis of the ruling of Rav Mohliver the members of the settlements performed all types of work by themselves—"for in order to allow non-Jews to work the land, the land did not need to be sold." Rav Kook responded to Mr. Lilienblum as follows: "The great scholar, Rav Shmuel Mohliver, may his memory be for a blessing, was of the view that in his day there was neither the need nor the possibility to arrange for the work to be done by non-Jews, while I am of the view that [nowadays] it is both possible and necessary, and Yiftah in his generation is as Shmuel was in his." See, as well, *Mishpat Kohen*, no. 86.

29. As a result of the difficult economic situation that prevailed in the land of Israel following the rebellion of Bar Kokhbah, Rav Yehudah ha-Nasi relaxed the strictness of various prohibitions limiting the use of fruit of the sabbatical year, on the basis of the halakhah that the sabbatical year nowadays is only a rabbinical ordinance. As opposed to his view, other Sages claimed that the sabbatical year, even nowadays, is still a biblical command and, therefore, in no case may one be lenient with regard to the four types of work that are biblically prohibited. Rav Kook ruled in accordance with the second view. See Gilat, "Le-Tokefan shel Ḥarishah," (above note 22), 271.

30. G. Yardeni, *Ha-'Itonut ha-'Ivrit be-Eretz Yisrael* (Tel Aviv, 1969), 130.

31. *Shabbat ha-Aretz* (Jerusalem, 1975), 8.
32. Ibid., 121.
33. *Meishiv Davar*, 2:58–59.
34. Rav Kook, *Orah Mishpat* (Jerusalem, 1979), 117–38.
35. For a thorough discussion of this issue, see M. Z. Neriyah, *Bi-Sedeh ha-Re'iyah* (Kefar ha-Roeh, 1987), 145–79.
36. Ibid., 152–53, 173–75.
37. *Orah Mishpat*, 119.
38. For a presentation of the history of this issue, see H. Peles, "Ba'ayot he-Halivah be-Shabbat be-Hityashvut ha-Datit," *Barkai*, (Jerusalem, 1985), 2:108ff.; and A. Nahlon, "Ha-Rav Herzog ve-Helko be-Pitron Ba'ayot ha-Halivah be-Shabbat," *'Amudim* (Dec. 1988–Jan. 1989), 132–36.
39. Rav Hayyim Hirschensohn (1857–1935), among the first and most active leaders of the Mizrahi movement, was born in Safed and died in New Jersey. For his thought and for the similarities and differences between him and Rav Kook, see E. Schweid, *Demokratiyah ve-Halakhah* (Jerusalem, 1978); and see, as well, Y. Cohen, ed., *Ha-Torah ve-he-Hayyim* (Jerusalem, 1989).
40. R. Hayyim Hirschensohn, *Malki ba-Kodesh* (St. Louis, 1928), 5:44.
41. Ibid., 40.
42. Ibid., 61–62. Two points in this letter are worthy of note, for it would seem that they reflect the general outlook of the religious pioneers at that time: (1) It is inconceivable that according to the Torah of Israel there should be no possibility for religious Jews to raise cattle and sheep in the land of Israel, or that they would have to use non-Jewish help on a regular basis; and (2) one may assume that the halakhah in the *Shulhan Arukh* pertains only to the living conditions of the Jews in exile and not to their mode of life in the land of Israel.
43. Ibid., 55.
44. Rav Ben-Tziyyon Uziel (1880–1953) served as the Chief Rabbi of Jaffa and Tel Aviv and eventually became the Sephardic Chief Rabbi of the State of Israel.
45. *Piskei Uziel* (Jerusalem, 1977), 87.
46. See *Hazon Ish, Orah Hayyim: Hilkhhot Shabbat* (Bnei Brak, 1973), 82: "Therefore, even if milking on the ground on the Sabbath would only constitute [work forbidden by] one rabbinical ordinance superimposed upon another rabbinical ordinance, one would still not be able to permit the action on the basis of potential monetary loss; but we may rely on those authorities who say that [such milking] is not considered work at all."
47. See *Tehumin*, (Alon-Shvut, 1980), 1:5–6.
48. Ibid., 7–8.
49. *Barkai*, 114.

50. *Teḥumin*, 8.
51. *Malki ba-Kodesh*, 2:7–9.
52. Rav Kook describes the members of a delegation from London to the land of Israel thusly: "These holy messengers are delegates appointed by the sentiment that derives from the very core of the national soul . . . from that holy force, that divine force which guides the whole world" (*Iggerot ha-Re'iyah* III, 167). It is clear that he also saw himself as occupying a similar position. An introspective revelation that borders on a prophetic vision is found in one of the manuscripts of *Orot ha-Kodesh*, but it was deleted from the published version. (Its proper place is I, 157.) "I listen and hear from the depths of my soul, from within the sentiments of my heart, the voice of God calling, and I tremble greatly—have I fallen thus far that I should be a false prophet to declare that God has sent me, while the word of God has not been revealed to me, etc." (I would like to thank my friend Rav Yaakov Filber, who is in the midst of publishing works of Rav Kook still in manuscript, for making this text available to me.) The editor of *Orot ha-Kodesh*, Rav David Cohen (the Nazir), hinted at this deletion by beginning the section found on 157 with a dotted line.
53. *Orot ha-Kodesh* IV (Jerusalem, 1990), 517.
54. See *Shabbat ha-Aretz*, 13.
55. It seems to me that the phrase "concocted practices" alludes to the outlook which advocates that work on the land of Israel be done by Jews only. Rav Kook, by contrast, viewed the existence of gentiles in the state of Israel as a component of the ideal order of the redemption. "It is impossible for a Jewish settlement to get along without the presence of a Shabbos goy" (*Oraḥ Mishpat*, 74). Also worthy of note is a comment of Rav Kook cited by Rav Szelensky: "Moreover, he said to me orally that the yishuv in the Land of Israel cannot be established contrary to the decision of the Torah which declared that gentiles will also live there; and it is for this reason that the Torah contains laws about the resident alien [*ger toshav*]" (*Likkutei Batar Likkutei*, 6).
56. *Teḥumin*, 1:8. See also Schweid, *Demokratiyah ve-Halakhah*, 166–167, who arrives at a conclusion identical to my own via a somewhat different path. He summarizes the opinion of Rav Hirschensohn as follows: "One should prepare for the future toward which the present points, but one should not prematurely anticipate the future by skipping over the present." About Rav Kook, he says: "From this standpoint, Rav Kook envisions that life itself, through the divine dialectic embodied in it, will rise to the level of the Torah, and he does not feel the need to bring the Torah to the present in the form it has assumed currently. He endures the present, and in enduring it he anticipates the already imminent future."
57. For a full discussion, see A. Morgenstern, *Ha-Rabbanut ha-Rashit le-*

Eretz Yisrael (Jerusalem, 1973), 119ff.; and M. Friedman, *Hevrah ve-Dat* (Jerusalem, 1988), 146–82.

58. Friedman, *Hevrah ve-Dat*, 149.

59. *Ma'amarei ha-Re'iyah*, 189–90.

60. Rav Hirschensohn ironically noted that "Rav Avraham Yitzhak Kook . . . wrote an ethical essay about the pursuit of peace, and his words are even more ethical than the halakhah" (*Malki ba-Kodesh*, 2:71).

61. *Ma'amarei ha-Re'iyah*, 190.

62. Ibid., 192–94.

63. Ibid., 192–93.

64. *Piskei Uziel*, no. 44, 228ff. Rav Zvi Pesah Frank, who was a member of the Rabbinical Council of Jerusalem during Rav Kook's time, issued a public proclamation directed at the religious circles, stating: "In order that we should succeed in ensuring that [the Jewish community] in the Land of Israel should continue in its behavior according to the Torah of Israel, we must make an effort so that the women, most of whom are righteous and still loyal to God, take part in the elections" (quoted by Rav Hirschensohn, *Malki ba-Kodesh*, 2:12).

65. *Piskei Uziel*, no. 44.

66. *Malki ba-Kodesh* 2, question 4.

67. Ibid.

68. Ibid., response to question 4. Rav Y. L. Maimon publicly announced that the Mizrahi movement refused to accept the ruling of Rav Kook: "The Mizrahi organization in the Land of Israel acknowledges the value of women participating in the rebirth of our nation and does not at all object to the granting of suffrage to the Jewish woman, neither on general grounds nor for any religious reasons" ("Doar ha-Yom," 5 Shevat 1920. For an even stronger version, see "Doar ha-Yom," 1 Iyyar 1920).

69. *Malki ba-Kodesh* 2:171, 201.

70. *Otzerot ha-Re'iyah*, 932.

71. *'Olat Re'iyah* (Jerusalem, 1962), I, 71.

72. *Iggerot ha-Re'iyah*, I, 176. Concerning sacrifices, Rav Hirschensohn had stated: "But knowledge and cognition cannot move backward and will not regress to consider something uncultured as being cultured" (*Malki ba-Kodesh*, 6). Rav Kook responded to this comment as follows: "Concerning sacrifices . . . we will not be overly impressed by the ideas of European culture, because the word of God that is with us will in the future raise up the foundations of culture to a level much more exalted than anything human reasoning can achieve. It is not proper for us to think that sacrifices only consist of the base idea of material service [of God], but rather they contain an inner natural holiness that can only be revealed in its splendor with the revelation of God's light to His nation, and [then] a holy rebirth will return to Israel—

and this will also be recognized by all the nations" (*Iggerot ha-Re'iyah* IV, 24).

73. *Da'at Kohen*, no. 199, 383.
74. *Piskei Uziel, Orah Ḥayyim*, 178–79.
75. *Orot*, 155–56.
76. Ibid., 156.

PART TWO

Faith, Culture, and Pluralism: The Perspective of Harmonism

CHAPTER 6

Harmonism, Novelty, and the Sacred in the Teachings of Rav Kook

Norman Lamm

I do not often indulge my mystical penchant for finding significance in names, but I shall do so here because of the felicitous coincidence of the names of Rav Kook and the appropriateness of their meaning to his personality. The name "Kook" in Yiddish means a look, a glance. The Hebrew acrostic of his name, "HA-R-A-Y-H," standing for *Ha-Rav, Avraham Yitzḥak Ha-*Kohen, means the look, the sight, the glance. Both names, therefore, imply vision.

This essay will treat three aspects of the grand vision of Rav Kook: his harmonistic approach; his conception of the new; and his view of the relations between the sacred and profane.

I

One of the major themes evident in all the writings of Rav Kook is that of harmonism. We all experience a degree of dissonance in our lives—our hearts and our minds are in almost constant and tragic confrontation; science and religion pull us into divergent paths; wherever we turn, intellectually or existentially, we are beset by dualisms, distinctions, and opposing concepts. Our lives don't seem to hang together, they lack coherence; our cognitive experience is pock-marked by antinomies and incompatible categories of all kinds; existence itself seems so very fragile, frangible, and fractured.

Harmonism is the desire to transcend all differences between opposing ideas as to the way to truth, viewing them as but transient obstacles to be overcome, and harmonizing them in a grand, cosmic, mystico-philosophical effort to achieve the *Alma de-Yiḥuda*, the World of Unity of which the Zohar speaks, and which is the worthiest goal of man's aspirations. Rav Kook sees this as the proper antidote to the *Alma di-Peruda*, the World of Disunity, characterized by man's atomizing tendencies and the fragmentary nature of his perilous existence. In the state of *Alma de-Yiḥuda*, man's integrated life reflects the uncompromised unity of God; in the *Alma di-Peruda*, man's experience of dissonance is both cause and effect of the broken and disrupted unity of God.

One must add here that for Rav Kook, unlike the Lurianic kabbalists, what separates the worlds of Unity and Disunity is not time—with the World of Unity relegated to the eschatological era—but perception. In an objective sense, unity and harmony exist and are, indeed, the foundation of all existence: "All is naught but the revelation of oneness that appears in a variety of 'sparks.'"[1] It is only subjectively that fragmentation and conflict seem to prevail. Indeed, Rav Kook is primarily subjectivistic, his interest almost exclusively centered on man's inner life.

Thus, while Franz Rosenzweig viewed the world as dissonant and fragmented, Rav Kook saw it as whole, and he attributed the experience of fragmentation to our flawed perception of reality. Hence, objectively, "The world is not torn and shattered. It stands as a powerful structure. The highest heavens and the bowels of the earth form one unit, one world, one existence."[2]

I do not recall who first used the term "harmonism" to describe the thought of Rav Kook, but it is a most felicitous one. Rav Kook himself alludes to harmony, although not to describe his own thought, and it expresses well the particular quality and flavor of his quest for unity. Thus: "Every mitzvah and every halakhah has its own particular musical quality, which Knesset Israel listens to and enjoys."[3] Musical tones ought to differ from each other by their very nature; yet they should not result in a cacophony but, approached properly, can be harmonized to produce a new, marvelous whole. Creation may now be little more than chaos, but man has the ability to make of it a divine symphony. Moreover, the proper and profound insight both into the world and into one's self will reveal that unity is already ubiquitous and underlies the apparent mass of dissonance and atomization that seems to prevail.

Rav Kook's harmonism has a multiplicity of significant consequences and implications. Because I have written about it elsewhere,[4] I shall not elaborate upon this aspect of the theme here, but just briefly adumbrate some of the areas that are comprehended in this grand conception of harmony. They include the spheres of metaphysics, education, epistemology, psychology, talmudic studies, Bible, war and peace, science and religion—to mention but a few. In other words, Rav Kook's striving for unity is totally comprehensive, indeed nothing less than a cosmic effort. And he does not lose sight of man's mundane interests in the drama of harmonization.

I alluded to the fact that Rav Kook's monism has its origin in the Zoharian concept of overcoming the 'Alma di-Peruda by establishing the 'Alma de-Yihuda. A more complete study of the history of this idea, in its various forms, would have to include the "SHeLaH"[5] and the subsequent development of the theme in the hands of the Hasidic masters, the immediate influences on Rav Kook. Space does not permit the presentation of the other side of the coin: the implicit rejection by Rav Kook of the pluralistic views of the Mitnaggedic world, as exemplified by R. Hayyim Volozhiner in his Nefesh ha-Hayyim.

It is hard to avoid one last comment on Kookian harmonism, and that is that his theories dovetailed beautifully with his personal proclivities. Not only was the mode of his thought dialectical in a harmonistic manner, but his personality was irenic. He was a peaceful, peace-loving leader (a difficult combination!) who preferred to resolve differences rather than allow them to fester and lead to ugly and destructive confrontation. He did not eschew differences of opinion; on the contrary, he encouraged and cherished them. He was himself a man of principle who suffered terrible vilification from circles which to this very day studiously refrain from mentioning his name except, perhaps, to smear him. The more he was attacked by critics, often mindlessly extremist, the more resolutely he maintained his position and the more stubbornly he asserted his independence. But he wished to transcend, not dissolve, differences and so have each play its own role in the divine economy or symphony.

It is for this reason that, over fifty years after his death, it is painful to behold how he has been ill-served by some of his own followers, those who presume to be the official and authoritative interpreters of Rav Kook. Of course, he was a great nationalist whose love of Eretz Israel was legendary. But he was not a jingoist! One wonders what he would have said had he known that those who speak in his name and the name of his thinking sow divisiveness in Israel, speak the rhetoric of power and coercion, and throw bombs at adversaries, Jewish and non-Jewish. "Even in times of war," the Midrash teaches, "one must seek peace."[6] Rav Kook was not a one-issue person. Eretz Israel was a cardinal part of his whole outlook, but it was not all of it. To highlight and absolutize the holiness of the Land and, at the same, time, to ignore or derogate the holiness of human life, all in the name of Rav Kook, is to betray him and his teachings. Rav Kook taught the principle of harmony, whether in the universe of ideas and precepts or in the realm of human relations or in the inner life of each individual. And in the symphony of creation, when one focuses on one note or one tone or one instrument to the neglect of others, one has not harmony but disruption and discord and divisiveness.

It is worth mentioning, in this respect, a beautiful *vort*, a homiletical insight, that has been repeated in his name. *Shalom*, Peace, according to the Sages, is one of the sacred Names of God; *Emet*, Truth, is His "seal." What is the difference between a "name" and a "seal," such that one characterizes Peace and the other Truth? It is this: A name or signature proceeds letter by letter, until the whole name is signed. A seal, however, imprints all in one act. So too, Truth is a seal—it is "all or nothing." Half a truth is a lie. But Peace is a name, a signature, and therefore can be attained only step-wise, bit by bit. Consequently, we must aspire for it piece by piece, and must not despair if we cannot win the prize of total peace all at once. Would that all of us, "Kookians" no less than others, bore this in mind in our politics as well as our theorizing!

II

Rav Kook's view of the New is exemplified in a posthumously published lecture—actually two introductory lectures to Yehudah Halevi's *Kuzari*, delivered in Rav Kook's yeshivah and recorded by his disciple, Rabbi Moshe Zvi Neriah.[7] Rav Kook singles out three philosophical works as the most significant of the medieval period: Baḥya's *Duties of the Heart*, Maimonides' *Guide of the Perplexed*, and Halevi's *Kuzari*. Each made a singular contribution. Baḥya's work is preeminent as an ethical treatise, Maimonides' as the great rationalistic achievement of the Middle Ages, and Halevi's *Kuzari* as the most spiritual—or, to use the direct translation of his term, *ḥavayati-elohi*, "theo-experiential." None of the three is reducible to either or both of the other two. Rav Kook's harmonism is here applied to literary criticism and philosophical analysis. Each of these works is different from the others; but while it is important to delineate their differences from and oppositions to each other, ultimately one must see them in the perspective of the totality of Jewish theology as each makes its distinctive contribution to that totality and thus complements the others.

Rav Kook then focuses on the uniqueness (and perhaps superiority) of Halevi as Rav Kook understands him. Rationalism both preceded and followed Maimonides, even though his version had clear advantages over others. Ethical works were written before and especially after Baḥya, although his interpretation of ethics, as representing that of the Torah and the Jewish tradition, is clearly superior. Neither Baḥya nor Maimonides can be said to have attained uniqueness. This achievement is reserved for Yehudah Halevi.

Halevi's theo-experiential vision is not that of the will or the intellect, but is singular: that of renewal, creation anew. Through the Torah we are recreated, born anew. We become genuinely new beings. We "create" ourselves by means of Torah. Rav Kook then quotes the talmudic comment on the verse *va-asitem otam*, "you shall do [or make] them" (Deut. 29:8). The Rabbis read *otam* as *attem*, hence: "you shall make yourselves; I [i.e., God] consider it as if you had made yourselves."[8] For Halevi, Rav Kook maintains, important as ethics and reason are, the theo-experiential view is the most significant of all because it teaches us to transcend ourselves, to renew ourselves in the fullness of our very existence, to become new beings by means of the divinity that flows into us from the Torah. The divine miracles at the Exodus as well as the commandments and laws of the Torah were genuinely new, unprecedented. The Torah itself came to us as something wholly new, and it therefore elicits from us the striving for the New. Indeed, the very last paragraph of his classical work, *Orot ha-Kodesh*, concludes on this theme of the New, speaking of the creation of "new souls."[9]

Now, Rav Kook's characterization of the three medieval works is not terribly novel or significant, although some attention should be paid to his interpretation of Halevi. What is remarkable—and we shall presently see why—is his treatment of the New, his esteem for the novel.

In truth, Rav Kook's enchantment with the idea of the New was not unprecedented in the history of Jewish thought. A theme that appears often in the Zohar is that of the sense of newness that must accompany one's divine service. Thus, "garments worn in the morning are not to be worn in the evening," that is, each of the daily prayers is specific to its own time—and they are not interchangeable.[10] While echoes of this idea already appear in rabbinic literature ("every day they should appear as new in their eyes"),[11] the kabbalistic treatment is deeper and more substantive than what appears to pass as a mere recommendation in the Midrash. The subject is further elaborated in Lurianic Kabbalah, and it is then more fully developed in Ḥasidism, which finds it compatible with its own emphasis on spontaneity and *devekut*. The following statement by R. Yisrael Meir of Gur, the renowned author of *Ḥiddushei ha-Rim*, may serve as an illustration of the Ḥasidic appreciation of the radical newness of time: " 'And if not now, when' [*Avot* 1:14] When will the 'now' come about—the *now* 'now'—this very minute that we are speaking? Since the creation there was none like it, and there never again will be. Before this, there was another 'now,' and after this, there will be another 'now.' And every 'now' is another [way] of serving God."[12]

Rav Kook's Ḥasidic background, which had such a seminal influence upon him, thus served as well to prepare him for the even greater valuation of the New that he was to develop.

In addition, I believe that it is clear that Rav Kook's emphasis on and delight with the New was influenced as well by the heady times in which he lived. For him, the pioneering spirit of Zionism, the adventurousness of the *ḥalutzim*, the social experimentation in the kibbutzim, the renaissance of Eretz Israel redeemed by its own children—all constituted harbingers of the Messianic redemption of the people of Israel and thereafter of all mankind. Of course, these stirring and momentous developments did not create the idea of the New for Rav Kook, but they did inspire him; they provided the right climate for Rav Kook's profoundly religious formulation of the New. There is no better proof for this thesis than Rav Kook's own words:

> The life of the Jewish people, which is constantly being renewed in Eretz Israel, causes us to renew and exalt our thought processes and our logic. The specific form of this novelty must be felt in all disciplines—in Halakhah and in Aggadah, in all areas of science and ethics, in our conception of life and in our *Weltanschauung*. The general content of this newness must be the establishment of all spirituality on the basis of the collective life of the nation and the establishment of all of national life on its highest spiritual basis, and the complete coordination of secular life with sacred life and physical life with spiritual life in general.[13]

This passage is important not only for the light it sheds on the influence on Rav Kook of the Zionist experiment and the novelty of the Jewish situation it was creating, but also for the insight it provides into the content of Rav Kook's conception of the New. New ways of thinking must be insinuated into the study of Halakhah, of Aggadah, of ethics and morality. The New must characterize our *Weltanschauung*, our very conception of life itself. The foundation of spirituality must no longer be that of the individual in his relation to his Maker, but that of the people, the nation—the sign of Israel's reentry onto the stage of history as a nation reborn— and that national foundation, in turn, must be based on the coordination or integration (or "synthesis") of the sacred and the profane, of the mundane and the spiritual.

What is remarkable about Rav Kook's conception of the New and his respect for novelty is the indomitable courage he displayed in formulating and advocating such ideas. He was, after all, no outsider to the religious establishment of his time. As Chief Rabbi, one would not normally expect revolutionary ideas of him; indeed, one would expect him to preach reverence for the Old, not striving for the New. Of course, his respect for the sacred tradition was boundless. Yet his courage led him to advocate the tenets of political Zionism, imperfect though it was, and the espousal of the New as the culmination of his—and Yehudah Halevi's—"theo-experiential" approach. This boldness earned him no peace and serenity.

Indeed, it is this that makes his views on the New so compellingly relevant to our contemporary situation. Two opposite attitudes characterize Jewish life in our stormy, riven, polarized times. On one side, our technological society is based upon the need for change and the desire for the New. The technological imperative is, at bottom, a quest for the novel. The atmosphere is thus created for the worship of the New—indeed, the newest. The quest for the New, whatever its nature and regardless of its quality, permeates every facet of life, from fashion to gadgetry, from education to scholarship to religion. Jacques Maritain has referred to this phenomenon as "chronolatry," the worship of the most recent, the most modern. It is an idolatry in which the icon is temporal rather than material; the latest page of the calendar and the latest position of the hour hand of the clock are the fetishes of this cult of the New. This is not only nonsensical but also dangerous. One wit once remarked that "he who marries the spirit of the times will soon find himself a widower." In the realm of religion, such mindless pursuit of novelty is noxious; not only does it ignore, at its own peril, the value of tradition and history in the life of the sacred, but it despairs of the search for enduring truth.

In a classical sociological illustration of Newtonian mechanics, this chronolatry—or what we might call "neophilia"—has evoked an equal and opposite reaction, what we may term "neophobia," the fear of the New. With Haskalah and Reform championing the New, traditional or Orthodox Jews have chosen to advocate the traditional, the tried and tested, and to abjure all that is new or modern. The most pithy expression of this view is the one offered by the renowned R. Moses Sofer, the venerable author of *Ḥatam Sofer*, who used an original halakhic ruling, out of context, as a metaphor for the problem of the New: *ḥadash asur min ha-Torah*, "what is new is forbidden by the Torah." Such neophobia has become as ingrained in Orthodox circles as neophilia has become the dogma of those modernist and anti-traditionalist circles who so proudly congratulate themselves on their rejection of all dogma.

Confronted with two such equally unattractive alternatives in
the orientation to the New, it is refreshing and encouraging to turn
to Rav Kook and discover that one need be neither a neophiliac nor
a neophobic, that it is possible to approach the new not as a neu-
rotic but as an open-minded and passionately spiritual person who,
without obsessions or phobias, can esteem the New in a discriminating manner for its high spiritual value and its redeeming potential
for man and society. The very reason he is ignored by the religious
left—his refusal to go along with the cultic adoration of the newest
and most modern—and the very reason that he is still reviled by
the religious Right—his rejection of atavism and spiritual recidi-
vism—are what make Rav Kook's *Gestalt* so appealing, now, a half
century after his death.

The two themes, Harmonism and the New, are not unrelated.
The successful perception of the underlying unity of existence and
the harmonious concatenation of all its diverse and multifarious
parts themselves lead to holy novelty. Thus, Rav Kook writes: "The
reason for combining Torah with Wisdom [i.e., secular knowledge]
is not to make up for some deficiency [in either of them], but in
order to create new combinations and phenomena." [14]

III

The principle of harmonism is not limited to the realm of the
ontological, that is, the different aspects of reality, but applies
equally to the realm of the axiological—the sphere of values.
Hence, the sacred and the profane too, the most significant of values, must be embraced in the harmony that prevails in all the rest
of existence.

Indeed, for Rav Kook, the very definition of the sacred is the
awareness of the wholeness of existence, of the harmonious interre-
latedness of the vast complexity of the universe. It is the perfection
and unity of all, the perception that all issues from the Creator
of all.

Since the holy is the vision of cosmic harmony, whereas the
profane is that of fragmentation, and, moreover, since in truth,
objectively, it is harmony that prevails, it follows that the profane
is never absolute. It is one of the functions of the mystical insights

of Torah that in the world one must view the profane from the perspective of the sacred, and hence realize that "there is indeed no absolute profaneness in the world." Thus, "all values are drawn together, and the unity of the world is revealed."[15] It is not difficult to hear the echoes of this teaching of Rav Kook in Buber's famous statement that there is no holy and profane, only the holy and the not-yet holy.

This vision of the holy is quite startling. The classical understanding of the sacred in the Jewish tradition is that which is separate, set apart, different. Thus, the Scriptural commandment "Ye shall be holy" (Lev. 19:2) is interpreted by the Sages as "Ye shall be separate."[16] In Rabbinic parlance too, the standard marriage formula, "You are hereby sanctified unto me," is a legal statement that means, "You are hereby separated from all other people." Rudolf Otto's description of the Holy as the "numinous" certainly seems closer to the traditional view of the holy than the creative and all-embracing definition that is propounded by Rav Kook.

It is important, therefore, to trace the antecedents of this rather novel view of Rav Kook and evaluate his contribution in the light of this background.

In classical Judaism, as mentioned, holiness implies separateness, and especially separateness from the profane and the mundane. The Torah is replete with lines of demarcation, and the Halakhah reinforces these distinctions and elaborates upon them—distinctions between Jew and Gentile, Sabbath and weekdays, kosher and nonkosher, the Holy Land and elsewhere, and so on. *Havdalah* is an integral part of *Kedushah*.

It is in Ḥasidism that, as a result of a certain line of development to which we shall return later, the blurring of such distinctions between the sacred and the profane began to reveal itself. The sacred, in Ḥasidism, gained greater power, a need to reach out and conquer new horizons, to encroach upon the secular and transform it into the sacred. This aggressiveness of the holy rejects sharp boundaries and clear limits. Thus, for instance, the Halakhah sets very clear limits to the prescribed times for each of the formal daily prayers, as well as to the recitation of the *Shema*. But Ḥasidic emphasis on holy intention and thought accentuated the pneumatic as opposed to the normative, the spiritual over the legal, and thus abided praying even after hours, in clear violation of the Halakhah, provided that the proper holy intentions were present. The sacred became irrepressible—at the expense of the profane.

Similarly, Ḥasidism saw opportunities for holiness even in areas that were *reshut*—adiaphora or neutral—from the point of view of Halakhah. It developed the theme of *avodah be-gashmiyyut*, serving God through corporeal means, and not only through formal mitzvot such as prayer, study, or tefillin. Again, the boundaries between the sacred and profane are blurred as the sacred expands outward.

I am convinced that, from a systematic point of view, this development was inevitable, given the high emphasis placed by Ḥasidism on divine immanentism, the presence of God within the universe and His closeness to man. If, indeed, "the world is filled with His glory" (Isaiah 6:3), the *locus classicus* of Ḥasidic theology, or—as the *Tikkunei ha—Zohar* puts it—"there is no place that is empty of Him,"[17]—then holiness too is ubiquitous and cannot be easily contained in neat halakhic categories such as those of time and place. The closer one perceives the presence of God, the more all-embracing becomes the sense of the holy and the greater its domain.

As a footnote, I believe that the immediate precursor to this Ḥasidic development is R. Isaiah Halevi Horowitz, the "SHeLaH" whom we mentioned earlier. In two separate but significant comments, he points out that, for Jews, the sacred/profane dualism is meant to be provisional and ephemeral, because ultimately all the profane will be sanctified; and second, that it is only the immanent presence of the divine that sustains existence, and thus even idolatry exists because it participates, in some way, in the divine. I see these two views as related—as they are, I believe, later in Ḥasidism and, later yet, in Rav Kook. It is immanentism that gives rise to the revolt of the sacred against the limitations imposed on it in its campaign to sanctify the profane. I might add that the bold view of the "SHeLaH" on the divine within the idolatrous has implications both for theodicy and for the liberal approach of Rav Kook to religious skepticism and denial.

The traditional rabbinic world did not take kindly to this innovation by Ḥasidism. The most intellectually objective, and least *ad hominem* polemicist of the Mitnaggedim, R. Ḥayyim Volozhiner, spells out the antinomian implications of this exaggerated immanentism and the consequent blurring of the sacred/profane distinction by the new movement that was sweeping Jewish Europe. In retrospect, from the vantage point of the late twentieth century, the issues that agitated the greatest thinkers of the early years of the last century seem so very quaint and ingenuous. Yet they were very real, if not so much in and of themselves, then as powerful symbols and harbingers of unwanted and unexpected consequences. R. Ḥayyim faulted the Ḥasidim for neglecting the halakhic times set for prayer, and also for their violation of one particular halakhah: the prohibition to meditate on words of Torah in a latrine or in other such unclean places. Ḥasidim, R. Ḥayyim tells us, inflamed with the consciousness of divine immanence, would declare that God is present anywhere and everywhere and, if so, He is present even in the latrine and dirty alley ways; to refrain from meditating on "words of Torah" in such places is in effect a denial of God's presence and hence a sin. R. Ḥayyim considered this aggressive monism a sign of the incipient antinomianism of Ḥasidism and, therefore, worthy of his strong opposition.[18] He pointed out that the Halakhah is built on the foundation of value pluralism, and that there are real differences within the realm of the holy itself, such as distinctions in the levels of divine emanations and, more important, halakhic distinctions in the sphere of holiness—thus the Mishnaic teaching of the "ten levels of sanctity,"[19] that there are ten degrees of holiness, as well as the various levels of sanctity in the three "camps" surrounding the Tabernacle.

Rav Kook was obviously well aware of this controversy. His own family background included both Volozhin and Ḥabad. He was not only a great mystic and religious thinker, but a renowned halakhic scholar who was profoundly committed to Halakhah. The issues were no longer possessed of the same high emotional quotient, but the lessons had become part of history. Thus, Rav Kook protects his flank and states, "The distinctions between the sacred and the profane are facts, and the attempt to blur their [separate] images is destructive. The profound understanding and intuiting of this matter of their differences are the source for great spiritual fruitfulness."[20]

It is true that all such distinctions are ephemeral, but in the reality in which we live such differences are highly significant and must not be ignored. True, the contradictions between sacred and profane will ultimately be eradicated as the world is swept up to the heights of holiness, but for us in the here-and-now, in this mundane sphere, an abyss separates them, and the gap cannot be bridged by any heroic leaps, but only gradually and surely. And it is precisely this gradual reconciliation and harmonization that constitutes our major challenge.[21]

This caveat notwithstanding, the harmonization of sacred and profane is not relegated to some distant eschatological era, but can be—nay, must be—achieved in this world, inasmuch as the scene of the unity that must be accomplished is internal and subjective. And the insights to be gleaned from this harmonistic softening of the sacred/profane dualism are available for us—here and now.

Thus, the approach of Rav Kook to the holy was dialectical: holiness is supernal, but it is also close to us. Our lives in the very realm of the profane are filled with holiness. Rav Kook's dialectic of holiness had Hasidic precedent. The Kotzker Rebbe explained the verse "Ye shall be holy men unto Me" (Exod. 22:30) to mean that one can be a "man" and "holy" at the same time. The profound Hasidic sage R. Zvi Elimelekh Shapiro, in a comment on the verse "Ye shall be holy, for I the Lord your God am holy" (Lev. 19:2), queried: If God wanted us to be holy, why did He create us with such gross natural appetites? He replied that it is precisely in the realm of nature that we are expected to attain holiness. This answer, he continued, explains how the end of the verse, "for I the Lord your God am holy," can serve as a rationale for the beginning of the verse, "Ye shall be holy." That is, just as My holiness is expressed in the coexistence of both My transcendence and immanence, so I expect of you to be holy by means of both involvement in and separation from the world.[22]

The relation of sacred to profane was expressed by Rav Kook in terms of the Aristotelian distinction, taken over by medieval Jewish philosophers, mystics, and exegetes, between matter and form: "The sacred must be built on the foundation of the profane. The profane is the matter of the sacred, and the sacred is its form. The more powerful the matter, the more significant the form."[23] Similarly, Rav Kook stressed again and again, spirituality is not only *not* contravened by physical health, but it requires it. For just as there is an ongoing dynamic in the cosmos as a whole from lower to higher and higher to lower, so in the microcosm of the human organism there is a constant reciprocal relationship between body and spirit.[24] Therefore, "the body must of necessity be healthy and whole in order for the spirit to flourish."[25] Rav Kook took this idea with the utmost seriousness, and emerged with a rather revolutionary thesis: that the very first level of *teshuvah* or repentance is that of physical health—not just that health is necessary for the life of the soul and proper repentance, but that physical health is *in itself* a spiritual value in the ladder of repentance.[26] Rav Kook is not here merely giving sophisticated expression to the folk wisdom of *abi gezunt*. Rather he is incorporating into his religious philosophy of *teshuvah* his own assessment of the relationship between sacred and profane and, ultimately, the Hasidic doctrine of *avodah be-gashmiyyut*, serving the Creator through corporeality.

Thus, Rav Kook adopts the Hasidic doctrine of the innate significance of even halakhically neutral acts when graced with holy intentions and applies it to a person's daily work. First, he counsels that whatever one does, one should do wholeheartedly and without distraction—advice already given by the Ba'al Shem Tov himself, and recorded in the *Tzavaat ha-Ribash*. Thus, a person should concentrate on prayer while praying, on understanding the material being studied during Torah study, and on trying one's best to help a friend when engaged in *gemilut hasadim*. This is so, he continues,

> in all that one does—for in truth there is nothing in the world that is not for His glory. Hence, whatever one does should be [for the purpose of carrying out] His command and His will, seeking thereby [to know] His Name, as one endeavors with all his reason and powers to do what he does in as perfect and whole a way as possible. Thus he will come to know the blessed Name in all ways. . . . When a man performs something in perfection, whether in thought or in deed, he ought to be happy with his lot, and not pursue anything else, for the entire world is then concentrated before him in that matter.[27]

This emphasis on the importance of the act in itself, and not merely as something propadeutic to a formal mitzvah, is straight Hasidic doctrine and fits in nicely with Rav Kook's views on the relation of the sacred to the profane. His conciliatory stance on the

Ḥasidic-Mitnagdic polemic comes through clearly. On the one hand, he follows R. Ḥayyim Volozhiner's view that the study of Torah *lishmah* (for its own sake) means for the sake of intellectual comprehension and not, as the Ḥasidim would have it, for the sake of ecstatic contemplation or *devekut*. On the other hand, his view that work be performed with total concentration on the work itself, as a means of carrying out the divine will even where no formal mitzvah or halakhah exists, is in line with Ḥasidic teaching and not in keeping with the view of R. Ḥayyim, who counseled a form of "double consciousness," whereby one could be physically engaged in the daily pursuits of earning a living and yet, at the very same time, could inwardly be cogitating in Torah in a purely intellectual fashion.[28]

Thus, forewarned by the often bitter yet illuminating history of the Ḥasidic-Mitnagdic controversy, and sensitive to the Mitnagdic criticism of Ḥasidic excesses, Rav Kook acknowledged man's rootedness in his existential context in which fragmentation and dissonance appear to hold sway, and yet felt free to press his teaching of harmonism even in the realm of the sacred and the profane.

Let us now temporarily put aside the question of the extent to which Rav Kook is indebted to and follows Ḥasidic teaching, and turn to an internal problem in his conception of the sacred and profane—a problem that may seem trivial, but which may give us an indication of how radical his teaching really is.

We mentioned that, for Rav Kook, holiness is the perfection of the whole, the ultimate in harmonism, while the profane represents its antithesis, that is, the quality of fragmentation and dissonance. Rav Kook acknowledges gladly that whole areas of life require the ability to look at phenomena in isolation. This requirement of *analysis* is particularly pertinent in the natural sciences. Yet, it is the function of holiness to overcome this separateness and embrace all in its *synthesizing* cosmic vision. Indeed, if holiness is universalized, it must perforce be found to include the profane. Now Rav Kook does not see in this embrace by holiness the destruction of the profane, but its inclusion in the larger scheme of harmonization by the sacred. But if by profane we mean the resistance to such all-embracing comprehensiveness, how can it be included in it? What we have here is a logical contradiction that cannot be overcome by dialectical reasoning. How can A include B, if by definition B represents noninclusion?

Of course, one might argue that Rav Kook is not a systematic philosopher, and that his mystical sweep and poetic style make for a certain degree of fuzziness so that such questions are irrelevant. But I do not think that this is the case, certainly not with regard to the present issue.

I propose to solve that problem in the old Jewish manner of answering one question by asking another. Rav Kook writes: "The foundation of the Holy of Holies bears within itself the element of the holy and the element of the profane."[29] This statement is somewhat puzzling. The "Holy of Holies" or the holiest is obviously more pure, more supernal, more holy than the merely "holy." One might have expected that Rav Kook should state that the "holy" includes the "Holy of Holies" and the "profane," thus allowing the "Holy of Holies" to retain its pristine purity while leaving it to the merely "holy" to include within itself, along with the "Holy of Holies," the profane as well. Surprisingly, Rav Kook reverses the order and places both the sacred and the profane within the wider context of the Holy of Holies.

Here again, one might dismiss this as quibbling, and insist that a lyrical and mystical writer like Rav Kook should not be read as, for instance, Professor Leo Strauss reads the *Guide* of Maimonides or a halakhist reads Maimonides' *Yad*. But I demur and believe that Rav Kook is telling us something of real importance: there are two levels of sanctity, the "holy" and the "Holy of Holies," and the latter represents the ultimate in holiness. While the holy confronts the profane in this contest of the whole versus the parts, synthesis versus analysis, comprehensiveness versus separateness, the impulse to include all—even the profane and all that it stands for—comes from the very highest level of holiness, the "Holy of Holies." Rav Kook means exactly what he says: because of his very definition of holiness as harmony in its widest and most comprehensive sense, it is the "Holy of Holies" that must include both the holy and the profane.

Thus, writing of the conflict between the sacred and the profane, he avers that the clash is only subjective, "but they are reconciled in the heights of the world on the foundation of the Holy of Holies."[30]

If that is indeed the case, our first question is answered: there is no logical trap here. The profane, in its aspect of separateness and fragmentation, is opposed to holiness which, in turn, is not assigned by Rav Kook with the task of embracing the profane itself. That duty is reserved for the "Holy of Holies," the highest level of sanctity, which thus makes it possible for the profane to retain its integrity when it is included in the ultimate harmony. The sacred and the profane continue their dialectical confrontation, as both are absorbed in the "Holy of Holies."

We now return to the problem of Rav Kook and his relation to his theological antecedents in Ḥasidic thought. It should be obvious that, on a theoretical plane, Rav Kook goes further than did Ḥasidism. For Ḥasidism, the raw power of the sacred seeks to break out of its halakhic and spiritual confines and annihilate the profane by sanctifying it, thus transforming even *reshut*, halakhically neutral acts, into holy deeds of a certain order. When this act of sanctification takes place, the profane acts are no longer profane; they are holy. For Rav Kook, however, the profane is not annihilated, but is included in the very highest realms of sanctity, the "Holy of Holies."

Thus, Rav Kook built on Ḥasidic thought but transcended it. His approach to the secular world was one that gave it religious credibility and enduring significance, and in this sense his contribution was original, bold, and radical. Whether or not he followed through on this premise and spelled out the consequences, such as in the curriculum he devised for his yeshivah, and whether or not his followers succeeded in implementing his insights—that is the subject for another essay.

Notes

1. *Orot ha-Kodesh* (Jerusalem, 1963), I, 16 (paragraph 12).
2. Ibid. I, 144 (paragraph 126).
3. *Eder ha-Yakar* (Jerusalem, 1967), 48.
4. Lamm, "Monism for Moderns," in *Faith and Doubt* (New York, 1971), 42–68.
5. Acronym of *Shenei Luḥot ha-Berit*, by R. Isaiah Halevi Horowitz. See ibid., 63, for an illustration of the Shelah's treatment of the *havdalah* as exemplifying the uniqueness of Judaism's monistic or harmo-

nistic approach. For further comment on the Shelah, see section 3, below.

6. *Sifre* on Deut. 20:10; cf. *Bemidbar Rabbah* 11:7.
7. *Mishnat ha-Rav* (Tel Aviv, 1980), 94–98.
8. *Sanhedrin* 99b.
9. *Orot ha-Kodesh*, III, 368.
10. *Tikkunei Zohar*, 22. Cf. *Nefesh ha-Ḥayyim* 2:13.
11. *Midrash Tanḥuma* on Deut. 26:16.
12. Quoted in *Likkutei Yehudah* V, 213–15.
13. "Ne'edar ba-Kodesh," in *Ma'amarei ha-Re'ayah* (Jerusalem, 1984), 413.
14. *Orot ha-Kodesh* I, 63 (paragraph 46). In an address published in the *New York Times Book Review* (February 7, 1993), Alexander Solzhenitsyn, protesting the mindless and destructive pursuit of the new and the newest in art, especially in literature, advocates an appreciation of the new tempered by a reverence for the old and the traditional that echoes the views and sentiments articulated by Rav Kook more than a half-century earlier with regard to more comprehensive and consequential issues. Solzhenitsyn writes:

> The divine plan is such that there is no limit to the appearance of ever new and dazzling creative talents, none of whom, however, negate in any way the works of their outstanding predecessors, even though they may be 500 or 2,000 years removed. The unending quest for what is new and fresh is never closed to us, but this does not deprive our grateful memory of all that came before.
>
> No new work of art comes into existence (whether consciously or unconsciously) without an organic link to what was created earlier. But it is equally true that a healthy conservatism must be flexible both in terms of creation and perception, remaining equally sensitive to the old and to the new, to venerable and worthy traditions, and to the freedom to explore, without which no future can ever be born.

15. Orot ha-Kodesh I, 143 (paragraph 125).
16. *Sifre ad. loc.*
17. *Tikkunei Zohar*, 57.
18. *Nefesh ha-Ḥayyim* 3:2–4. See my *Torah Lishmah: Torah for Torah's Sake in the Works of Rabbi Ḥayyim of Volozhin and His Contemporaries* (New York, 1989), 14–18, 98–99.
19. *Kelim* 1:6–9.
20. *Orot ha-Kodesh*, II, 312 (paragraph 19).
21. Zvi Yaron, *Mishnato shel ha-Rav Kook* (Jerusalem, 1974), 111–12.
22. *Iggera de-Kallah* (Jerusalem: 1980), 2:80.
23. *Orot ha-Kodesh* I, 145 (paragraph 127).
24. See Ibid. I, 70 (paragraph 54); and II, 416 (paragraph 14).
25. Ibid. I, 65 (paragraph 49).
26. *Orot ha-Teshuvah*, 5th ed. (Jerusalem, 1970), 21. Cf. Yaron, op. cit., 128.
27. *Musar Avikha u-Middot ha-Re'ayah* (Jerusalem, 1971), 39–40. For more

on this theme, especially as it relates to the relations between Torah and "secular" studies, see my *Torah Umadda: The Encounter of Religious Learning and Worldly Knowledge in the Jewish Tradition* (Northvale, N.J.: 1990), chaps. 6, 10, 11.

28. See *Nefesh ha-Ḥayyim* 1:8; and my *Torah Lishmah*, 130 n. 8. Cf. Yaron, op. cit., 114–15, espec. n. 11.

29. *Orot ha-Kodesh* I, 64 (paragraph 48).

30. Ibid. II, 311 (paragraph 17).

CHAPTER 7

Tolerance and Its Theoretical Basis in the Teaching of Rav Kook

Benjamin Ish-Shalom

In memory of Professor Moshe Schwarz
who knew that the truth is God's seal
and never wearied
in his search for it

Introduction

As the Enlightenment evolved in the second half of the eighteenth century, the idea of tolerance grew increasingly widespread, until it became a value central to modern Western society. Tolerance is one of the distinguishing characteristics of modern democracy, and is undeniably linked to the process of secularization undergone by Western society.

Within the framework of a religious worldview, however, the value of tolerance is not self-evident. Indeed, its problematic nature served many in their claim that religion is the source of intolerance. This contention was very common in the writings of the European Enlightenment, particularly those of Voltaire and other thinkers in his wake. But from a more balanced sociological and anthropological perspective, tolerance is clearly not only a religious problem but a social-psychological one as well, related both to cultural structure as a whole and to cultural dynamics; and religion, in its theological manifestations, is but one of its aspects.[1]

Nevertheless, the claim that religion, and particularly monotheism, based as it is on the idea of revealed absolute truth, is characterized by intolerance is not unfounded. It is only natural that religion, which is concerned among other things with truth, or, more precisely, which attempts to represent absolute, final truth, would have difficulty adopting a pluralistic point of view and would not place tolerance high on its scale of values. Yet already in the Bible and the writings of the Rabbis we find the roots of tolerant views founded on the conception of man created in God's image and on the idea of the covenant made with Noah.[2]

Still, in the modern Western world at least, tolerance as a human social value was not rooted in the soil of religion. The tolerance of eighteenth-century rationalism stemmed not from a true understanding of the essence of religion but rather from a critique of particular religions and an attempt to uncover the rational and "natural" basis common to all religions.[3] "Natural religion" or "enlightened ethical religion" affirms tolerance, a tolerance that implies both rejection of the pretensions of historical religions and indifference to the specific values and special forms of these religions. Skepticism provided further support for the imperative of tolerance. If truth cannot be known, one approach cannot be preferable to another.

This sort of tolerance would clearly be very difficult for a traditional theologian to accept, and it is no accident that in the middle of the nineteenth century the Catholic church staunchly opposed such values as liberalism and tolerance, viewing them as flowing from indifference and lack of commitment to religious values.

In modern Judaism, beginning with Moses Mendelssohn, the ideals of tolerance grew increasingly accepted in the wake of the hard and bitter battles waged in the sixteenth and seventeenth centuries. Yet at the same time, intolerant tendencies gained force within Orthodox Judaism, spurred by the sense that traditional faith and ways of life were endangered by exposure to general culture and the *haskalah*. It was against this background that the unique view of Rabbi Abraham Isaac Kook stood out with particular prominence.

Rav Kook's path and worldview were characterized by anything but indifference. On the contrary, the sight of Jews transgressing the laws of the Torah troubled him greatly, and his pain found clear and unequivocal expression both orally and in writing.[4] He vigorously spoke out on contemporary public issues, and his voice of protest was never stilled. Rav Kook was not a compromiser, and it was contrary to his nature to abandon the truth in which he believed. Yet, at the same time, as I hope to show, a pluralistic and tolerant approach, originating not in a notion of liberalism but rather in a deeply religious conception, is expressed in Rav Kook's essential theoretical stance.[5]

The contradiction between the extremist positions Rav Kook took more than once (albeit always in a moderate and affectionate manner) on current questions, and indications of a pluralistic and tolerant stance expressed in his theoretical works is not a unique phenomenon. In any discussion of the concept of tolerance, we must distinguish between theoretical and practical tolerance, that is, one approach may truly respect various opinions and recognize their legitimacy while holding that in certain concrete circumstances they must be contested. Another approach, in contrast, may hold that practical considerations or indifference dictates a tolerant attitude toward differing opinions and ways of life, yet will not truly see such ways as valuable or legitimate.

We must distinguish, as well, between a tolerant approach to the outside world, in the sense of the verse, "For let all people walk every one in the name of his god" (Micah 4:5), and a simultaneous extremist approach directed inward, according to which a Jew is not permitted to think or do as he wishes. It is one thing to grant limited and relative legitimization and appreciation to an individual's experience and existence and quite a different thing to honor the authenticity of that experience and existence in all its manifestations. In the light of these distinctions, the question arises whether partial forms or versions of tolerance deserve that name, and more important, what the practical meaning of theoretical tolerance might be. At the end of our discussion I would like to propose an answer to this critical question, but our main concern throughout will be the theoretical and metaphysical principles on which Rav Kook's view of the issue is founded and their consequences for the formation of that view.

Metaphysical Principles

Rav Kook's tolerant view is based on two primary intuitions, which may in fact be considered as different versions of a single basic intuition. The first could be phrased in the words of Quintus Aurelius Simacus, one of the eminent Roman rhetoricians of the fourth century, who said: "No single way can grasp the full greatness of the secret" *(Uno itinere non potest pervenite ad tam grande secretum)*. In Rav Kook's view, the truth is too great, too rich, and too multifaceted to be grasped or exhausted by any one particular theory.[6] The second intuition is related to Rav Kook's conception of revelation[7] whose roots are kabbalistic-Neoplatonic, and some of whose formulations are marked by a certain spiritualization of the idea of revelation, under the influence of nineteenth-century philosophic trends. According to this intuition, all dimensions of reality, including history and human culture, should be seen as a sort of revelation or manifestation of the divine, and as the divine is infinite, it reveals itself in an infinite number of forms and modes.

These two intuitions play a decisive role in Rav Kook's views, both in the realm of philosophical discussion and his relationship to other philosophical methods and in the realm of his attitude toward the heresies of the second aliyah and toward general culture and the various religions.[8]

The premise that reality cannot be grasped or exhausted by any single theory—inasmuch as no theory can circumscribe the infinite but can only express or describe one of its aspects—prevents Rav Kook from holding a dogmatic position in the domain of metaphysics. Rather, his position vis-à-vis all metaphysical systems is relativistic; all systems, including his own metaphysical formulations, have the status merely of *hypotheses*.[9] This approach leads Rav Kook to accept the contribution of every philosophic method toward a more complete understanding of reality. His readiness to concede the grain of truth in every theory, however, does not impede him from criticizing the pretentiousness of any system claiming exclusivity. Thus, for example, when Rav Kook polemicizes against Schopenhauer concerning the nature of will and its status as the basis of reality, he in fact accepts Schopenhauer's view that will, in and of itself, or in Rav Kook's words, "in its own precise

essence, which is pure will, unaccompanied by other positive attributes" (*OHK* II,484), is indeed blind. He rejects, however, the pretension to totality of the Schopenhauerian method. As he states,
"Schopenhauer's conception of will itself is not unreasonable. Its
defect is that Schopenhauer, instead of seeing it as one phenomenon
of reality, perceives it as all of reality and its very cause" (Ibid.).

Rav Kook uses the same criterion in his criticisms of the systems
of Spinoza and Bergson. He accepts the basic position of each of
them, although they are fundamentally opposed. Both Spinoza's
perception of static completeness and Bergson's perception of dynamic evolutionary reality seem to him different aspects of reality,
and he rejects the pretension to totality advanced by both systems
(*AT*, 2).

The basic lack of certainty that characterizes Rav Kook's metaphysical reflections[10] is only one side of the issue. For when every
view and idea are seen as modes of revelation, skepticism and
relativism become transformed into certainty regarding the truth
value of any particular view, on the condition that awareness of
its relative status within the framework of the all-inclusive unity
is preserved.

Thus Rav Kook sees culture, in all its manifestations, as a revelation of the holy, or, more precisely, as a revelation of divine will.
All systems of thought, all ideas, systems of ethics, laws, sciences,
artistic creations, and human aspirations are, for him, revelations
of divine will (*AT*, 2; *OHK* II, 289). To be sure, the degree of
intensity and the quality of the revelation vary, but these differences are not fundamental, as we will see later. Rav Kook himself
makes explicit mention of many phenomena and cultural creations
that he perceives as revelation of the holy, among them even the
political system and its institutions and activities. Culture as a
whole, in his opinion, is a less explicit expression of the holy, while
certain acts in the realm of culture, formally described as *mitzvot*
(commandments), are more explicit revelations of divine will. He
compares the relation between culture as a whole and its individual
manifestations to the relation between the *tallit* (prayer shawl)
and the *tzitziyot* (fringes); in the same way individual events reveal the holiness that inheres, albeit hidden, in the whole (*AT*, 5).

This understanding of revelation does follow from a stringently monistic position like that of Rav Kook, yet at the same time it allows the pantheistic, acosmic nature of reality to be bounded and circumscribed, for all creation is perceived as "revelation"—a concept that posits a distinction between the divine and the world. The domain of revelation is the reflection of the divine in reality, a sort of path or gateway to the inner chamber. Creation itself, nature in all its beauty and glory, and even man with his intellect and his emotions, are the royal road leading to the divine (O, 119).

Since all of creation is an aspect of revelation, it is only natural to perceive the ideas of every thinker and the artifacts of every human creator as modes of revelation as well. Moreover, because of the infinite nature of the divine, the realm of revelation is even broader than all that exists in actuality, for "the speculations concerning the *possible* in the realm of the holy are the most sublime poems, and the most supernal truth is revealed in them and by them" (AT, 4).[11]

It must be noted that in his perception of revelation as a manifestation of divine-cosmic "will," Rav Kook uses the term in its twofold meaning: will or freedom, and wisdom or necessity.[12] In his understanding, reality, in all of its complexity, reflects the paradoxical nature of will, which includes the element of freedom together with the element of necessity. Will is perceived as the essence of life, as the force of existence comprising the whole of reality; its general tendency is informed by a necessary order, but the particulars in the process of its revelation are not predetermined and are characterized by absolute freedom.[13]

This phenomenon itself, "the revelation of two apparently contradictory visions," can be seen not only in existence as a whole but in the human soul, in the life of every individual, as well as on the level of social, cultural, economic, and political life.[14] The phenomenon of human will is described as a miracle that can only be comprehended as a "spark . . . of the larger will that invests all of being" (OHK III, 39).

Human life is therefore a revelation of two cosmic principles in their dialectical relationship. Rav Kook takes care to explain that our reason and will, like everything in existence, is "a spark from the All," and "from the All it emerges" (OHK II, 559), and that, at the same time, the human and cosmic will are bound by ties of mutual dependence (*AT*, 7).[15] On the one hand, all manifestations of the human spirit, "every aesthetic order of life, every endeavor to arouse man's aesthetic sense," as well as "all visions and ideas, desires and imaginings," insofar as they are manifestations of the supernal will, "are much more influenced by the constant emanations [of that will] than by the value of human deeds" (*OHK* III, 59). On the other hand, these very same manifestations serve as instruments preparing "paths for the appearance of supernal lights from the supernal spiritual treasurehouse that flows without cease and seeks to become active in every place that can contain it" (*AT*, 7). Here as well there are varying degrees: the moral virtues are a more effective means to the revelation of the supernal holiness than are aesthetic modes of life and the aesthetic sense, and superior to them are other activities in an ascending order of importance. "The practical commandments [are higher than moral virtues], and higher still is the Torah, and the inwardness [*penimiyut*] of the Torah is higher still. And the pure supernal mystical intentions [*yihudim*], after all of the previous preparations have been completed, are on the highest level of all" (Ibid.). As far as human consciousness is concerned, this conception embodies two aspects of the human spirit: one is passive—man's spirit as an instance of the supernal spirit; and the second active—the human spirit as a creative force, forging the countenance of reality by serving as the instrument that creates the conditions for the revelation of the general will.

One further step brings us to Rav Kook's contention that "all the upright views of the multitude flow from the source of inner illumination of the supernal wisdom" (*AT*, 24). This contention comes as no surprise in the context of a view that, as we have seen, considers all of reality as an aspect of revelation. What is interesting is the emphasis on the special status of the views of the multitude precisely by virtue of their popular nature. Rav Kook accredits the more primitive levels of existence with a greater measure of authenticity, considering them closer to the source, the essence of being.[16] Here this view is applied to the creations of the human spirit: "The more upright the multitude, the more its views and tendencies are rooted in the source of enlightened knowledge and the more there is to learn from them" (*AT*, 24).[17] That is, to the extent the perceptions of the multitude become increasingly simple and are less influenced by intellectuals, the element of authentic revelation in them grows. Indeed, it would follow, *a fortiori*, that the views of the "people of pure heart," who are occupied with Torah and mitzvot, stem from the source of the holy (Ibid.), yet the common multitude still possesses a definite advantage: the less sophisticated the mind, the more "natural" and "healthy" it can be. Rav Kook rejects the view of the aristocratic intelligentsia who held that their own good demanded their dissociation from the multitude. In his view, the uneducated multitude, as yet "unspoiled" by the sophistication of culture, is endowed with "natural senses" and "natural cognitions"—while the intelligentsia possess instruments of conceptual definition, analysis, and formulation to aid them in dealing with intellectual perplexities and with alien worldviews opposing their own. Thus it seemed to him that the intelligentsia and the multitude should be reciprocally related one to the other so that each might contribute its special qualities for the other's good (*OHK* II, 364–65).[18]

It is in fact simplicity, the absence of the cultural sophistication and refinement, that guarantees the authenticity of revelation. From this perspective, Rav Kook preferred emotion over intellect (*OHK* I, 251) and held instinct in high regard (*AT*, 7, 14; see also *OHK* I, 213, section 44). But while such simplicity would seem to guarantee the authenticity of revelation, it also harbors the threat of absolute anarchy. Rav Kook thus takes care to include qualifying remarks that clearly delimit the bounds of what is possible or legitimate in terms of human action: "As long as we are occupied with Torah and wisdom, with deeds of loving kindness and social welfare, with love of humanity and proper conduct, we need not fear an outbreak of our imaginings" (*OHK* I, 231). In other words, it is the intellectual involvement in learning Torah and wisdom, along with ethical, political, and social action that are the best guarantees against anarchy.

This reservation is no mere external element of Rav Kook's thinking which he was forced to include out of extraneous considerations. Both the undertone of reservation regarding the dangers concealed even in authentic revelations and his affirmation of the necessity of the concrete performance of mitzvot and ethical action as highly effective instruments of revelation are fundamental elements of his doctrine (*AT*, 9–10).

Undeniably, Rav Kook's conception of revelation is founded on a paradoxical combination of both radical and limiting conservative elements.[19] In any event, it is important to emphasize that we have here a clear recognition that the honest views of the multitude are an authentic expression of revelation, and a daring legitimization of other realms of revelation that seem removed or even opposed to the holy: "great souls," "the upright" reveal the living light of all inclusive holiness in "secular wisdom, in strange matters, magic, and strange and impure beliefs" (*AT*, 3; *OHK* II, 291).[20] Still, we find in Rav Kook's writing no call to a revolutionary, *a priori* change, but rather a *post facto* religious interpretation of processes and events that have already occurred.[21]

Rav Kook's View of Secularism

In light of the above, Rav Kook's relativistic stance toward the value and status of faith and heresy, and of beliefs and opinions in general, is understandable. An outlook that sees all manifestations of existence as an expression of divine revelation and claims that "all the wonderful aptitudes possessed by living creatures . . . the light of their lives, are shards of the great, supernal soul filled with wisdom and aptitude that was divided into many parts" (*OHK* II, 358) — such an outlook must see all manifestations of the human spirit as an aspect of revelation and, further, as we have seen,[22] must concede that they possess some truth value. In recognition of the divine source of all thoughts, Rav Kook adds: "All thoughts are reasonable and may be systematically linked one with the other . . . and, consequently, we know that no thought in the world is vain" (*OHK* I, 17).

However, it is impossible as well as undesirable to ignore the distinctions among levels of revelation. As Rav Kook states, "The differences between sacred and profane are facts; to blur their distinct nature would be disastrous" (*OHK* II, 312). Yet at the same time one must keep in mind that these differences are really only an epistemological problem, possessing no ontological status. The "facts" of which Rav Kook speaks have no relevance outside the

ken of human cognition. "As for the distinction between spirituality and materiality, the essence of the difference is only in relation
to our mental and sense perceptions; in and of itself, and all the
more so in relation to the supernal wisdom, there is no place for
such a distinction. . . . And in the divine source, everything, great
and small, exists in completeness, reality revealing itself in accordance with the disposition of the recipients" (IR II, 39).[23]

Thus one can make "no absolute division between existents, but
only a division of degrees" (OHK II, 393; AT, 33).[24] This notion is
in keeping with Rav Kook's basic metaphysical structure, according
to which all things and events of the world are ordered in ascending
movement, and the differences in degree between upper and lower
are only relative. "Every particular [entity] becomes the base for its
fellow [entity] and the higher entity becomes its [the lower entity's]
center, soul and light" (AT, 2–3; OHK II, 289). From this it follows
that "proper" thoughts (maḥshavot kesherot), as well as "fallen"
thoughts, need to be elevated (AT, 1).

Without a doubt, despite his many reservations about heresy,[25]
the legitimacy Rav Kook attributes to it as a phenomenon containing positive elements, as a catalyst to the national revival,[26]
and as something supposed to purify the concepts of faith itself[27]—
this legitimacy issues from his view of heresy as a certain degree
of revelation.

> Compared to the supernal divine truth, there is absolutely no differ-
> ence between imagined faith and heresy, for neither contains the
> truth; but, from our perspective, [legabei didan], faith approaches
> truth while heresy approaches falsehood. Consequently good and evil
> derive from these two opposites; "the righteous will walk on them,
> while transgressors stumble on them" [Hos. 14:10]; and the whole
> world, with all its material and spiritual values, all is with respect to
> our worth, and with respect to our worth the truth is revealed in
> faith and it is the source of good, while falsehood is revealed in
> heresy, and it is the source of evil. But in the light of the Infinite One
> all are equal, and even heresy is a revelation of the life force. For the
> living light of the supernal splendor clothes itself in it, and therefore
> the valiant in spirit draw good sparks from it, and turn its bitterness
> to sweetness (AT, 2).[28]

Clearly, then, the source of heresy is in holiness, and this grants
great moral and ideological validity to the battle waged by heresy,

in the person of the "free" *(hofshiyyim)* or secular Jews against the "bound" *(meshubadim)* or observant religious Jews.

> The war is fierce and both camps are justified in their battle; the secularists *[hofshiyyim]* fight for the sparks of good in their will not to suffer needless bondage, while the religious *[meshubadim]*, who remember the past and apprehend it in all the splendor of its goodness, defend their bondage, so that the noble edifice of the world not be destroyed by the defiled elements of the will. Great souls are required to establish peace between the combatants by showing each his true and proper boundary *(OHK* II, 544).

One may well be amazed at Rav Kook's analysis and description of the two warring camps, as if undertaken from the perspective of someone removed from the conflict. It is not mere objectivity that determines his perspective; rather it is an expression of the sense of freedom that, more than anything else, characterized his thought. Rav Kook evaluates the limited *haredi* (non-Zionist Orthodox) way of thinking with this standard of freedom, and does not spare it the rod of criticism. In his opinion, the widespread hatred of culture and opposition to the sciences and political activity within the *haredi* community derives from a "petty type of faith," from envy, or even from "lack of faith." As he sees it, true faith obligates one to view every manifestation of culture as a "divine manifestation." A person, therefore, ought to consider each movement, idea, or enterprise individually. Nothing should be categorically disqualified, but rather should be subjected to relevant, substantive criticism, and all ideas and projects evaluated according to the measure of benefit or harm they generate *(AT,* 47).[29]

Rav Kook's View of General Culture and the Various Religions

Throughout Rav Kook's writings, we find a very positive, principled attitude toward culture in the widest sense. Rav Kook repudiates zealotry, claiming that even non-Jewish sages deserve respect, and that the truth should be accepted because it is true. He writes:

> I do not understand the necessity of this excessive zealotry, for if all the paths of human intelligence are forbidden to Israel, where then is the beauty of Yephet in the tents of Shem, and where is the universal

bond [joining all men], deriving from the universal divine image, which the Holy One, blessed be He, bestowed upon man, as a result of which we honor all wise and upright men and accept the truth from whoever utters it. In our tradition, he who speaks wisely, even if he be a non-Jew, is called a wise man.[30]

Rav Kook's fundamentally positive view extends not only to neutral cultural creations but also to faiths other than his own, including Christianity.[31] Yet he was never indifferent to qualitative value distinctions, and did not ignore virtues and deficiencies.[32] However, what view or deed is completely free of deficiencies? Rav Kook appears to ground his view of faith and heresy on the assumption that both are deficient. To him, faith and heresy are interdependent and interrelated, and they join together in building the world of spirit in its wholeness—that of the Jewish people in particular and of human creativity in the broadest sense (OHK III, 34). Religious thought, deriving from cognition and feeling that are whole and complete, has no deficiencies. But there are religious views that do not derive from a profound cognition, and such views, says Rav Kook, "restrict life, diminish energy, ruin man's physical powers and spiritual abilities." The "weakness" caused by unenlightened religiosity finds its remedy in the appearance of heresy in literature and journalism; the harsh words of heresy and their aggressive character arouse dormant strengths in the religious camp and instill even the pious with renewed will.

Rav Kook understands modern heresy against the background of modern philosophical developments, as a legitimate demand for a rational explanation of reality.[33] "The insolence preceding the coming of the Messiah [ha-hutzpah de'ikkeveta di-meshiha][34] occurs because the world is at the stage that it demands to understand how all the details are related to the whole. No detail unconnected to the greatness of the whole can prove satisfactory" (AT, 1).[35] In the Age of Enlightenment the world has reached the level where it demands to comprehend the rationality of life. This demand for a rational explanation of reality is tantamount to an attempt to abstract and generalize the myriad details of the world into general principles. An act is considered rational if it accords with a general principle.[36] In the modern age, the commandments of the Torah seem irrational, for we do not see how the details are connected to the whole. When modern man examines individual ideas and deeds and fails to understand the principles that serve as their basis and unifying force, they seem completely meaningless to him.

When we speak of the crisis or decline of religion, we must distinguish between the universal crisis and the crisis that befell Judaism, for, in Rav Kook's view, the roots of the general religious crisis and of the specifically Jewish crisis are completely different. He wishes to eradicate the—in his view—mistaken assumption that the collapse of religion in the Western world and the collapse of religion among the Jewish people had common or similar causes. According to that assumption, the cultural development and progress ushered in by the Age of Enlightenment left religion far behind and exposed it to a negative light (*NBK*, 19).

Rav Kook disputes the theory, commonly accepted in his time by students of religion, that religion is just an anachronism, a "remnant" of the past, a mode of thinking that enlightened humanity has transcended.[37] He does, however, accept this theory as it pertains to the nations of the world. For, in his view, "the pagan elements of Western religions are in fact crumbling in the face of the fortification of the intellect and human progress in general, and since these idolatrous elements are inherent to these religions, the religions themselves are in a state of collapse" (*NBK*, 19). But the same is not true of the Jewish people. For the basic principles of Judaism are not interwoven with pagan elements, and nothing therefore prevents their acceptance even at the stage of the high culture of the modern era.

The roots of the religious crisis in Judaism, then, are grounded in another cause: the narrow and depressing quality acquired by religiosity over the generations. In Rav Kook's own words:

> Fear is deficient in its external aspect, in that it softens the heart too much, depriving man of his innate strength and giving rise to a sense of impotence. In this way, any experience of fear, even it if be the fear of God deriving from a pure tradition, *prevents the improvement of the world and perfection of the human image*. And when this state is reached, when the attribute of fear becomes filled with great bitterness, so that its influence serves to greatly *oppress* the heart, when the spirit is overwhelmed by this fear, then the time is ripe for a new spirit to arise in humanity, a spirit of lawlessness, which

comes to counteract the venom of this external fear. When these two *external* spirits clash, the world becomes drunk, dust rises to the Heavenly Throne, *weakness, extremism, hypocrisy, and great wickedness* on the one side and *insolence, competitiveness, lawlessness, absence of spirit* on the other side fell many a mighty warrior. And the multitude continues to decline until that time when the light of justice will shine, and the supernal divine knowledge will appear in all its power, bearing on its wings a healing remedy.[38]

Secularization and nihilism are thus seen as a reaction to a long period of religion's oppression of man's spirit and his natural aspirations. "The need for this revolt comes from an inclination toward the material aspect of existence, that, of necessity, must have arisen in an exceptionally intense fashion among large segments of the nation after so many years in which both the necessity and possibility for the nation to occupy itself with material concerns became as naught" (*AT*, 60). And when "the profane is cruelly treated by the holy, so that matter itself becomes impoverished," then, Rav Kook claims, an era is reached "when matter demands justice on its own behalf, and the creditor is urgent, and the profane recovers the debt owed it by the holy with interest, and insolence increases" (*NBK*, 4).

The outcome of the struggle between these two distorted spiritual movements is that the element of truth and authenticity in both is lost. Weakness, extremism, hypocrisy and cruelty seize hold of the religious camp; insolence, lawlessness and emptiness characterize the secular camp. Rav Kook's neutral approach in describing and analyzing the process of secularization within the Jewish people is founded on the metaphysical principles discussed above. The fact that even heresy, like faith itself, is seen as a revelation of a life force, in which "the living light of the supernal luminousness clothes itself"[39]—allows us to perceive its positive aspects and to discern the positive role it plays.

> The principle of negation was created in order to cleanse the soul of the individual and of society from the frightful and debilitating dross present in the fear of punishment. And the poison of crude heresy destroying the world came into being primarily to serve as an antidote against this dross contained in fear of punishment that forever spreads downwards and detaches itself from the light of Torah, from the supernal fear, and from the true love [of God].[40]

This tolerant attitude was not limited only to Rav Kook's approach to the phenomenon of secularization. It was precisely his profoundly religious worldview that enabled Rav Kook to see what was useful and even true in other religions and beliefs. Thus he writes: "And because the nature of the bond between human thought and feelings and the most supernal, unlimited divine light must be of many and varied shades, for this reason each and every people has its own distinctive spiritual life" (*OHK* III, 15). That is, the particular form characterizing every national culture and every religion is but a particular revelation of divine light, and, therefore, it is rooted in truth.

The question of tolerance is above all an ethical question.[41] Rav Kook was, to be sure, well aware of the problematic nature of tolerance from the standpoint of the man of faith.[42] He was convinced that tolerance was fundamentally opposed to natural faith and the stronger faith becomes, the more fanatical it becomes as well. "Conventional theology believes," he claims, "that religions must, unavoidably, be opposed to each other."[43] A religious position, however, is motivated by more than the natural feeling of religiosity. Rationality is an intrinsic element of faith,[44] and from the point of view of religious cognition, tolerance is the clearest expression of understanding divine revelation in all its variegated forms. In Rav Kook's words:

> Faith is composed of both a natural element and a cognitive, rational element. In terms of its natural element, faith is a fiercely burning fire, tolerating no opposition; and it cannot tolerate not only that which opposes its essence but even that which is contrary to its particular way, its special style. This is why different faiths cannot live together and blend together, without all of them suffering natural damage. And the more splendid and healthy, the more significant and mighty the faith, the more its natural power grows, and its zealotry and concern for maintaining its own purity becomes exceedingly great. In terms of its cognitive elements, however, faith is filled with broad-minded knowledge and crowned with mercy and great tolerance. For, via this cognitive element, faith knows full well that the inner spirit of the divine longing and the supernal wholeness for which it yearns is also so richly variegated, that it can clothe itself in many different guises, even in contrary descriptions, as a result of which it transcends all contradiction and is higher than any opposition.[45]

This view of Rav Kook does not remain on the theoretical level, a phenomenological analysis without practical implications. On the contrary, Rav Kook, with great daring, draws practical conclusions from his fundamental position:

> We must study all the sciences of the world, all the teachings of life, all the different cultures, and the religious and ethical doctrines of every nation, and with great broad-mindedness must understand how to purify them all (*AT*, 32–33).
>
> Despite differences of opinion among religions and faiths, among races and climes, we should try to comprehend the different groups and peoples of the world to the best of our ability, to learn their nature and their characteristics so that we might know how to build human love upon practical foundations. . . . And narrow-mindedness, which causes one to see all that is outside the bounds of one's own nation, even if it be outside the bounds of the Jewish people, as naught but ugliness and impurity is one of the worst kinds of darkness, which completely destroys the whole structure of spiritual good for whose light every noble soul yearns.[16]

We must emphasize that Rav Kook's pluralistic view does not imply indifference to the differences in rank and value among the religions and faiths. Although he believed "all facets of the spirit are an organic whole," he did not ignore distinctions "between essential and incidental, high and low, greater holiness and lesser holiness, and between these and the secular."[47] Moreover, Rav Kook adds, "We rise above the decadence in which the nations are sunk, i.e., the intense concern and study by their most distinguished scholars about the differences between the Semitic spirit and the Aryan spirit. We glorify in Lord of the Universe who created all mankind in His image, in the image of God He created him. Each branch grows its own way, this one to the right and that to the left, for they do possess above and below, left and right, but in their essence they all ascend to a single place. And all will be elevated, to mend the world under the kingdom of the Almighty, and all humanity will call upon Your Name."[48]

This rejection of all racial or national distinctions and differences in the domain of the spirit is of great interest. Rav Kook's formulation of his view in this passage is particularly surprising in light of his view concerning the metaphysical-mystical essence of the Jewish people.[49] The difficulty in harmonizing these two ideas is obvious, unless we assume that both are to be understood in a qualified manner, as seem to be implied by Rav Kook's own statement regarding the differences in value between and the varying functions of the limbs of a physical organism.[50]

In what, then, do the differences between Judaism and other religions come to light? Clearly, the difference is in spiritual and ethical orientation, rather than in metaphysical insights.[51]

It is impossible, however, to overlook the clear relation between the Jewish metaphysical conception, which Rav Kook understands as a monistic outlook, and the spiritual and moral orientation of Judaism, which he understands as a unifying orientation. In various contexts, Rav Kook describes the nature of the spiritual-ethical orientations that characterize other religions. He distinguishes between four basic aspirations of the human spirit: (1) the aspiration to impose the reign of absolute evil in all spheres of life, a tendency basic to idolatry; (2) the aspiration to annihilation, grounded on the premise of the total reign of evil in reality, which is characteristic of Buddhism; (3) the aspiration attributed to Christianity, described as "partial despair," despair of the material world and consigning it to the reign of evil, and the desire for the soul's salvation alone; (4) the aspiration characteristic of Judaism, to strive "to save everything . . . body as well as soul . . . evil itself as well as good . . . to elevate the world and all the fullness thereof, in all its dimensions and aspects" (OHK II, 488).[52]

The most prominent deficiency that Rav Kook ascribes to idolatry and Christianity is their fragmentation of reality. "The heathen world," he says, "aspires to be connected to nature as it is" and sees in it "its own final aim."[53] Christianity, by contrast, distanced itself from and negated nature, and by seeing every aspect of natural life as opposed to religion, "poisoned the aggadic (theoretical-spiritual) dimension and set it in opposition to the firm and mighty structure of halakhah."[54] In other words, it was Christianity's negation of life that induced the Church to abrogate the commandments.

These varying tendencies indelibly mark the religious consciousness of the faithful of these religions, naturally influencing their ritual as well. Rav Kook believed these differences originate in the vastly disparate basic religious experiences of each of the religions. In all other religions, he claimed, the source of religious worship is in the experience of "horror and shock," a clearly negative experience. The experience that is the life blood of Judaism, on the other hand, is described as "love" and a "powerful aspiration toward divine ideals," a clearly positive experience.[55]

Religious consciousness, derived from negative experience, is by nature dependent and servile. It is, as Rav Kook said, "the service of a slave."[56] In contrast, "enlightened service of God," founded on positive feeling, gives rise to a creative and constructive consciousness. "And it transforms the divine ideals, cultivating them, perfecting them, striving to exalt them, glorifying them among the people, among mankind, and the cosmos as a whole."[57] Rav Kook contrasts the servile consciousness, the legacy of primitive belief, with the religion of freedom, the attainment of which is the ultimate aim in the battle against idolatry *(avodah zarah)*.[58]

> When adhesion *[devekut]* is distorted, misdirected away from the true God, . . . when appeal to the divine is directed toward something other than God, then the ascent of creation is impeded. . . . The world's freedom and its flight aloft depend on the radical extirpation of all idolatry from thought, language, deed, emotion, attitude and inclination, from national, religious and psychic design. This is the aspiration of *Keneset Israel*, and on that day the Lord alone shall be exalted, and the idols shall utterly be abolished.[59]

The Limitations of Pluralism

The freedom Rav Kook accords the realm of thought has its roots in the idea that every belief and conjecture contains an element of holiness in accordance with the strength of the divine revelation embodied in it.

> All the wisdoms of the world, internal and external, pure and impure, serve a purpose for the [supremely righteous], and whatever [body of wisdom] they incorporate into the orbit of their knowledge becomes elevated with their ascent. To be sure, in [the realm of] practice no human being can reach that measure, for the Torah has set eternal boundaries for all. But as for [the flight of] thought, there are no such limitations; there the adversary and evil inclination do not reach.[60]

On the level of action, we are confined by the boundaries set by the Torah, everlasting and binding upon all; it is dangerous to breach them. Thought, on the other hand, knows no bounds and even limitless freedom holds no danger. What is more, intellectual honesty and an objective approach are perceived as assuring that truth will triumph, and with it Judaism.

In Rav Kook's view, "the evil heart alone . . . is what causes all the confusion and the troubles[61] of Israel and of man" (*EY*, 52). Free thought and scientific research for the sake of truth are not intrinsically harmful. The danger resides in tendentious and unobjective research. His writings abound with confidence in the power of the Jewish faith to emerge victorious in all her ideological battles. From this derives his insistence on the necessity of serious and profound study, for it is superficiality that gives rise to narrow-mindedness. Limited, restricted thought is described by Rav Kook as sickness and slavery, and he calls for an arduous effort to free ourselves from it, "to deliver our soul from the oppression of its confines, from its house of bondage" (*OHK* I, 177).

As we remarked earlier, Rav Kook was convinced that ignorant and unenlightened "fear of Heaven" breeds superficiality and narrow-mindedness, and inasmuch as it arouses fear of free thought it serves to degrade man's spiritual stature.[62] Worse yet, faith itself, man's conception of the divine, does not survive this brutish ignorance unscathed, for the level of faith is commensurate with the level of enlightenment. "If man's enlightened knowledge of God is small, the idea he conceives of God will be small as well; and since the concept of the divine makes clear man's infinite insignificance as he stands in God's presence, man becomes inestimably demeaned and useless by such a fear of Heaven devoid of understanding" (*AT*, 32–33).[63]

We need not emphasize that Rav Kook shrank from narrow, apologetic thought.[64] The uncompromising quest for truth does not permit one to adopt any single view to the exclusion of all others, denying even the legitimacy of their existence. On the contrary, the identity of "truth" with "existence" means that just as existence is not unidimensional, so truth is multi-faceted.[65] The idea that all views are expressions of divine revelation mandates respect for all instances of human creativity. "Anyone who reflects upon divine matters in their purity cannot hate or despise any creation or aptitude that exists, as God's exaltedness and strength are revealed in everything" (*OHK* III, 327; see also 100).

It would be wrong, however, to assume that freedom of thought has no bounds. Rav Kook enumerates at least three grounds for limiting such freedom. The first ground determines that the principle of freedom of thought possesses ethical value only when research, speculation, and study are undertaken in pursuit of the truth. In this instance freedom is constructive and meaningful. But the concept of freedom of ideas is meaningless when this freedom is not active and effective, that is, in the case of the masses guided by their imagination and blown hither and yon by every wind (*AT*, 13). The two other grounds are related to the danger of nihilism and the undermining of the people's status and existence that may result from unbounded freedom. "There is no attribute in the world," Rav Kook claims, "that would not be harmed by extremism" (*IR* I, 19–20). He maintains that any view which would threaten to throw off the "yoke of commonly held moral values" or the spread of which would stimulate the destruction of "the world's existence" would not be protected by the principle of freedom of ideas.[66] Still, Rav Kook remains aware of the difficulty involved in formulating the precise boundaries of freedom, especially in light of the relativity of ethical conventions. Circumscribing the boundaries of freedom of ideas must, by nature, differ from one society to another, from culture to culture, just as rules of behavior in many other domains are determined by the concepts of justice and beauty unique to each people and by the particular circumstances of each.[67] These considerations lead Rav Kook to the conviction that inasmuch as the definition of Jewish nationality is inextricably linked to a certain faith, that faith cannot be compromised by unbounded freedom of ideas. Because the very existence of the people is conditional upon a particular view, Rav Kook perceived any modicum of tolerance on that question as "laziness [of the people] in defending itself," and thoroughly condemnable.

Conclusion

Our discussion leads us to the conviction that Rav Kook's idea of tolerance was rooted in the fundamental principles of his metaphysical outlook, and found expression in his basic attitudes toward secularism and heresy, general culture, other religions, and all opinions, ideas, and philosophical systems. His view is characterized by principled openness to understanding the truth of every approach, engendered in turn by an all-inclusive insight into the unity of all opposites as aspects of an unbounded whole. Rav Kook, at the same time, took note not only of the essential and true elements but also of superfluous and false elements inherent in each approach. That is, although he showed his understanding of those who held varying views, by no means did he grant unreserved legitimacy to those views. The extremist and uncompromising positions that Rav Kook adopted on more than one occasion on issues of public interest were not generated by passion alone but rather by the realization that the war of ideas, which highlights the singularity of every view, is critical if a healthy balance among disparate views is to be maintained. Only when such balance exists can wholeness be revealed in its totality, in the sense of "Torah scholars increase wholeness/ peace [shalom] in the world" (OR I, 330). That is, through their clashing with each other over halakhic issues, Torah scholars expose and refine the diverse aspects of the truth, and it is this *multiplicity* of aspects that gives birth to wholeness. Deriving from that recognition, coupled with sharp criticism of its path, Rav Kook understood the justice of the claims made by the secular camp and the legitimacy of their battle,[68] just as he recognized both the justice and the deficiencies in the path taken by the *haredi* camp.

The practical application of this complex conception of tolerance is clear: it is what enabled Rav Kook to perceive the highest human and Jewish qualities even in those who were considered by him as well as "Jewish transgressors," i.e., the secular Jews in the early years of Zionism, and to recognize the positive value of heresy despite its falsity and ethical distortions; and it allowed him to work exceptionally closely with the "impudent" secular pioneers [*"ha-ḥutzpanim"*],[69] for they, after all is said and done, are the harbingers of the rebirth of Judaism[70] and of the renewal of Israel's original and authentic spirit.[71]

Notes

This chapter is based on a lecture presented at a conference in memory of Rav Kook, June 1985, at Bar Ilan University, Ramat Gan, Israel.

The following abbreviations are used in some of the parenthetical references to Rav Kook's works in the text of this essay:

AT—*Arpelei Tohar* (Jaffa, 1914) [All citations are from this edition, which Rav Kook himself saw through publication.]

EY—*Eder HaYakar ve-Ikkevei HaTzon* (Jerusalem, 1963)

IR—*Iggerot HaRayah* (Jerusalem, 1962)

NBK—*Ne'edar BaKodesh* (Jerusalem, 1933)

O—*Orot* (Jerusalem, 1963)

OHK—*Orot HaKodesh* (Jerusalem, vols. I–III, 1964; vol. IV, 1990)

OR—*Olat Rayah* (Jerusalem, 1963)

1. See Raphael Yehudah Tzvi Werblowsky, "Tolerance as a Value" (Heb.), in *Sefer Shaḥar*, ed. Shlomo Kodesh and Kalman Yaron (Jerusalem, 1984), 176–87.

2. A. Altmann, "Tolerance and the Jewish Tradition" (Heb.), in Altmann, *Panim shel Yahadut* (Tel Aviv, 1983), 217–32; Jacob Katz, "The Transformations of Three Apologetic Statements" (Heb.), in Katz, *Halakhah ve-Kabbalah* (Jerusalem, 1984), 270–90, 291, 307–10.

3. On Deism and the view of religion in the Enlightenment see E. Troeltsch, "Der Deismus," 1898 (*Gesammelte Schriften* [1925], 4:429–87), and E. Cassirer, *The Philosophy of the Enlightenment*, 1951; A. Altmann, *Moses Mendelssohn: A Biographical Study*, (Tuscaloosa, Al., 1973). Concerning the "battles" referred to below that led to the increasing acceptance of tolerance as an ideal, see A. Altmann, "Gewissensfreiheit und Toleranz; Eine Begriffgeschichtliche Untersuchung," in *Mendelssohn Studien*, ed. Cecile Lowenthal-Hensel and Rudolf Elvers (Berlin, 1979), 4:9–46.

4. A clear expression of his approach can be found in his essay "Al Bamoteynu Ḥallalim," written for the collection *Yizkor: Matzevat Zikkaron le-Ḥallelei ha-Po'alim ha-'Ivrim be-Eretz Yisrael* (Jaffa, 1912), ed. A. Z. Rabinovitz, first published in 1945 in the collection *Azkarah*, ed. Rabbi J. L. Fishman (Maimon); reprinted in *Ma'amarei HaRayah* (Jerusalem, 1984), 89ff. This approach is expressed in many letters, too numerous to list here. See also Zvi Yaron, *Mishnato shel ha-Rav Kook* (Jerusalem, 1974), chap. 12 ("*Sovlanut*"), 323ff.

5. Yaron, op. cit., 365, summarizes his discussion of the conception of tolerance with the observation that there are three stages in Rav Kook's view: (1) The large number of opponents to religion warrants an extreme reaction; (2) social reality does not permit extremist activity; (3) this practical impediment leads to the rejection of extremism "under the existing circumstances of a society in which many oppose

religion." In my own discussion, I would like to indicate the principal theoretical roots of Rav Kook's conception of tolerance and to demonstrate that it is not the mere outgrowth of a "practical impediment."

6. See Benjamin Ish-Shalom, *Rav Avraham Itzhak HaCohen Kook: Between Rationalism and Mysticism* (Heb.) (Tel Aviv, 1990), chaps. 1, 7. (An English translation with this title was published by SUNY Press, 1993.)

7. Ibid., chap. 2.

8. All these subjects are discussed extensively in Ish-Shalom, *Rabbi Kook*.

9. Ibid., chap. 1.

10. See Ibid., 47–57.

11. Note his discussion concerning the ontological status of the "possible," and compare *Orot HaKodesh* (Jerusalem, 1964), III, 27. See also my book, Chap. 1, 57–66. Compare Spinoza, *Short Treatise on God, Man and His Well-Being*, ed. Yosef Ben Shlomo (Jerusalem, 1978), 41.

12. See *Orot HaKodesh* III, 108–10. Both will and knowledge are perceived as revelations. See also Ish-Shalom, chap. 1.

13. See "Kirvat Elohim," *Tahkemoni* (1911), II, 5 (reprinted in *Maamarei HaRayah*, 34–35). See also Ish-Shalom, 82–92.

14. "Kirvat Elohim," 3–4 (reprinted in *Maamarei HaRayah*, 32–34).

15. This was also Rav Kook's stance on the question of the relationship between the holy and profane in general. See ibid., 6–7, and *Orot HaKodesh* (Jerusalem, 1963), I, 145.

16. See Ish-Shalom, 66, 90–91. See especially *Orot HaKodesh* II, 362.

17. The influence of romantic conceptions are clearly discernible.

18. Compare the view of Claude Levi-Strauss on the value of primitive cultures, *Le Totémisme Aujourd'hui* (Paris, 1962); Z. Levi, *Structuralism* (Heb.), (Tel Aviv, 1971), espec. 119.

19. See Ish-Shalom, chap. 6, 190.

20. The words "magic, and strange and impure beliefs" were deleted from *Orot HaKodesh*. An echo of the hassidic idea of "raising the holy sparks" is unmistakable.

21. See *Arpelei Tohar*, 11 (Sheilat edition, 15). See also Ish-Shalom, 190 and 321 n. 115 on the changes in the new edition.

22. See above, note 10.

23. The allusion is to *Genesis Rabbah*, ed. Theodor and Albeck, chap. 8, 60. See Ish-Shalom, 224.

24. Compare the two versions. The passage in *Arpelei Tohar* is phrased in the singular, while in *Orot HaKodesh* it is phrased in the plural: "I cannot make an absolute division"; "We cannot make an absolute division."

25. See *Iggerot HaRayah* I, 146 (on the desecration of the Sabbath in the land of Israel: "It wounds our heart deeply, mortally"; "Boorishness and crude, contemptible heresy"); *Te'udat Yisrael u-leumiyuto*, 62; *Orot HaTeshuvah* (Or Etzion, 1970), 40 (the ethical invalidity of her-

esy); *Iggerot HaRayah* I, 201, 369; *Iggerot HaRayah* II, 87, 90; *Orot*, 99–101 (heresy distorts a person's natural aspiration); *Orot HaKodesh* III, introductory remarks, 24, 34; *Arpelei Tohar*, 20, 75. In Ms. *Kovetz* B, 34b [*Orot ha-Emunah (OHE)*, Jerusalem, 1985, 17], Rav Kook views the heretic as a "lost soul" whose "life is not life."

26. *Orot*, 84–85; *Te'udat Yisrael u-Leumiyuto*, 62.
27. *Eder HaYakar* (Jerusalem, 1963), 32; *Iggerot HaRayah* I, 50; *Orot*, 79, 87, 124–27; *Orot HaKodesh* I, 14.
28. See also *Arpelei Tohar*, 19: "All ethical ideal morality must become revealed in the divine governance, and one of these revelations is the element of ideal, simple loving kindness, in which even gratitude plays no part. Thus [the existence of] heresy *(ha-kefirah)* is one of the ideal revelations of divinity, and its resulting blasphemy and sacrilege are the highest stage of this revelation" [i.e., God displays His loving kindness to scoffers despite their lack of gratitude, despite their blasphemy and sacrilege]. See also *Orot*, 127: "Whoever can discover the inner nature of heresy, can, in this respect, suck its sweetness and return it to the source of its holiness." See above, note 20.
29. See also *Ne'edar BaKodesh*, 14: "The culture of our times, greater than any other, is a vital revelation of a vital secular value. We must know it well in all its details, aspirations and roots, and our familiarity will guide us in establishing the revelation of the religious cultural values that soar above secular cultural values as heaven soars above earth."
30. "Ma'amar Meyuhad," in *Ma'amarei ha-Reayah*, 111.
31. See *Arpelei Tohar*, 73, 23 ("The source of the impulse to *avodah zarah* is in the holy"); *Iggerot HaRayah* I, 142; *Tahkemoni* (1910), 17. See Ish-Shalom, chap. 4.
32. Rav Kook acknowledges that "there are very precious things that can only be revealed under the guise of deficiencies." Therefore, "We value those deficiencies because they point to the good that is the cause of their being." See *Arpelei Tohar*, 13.
33. See R. Schatz-Uffenheimer, "Utopia and Messianism in the Teaching of Rav Kook" (Heb.) *Kivunim* 6, 24.
34. Cf. Mishnah Sotah 9:16. "In the footsteps of the Messiah insolence will increase."
35. Cf. *Arpelei Tohar*, 20. Rav Kook also cites other, less fundamental reasons for this "hutzpah." See *Orot HaKodesh* II, 298; *Arpelei Tohar*, 60.
36. For example, in Kant's conception of ethics, an act is ethical as well as rational only if it corresponds to the categorical imperative (in both its formulations) that is a rational imperative.
37. Cf. William James's critique of the "survival theory" in Lecture 20 (conclusion) of *The Varieties of Religious Experience* (New York, 1902).
38. Ms. *Kovetz Kadum*, 57a [*OHK* IV, 421–22] (emphasis mine).
39. See above, note 27.

40. Ms. *Kovetz* C, 21 [*OHK* IV, 421]. Still, as we remarked above, Rav Kook does not hesitate to criticize both heresy and heretics on many grounds. See *Arpelei Tohar*, 1.

41. "Talelei Orot," *Tahkemoni* (1910), 17.

42. On the problematic nature of tolerance within the framework of religious tradition, see above, note 2.

43. "Talelei Orot," loc. cit.

44. See R. Otto, *The Idea of the Holy*, trans. John W. Harvey (London, 1959), 15. Rav Kook also takes note of the rational principle as one of the components of religion, although his analysis of this phenomenon differs from that of Otto. In his essay "Li-Demut Diyukno shel ha-Rambam," published in the Passover Eve issue of the newspaper *Ha-Aretz* (1935), Rav Kook affirms, in a manner similar to Otto, that the religious phenomenon is composed of two principles: the emotive and the rational. In his view, the emotive principle expresses itself in the natural desire to draw closer to God, a desire that also gives rise to accompanying negative results. The role of the rational principle is to curb the emotive components and refine religious thought. The difference between Rav Kook and Otto lies in their conception of these two principles. For Otto, the emotive principle, or, to use his phrase, the numinous, expresses itself in the fear of and recoil from the divine and mysterious *(mysterium tremendum)*, while the rational principle generates descriptions and concepts to facilitate a rational perception of God. For Rav Kook, the emotive principle is not an expression of man's fear and recoil from the divine, but rather, as we have said, of his desire and aspiration, and the rational principle does not engender descriptions and concepts but, on the contrary, negates all description and conceptual analysis in its attempt to purify religious thought.

45. Ms. *Kovetz* 5, 76b [*OHE*, 49]. See also above, note 30.

46. Ms. *Kovetz Kadum* 128 [*OHK* IV, 405].

47. "Talelei Orot," 17.

48. Ms. *Kovetz Katan* 97.

49. See Ish-Shalom, 109–12, 223.

50. See above, note 48, and "Talelei Orot," 17. Compare the view of R. Yehuda HaLevi in the *Kuzari* 2:36 on the organic relation between Israel and the nations.

51. "Avodat Elohim," in *Ikkevei HaTzon* (printed together with *Eder Ha-Yakar*), 148.

52. See also ibid., 486, 491.

53. Ms. *Kovetz* 2, 16b.

54. Ms. *Kovetz* 5, 103b [*OHE*, 12].

55. The preceding paragraph is based on "Avodat Elohim," 147–48. See above, note 44.

56. It should be mentioned that Schleiermacher also extolled the "feeling of dependence" as a central and characteristic factor in the phenomenon of religion. See Rav Kook's "Avodat Elohim," 145.

57. "Avodat Elohim," 145.
58. See *Orot HaKodesh* III, 75: "One of the aims of the holy Torah is to lighten man's burdens." Cf. *Guide* II, 39; III, 47, 49.
59. Ms. *Kovetz* 3, 9a [*OHK* IV, 451].
60. *Arpelei Tohar*, 19. Also compare loc. cit. 17 (on the eternity of the Torah in Maimonides' teaching). See loc. cit. 11. In Ms. *Kovetz Katan*, 270 [*OHK* IV, 423], Rav Kook writes: "The essential quality of fear of Heaven is suitable for [man's] physical powers. The intelligence [by contrast] must be exalted in all its splendor, in the mighty purity of its freedom."
61. Cf. Deut. 28:30.
62. *Orot HaKodesh* III, introductory remarks, 26. See Ish-Shalom, *Rabbi Kook*. In an extended passage in Ms. *Kovetz* 4, 18b [*OHE*, 67–68], Rav Kook sharply attacks a particular ultra-orthodox approach that would suppress intelligence for religious reasons: "The enslavement of the intelligence and its stupefaction as a result of whatever influence constitutes destruction of the world. And the more holy the influence, the greater the damage done. Such an influence resembles the infamy of false prophecy in God's name, calling to actions of wickedness and impurity, idol worship and abominations. Thus, when the attempt to stupefy the intelligence is presented in the name of faith, of fear of Heaven, of diligence in Torah and fulfilling of mitzvot, it becomes a terrible lie and a vile impurity. Then the holy ones of the Most High, God's pure servants, must go forth to enlighten the world and Israel, the Torah, faith and all that is holy to the Lord from these destroyers, whoever they may be, whether they be liars who want only to cheat their fellows by cloaking themselves in a garment of piety, or whether they be people weak of spirit and small of mind, whose own intellectual light has been obstructed, whose feelings have been dulled, and whose imagination has coarsened, and a result of which, who purposefully and thoroughly trample down the reality before them, being rooted in mere fables of faith."
63. See *Orot HaKodesh* I, 217; "Derishat A-donai," in *Ikkevei HaTzon*, 129.
64. In a letter written to Rabbi Meir Berlin in 1911, Rav Kook deprecates apologetics and tendentious criticism and affirms that the truth is more beloved than anything, and precisely in it will the Most High, blessed be He, be praised and will the honor of enduring faith be exalted. See *Iggerot HaRayah* II, 20.
65. See *Orot HaKodesh* I, 120–21; *Olat Rayah* I, 330–31; *Orot HaKodesh* II, 544–45. See *Arpelei Tohar*, 2; *Orot HaKodesh*, II, 289.
66. Compare John Stuart Mill, *On Liberty*. According to Rav Kook, the limitations of freedom of speech must be set not by fanatical insistence on any one view, but rather out of a sense of responsibility that is aware of differing perspectives and carefully examines the implications of giving open expression to certain views. See *Orot HaKodesh* III, 282. "One should be wary of saying anything that will undermine the moral

framework of any individual. Even if such views seem correct in and of themselves, they harm the listener, if he is bound to his own moral circle by beliefs that are contradicted by the one being expressed to him."

67. See *Iggerot HaRayah* I, 19–20.

68. E. Schweid rightly claims that Rav Kook's view of secular Jews was guided by the religious gloss he ascribed to the motives and actions of the men of the Second Aliyah in the Land of Israel. See his essay, "Secularism from a Religious Perspective" (Heb.), in his book, *HaYehudi ha-Boded ve-ha-Yahadut* (Tel Aviv, 1974). Yet it must be noted that Rav Kook had great regard for the sincerity, honesty, love of truth, love of humanity, and love of Israel that came to expression in the heretical protest and revolt of his generation. For him, these qualities were of value in and of themselves, and for this reason alone, he interpreted them as an expression of motives to be understood within the framework of religious categories. (See my essay, "Religion, Repentance, and Human Freedom" (Heb.), in *Yovel Orot*, ed. Benjamin Ish-Shalom and Shalom Rosenberg [Jerusalem, 1987].)

69. This was Rav Kook's name for the heretical *halutzim* (pioneers), based on the saying of the Sages: "*Be'ikvot meshiḥa ḥutzpah yisgeh*" [In the footsteps of the Messiah "ḥutzpah" (insolence) will increase]. See above, note 34.

70. His writings overflow with faith in the renaissance of Judaism that would be, to use his phrase, a "*tehiyah toranit*" (Torah renaissance). On this subject, see Ish-Shalom, *Rabbi Kook*, 150.

71. See *Arpelei Tohar*, 29: "Without the insolence of the footsteps of the Messiah, the secrets of the Torah could not be fully revealed. Only by coarsening the emotions through this insolence can the most supernal intellectual illuminations be received, and in the end everything will be brought back to its perfect state." Rav Kook goes even further: "The children of the rebellious insolent ones will become prophets of the highest rank, of the rank of Moses, our Master and the supreme luminousness of Adam ha-Rishon [primordial Man]. The entire Tree of Life in all the depths of its goodness will be revealed in them and through them" (ibid., 12, the same text appears, with variations, in *Orot Ha-Kodesh* II, 298). In *Raya Mehemna* and *Tikkunei Zohar*, the Tree of Knowledge and the Tree of Life symbolize *tzimtzum* (contraction, retreat) and limitation, prohibitions and restrictions on the one hand, and freedom and lack of distinction between good and evil on the other. The Tree of Life is the tree of freedom, symbolizing the utopian aspect of the Torah. See Gershom Scholem, "The Meaning of the Torah in Jewish Mysticism," in *On the Kabbalah and Its Symbolism* (New York, 1965), 68–69.

CHAPTER 8

Dialectic, Doubters, and a Self-Erasing Letter: Rav Kook and the Ethics of Belief

Shalom Carmy

A belief to which the intellect does not assent encourages vexation and cruelty, because the supreme aspect of man, namely the intellect, is impoverished by its impact. The immanent demand that actions correspond to the highest, most refined opinions and affects, is a special characteristic of Israel.[1]

When they were about to publish *Orot ha-Kodesh*, they asked Rav Kook what of the book to print and what not to print, and he said: "In my opinion it should all be published, but one must ask my 'censors.' "[2]

When we think of Rav Kook's approach to the question of belief, we reach almost instinctively for a conventional, by now routine, account of his philosophy. I call this account conventional, not in order to disparage it or to replace it by another; indeed I subscribe to it myself.[3] The standard account is, in my opinion, a reliable guide to Rav Kook's epistemology and a key to much of his ontology. No less important, it helps to explain how Rav Kook's much discussed interpretation of the nonreligious Jewish national awakening in his time is to be understood as an integral component of his general philosophical-religious *weltanschauung*. Precisely because the standard account works so well in so many crucial areas, however, it tends to dim our awareness of other Kookian concerns.

A quick review of the conventional account will enable us to locate lacunae lurking, as it were, in the shadows.

The Spirit of Dialectic

If one word can be denominated to sum up Rav Kook's theological distinctiveness, most people would designate "unity" as that word.[4] All features of the world are to be viewed eschatologically and monistically, under the aspect of eternity, as ultimately good. If this is so then even mistaken intellectual and spiritual movements contain some valuable kernel of truth. They are to be appreciated for the insight they affirm, even as they are to be rejected for their failure to encompass the absolute Ideal. This fundamental doctrine, rooted in Kabbalah, is formulated and applied in a highly original manner (itself not innocent of exposure to the Hegelian, evolutionary *zeitgeist* of the nineteenth century).

An example will illustrate how Rav Kook does this. "That wicked, pessimistic, extreme perspective that is expressed in modern philosophy by deniers like Schopenhauer and his confreres, like all aspects of reality, has a place, and for everything in general—there is no thing which has no place."[5] Even the pessimism of Schopenhauer thus manifests the correct perception that reality is ultimately determined by a Will concealed from man; it is utterly wrong, however, in the conclusion it draws from this, as Rav Kook goes on to state. Similar readings of "alien" culture abound in Rav Kook's writings[6] and constitute an important element of the influential doctrine of tolerance associated with his name.[7] Only in the Torah do we confront an outlook on the world that comprehends the absolute Ideal and overcomes the finitude of human perspectives.

To acknowledge the Torah as the final, inclusive account of reality is not to claim that all its adherents are in identical possession of the perfect Truth. "There is no awareness and knowledge in the world . . . that does not engender oblivion and errors."[8] Most individuals are not equally engaged in all disciplines. They differ in character and attainments. The opening chapters of *Orot ha-Kodesh* are a sustained and eloquent attempt to classify various intellectual temperaments, the strengths and weaknesses of each and their interdependence as components of the supreme synthesis. Accordingly Aggadist is contrasted with Halakhist; the esoteric with the exoteric; intellectual concentration with diffusion; the comprehensive thinker with the scholar of the particular.

The work of synthesis in which Rav Kook calls his reader to take part is painful, incomplete, and gradual. The following excerpt, though frustrating in its abstractness, nonetheless captures the dialectical tension typical of Rav Kook:

> There are such ideas that must, according to the nature of man, engender by their dissemination harmful consequences, although they are in themselves useful and true. Therefore it is in the nature of man's spirit to struggle for his existence, and to oppose those ideas, so that he will not be harmed by their ramifications.
>
> The war grows longer . . . until he feels that his position fears not the diffusion of the ideas against which he had struggled. And that power itself that strengthens his spirit was granted him by the war itself. . . . And he knows how diminished he would have been had he not struggled against the diffusion then harmful to him. . . .
>
> But just as the man has been elevated so have his spiritual concepts been elevated, and those same ideas, though they appear to be the self-same ideas against which he had struggled, in truth it is not so. Only in their external expressions are these similar to those, but under the aspect of their inner value, they are separated one from the other, like the distinction between sacred and profane, and between light and darkness.
>
> And what he rejected then he finds that he had rightly rejected, and that he accepts those ideas after they were elevated he rightly accepts them. Precisely the discarded ideas that return to view—in them we find the dew of life, steadfast and very holy.[9]

Now when we ordinarily conceive of Rav Kook having a doctrine of belief it is this cluster of ideas that we tend to think of. The kind of *emunah* implicit in most of Rav Kook's discussions, whether he is treating the "alien" philosophies or those deriving from authentic Jewish thinking, is a feel for reality, a way of perceiving the world, rather than an assent to well-defined propositions. The salient propositions offered by Schopenhauer, as we have seen, are to be rejected: they are false; they are wicked. Taking their measure in the cold light of ordinary Aristotelian logic, the theses propounded by the alien philosophies can only be described as categorically false.

They are redeemed only through the kind of dialectical sublation conducted by Rav Kook.

The converse is the case when Rav Kook deals with views expressed by thinkers who are part of the Torah community. When, for example, the historian and man of letters Zeev Jawitz, a friend and correspondent of Rav Kook, questioned the Jewish authenticity of Maimonides' *Guide*, the Chief Rabbi avoided staking his rebuke on the truth value of Maimonides' positions.[10] To be sure he argues, case by case, that Maimonides does not subscribe to theologically objectionable propositions; if he errs, it is for "philosophical" reasons irrelevant to their Jewish legitimacy. But Rav Kook's primary line is that the *Guide* represents a religiously healthy intellectual path:

> Our master Rambam for whom God's Torah was the source of his life found his heart faithful to God and His Torah with these ideas. This itself is the decisive aspect. . . . And the decision on this is granted according to the spiritual state and the conception of spiritual images of each one according to his character and according to his measure as a human being. There is no doubt that there are people upon whom certain ideas exert a favorable effect . . . and there are other people for whom other ideas are able to bring their hearts near to those holy and sublime things.[11]

Later in the essay Rav Kook asserts that the prevalent anthropocentric thesis, according to which man is the purpose of creation, and Maimonides' rigorously anti-anthropocentric doctrine, are complementary rather than contradictory; each reflects a moment in man's experience of his place in the universe.[12]

Clearly, based upon the representative examples cited, Rav Kook's meditation on the spectrum of methods and doctrines within the tradition is indifferent to their categorical truth or falsehood. All is grist for the dialectical mill; better yet, given the tenor of that dialectic, all is thread to be woven into the eschatological tapestry.

All this can only confirm our conviction that Rav Kook has little interest in quotidian judgments of propositional truth and falsehood. This is consistent with the commonplace judgment that Rav Kook is to be classified as the luminous mystic and God-animated poet, not as a traditional analytic philosopher. If we were to adopt Buber's distinction[13] between *emunah* (faith) and *pistis* (belief), we should no doubt expect Rav Kook to teach us about the former rather than the latter.[14] Indeed a perusal of Rav Kook's voluminous effusions reveals much about the experience of faith, the feelings it inspires, its omnipresence even where it is apparently absent.[15]

But this orientation may engender a partial, hence misleading, picture of Rav Kook's thought. For it may lead us to overlook Rav Kook's attention to the matter of propositional belief.[16] To place such concern in its appropriate context we must consider for a moment that Rav Kook, as one of the foremost rabbis of his era, devoted the major part of his intellectual energy, for over three decades, to the resolution of halakhic queries. These questions required rational categorical judgments of the permitted and the prohibited, the mandatory and the aleatory, and Rav Kook was recognized as a master respondent.

The standard approach, by virtue of its inherent preoccupation with the social background of his ideas, concentrates on Rav Kook's attitudes toward rejected beliefs and worldviews alien to him. Turning to the immanent nature of Jewish belief, we again look to the dialectical, synthetic features so ubiquitous in Rav Kook's writings. But what of the prosaic bread-and-margarine problems connected with dogmatic religious belief? What ought an intellectually honest individual do when the evidence for the required belief seems to fall short of adequacy? How should one act if there is a discrepancy between the beliefs I consider true and those adopted by the rest of the observant community? Once we formulate the questions of belief in this manner, we have moved from the poetic-mystical realm where Rav Kook discusses the nature of reality and its eschatological destiny and entered the province of Halakhah.

It is not surprising that Rav Kook was called upon, as the halakhic authority of first and last resort for many individuals struggling with the questions of normative belief on their own behalf and on behalf of their communities, not only to communicate his own faith but also to state its halakhic parameters. He took it upon himself, as we all know, to instruct the faithful on proper attitudes and behavior toward the deviant. But it was also his task to define what was, or was not, deviant, to guide the faithful away from the prohibited, to encourage their flourishing within the precincts of the permitted and the desirable.

Once we recognize the philosophical interest in Rav Kook's treatment of these issues, we have permitted Halakhah to invade the kingdom of theology. To that extent we will have chosen to understand Rav Kook as he truly lived, with one foot firmly planted in the four cubits of Halakhah and the other (excuse the image) exploring the infinite expanses of the spiritual world. By subjecting Rav Kook's arguments to analysis we are also, of course, exposing his halakhically informed position to the critical perspective of the uncommitted reasoner whom Rav Kook would persuade.

The discussion that follows will posit the experiential dimension of Rav Kook's faith, as recorded copiously in his writings. Likewise we accept, as an integral part of Rav Kook's harmonistic ideal, his conviction that "a belief to which the intellect does not assent encourages vexation and cruelty."[17] We shall not make our task the construction of Kookian arguments for particular propositions (though this will come up peripherally). Our subject is rather the "ethics of belief," the right or duty to believe a proposition under certain circumstances, and only indirectly the content or rationality of the belief itself. To this purpose I would like to present, and interrogate, two letters in which Rav Kook addresses the difficulties faced by the honest doubter and by the maverick whose ethical (and perhaps theological) orientation differs from that approved by the observant community as a whole.

The Honest and Dishonest Doubter

In June 1905, early in Rav Kook's highly productive Jaffa period, he responded to the query posed by Moshe Seidel, a disciple to whom many of Rav Kook's most significant theological epistles were first written, on the subject of intellectual liberty.[18] Must we accept freedom of thought grudgingly, as a necessity of modern society, or can it be justified from a Torah perspective?

Rav Kook argues that freedom of thought cannot be unlimited. To begin with, all values, when carried to extremes, are wrong. Moreover, untrammeled freedom of thought will inevitably lead to moral anarchy that cannot be tolerated.[19] What limitations are necessary, however, is something that varies, like the limits of tolerated behavior, among different societies. The entire being of the Jewish nation qua nation is tied up with "the proclamation of God's Name in the world." For any nation whose existence is essentially connected to some idea, "it is completely permitted, nay an obligation, that with respect to that idea there would not be found within it freedom of opinion. For that would not be freedom but indolence in self-defense." He goes on to qualify this thesis:

> Indeed sometimes there are found individuals who may rebel against their nation, when they discover that the idea which consolidates and sustains their nation is harmful to humanity as a whole. Therefore they forsake the nation for the sake of the truth. But so long as the idea that fortifies the nation is not a harmful idea at all, more so when it is an idea that is beneficial beyond its border . . . there is no place for toleration.[20]

The first part of Rav Kook's letter thus provides a nonhalakhic rationale for the Halakhah's refusal to endorse unlimited freedom of thought. Nonetheless Rav Kook does not advocate the use of political coercion to impose right theology under contemporary circumstances. The Divine cunning has seen to it that diminution in the spiritual vigor of the nation is accompanied by a proportional diminution in its powers. As a result the nation is prevented, whether by external weakness or inner obstacles, from the enforcement of doctrinal uniformity: "We are content with this, because we recognize that it is the Will of supreme Providence in such times."

Rav Kook furthermore feels a need to counter an implicit argument against punishing the denier—namely that people cannot be held culpable for failing to accept beliefs unsupported by reason. Surely the Halakhah prohibits entertaining any kind of doubt about normative belief.[21] The status of heretic (apikoros), however, is reserved for the denier (kofer), "i.e., one who decides the opposite." Such a resolute denial is impossible among Jews,[22] asserts Rav Kook, unless the individual is maliciously and deliberately dishonest, and such an individual fully deserves the stringent penalties set down by Halakhah.[23] Were contemporary heretics intellectually honest, they could assert no more than uncertainty; the humble admission of uncertainty would swiftly issue forth in the resolution of their doubts, and all would be well.

Reviewing this letter, we can isolate three philosophically interesting theses presented by Rav Kook:

1. All things being equal, one is morally obligated to believe a proposition, if belief in that proposition is a necessary component of his/her national identity.
2. The aforementioned obligation is overridden when an essential national belief is inimical to the welfare of humanity.
3. If an essential national belief is *refuted*, the obligation to believe it is overridden as well. (I infer this from the fact that Rav Kook must insist that the essential Jewish beliefs can, at the very worst, be doubted, but not disproved.)

Each one of these views requires further clarification. To this we now proceed.

Thesis 1

That belief in the Torah is a necessary component of Jewish national identity is an idea explicitly formulated as early as Saadia Gaon. The Torah must be eternal, he maintains, because, as the prophets tell us, Israel is, and Israel is a nation only by virtue of the Torah.[24] Saadia, however, can presuppose, by this point in his exposition, acceptance of the Torah; he seeks a demonstration of its eternity. Rav Kook, confronting the secularist challenge in an age of nationalism, invites additional questions: What defines a nation in the sense pertinent to Rav Kook in our context, and how do we recognize an essential national idea? And why is one obligated to subscribe to the essential idea?

Regarding the concept of nationhood, I find two distinct strands in Rav Kook's writing, both of which are alive in the letter we are considering. The first ("metaphysical-juridic") account would recognize the Jewish people as the only available candidate for nationhood in the appropriate sense of the term. This view could draw on Rav Kook's claim that other nations are constituted by the consent of individuals and hence form a merely atomistic, nominalistic aggregate; the Jewish people, by contrast, is constituted by

Divine election and is therefore bound together organically and essentially. "If [the Jew] considers detachment from the nation, he must detach his soul from the source of its life."[25] It can also boast kabbalistic antecedents.[26] Rav Kook is consistent with this formulation when he declares, in introducing the concept of the essential national idea, that "with respect to belief [emunah] there is a great distinction between Israel and the nations." And he goes on to state, "The national content of no other nation or tongue is at all bound to the nature of their being with the knowledge of the Name of God in its midst and in the world."

The metaphysical account is not susceptible to a posteriori refutation. Despite its apparent universality ("any nation in the world"), it really commits Rav Kook to only one case, that of the Jewish people. In our context this is a weakness: it renders the pretense to universality empty, arguing that the fundamental doctrines of Judaism must be accepted by appealing to a relatively abstruse theory of Jewish identity.

In fact Rav Kook is careful to incorporate an additional ("empirical") contention. There might exist "an isolated people, of base faith, whose faith is national." Such a faith-nation would presumably be so petty that its expansion would place obstacles before all humanity.[27] Moreover, as this putative nation would have little likelihood of perpetuating itself (because of its size), it would have no right to demand that its members obligate themselves to its sustenance. The intuitive force of the "threshold" criterion for viable nationhood will be evident to anyone who considers for a moment the implications of the term "Balkanization." Rav Kook offers two justifications for his theological variation on the principle. One is moral: the petty faith-nation would damage humanity.[28] The second is pragmatic: the too-small nation is simply not feasible and hence cannot claim commitment.[29] But as Rav Kook is skeptical about the possibility that a group so small be regarded as the bearer of an essential national idea, it is not clear how much weight he intends this branch of his argument to carry.

Let us note, at this point, that Rav Kook elsewhere has no difficulty speaking—and in a positive vein—of the ethos distinctive to various nations. Precisely when Rav Kook is elaborating on the uniqueness of Israel, to take one instructive example, he acknowledges the specific qualities of Gentile cultures: "There are many peoples who have some specific capability in greater measure than is found in Israel, but Israel, as the quintessence of all humanity, collects in its midst the singularities *[segulot]* of all the nations and they are united in their midst in a holy ideal form, in a sublime unity."[30] If Rav Kook does not permit the conservation of the Gentile singularities to engender a moral obligation (as Jewish singularity obligates the Jew to adopt the essential national idea), this may be because a Gentile singularity is, from the aspect of eternity, a metaphysically unstable (id)entity. It exists in order to be transcended in the "sublime unity" of Israel.[31]

Why does the existence of an essential national idea obligate members of that nation to believe (in) it? The possible justifications can be divided into two main categories: epistemic and ontic.

An epistemic justification of believing in the essential national idea would be something like the following: All things being equal, the fact that my parents or my society believe a proposition may be said to give me a reason for believing it too. At the very least, the fact that a belief is "tenured," that it is part of my tacitly or explicitly accepted culture, creates a presumption in its favor, in the sense that the burden of proof rests upon the denial of that belief; I am unreasonable to reject the belief (even to suspend judgment?) without adducing grounds for so doing. That many people outside my culture do not subscribe to our beliefs, that they in fact are firmly committed to beliefs that contradict ours, does not necessarily give me reason to abandon my received beliefs or even to hold them at arm's length. On this account, epistemological commitment to the essential national idea resembles in structure, though it surpasses in intensity, that accorded other tenured beliefs.

The crucial difficulty with the religious incarnation of this approach is its bare-faced relativism. Epistemic justification, in itself, provides no reason to regard one ethos or opinion as inherently more true than the other. At the risk of sounding paradoxical I would say that we are given a reason to adopt the belief but not a reason to believe that it is true. This is not, of course, a personal problem for Rav Kook, who possessed ample grounds for his faith in the absolute superiority of Judaism. In this letter, however, his purpose is not to convince himself that Judaism is true; he is supposed to be arguing that even Jews lacking his certitude ought to accept it as well. Rav Kook could try to enhance his position by claiming that Jewish tradition is more reliable than the skeptical alternative because of the antiquity of the tradition, the saintliness of its purveyors, the moral corruption of its disparagers. But, for reasons we can readily speculate on, Rav Kook chose not to make his case on this basis.[32] Hence, if we limit Rav Kook to the epistemic approach, he appears to be stuck, as it were, pushing a relativistic outlook reminiscent of seventeenth-century Europe and its *cuius regio eius religio* or the therapeutic civil religion of late modern America, a saline and cynical soil where nothing more salubrious can grow than a shrewd Montaigne-like skepticism.[33] There is no reason to assume that Rav Kook would find a nationalistic relativism adequate to his idea of religion, even as a temporary apologetic stopgap.

All this makes an alternative desirable. I have called the alternative approach ontic because it proceeds from an assertion about the conditions of the believing individual's being himself/herself and not somebody else. One is subject to a moral-juridic imperative that compels him to subscribe to the required belief. Failure to maintain the belief threatens the very identity of the individual so addressed. In our case, the required beliefs have two peculiar characteristics: they are *not* required of the entire human race; they *are* required of all members of the Jewish people.

An intriguing variation on this theme might run as follows: Under ordinary conditions, it is virtually tautological that an individual believes a proposition when *he or she* in fact believes it to be true. To demand of an individual that he believe a proposition when, in fact, he does not, offends our moral sensibility, according to the present account, because it violates the individual's autonomy, his sense that his beliefs must be his and not somebody else's. This presupposes that the self to which the beliefs must "belong" is the individual self. What if one were to challenge this presupposition and maintain that the autonomous self whose integrity is to be respected is not that of the human individual, but rather that of the collective organism—the nation? Thesis 1 would be there for the taking. The appeal of the epistemology thus delineated would be limited to thinkers with a very strong bias against individualism.[34] While it is always dangerous to speculate counterfactually as to how a thinker would react to a novel, conjectural reconstruction of his position, I suspect that Rav Kook, despite his commitment to the organic community, might balk at the "postmodernism" of this formulation.[35]

In any event, he who would champion the ontic justification of belief in the essential national idea must be willing to carry substantial metaphysical baggage. Rav Kook, of course, embraced the metaphysical burden with enthusiasm. He had no doubt that the spiritual vocation of the Jewish people is not an external imposition, but expresses the true nature of the kingdom of priests. Nevertheless the skeptical reader might protest the Rabbi's seemingly circular logic: he demonstrates the moral necessity of the essential national idea on the basis of a concept of Jewish peoplehood that is, from the outset, steeped in theological dogma. For whom did Rav Kook toil? Did he intend to convince the honest doubter or was his reasoning merely rationale, sufficient to explain himself to himself and to impress sympathetic listeners like Seidel, but inadequate to compel assent where assent was not already in the offing?

Professor Schweid, among others, has pointed out that Rav Kook's audience of doubters and deniers were, as a group, more amenable to his approach than observation of their modern counterparts would lead us to surmise.[36] Given their thoroughly Jewish background and nationalistic program, Eastern European Zionists[37] might well bear with them the unforgettable sense of belonging to the abiding community of Israel and a categorical responsibility to abide with it. Having no experience of a Jewish national ethos not rooted in religious commitment and belief, they had reason to suspect the viability of the people of Israel divorced from the God of Israel and the Torah of Israel. For many of them this intuition may have spoken more powerfully than the theological doctrines that Rav Kook's interpretation of that intuition presupposes.[38]

Another factor in the possible appeal of the ontic account for Rav Kook's contemporaries derives from the ideas associated with late nineteenth-century biology. The analogy between the individual's instinct of self-preservation and the nation's obligation to perpetuate itself was much favored by Aḥad Haam. Rav Kook, whose awareness of evolutionary biology as the intellectual wave of the present is well-attested,[39] had every reason to exploit the biological analogy to the utmost.

Contemporary hindsight, of course, has joined Berdyczewski and Brenner in their attack on Aḥad Haam. And the attempt to derive moral imperatives from evolutionary biology appears to us as no more than a spectacular display of the naturalistic fallacy. We subsume such recourse to the "biological" nature of human societies under the epistemic, relativistic model rather than the moral-juridic imperative character of the ontic analysis. Yet insofar as the relation between "is" and "ought" continues to intrigue men and women trying to explain their destiny in this world, and insofar as Rav Kook's thesis about the central place that God and Torah occupy in Jewish life continues to find a resonance in the meditations of Jews, the issues argued by Rav Kook remain alive.

Thesis 2

Why does Rav Kook believe that the essential national idea is not to be believed when it leads to general harm? How can one justify the introduction of moral factors into the judgment of truth and falsehood? Again one might classify the possible justifications under two headings: moral and epistemological.[40]

The moral argument would maintain that we reject certain beliefs, not because we have reason to believe them false, but because we believe that believing them to be true is morally wrong. The fact that the belief is morally wrong does not give us a reason to believe it false, but it does give us a right and duty to want it to be false. The immoral character of a proposition whose only claim to our allegiance is its status as an essential national idea does not establish that the belief is false; rather it relieves us of the obligation to believe it true. The weakness of the moral argument for Thesis 2 is its relativism; in this it resembles the epistemic argument for Thesis 1.

The epistemological argument aims at a stronger result: if successful, it not only gives us reason to withdraw our assent from the immoral proposition, but provides grounds to regard it as false. Several such arguments can be constructed on the basis of premises congenial to Rav Kook. If, for example, we assent to the existence of a benevolent God, one might validly infer that God would not countenance the existence of a nation whose essential idea is immoral. Even the agnostic about the existence of God (for whom the existence of God is an unconfirmed possibility) would concede that *if* there is a God, His benevolence would exclude from existence the nation with the immoral essential idea.

Along different lines, the Kookian could argue that Thesis 1 applies not only to nations but also to humanity as a whole. This would yield "All things being equal, one is morally obligated to believe a proposition, if belief in that proposition is a necessary component of his/her *human* identity." Since humanity is more inclusive than any national identity, allegiance to the human race would take precedence over the national ethos. Thus Thesis 2 becomes a corollary of Thesis 1. This reading might be supported by Rav Kook's emphasis on harm to humanity as the defining characteristic of the immoral national idea.[41] It gains further strength from Rav Kook's statement that the justified rebels against the immoral nation "forsake the nation for the sake of the truth."[42]

That Judaism passes the test of Thesis 2 with flying colors is something that Rav Kook would hardly question. He frequently insists that the Torah does not contravene man's natural ethical sense, but on the contrary fulfills it.[43] But if he took the beneficial consequences of Judaism for granted, others among his contemporaries did not, as witnessed by his need to reiterate this very point. A letter he wrote in 1910 gives us a thumbnail idea of how he went about establishing, to an anonymous questioner, the superiority and uniqueness of the Jewish people's ethical mission:[44] though we Jews ought to take pleasure in points of idealistic light flashing out their messages amid the darkness, we must recognize that those who ape "our Divinely compassed historical activity," were they disconnected from the Jewish spiritual influence—"Would anything remain of the goals of their wars except for the spilling of blood and despicable murders?" To be sure, Rav Kook straightforwardly confesses, the Jewish people are not morally impeccable: indeed, it is no secret that the Rabbis utter words of reproach against some actions of our greatest leaders. Yet isolated instances should not overshadow the ideal that embraces the national soul, and even these flaws are to be transcended from an eschatological perspective that comprehends them as stages in man's progress to a redeemed existence.

Thesis 3

Rav Kook is quite certain that the beliefs he would have his compatriots accept as their national duty cannot be proven false. There cannot be a duty to regard as true what one knows to be false, even if such a feat were psychologically possible. This is, to put the matter simply, as analytic students of Plato's *Theaetetus* often do, a consequence of the grammar of the verb "to know": you can't *know* something that's not true.

What, though, is the standard of certainty sufficient for knowledge? That is the crucial question. We are duty-bound to note that Rav Kook's apologetic zeal occasionally led him to set extraordinarily high standards of proof for propositions the negation of which he sought to defend. An example from Rav Kook's vindication of Maimonides against Jawitz will suffice. Rebutting the charge that Maimonides' belief in the intelligence of the celestial spheres introduces Greek doctrine into Jewish thought, Rav Kook calmly states: "I don't know if there is any right-thinking man who can deliver a conclusive verdict, that there is no willing, animate, intelligent cause, in all the cosmic motions even now, when universal gravity has been discovered, for we find living beings wherever we turn. If the diseases are progressively explained as the effect of living creatures, why should not the great occurrences in the entire universe be the outcome of forces in which inheres life?"[45] Such tendentiousness takes something away from the persuasiveness of Rav Kook's Thesis 3.

Before we leave our discussion of the three theses, it is instructive to compare Rav Kook's analysis with William James's well-known "Will to Believe."[46] James advocates basing one's decision on the will to believe when the option we choose is live, forced, and momentous. Clearly the religious commitment required by Rav Kook is forced and momentous. Given Rav Kook's metaphysical assumptions, the option of Jewish existence is inevitably a live one to every Jew. As we have seen, many of his contemporaries who lacked his *a priori* assurance of the integral bond between the Jew and his religion would yet know belief as a live option.

James recommends the will to believe when accepting that the candidate for belief has beneficial consequences. This is parallel to, but significantly different from, Rav Kook's Thesis 2. For Rav Kook, the fact that a belief is essential to the national identity precipitates the duty to believe. That duty vanishes only when the belief is positively harmful to humanity. To square this with James's position requires adding a premise (one to which Rav Kook would heartily subscribe) asserting that sustaining essential national ideas is beneficial and therefore a worthy repository of our will to believe.

Another point of apparent agreement is Rav Kook's Thesis 3. James, like Rav Kook, does not expect the will to believe to operate where the truth or falsehood of the proposition can be determined independently. The difference in application of this principle is far more impressive than the element of accord. For James, will to believe enters where science has given up. For Rav Kook, on the other hand, faith in the essential national idea bears a secure presumption of truth; he can tolerate its abdication only when it is undermined by conclusive evidence. And we have already discovered how strong evidence must be before Rav Kook regards it as decisive.

Lastly, the two turn-of-the-century thinkers[47] diverge radically with respect to the normative character of belief. Rav Kook, as an exponent of halakhic Judaism, could not but view certain beliefs as halakhically required. He can sympathize with the honest doubter but not commend him for suspending judgment. While James sometimes seems to be saying that one *must* exercise the will to believe, it is not clear whether this "must" is moral or prudential. At other times James rued the notorious title of his essay: if only he had called it "The Right to Believe," his meaning would not have been misconstrued so easily.[48]

Critics of James have likewise argued plausibly (though not necessarily conclusively) that the verb "believe" could readily be replaced in his analysis by "pretend" or "gamble" without losing anything in translation. After all, the benefits of believing can be reaped by acting and/or feeling as if the belief were true without the cognitive occurrence of the belief. Although Rav Kook might deem "pragmatic"[49] faith to be better than nothing, insofar as it would conduce to "cognitive" belief and might well testify to an irrepressible unconscious belief, in the final analysis the belief to be achieved should be no less than full-bodied cognitive belief.[50]

The letter we have examined prescribes for the situation of the honest doubter, the individual who stands in the presence of the believer, on the periphery of his belief. Such individuals are not uncommon in times of rapid cultural change. But the same conditions that make for doubt at the edges of the community precipitate another kind of dilemma within it. Imagine the believer fully committed to the revealed faith of his/her ancestors, who, in the course of formulating those beliefs to himself, finds himself holding opinions the rest of the observant community shuns. What is the honest believer to do, faced by a hostile consensus?

The Honest Conformer

Rav Kook, stranded in Switzerland with the beginning of World War I, addresses an unnamed interlocutor.[51] The subject is the proper balance between humility and pride and Rav Kook endorses his correspondent's view that "in matters of character [middot] that are given to the heart no human being can mete out judgment about his fellow." But he is in doubt whether, in the event that the individual's determination of the correct measure deviates from that of the community, "one can say that there is an obligation to conduct oneself so that there would be no transgression according to the agreement of the world."

Rav Kook's response is formulated in strictly halakhic terms. The halakhic give-and-take touches, as is often the case, upon a wide range of sources. Among other matters Rav Kook considers Isaac's behavior in Genesis 26: having told the Philistines that Rebecca is his sister, thus creating the public impression that she was prohibited to him, he nevertheless did not abstain from conjugal relations in private. He also alludes to a halakhic discussion in the laws of sacrifices: do witnesses oblige an individual to bring an offering to atone for unintentional transgressions when the alleged sinner is certain that he is not liable?[52] And desecration of God's Name (ḥillul haShem) also makes an appearance.

Surprisingly, Rav Kook fails to mention here a relevant dictum of

Maimonides. In the *Commentary on the Mishnah*, Maimonides states that, when a dispute among talmudic rabbis has no ramifications in practice, it is unnecessary to rule which view is correct.[53] This position would seem to support individual freedom in matters of belief. In an earlier letter Rav Kook had cited Maimonides' position.[54] There he aligns Maimonides with other decisors who maintain that "although it is forbidden to decide in [a matter connected to] practice against the editors of the Talmud, it is nonetheless permissible to choose, on the basis of inquiry, which opinion is more plausible to each one, according to his own opinion, if it too is founded on the totality of Torah and the opinions of the Sages." Rav Kook identifies this view with that of the Babylonian Talmud. The rabbis of the Jerusalem Talmud disagree, in Rav Kook's opinion, maintaining that Aggadic matters are also given to final determination by the talmudic Sages.

Why did Rav Kook ignore a source he had probed only a few years earlier? There are two possible reasons for dismissing the relevance of Maimonides' statement in this context: (1) In the cases discussed by Maimonides, the beliefs in question—whether the ten tribes will be restored, the precise supernatural torments visited upon the *sotah*, the details of supernatural atonement—carry no obvious existential import. Rav Kook, by contrast, is directly concerned with beliefs that affect moral attitudes. (2) Maimonides deals with matters disputed by the rabbis: where there are practical implications, one ought to rule one way or the other; where there are none, authoritative decision is not required. Rav Kook, however, addresses the situation in which the isolated individual confronts an apparently monolithic body of opinion.

In any event, the primary concept governing Rav Kook's discussion is that of *mar'it 'ayin*—the appearance of sin. The rabbis prohibited certain kinds of otherwise permissible behavior because of *mar'it 'ayin*, lest others mistakenly identify the permitted act with a prohibited one. "Whatever is prohibited because of *mar'it 'ayin* is prohibited even in one's inner chambers"[55] is a corollary of this principle. Thus one is to avoid the appearance of transgression even when it is highly unlikely that he/she will be observed. For example, the consumption of human blood (or for that matter fish blood) does not come under the biblical prohibition of drinking animal blood. Nevertheless one may not partake of human blood because it has the appearance of animal blood and thus brings mar'it 'ayin into play. Even when an individual eats in seclusion and blood from his own gums discolors the bread in his hand, he is obligated to scrape off the evidence of bleeding. Why? Because mar'it 'ayin applies as soon as the blood becomes visible.

What if the blood is not visible outside the body? Were one to eject the food inside one's mouth it would no doubt exhibit the telltale redness. Do we apply the principle "whatever is prohibited because of mar'it 'ayin is prohibited even in one's inner chambers?" Is the inside of one's mouth an inner chamber? No, rules the Halakhah: unlike the private chamber, the inside of the human body is not, even theoretically, accessible to public inspection.

Now, infers Rav Kook, if the inside of your mouth is exempt from concern about appearances, the same should apply to the inner sanctum of the mind. If I am convinced that my judgment is correct I am not obligated to abrogate it merely because the community, were it to know my ethical view, would regard it as halakhically prohibited.[56] As Rav Kook puts it: "With respect to middot in the chambers of the heart it is between a man and himself and we do not follow the opinion of the world." Note that Rav Kook's logic, at first blush, clearly implies the same freedom with respect to theological beliefs: these too, take place, as it were, in the privacy of heart and mind.

This freedom, however, is not unqualified: "What is revealed in writing or speech in matters of middot one must indeed beware lest it appear to be an improper middah according to the estimation of the world." Freedom of thought in matters of middot, yes; freedom of expression, no![57]

It is not clear what kind of limitation Rav Kook has in mind. Many contemporary Orthodox ideologists would grant halakhic authorities the right to determine what is, or is not, correct in areas that are not halakhic in the narrow behavioral sense (Da'as Torah).[58] Rav Kook does not allude to halakhic authority: he respects the judgment of his interlocutor since "in matters of character [middot] that are given to the heart no human being can mete out judgment about his fellow." Does this apply to (at least some) theological approaches as well? I would answer in the affirmative, given Rav Kook's forthright avowal that different philosophical perspectives are suitable to different individual tendencies.[59] But respect for subjectivity does not imply indifference to authoritative halakhic judgment. Would Rav Kook extend the same right of decision to persons less responsible than his obviously erudite interlocutor? Presumably not. Does Rav Kook fail to counsel resort to halakhic authority in this case for the simple reason that a halakhic authority (namely himself) has already been consulted and has authoritatively ruled that the individual should rely on his own judgment? Perhaps. And how much weight should we attach to Rav Kook's suspicion[60] that, under contemporary circumstances, very few people are capable of exercising genuine freedom in determining which beliefs to adopt?[61]

Moreover, there is a significant distinction between the classical examples of mar'it 'ayin and the ethical issue facing us here. In the former case nothing is lost if one is more stringent than would otherwise be necessary; in the latter case, deviation from the optimal attitude (or belief) for the sake of social appearances involves the real sacrifice of one's own spiritual excellence. Furthermore, when an individual keeps his intellectual (or ethical) convictions to himself because society disapproves, he may be consigning to religious alienation others who, believing these attitudes to be proscribed by Judaism, conclude there is no place for them within established religion.

This difficulty may be tied to the obscure referent of Rav Kook's term "the opinion of the world" ('olam). Who is this "world" of which one's public utterances must be so endlessly solicitous? Jewish society as a whole? Orthodox society? The Rabbinic elite?[62] Here too Rav Kook seems to be advising his interlocutor to exercise his own judgment. He is counseling no more than theologically prudent care and restraint in revealing views that are liable to misunderstanding.

On reflection Rav Kook's instruction here is stated elsewhere as an ethical dictum about the significance of careful speech: "One ought to beware of expressing any utterance that would cause the weakening of the ethical system in the life of any man. Even if the matters in themselves appear correct, they harm the listener, if his ethical circle is bound up with a content that conflicts with that which he is able to hear at that stage."[63]

The Self-Erasing Letter

This last discussion appears in the 1923 collection of letters[64] that Rav Kook chose to reveal to the reading public. According to the editorial note by his son, R. Zvi Yehudah Kook, the letters selected[65] offered guidance "in the way of Torah and the service of God in Halakhah and Aggadah, literature and deed, the life of the individual and the life of the community, on questions that come up and in attitudes and assessments of parties, currents and various aspects of the building of the house of Israel and its renaissance on its holy land." He informs us that three or four letters contain detailed halakhic discussion, to the point where that analysis takes up more space than "the general issues of opinions and beliefs, ethics and worship and the life of the community."[66] By the time the collection was reprinted, twenty years later, Rav Kook was no longer living. R. Zvi Yehudah had full responsibility. The letter we have just examined was removed from the posthumous book. Why?

The only direct clue to resolving the mystery of the vanishing letter is R. Zvi Yehudah's preface, in which he reviews his editorial policy. His words deserve full citation:

> Omitted now are only a few isolated matters, that were pertinent to other people and belonged to that time, and so too halakhic matters, which are for the determination of practical halakhah or the elucidation of entire issues through the give-and-take of Halakhah. These were omitted here and set in their places, in the appropriate frames of reference that I have indicated. Only brief notes, albeit great in quality, remained here.[67]

How does this explain the excision of our letter? Perhaps R. Zvi Yehudah considered the content too heavily halakhic. But in that case it should have been transferred to one of Rav Kook's halakhic works. This did not happen.[68] To maintain that the letter we have just examined was pertinent in 1916, when it was written, and in 5683 (1923–24) when the author made it public, but was no longer relevant in 1943, says a great deal about the views of the editor. Are we really to believe that the kind of situation addressed by Rav Kook in 1916, which he considered to be worth a public airing several years later, no longer came up in 1943?

Let us consider another, rather poignant way of explaining the deletion of the letter. According to the letter, as we have seen, an individual who has concluded that some series of propositions p_1. . . p_n is a true and legitimate expression of the Torah's teaching is right to believe it, even if the community disagrees with that evaluation. However, as we have also seen, the individual is not justified in expressing his/her belief publicly when that utterance is liable to misunderstanding and condemnation. If we instantiate Rav Kook's theory of belief expressed in the letter for p_1. . . p_n we get the following thesis:

> If Rav Kook believed the theory stated in his 1916 letter as a true and legitimate expression of the Torah's teaching, he was right to believe it. However, this does not justify the publication of his belief insofar as that utterance was liable to misunderstanding and condemnation.

Perhaps, reasoned R. Zvi Yehudah, his father had his reasons for putting his marginal views before the public. Yet these were hardly the kind of assertions that would win Rav Kook the approbation of the "world."[69] Therefore Rav Kook's own letter provides the justification for its censorship!

We have arrived full circle. At the outset of this analysis I suggested that the standard portrait of Rav Kook, the one promoted by academicians, fails to take into account his vocation as a working halakhist and communal leader. We have sought to recover philosophically significant passages in his legal and communal corpus in order to arrive at a more rounded sense of Rav Kook. We end with the melancholy insight that one factor preventing us from the full possession of Rav Kook's legacy is the censorship of his writings by those who would conserve it, and furthermore, that this erasure of a halakhic discussion can be justified by Rav Kook's halakhic reasoning itself. Thus a not insignificant component of Rav Kook's contribution recedes into oblivion, consumed by that which he had nourished.[70]

Notes

1. *Arpelei Tohar* (Jerusalem, 5743), 105.
2. H. Lifshitz, *Shivḥei haReiyah* (Harry Fischel Institute, Jerusalem, 5739), 296. Cf. the magazine *'Ayin be-'Ayin* (ed. Pinhas Peli) for *Vayehi*, 5719, recorded by Agnon in *Sefer, Sofer ve-Sippur* (Tel Aviv, 1978), 352: "R. Zvi Yehudah Kook recounted that when he was arranging the book *Orot* by his father Rav Abraham Isaac Kook of blessed memory, he brought him the entire work for examination before giving it to the printer. Meanwhile he remarked that it might be worthwhile to omit from the book the section on young Jews engaging in gymnastics, insofar as this section would likely be misunderstood by many and enemies would exploit it in their instigation. Rav Kook responded to him: 'Do you wish to do this because of the fear of Heaven? Rather it is the fear of flesh and blood, and I don't have this fear.'" The controversial material alluded to is 80, section 34. The aftermath to the first publication is described in Moshe Ganz, *Toratekha le-Yisrael* (Jerusalem, 5750) 68: "In 1921 . . . a group of zealots opposed to Rav Kook . . . bought up the edition, so that the book would not reach the public, and printed section 34 . . . on the walls of Meah Shearim, in order to expose the supposed depravity of Rav Kook's approach. . . . Prof. Nahum Arieli recounted in the name of his father, the eminent Rabbi Yitzhak Arieli, that there was a meeting, in which Rav Kook, R. Zvi Yehudah and R. Arieli took part, where it was decided to go ahead immediately with a second edition because the first was not available. R. Arieli suggested omitting the passage on physical exercise to calm the zealots. Rav Kook answered that if he did this, he would be, in his own eyes 'a prophet suppressing his prophecy.'" (I owe the Ganz reference to my friend and former student Yaakov Genack.)
3. My "Rav Kuk's Theory of Knowledge" (*Tradition* 15:1–2, 193–203) differs from the standard version primarily in its stress on the imagination and my effort to enlist Rav Kook as a participant in an Eastern European "Copernican revolution."
4. N. Arieli, to take a recent example, opens his essay "Integration in the Thought of Rav Kook: Aspects of His Practical Approach to Society and Culture" (in *Yovel Orot*, ed. B. Ish-Shalom and S. Rosenberg [Jerusalem, 5748]; in English, *The World of Rav Kook's Thought*, trans. S. Carmy and B. Casper , [New York, 1991]) with the following statement: "The central concept of Rav Kook's teaching, one coined by him, is 'the inclusive unity' *(ha-aḥdut ha-kolelet)*." Professor Rotenstreich starts with "harmony," which rapidly becomes identified with unity (*Jewish Philosophy in Modern Times* [New York, 1968], 219ff.). Cf. also Norman Lamm, *Faith and Doubt* (New York, 1971), chap. 2.
5. *Orot ha-Kodesh* (Jerusalem, 5724) II, 482–84. All translations from Rav

Kook are mine. On Rav Kook and Schopenhauer, see S. Rosenberg: "Rav Kook and the Blind Sea Monster," *Be-Oro*, ed. Ḥ. Ḥamiel (Jerusalem, 1986), 317–52.

6. E.g., the treatment of other religions in *Arpelei Tohar*, the discussion of Spinoza in *Eder haYekar*, (Jerusalem, 5727), 133–34.

7. The development of Rav Kook's views on tolerance is recounted in Z. Yaron: *Mishnato shel haRav Kook* (Jerusalem, 1974) chap. 12, especially 365. The title of Benjamin Ish-Shalom's essay "Tolerance and Its Theoretical Basis in the Teaching of Rav Kook" in this volume speaks for itself.

8. *Orot ha-Kodesh* I, section 8.

9. Ibid., section 10 ("The Value of the War of Ideas").

10. Rav Kook's critique of Jawitz appears under the title "Special Essay" as an appendix to Volume 12 of the latter's *Toledot Yisrael* (Tel Aviv, 5695) (211–19), reprinted in *Maamarei haReiyah* (Jerusalem, 5740), 105–12. On Jawitz, see *Encyclopedia Judaica* 9: 1303–4 and bibliography, to which add M. Bar-Lev, "R. Zeev Jawitz as Annunciator of Religious-National Education in Israel," *Bi-shevilei ha-Teḥiyyah* 2, (Bar Ilan, 5747). On Rav Kook's relation to Maimonides, see Jacob Dienstag's bibliography (forthcoming, in *Daat*). On criticism of Maimonides' philosophy as an adulteration of Jewish belief on the part of intellectuals preceding Rav Kook's era, see J. Harris: "The Image of Maimonides in Nineteenth-Century Jewish Historiography," *PAAJR* 54: 117–40, in addition to the references on Rabbinic ambivalence toward the *Guide* cited by J. J. Schacter, *Rabbi Jacob Emden: Life and Major Works* (Ph.D. diss., Harvard University, 1988), 644–45 n. 279. Also note, for early Haskalah, Moshe Pelli, *Be-Maavakei Temurah* (Tel Aviv, 1988), 123 n. 15; on more recent writers, Marvin Fox, *Interpreting Maimonides* (Chicago, 1990), 9ff.

11. Op. cit. 211–12. Cf. Rav Kook's description of the role of principles of faith in "The Dogmas" (*Maamarei ha-Reiyah*, 14–15).

12. One of the most ferocious contemporary critics of Rav Kook's mystical orientation has recently reconstructed a 1928 conversation in which Rav Kook regards Maimonides' philosophy as a corrective to the potential dangers of Kabbalah: M. Shashar, *Yeshayahu Leibowitz al Olam uMelo'o* (Jerusalem, 1988), 93–95. The remarks quoted are consistent with the general tenor of Rav Kook's published writings, even as they reflect Professor Leibowitz's own preoccupations. When, however, Leibowitz insists that "the term Kabbalah does not appear in his writings at all. Many fail to notice this," he is himself failing to notice *Orot ha-Kodesh* I, sections 85–86, *inter alia*.

13. See his *Two Types of Faith*.

14. David Shatz, in "The Integration of Religion and Culture: Its Scope and Limits in the Thought of Rav Kook" (see note 12 in the introduction to this volume), has demonstrated how Rav Kook's orientation may limit

his usefulness in confronting many of the intellectual problems of modernity.

15. See *Orot ha-Emunah, passim*, and countless passages in the Kookian corpus.

16. Professor Fox, in his contribution to this volume, bluntly insists on the unsystematic nature of Rav Kook's characteristic mode of thought. Noting that Rav Kook rarely presents rigorous argument in support of his assertions, he goes on to infer that we are unlikely to benefit from trying to supply the missing lines of reasoning and justification, either because it can't be done or because analysis diminishes the visionary force of Rav Kook's poetic prose. Whether this is true is, to my mind, a moot question: the struggle for precision will not dispel the mystery, but it can help ensure that we encounter the right mystery. (Parenthetically, it may be instructive to examine Fox's thesis in the light of H. O. Mounce's comments on Anthony Kenny's analysis of St. John of the Cross's mysticism; see "The Aroma of Coffee" (*Philosophy* 64 [1989]: 159–73). In any event Rav Kook, like other mystics, undertook to communicate his most intimate thoughts in words; unlike many mystics, he accepted the responsibility of guiding others along the paths of propositional belief. The account that emerges is, as the present study demonstrates, highly problematic. Nonetheless I find it a challenging and rewarding attempt to respond to modern perplexity.

17. See epigraph at note 1 above.

18. Text in *Iggerot ha-Reiyah* (Jerusalem, 5703) I, 19–21. For an English translation, see T. Feldman, *Selected Letters of Rav A. Y. Kook* (Maale Adumim, 1986), 31–36. On Seidel, see Y. Kil's introduction to Seidel's *Ḥikrei Mikra* (Jerusalem, 1978), 7–11.

19. *Arpelei Tohar*, 18 (cited by Ish-Shalom in his essay in this volume, p. 197) offers an additional reason to limit free thought, namely the weakness of intellectual fiber among the masses.

20. At this point in my first draft I find a note, in Professor Lawrence Kaplan's hand, referring to Maimonides' *Guide* III, 28. To follow up on his comparative suggestion would require a full elucidation of that chapter; I will not undertake it here.

21. E.g., Rambam, *Hilkhot Avodah Zarah* 2:3.

22. Why "among Jews"? The phrase is probably a rhetorical flourish, testifying to Rav Kook's confidence that the great majority of contemporary rebels do not, God forbid, belong to the category of heretic. Cf. *Iggerot ha-Reiyah* I:138, p. 171 (trans. Feldman, 51–54), where Rav Kook suggests that the pressures of modern culture, rather than deliberate denial, are responsible for contemporary falling away; and see the additional letters 113, 332 (trans. Feldman, 40–50). Cf. N. Lamm: "Loving and Hating Jews as Halakhic Categories" (in *Festschrift in Honor of Walter S. Wurzburger*, ed. H. Goldberg [*Tradition* 24:2]), especially 110–11. It is possible (but not likely) that Rav Kook may hold that

Jews, whether individually or collectively, have more assurance of the truth, and therefore that Jewish heresy testifies more clearly to intellectual-moral bad faith.

23. The apparent equanimity with which Rav Kook pronounces his verdict is belied by the tormented, magnificent "aborted" eulogy for the dead watchmen *Al Bamotenu Halalim* (in *Maamarei ha-Reiyah*, 89–93), where he is torn between the harsh judgment of Halakhah and his admiration for men who devoted, and sacrificed, their lives to build up their people and their land. This leads him to explore halakhic grounds that would permit a eulogy to be said over those who rejected the sancta of Israel so long as they did not maliciously reject their national identity.

24. *Emunot veDeot* 3:7.

25. *Orot*, 144. This passage coheres well with R. Yoel Bin-Nun's thesis, on which see below, note 30. For Rav Kook's halakhic application of this principle, see *Responsa Mishpat Kohen* (Jerusalem, 5726), #124, 273–74.

26. See M. Hallamish, "Some Aspects concerning the Attitude of Kabbalists to Gentiles," in *Philosophia Yisraelit*, ed. A. Kasher and M. Hallamish (Tel Aviv, 1983), 49–71, e.g., his quote from *Shelah:* "Indeed there is no people *['am]* but Israel."

27. The subject-pronoun in the phrase *Hi vaddai kol kakh ketannah* is feminine, implying that the faith *(emunah)* is small (see the translation by Feldman, op. cit. 34) and that this "smallness" is an obstacle before all humanity. But smallness is not ordinarily the defining characteristic of a faith; hence Professor Kaplan (in private communication) treats *ketannah* as a moral term, translating it as "limited and narrow." It seems to me that Rav Kook did not need *ketannah* to express this idea; he had at his disposal perfectly serviceable Hebrew words like *shefalah* ("base," which he had just used to describe the faith of the small nation), *mugbelet ve-tzarah* (limited and narrow). This is why I prefer to take the smallness literally and assimilate the meaning of the phrase to the next phrase, which clearly refers to the isolated nation's prospects for survival. The subject of *Hi vaddai kol kakh ketannah* then becomes the "wide scope" masculine *'am*; the feminine form *hi* results, according to this reading, from the influence of the interposed feminine noun *emunah*.

28. Cf. John Stuart Mill (1861): "Nobody can suppose that it is not more beneficial to a Breton, or a Basque of French Navarre, to be brought into the current of the ideas and feelings of a highly civilized and cultivated people—to be a member of the French nationality . . .— than to sulk on his own rocks, the half-savage relic of past times, revolving in his own little mental orbit, without participation or interest in the general movement of the world" (*Considerations on Representative Government* [Chicago, 1962], 313f.). Note that Mill, for

whom the essential national idea is not a value in itself, calculates the benefit to be gained by the member of the small group associating itself with a larger entity, whereas for Rav Kook it is the presumed damage wrought by the small nation's perpetuation that undermines its right to exist.

29. For instances of the common nineteenth-century argument from unfeasability against unlimited national self-determination, see E. J. Hobsbawm, *Nations and Nationalism since 1780* (Cambridge, 1990), 30ff. The idea that all nations, however small, may claim the right of political self-determination gains momentum late in the century and becomes dominant under the impact of the Wilsonian commitment to small-state nationalism in the aftermath of World War I. A. Margalit and J. Raz, at the end of a rather ahistorical analysis ("National Self-Determination," *Journal of Philosophy* 87 [September 1990]: 439–61), raise the problem of damage to other groups caused by self-determination (459, conditions 4 and 5) and apparently leave the feasibility problem to the discretion of the seceding group.

30. *Orot* (Jerusalem, 1961) 130. This passage, among others, militates against Y. Bin-Nun's theory that Rav Kook denied the legitimacy, for non-Jews, of all categories other than the human individual and the entire human race. See his "Nationalism, Humanity and *Knesset Israel*" (in *The World of Rav Kook's Thought*, 207–54). His analysis is more convincing at the eschatological level, which would be consonant with the position I take in the text. The best proof for the last statement is *Orot* (143): "The elevation of Knesset Israel at its highest level, so long as there is a distinction of peoples in the world, that is the level of the point of Zion." So too Ibid. (156): "Humanity is worthy of being united as one family, then all aggression and all bad traits deriving from the distinctions of peoples and their boundaries would cease. But the world requires an essential refinement. . . . This deficiency was supplied by Knesset Israel." See also Yaron, chap. 11.

31. Notice how the dialectical thrust prominent in Rav Kook's philosophical writings makes itself felt in our supposedly more sober, prosaic discussion.

32. "Negative campaigning" is, for better or for worse, quite prevalent in certain circles of recent Orthodoxy, the guiding light being R. Elḥanan Wasserman *(Kovetz Maamarim)*. As far as I can tell, Rav Kook never explains away the failure of his opponents to assent to his positions by denigrating their characters and motives.

33. I need hardly note that the problem of relativism is also the Achilles' heel of neo-Wittgensteinian and Gadamerian philosophies of religion, whatever their value in assisting to the recovery of religious language.

34. The idea that the ethics of belief are connected with the principle of autonomy was suggested to me by R. Gale's very different argument in "William James and the Ethics of Belief" *(American Philosophical*

Quarterly 17 [1980]: 1–14). The notion that the collective, rather than the individual, can function as the epistemological subject owes something to ideas about the autonomy of linguistic (i.e., social) institutions current among some neo-Wittgensteinians. See, for example, F. Kerr, *Theology after Wittgenstein* (London, 1986), especially his critique of Karl Rahner, 7–14, which concludes with the judgment that "this mentalist-individualist conception of the self seems difficult to reconcile with the insistence on hierarchy and tradition that marks Rahner's Roman Catholic ecclesiology." It would be worthwhile to compare Rav Kook's attempt to found religious commitment on the essential national idea with Isaac Breuer's explicit view of the Torah as juridically binding on believer and nonbeliever alike as the collective will of the nation of Israel. See his "Torah, Law and Nation" (in *Tziyyunei Derekh*, [Jerusalem, 1982]), 17–19.

35. N. Murphy, for example, in *Theology in the Age of Scientific Reasoning* (Ithaca, 1990), 200–202, regards the authority of the community, rather than that of the individual, as one of three major contrasts between postmodern and modern thought. While Rav Kook shows affinity with another of Murphy's pillars of postmodernism, namely holism in epistemology, and might even incline toward the third (a holistic doctrine of meaning), he can be described, at most, as a precursor of postmodernist philosophy.

36. E.g., *Ha-Yahadut ve-ha-Tarbut ha-Ḥilonit,* 111–42; "Repentance in Twentieth-Century Jewish Thought" (in Ish-Shalom and Rosenberg, *The World of Rav Kook's Thought,* 349–72).

37. Individuals who had lost their Orthodox theological moorings but wished to continue, not only their Jewish affiliation, but the Orthodox (or rather Orthoprax) way of life notwithstanding, existed at this time in Germany too. See J. Levinger, "Life and Achievement of Isaac Breuer," in *Isaac Breuer: Studies in His Thought,* ed. R. Horwitz (Ramat Gan, 1988), 15.

38. For the actual state of religious commitment among the Zionists entering Palestine at this time, see D. Knaani, *Ha-Aliyah ha-Sheniyah ha-Ovedet ve-Yaḥasah la-Dat ve-la-Masoret* (Tel Aviv, 1976), and Agnon's unforgetting and unforgettable portrayal in his novel *Temol Shilshom.* On Rav Kook's 1914 repentance campaign in the Galilee settlements, see M. Eliav, *Massa' ha-Rabbanim le-Moshevot ha-Galil bi-Shenat 5674, Katz Jubilee Volume* (Jerusalem, 1980), 379–96), and A. Frankel, "These Were the Journeys," *Sinai* 97:1–6, 16–60. N. Govrin's *Meora' Brenner* (Jerusalem, 1985) reports on the fascinating affair precipitated when Brenner (in 1911) wrote an article in which he contemplated with equanimity the possibility of a national Jew whose religion is Christian. Many secular Zionists were scandalized and the newspaper was threatened with withdrawal of financial support. Rav Kook is

conspicuous in the ensuing debate by his absence. His sometime confidant A. Z. Rabinowitz abstained from attacking Brenner. On Brenner's attitude to Rav Kook, see *The Traditional Jewish World in the Writings of Joseph Hayim Brenner* (Ph.D. diss., Yeshiva University diss., 1979) by my colleague Shmuel Schneider, 157–71; on Rav Kook's view of Brenner, see 164 n. 18.

39. Most notably in *Orot ha-Kodesh* II, 537ff. (the first section available in my English trans. in *Shevivim* [World Zionist Organization, 1987]), 22–23. See also Yaron, 96–98.

40. A similar inquiry can be started up with respect to the position taken by my mentor, R. Joseph Soloveitchik, who writes: "Regardless of the shortcomings of pragmatism as a solution to our most perplexing epistemological problems . . . [t]he ethical implications of any philosophical theory, as to its beneficence or detriment to the moral advancement of man, should many a time decide the worth of the doctrine" (*The Halakhic Mind*, [Philadelphia, 1986], 52). This inquiry would, I believe, connect up with Rav Soloveitchik's espousal of what he calls "pluralism."

41. Alternately, one might counter that Rav Kook simply chose the most clear-cut instance of an immoral essential national idea.

42. One might cavil with this inference too. Perhaps the morally motivated rebels in Rav Kook's text are forsaking their nation for the sake of that which is objectively true, though *they* themselves do not have adequate grounds for judging their position to be true as well as moral.

43. See *Orot ha-Kodesh* III, proem 27, which serves as the epigraph to R. Yehudah Amital's "The Significance of Rav Kook's Teaching for Our Generation" (Ish-Shalom and Rosenberg, *The World of Rav Kook's Thought*, 423–35).

44. *Maamarei ha-Reiyah* 507–10.

45. Jawitz, op. cit., 217. Cf. Rav Kook's differing justifications for *metzitzah* (sucking of the blood) at circumcision, collected in *Tov Ro'i al Massekhet Shabbat*, ed. B. Elon (Jerusalem, 5747), 126–128 as well as 78, and Elon's notes ad. loc.

46. Reprinted in James, *Essays on Faith and Morals*, selected by R. B. Perry (Cleveland, 1962), 32–62, and many other collections. G. McCarthy, ed. *The Ethics of Belief Debate* (*AAR Studies in Religion* 41 [Atlanta, 1986] collects many documents pertaining to the late nineteenth-century Anglo-American context to which James is contributing. See the discussion in G. Myers, *William James: His Life and Thought* (New Haven, 1986), 446–60 and bibliographies in J. Wernham, *James's Will-to-Believe Doctrine* (Montreal, 1987) and Myers, 604 n. 13.

47. James had been exploring these ideas as early as 1875. His famous essay appeared in 1897. It is virtually impossible for Rav Kook to have been aware of James's writings in 1905. On Rav Kook's access to philosophi-

cal developments, see E. Goldman, "Rav Kook's Relation to European Thought," *The World of Rav Kook's Thought*, 139–48.

48. Myers, 453.
49. This terminology was introduced to contemporary Orthodox thought in the title essay of N. Lamm's *Faith and Doubt*, who places his analysis in an avowedly Kookian frame of reference.
50. I assume throughout my discussion that Rav Kook, like James, would adopt a version of epistemological voluntarism. It would not seem to matter if he is a direct or an indirect voluntarist. Rav Kook's Thesis 2 and even more so Thesis 3 *might* reflect the inability of the will to believe certain propositions (though one could say more simply that they proscribe belief in these propositions as unreasonable). For a classification of the classical philosophical views on the subject, see L. Pojman, *Religious Belief and the Will* (London, 1986). I am more sanguine than Pojman about the truth of some version of voluntarism.
51. *Iggerot Reiyah* (Jerusalem, 5683), #74, 200–204. This first selection of letters was, please note, published in Rav Kook's lifetime.
52. The reference to Maimonides on the bottom of 201 should read *Hilkhot. Shegagot* 11:8 (not 11:5 as printed).
53. Sanhedrin 10:3; Shevuot 1:4; Sotah 3:3, listed by Fox, *Interpreting Maimonides*, 44–45 n. 25. In *Guide* III, 48, Maimonides prefers one mishnaic view over another. See also *Mavo ha-Talmud* by R. Shmuel ha-Nagid (printed in the back of the standard BT *Berakhot*), 45b-46a.
54. *Iggerot* I, #302 (letter of 25 Iyyar 5670 [1910]).
55. Shabbat 64b, *inter alia*. The example of human blood discussed below is codified *Shulḥan Arukh, Yoreh Deah* 66:10. For a detailed discussion of *mar'it 'ayin*, see *Entzyklopedia Talmudit* 17, s.v. Ḥashad, columns 567–756, especially sections 3–4; for the prohibition of human blood, see vol. 7: s.v. Dam, columns 426, 428–30.
56. Would *mar'it 'ayin* apply if people became mind readers? If they could render their neighbors' skin transparent? As a halakhist one might simply say that later generations have no obligation to expand the stringencies of the Talmud. See *Entzyklopedia Talmudit* 7:428 and n. 118.
57. Is there an affinity between this position and that of Maimonides' introduction to the *Guide*, which justifies the oblique expression of esoteric views so as to prevent the masses from becoming involved in matters beyond their ken? Cf. Kierkegaard's ironic aphorism: "How absurd men are! They never use the liberties they have, they demand those they do not have. They have freedom of thought, they demand freedom of speech" (*Either/Or*, trans. David F. Swenson [Princeton, 1971], I, 19).
58. To the brief bibliography on *Da'as Torah* in my "Who Speaks for Torah—and How?" (in *Religious Zionism*, ed. S. Spero [Mesilot, 1989]),

165 n. 10, add now two essays in *Rabbinic Authority and Personal Autonomy*, ed. Moshe Sokol (Northvale, N. J., 1992): Lawrence Kaplan, *"Daas Torah:* A Modern Conception of Rabbinic Authority," and Chaim I. Waxman, "Towards a Sociology of *Psak"* (the latter is also found in *Tradition* 25, n. 3 [Spring 1991], 12–25). Dov Frimer has work in progress on the same topic. The studies by Kaplan and Waxman were presented at the First Orthodox Forum, convened by Dr. Norman Lamm, President of Yeshiva University, in 1989. See also M. Piekarz, *Ḥasidut Polin bein Shtei haMilhamot u-biGezerot 5700–5705* (Jerusalem, 1990), 81–96.

59. See the critique of Jawitz in the text above at note 10.
60. See, for example, *Arpelei Tohar,* 18, and *Maamarei ha-Reiyah,* 41.
61. I have touched upon the question of individual responsibility for decisions involving inwardness in "Synthesis and the Unification of Human Existence," *Tradition* 21 (4): 37–51.
62. Cf. R. Simḥa Zissel of Kelm, *Ha-Torah ve-ha-Ḥokhmah* (Jerusalem, 5724), 88–90, who stresses the importance of getting one's legitimate point of view across to the Torah elite. Thus it is "the beginning of wisdom that a man should see to it that his Torah and actions conform to the depth of true Halakhah according to his abilities to fulfill his duty to Heaven, and then he must demonstrate to the few discerning sages—for not many are wise—that they too will concur to his Torah, his actions and his conduct. For without this it will not be accepted on high."
63. *Orot ha-Kodesh* III, 282. The pertinence of this passage, ostensibly dealing with the ethics of asceticism, was brought home to me by B. Ish-Shalom, *HaRav Kook: Bein Ratzionalism le-Mistikah* (Tel Aviv, 1990), 320 n. 100.
64. R. Zvi Yehudah Kook (introduction to the posthumous edition of 5703, viii) gives the year of first publication as 5685 (1924–25).
65. Selected by whom? The second epigraph to this study points to the complicated relation between Rav Kook's judgment and that of his "censors."
66. Prefatory remarks on reverse of the title page, 5683 edition.
67. *Iggerot ha-Reiyah* (1943 edition!), prefatory page viii.
68. Elon cites part of it in his collection *Tov Ro'i al Massekhet Shabbat,* 62–63. It is perhaps not irrelevant that this volume was published after R. Zvi Yehudah's death and that, like *Maamarei Reiyah,* it does not bear the Mosad haRav Kook imprimatur. The letter is also cited in Moshe Tzuriel's bibliographic *Otzerot ha-Reiyah* (Shaalvim, 1988), 2: 824ff., among "halakhic letters omitted from *Iggerot ha-Reiyah"* (see 820 and table of contents).
69. N. Gutel has recently suggested that in some cases R. Zvi Yehudah censored the 1923 edition only to restore Rav Kook's original words in

the posthumous edition: "Our master [Rav Kook] did not lack controversies and R. Zvi Yehudah saw no reason to add to them" (*Matzot
Yad o Matzot Mekhonah, HaTsofeh*, 14 Nisan 5750, 7–8).

70. It is a pleasure to thank Lawrence Kaplan and David Shatz for valuable
editorial commentary, both stylistic and bibliographic. My student
Mitchell Waxman wisely urged me to expand the first draft of the
opening section.

CHAPTER 9

Immortality, Natural Law, and the Role of Human Perception in the Writings of Rav Kook

Tamar Ross

In an oft-cited article, the noted Israeli philosopher S. H. Bergman discusses what appears to him to be the startling suggestion made by Rav Kook that a person, through *teshuvah* (repentance), is capable of overcoming death and attaining immortality.[1] As Rav Kook writes: "Our temporal existence is but a spark of the grandeur of eternal existence; and it is impossible to actualize the precious treasure concealed in temporal life without a measure of alignment to eternal life."[2] Thus, it is claimed, instead of Heidegger's conception of civilization being propelled by the awareness of the finality of all individual experience, Rav Kook sees the struggle to achieve a oneness with eternity as the basic factor generating all human endeavor and all movement of the cosmos at large.[3]

I

While all this is true, one is still left wondering exactly what Rav Kook meant by these views. Anyone who has had any experience in reading Rav Kook will recognize a familiar frustration here: despite the beauty and exalted quality of expression, one is often left with the annoying business of trying to understand what precisely is being said, fortified by the conviction that behind all the poetry there is a well-defined vision, waiting to be extracted.[4]

In the attempt to spell out more specifically the mechanics in-volved in the process of overcoming death, two alternative—possi-bilities present themselves. Rav Kook may have meant (1) that as a result of *teshuvah*, man will quite literally bring about a change in the physical world and abolish death as we know it in everyday life; or (2) that as a result of *teshuvah*, some sort of cognitive change will take place in man's perception of the cessation of his physical being, so that what was previously understood to mean death will now be understood merely as passage to another form of existence.

One might direct a query to Professor Bergman as well: Exactly what view of Rav Kook does he find to be so remarkable and what is so remarkable about that view? Bergman cites various modern thinkers that have demythologized the concept of immortality and spiritualized it beyond recognition, and points out that Rav Kook moved in the other direction. But what *is* this other direction? Certainly Rav Kook wasn't the first to suggest that there is an afterlife; this is a thoroughly classic Jewish belief! And if what is meant, then, is not the abolition of physical death itself, but merely the abolition of the fear of death, surely this is merely a question of the personal degree of one's religious conviction, and therefore rela-tive to the individual concerned. So perhaps what Bergman and Rav Kook are affirming is, after all, the first alternative—that man will quite literally abolish physical death as we know it.

Bergman himself is aware of the possibility of different interpre-tations and, in a debate with the equally noted Israeli philosopher Nathan Rotenstreich over this very question, seems to opt for the first alternative.[5] But he does not reject the role of cognition in the process. Instead, he introduces a subtle distinction between the call for a change in man's "perspective" (which he identifies with the interpretation that Rotenstreich attributes to Rav Kook) and the call for a change in man's "consciousness" (which is what Bergman understand Rav Kook as calling for)—the difference being that the first is not capable of effecting any objective change in reality, whereas the second somehow does.

An initial glance at the original cluster of passages in *Orot Ha-Kodesh* to which Bergman refers[6] would, however, seem to support Rotenstreich's view and not Bergman's. For these passages create the definite impression that Rav Kook, in his discussion of immortality, refers to a transformation of man's *perception* of reality, rather than to a transformation of reality itself. Thus, for example, Rav Kook writes "Death is an optical illusion. Its impurity lies in its false nature. For what people call death is really only the intensification of life and its strength."[7] Moreover, he continues by suggesting that it is merely the absorption with materialism and its petty, fleeting values that blinds us to the true nature of life and breeds in us a misguided dread of physical mortality.[8] True, Rav Kook does make reference to the latest advances of medicine in his day which have succeeded in prolonging longevity,[9] but the importance of these could be mainly psychological: the fact that we know today that we have relatively more time on this earth to fully accomplish all that we would like allows us to feel less pressured by the limitations of our physiology and fear of death. As a result, we are more open to an appreciation of life for positive reasons (i.e., the windows to eternity that it affords) and can thus view it on its own intrinsic merits, rather than out of the negative fear that, whatever it is worth, it will in any case be snatched away all too soon.

Nonetheless, I think Bergman is right, and I would like to offer an interpretation of Rav Kook's views that is close to his. I believe that in welcoming the advances in medicine that have extended longevity and in stressing their psychological value, Rav Kook is not negating the possibility of abolishing physical death as well. In other words, I think Rav Kook esteemed man's capacity to improve his this-worldly, physical situation, not just for the psychological benefits it offers, but also because it is directly relevant to the process of conquering death. This capacity, that is, serves as a precursor; it gives us a taste of the eventual eschatological situation in which physical death will no longer take place and immortality will belong to both soul and body. The "world to come" in Rav Kook's eschatology is not merely the purely spiritual state of affairs that already exists, as it is in Maimonides, for example. Rav Kook, rather, supports the rival tradition, formulated by Rabbenu Saadya Gaon and the Ramban (Naḥmanides), and understands the "world to come" as something to be revealed, from *our* point of view, within the dimensions of time and history. And his emphasis on the necessity of overcoming death even in this world (*'olam ha-zeh*) is related to his general "gradualism," in which the later period does not suddenly replace the former, but grows out of it, bit by bit.

In order to further explicate and defend this interpretation and pinpoint exactly what Rav Kook had in mind, it would be helpful to map his views onto a spectrum of similar opinions about these issues held by other thinkers, both early and more recent. An additional benefit of this exercise will be a new definition of the relationship between miracle and natural law and a heightened understanding of the value of human effort in Rav Kook's world view.

II

The notion that man is capable of increasing sovereignty over his existence by way of extending his perceptions beyond the level of the material is hardly an innovation of Rav Kook. Several important Jewish thinkers have pursued this line of thought—particularly those of a mystic bent.

We might do well by beginning with the Ramban and his distinction between *nissim mefursamim* (publicized miracles) and *nissim nistarim* (hidden miracles).[10] Now both *nissim mefursamim* and *nissim nistarim* are to be distinguished from blatant abrogations of the laws of nature (which are nowadays generally termed *nissim geluyim*). The Ramban acknowledges the occurrence of such blatant miracles but relegates them to the formative stages of Jewish nationhood in the distant past. Such occurrences were effected on rare occasions for pedagogic reasons, in order to inculcate belief in God, creation, and providence. These occasions in fact were so rare that they were enshrined as the pivotal content of key *mitzvot*, whose object was to commit them to the collective national memory. However, when the Ramban refers to miracles in general, he is referring to either *nissim mefursamim* or *nissim nistarim*. Because such miracles are not intended as pedagogical devices designed to impress, but rather are tools of divine providence, neither *nissim nistarim* nor *nissim mefursamim* need involve any obvious deviation from the normal course of events. They are rather to be understood as a timely coincidence of certain "chance" occurrences, which were possible within—though not enjoined by—natural law. These "chance" occurrences are, however, in accordance with a higher, moral set of considerations. Thus, if a certain individual is miraculously saved from what seemed to be almost certain death, this could be explained by a fortuitous coincidence of perfectly natural, but chance factors (e.g., his sweater stuck to the ridge of the window and caught him in mid-air, just as he had begun falling from the top of the Empire State Building). The fact that the man concerned was saved in the course of trying to perform a great *mitzvah* (preventing an innocent child from falling off that same building) is significant and evidence of divine providence. But the miraculous character of the occurrence need not necessarily be regarded as an abrogation of natural law. So too, if a whole nation continuously wins its wars even at great odds when it adheres to the *mitzvot*, and consistently suffers defeat when it transgresses the will of God, this need not involve any change in those areas determined by natural causality. That such events occur is not impossible in accordance with natural law, only unlikely. But this improbability is still only statistical. Therefore, this "miracle" is, intrinsically, no more miraculous than the "miracle" of the tzaddik saved by his sweater. The only reason why the example of the tzaddik saved by his sweater is termed a *nes nistar*, while the example of the people whose winning or losing battles correlates precisely with their obedience or disobedience to God is termed a *nes nigleh*, is that in the latter case large groups of people are amazed at the occurrence of this series of events.

To be sure, the man who is cognizant of the existence of a higher moral law can and should use this knowledge to his advantage. This is the meaning of Ramban's declaration[11] that were the Israelites, when living in the land of Israel and observing *mitzvot*, to choose to turn to God to be cured of disease, they would be assured of their cure in accordance with their individual merit. On the other hand, if they turn to doctors, as they have consistently done in the past and present, they will be left to the whims of chance. Some will be cured by doctors, others will not, and the outcomes, whether positive or negative, will be in accordance with their fate and not necessarily in accordance with their merit. But even though this knowledge can influence the course of man's destiny, in no way does the Ramban indicate that a heightened level of perception on the part of man can abolish or even mitigate the inescapability of physical death.

A bolder estimate of the role of heightened awareness of metaphysical law in controlling human destiny is taken by the Maharal (Judah Loew Bezalel of Prague). The Maharal, even more than the Ramban, is committed to the fixedness of the laws of nature.[12] Nevertheless, he allows for the possibility that those who are attuned to the moral or metaphysical laws of the universe are capable of determining not only the chance factors within the parameters of natural law (thus effecting a *nes nistar*), but also of determining their destiny by means of factors beyond those limits (thereby initiating *nissim geluyim*). Thus the Maharal, in discussing Joshua's miraculous ability to stop the sun's motion at Givon, writes: "This is why Joshua stopped the sun—because the sun is physical, and Joshua who was possessed of the metaphysical Torah *[Torah Sikhlit]* was able to govern the sun . . . the principle thus being that a virtuous man is superior to the sun, for his soul is divorced from matter."[13] But here too it must be emphasized that even the Maharal does not believe that the tzaddik's heightened ability to manipulate the course of his destiny involves any modification of existing law; rather it only makes use of an added perspective outside of its domain. The implications of a metaphysical law can be brought to bear on the natural scene, thereby revealing hitherto unimagined possibilities, but they do not actually violate the immutability of actual constraints in the realm of nature. Thus, miracles and nature can coexist side by side, and the experience of the wonder-working tzaddik should be likened to that of a creature ordinarily experiencing a two-dimensional universe who is suddenly exposed to the possibilities inherent in the perception of a third dimension.[14] This should serve to explain the ground for the Maharal's apparently preposterous claim that "tzaddikim . . . because they are tzaddikim . . . by right ought to be granted [everlasting] life by God, and never die, even though this violates nature. . . . And were it not for the fact that the tzaddik does not desire a change in the order of things [for death is called for in the order of reality], God would institute miracles for [or with] them, so that the tzaddik would not die." Only because "tzaddikim do not cast aside nature, for nature is the worthy way of running the world . . .

and they do not desire the world to exceed the bounds of true order . . . does death come."[15] Because a supernatural order exists alongside a natural one, it is possible for tzaddikim to recede at will to a mortal existence without being bound by the reality of immortality on the metaphysical plane. Thus, even according to the Maharal, the heightened control that the tzaddik has over his fate, due to his greater awareness of, or sensitivity to, the spiritual laws of causality, does not involve abolishing the inevitability of death in the physical domain.

An even more dramatic view of the power of spiritual perception to control human destiny in the physical realm can be discerned in the teachings of a near-contemporary exponent of the Lithuanian Musar (ethics) movement, Rav Eliyahu Dessler. Rav Dessler—inspired by a kabbalistic version of post-Kantianism[16]—expresses a Hume-like view of natural law as no more than a construct of our psychological expectations. He therefore asserts that the only limits to physical possibilities are those imposed on it by our illusions. In a manner similar to the Ramban, he too distinguishes between *nes nistar* and *nes galuy*.[17] However, while for the Ramban this distinction is fundamental, for Rav Dessler it is superficial. This is because Rav Dessler denies the reality of natural law altogether. The normal running of the universe according to "laws" of nature is in itself an illusion. It results from God's own voluntary response to our obtuseness to the immediacy of His control over all affairs of the world. When the tzaddik, by virtue of his complete trust in God, demonstrates that he has pierced this veil of illusion, God no longer feels the need to "play games" with him, and throws to the winds all the arbitrary constraints of natural causality. It is no more natural that a seedling buried in the ground should rot and then sprout new life than that a corpse should be buried, decay, and then be resurrected. To the extent that we internalize this understanding, we lay ourselves open to the possibility of its occurrence.

Although Rav Dessler phrases his views mainly in the religious idiom of a personalist God who reacts to our degree of trust in Him on the level of artificially constructed rewards and punishments, rewards and punishments that are extraneous to the position we hold and are imposed from without, it is obvious that he has a more sophisticated view of the integral relationship between faith perceptions and their real life consequences. The would-be Sabbath observer will never discover that closing his business on the Sabbath is an economically viable proposition so long as he bases his decision on practical "scientific" calculations,[18] not because God punishes him for his lack of faith, but because he hasn't opened himself up to that realm of experience that transcends such considerations, and evokes its rewards as a natural effect of such exposure. So too, the belief in immortality brings immortality with it, not because God decides to reward us for our faith, but because the belief itself leads to the way of life that will make it possible. The skeptical rationalist might easily object that Rav Dessler's theory is self-justifying and does not lend itself readily to empirical testing; obviously the would-be Sabbath observer who believes fiercely enough in the possibility of "making it" financially will do so, because the very definition of what is the necessary minimum required for his livelihood will adjust itself accordingly. If the called-for effects do not occur, the handy explanation might be that his resolve was not strong enough. Nevertheless, even such naturalistic attempts to explain away Rav Dessler's theories regarding the relationship between human perception and physical reality are not capable of disproving the power of faith to alter the physical course of events. Unlike the Ramban and the Maharal, Rav Dessler can continue to maintain that the barrier between the everyday and the fantastic does not exist. He might merely concede that it is not theurgic magic that is involved in this concept of the miraculous, but the perfect synchronization of man's will with that of the Divine.

III

Reverting back to Rav Kook, if we would refer merely to the passages from his writings cited above, it might seem that his claims for the power of perception to actually modify events are the most modest of all these thinkers. What is involved in the ability of the ba'al-teshuvah to achieve immortality would seem to be merely a redefinition of what "life" is, a redefinition that divorces it from its material trappings. No supernatural mumbo-jumbo here, not even the minimal tampering with the loopholes of destiny provided by chance. However, even in the context of the passages described above, Rav Kook gives the lie to an overspiritualized rendering of his view in a section that reads as follows:

> Why should the soul not attach itself to the body to give it life always; why should it not realize the full extent of its scope, orchestrating the task while residing in its exalted center, the body and its accoutrements? Only because the will has caved in under the darkness of lowly subjugation to the slavery of the physical and the bestial, and this filth has stamped itself indelibly on man.[19]

Rav Kook then goes on to indicate that the control of the soul over the body will increase in direct relationship to the measure of purity the former achieves. The ultimate conclusion of the process will take place when the will to exalt and improve life will overcome all base materialist tendencies and purge the creative spirit completely. He visualizes this climax in the destruction of our present-day souls and the appearance of new ones that "transcend the body, create it, draw from it, and through it reach exalted heights," leading to a will for an elevated life that will banish death forever.[20]

From these passages it becomes apparent that, on the one hand, Rav Kook does not regard natural, everyday, physical categories of existence as irrelevant to the exalted life of the spirit. Immortality does not preclude physical existence. On the other hand, he indicates that with the advent of everlasting life, nature will not remain in its current state of existence but will somehow be transformed. In accordance with Rav Kook's general disposition to think in kabbalistic terms, he brings to bear notions of the refined type of matter that various mystical midrashim, later amplified upon by Zoharic and Lurianic literature, attributed to Adam ha-Rishon, Primordial Man.[21] According to these notions, it was only as a result of eating the forbidden fruits of the Tree of Knowledge of Good and Evil that this higher type of matter became gross to the point of functioning as an impediment to spirituality, rather than clothing and protecting it. Rav Kook, as did various Musar teachers before him who were influenced by the Kabbalah,[22] interpreted this sin of eating the forbidden fruit as a cognitive one. But, whereas the more usual understanding assumes that Adam's cognitive lapse resided in his attributing any reality at all to a will outside of God's, Rav Kook understands the lapse as residing in Adam's attributing to nature an existence independent of the world of the spirit, as opposed to his seeing it as part of a continuum. Thus, the key to restoring the blissful state of material existence enjoyed by man in the Garden of Eden lies in destroying the false dichotomy we now perceive to exist between the physical and spiritual. What Rav Kook concludes from this is not only that spirituality includes some enhanced form of material existence, but also that the very mechanism of enhancement is facilitated by the very spiritual vision of a continuum between the physical and the spiritual.

Man creates cultures by changing natural conditions in order to maintain his spiritual self. In Rav Kook's estimation, the fact that our century has witnessed dramatic advancements in medicine, technology, the intercommunication between individuals, communities, and nations, and our knowledge of the cosmos at large[23] is not an accident of fate; it is born of the gradual collapse of the previous models, or controlling images, of our civilization that until now served to symbolize the relationship of humanity to its environment. The current need for establishing a heightened sense of immortality through these advances should be seen neither as a compensatory escape, nor as a pathological refusal to face facts, but rather as the natural by-product of a new sense of the ties that we now begin to perceive with other forms of life related to us physically, biologically, sociologically, or historically, in the past and in the future. The traditional imagery of separation, fragmentation, and helpless immobility in approaching the subject of the human lifespan and the relationship of the human organism to larger contemporary contexts yielded limited and distorted insights regarding the potential of human experience. Because we now sense greater connectedness, integrity, and freedom of movement as a more adequate representation of the self-world relationship, we actively seek to express these unitary visions in a new mode of interpretive anticipation of interaction with our environment as a base for cultural activity. This is what is meant by teshuvah.[24]

Stated baldly, the interaction between mental attitudes and our physical welfare is completely mutual and reciprocal. Our technological advances in prolonging life work psychologically to promote appreciation of spirituality per se, while, at the same time, our sensitivity to spiritual values enhances our ability for scientific advances (just as the religious consciousness makes for a better artist, poet, philosopher, moralist, and the like, by providing these with their life-sustenance). I am not trying to suggest by this that Rav Kook would celebrate science-fiction fantasies of freezer survivals and other futuristic prescriptions for bypassing everyday ideas of death as ideal responses to physical mortality. Ultimately, Rav Kook would agree with Maimonides that these palliatives have nothing to do with the true transcendence of death.[25] What I am arguing is that in Rav Kook's eyes, the very ability of human technology to provide such psychological palliatives that facilitate true immortality is itself the type of break with the natural order beyond the level of cognitive change that is made possible only through *teshuvah*. It is a moot point whether Rav Kook's understanding of the aggadic description of the end of days as a time when ready-made buns will spring out of the earth is strictly literal or loosely metaphoric.[26] In either case, he obviously regards an easy life in physical terms as an inevitable, concomitant, fringe benefit of elevation of the spirit. By the same token, it is a moot point whether immortality involves the prolonging of physical existence as we know it, or a more rarefied version of physical existence. But whatever the specific form physical life will take in the future, the very possibility of its prolongation will be ensured by the fact that such questions pale in the face of our concern for the more intense, spiritual concentrate.

IV

This interpretation of Rav Kook's view of the relationship between man's capacity to increase his life span and cognitive achievement is reminiscent of both the Maharal and Rav Dessler. These three thinkers, unlike the Ramban, see in man's escape from mortality palpable evidence of the automatic effect of changed perceptions, unconcealed by the category of "chance" divine intervention. But while the Maharal allows for the possibility of the miracle to exist only *alongside* nature in the life of the tzaddik, Rav Dessler insists that nature is completely obliterated for the tzaddik. It is here that Rav Kook intercedes with a solution that lies somewhere between the two.

In a significant passage that deals with his futuristic visions in a different context, Rav Kook states as follows:

> With the ascension of the world, nature will appear as a miracle, full of revelations of ideal inclinations and a general vibrant will, exact and grand, with all the grandeur of the highest refinement. And even then a concealed light will appear as higher miracle, the revelation of whose light will radiate and vitalize the light of the ordinary miracle, which will then be as the substance of nature today.[27]

This passage requires careful consideration. In ideal terms, Rav Kook does not require miracles as part of his religious scheme. For him the world as it stands should be sufficient evidence of God's existence. Therefore, the first sentence of this passage contends that with *teshuvah*, nature will appear as miracle because the *ba'al teshuvah*, having internalized spiritual values, will see in the existing expression of God's will not a restricting impediment, but rather the perfect expression of what should be. His transformed perception of what is important and what is trivial will allow him to live in peace and harmony with what does in fact exist, and see in it the best of all possible worlds. His physical death will not appear to him as tragic or untimely; he will welcome it because he will be capable of regarding it as the happy occasion for advancing into a higher form of existence.

Despite the fact that Rav Dessler would abolish the category of "nature" altogether, this interpretation is virtually consonant with Rav Dessler's views. But the second sentence of the above passage does not allow us to remain with so fixed and passive a view of man's role and of nature in the process of self-determination. For Rav Kook recognizes that a person, as a result of the weaknesses of human nature and the limitations of human vision, requires from time to time a fresh reminder of the supremacy of the spiritual; and it is precisely this supremacy of the spiritual that, according to the mainstream traditional view, miracles are all about (as the Ramban and the Maharal strove to stress).[28] This is effected by man's discovery of a new possibility—beyond the reach of what was previously regarded as the limits of normal modes of existence—which now becomes operative in our lives and renders our previous notions of nature obsolete. Each new conquest stretches the former

definition of nature further, by including within it a fresh understanding of what God's infinite power does in fact entail. It also
serves to open up new vistas of the miraculous and beckons us to
higher levels of aspiration and understanding yet to be disclosed.[29]
The dialectic between life and death, spirit and matter, miracle and
nature is a never-ending one, but by eliminating the element of fear
we can narrow the gap between the apparent opposites and transform the dichotomy into a continuum. The actual efforts of civilization to do so thereby acquire a significance of metaphysical pro-
portions, blurring the lines of demarcation between Creator and
created being.[30] This would explain the diametrically opposed attitudes that Rav Kook and Rav Dessler exhibit regarding the importance of involvement in worldly concerns.[31]

V

In sum, it may be said that what distinguishes Rav Kook's attitude
to the obscenity—as he sees it—of physical death in the present
unredeemed universe is his gradualist version of cognitive activism.
Our present-day world is continuously moving in the direction of
the ideal world, which will exist in the end of days. The optimistic
conviction that the continuous dialectic between this-worldly visions and those beyond must in the long run be forward-moving
is nourished by the basically acosmic orientation of Rav Kook's
worldview,[32] which understands the negative end of any polarity as
negative merely *in appearance*, due to its partial, restricted view of
the whole. The fact that we will never completely obliterate the
distinction between part and whole (if only because our memory
includes the past)[33] is what makes evolution necessary and forces
eternity to be perceived, from our point of view, via the prism of
history, development, and change, as a gradual process rather than
in absolute terms. But it is within our power, by rising above the
restricted, everyday conception of what happens around us, to hasten the process, both for ourselves and for mankind in general. We
can literally work in the direction of conquering death and not
merely the fear of it. For death itself and not merely the fear of it—
is a product of the limits of our vision.

Rav Kook is revealed here as bringing to fruition several parallel lines of thought that have been fermenting ever since the first open influences of mystic thought in the Ramban's era:

1. that immortality includes a physical element;
2. that the "world to come" will be ushered in by concrete events within the realm of time and history;
3. that immortality is effected by cognitive development. (This last strand has its parallels in European idealism from the time of Kant to such contemporaries as Nelson Goodman.)[34]

We have seen the limited extent to which one or two of these strands appears in the Maharal and Rav Dessler. We could also have elaborated upon their crystallization in some recent thinkers, but omitted to do so for reasons of space.[35] The particular contribution of Rav Kook lies, first, in his ability to transform the blurring of the distinction between the natural and the miraculous into an actual historical process happening before our eyes, a process to which we can contribute, and second, in his assertion that this is done not by ignoring the everyday world and its concerns, but by relating these to the broader spiritual context. That this task is the unique responsibility of the Jewish people[36] is due to the fact that it is the Jewish version of monotheism which understands the profound dialectical truth that while God's unity is all-inclusive, this unity can only be approached through the world of appearances. And in so approaching this divine unity, we bear witness to the process through which, as Rav Kook says, "nature will appear as miracle."

Notes

1. See "Death and Immortality in the Thought of Rav Kook" (Hebrew), in *Hogim u-Ma'aminim* (Tel Aviv, 1959), 101– 111.
2. *Orot ha-Kodesh* (Jerusalem, 1964), II, 377.
3. Ibid., 376, 378.
4. Rav Kook was not unaware of this criticism leveled against his literary style and offered several responses. See, for example, *Iggerot Re'iyah* (Jerusalem, 1943), I, 151, 265; ibid. (Jerusalem, 1946), II, 7, 36; *Orot ha-Kodesh* (Jerusalem, 1963), I, 108, and the passage from Rav Kook's diary quoted by Z. Yaron in *Mishnato shel ha-Rav Kook* (Jerusalem, 1974), 23. Various scholars have also offered their theories. See Rabbi

Adin Steinsaltz, "The Problematics of *Orot ha-Kodesh*," in *Ha-Re'iyah*, ed. Y. Rafael (Jerusalem, 1964), 102–6, and B. Ish-Shalom's debate with him in *Ha-Rav Kook: Beyn Ratzionalizim le-Mystikah* (Tel Aviv, 1990), 214–19.

5. Bergman, op. cit. 106.
6. *Orot ha-Kodesh* II, 373–385.
7. Ibid., 380.
8. Ibid.
9. Ibid., 381–82.
10. For a more elaborate discussion of this distinction made by the Ramban, see David Berger, "Miracles and the Natural Order in Nahmanides," in *Rabbi Moses Nahmanides (Ramban): Explorations in His Religious and Literary Virtuosity*, ed. I. Twersky (Cambridge, Mass., 1983), 107–28; M. Nehorai's critique, "Nahmanides on Miracles and Nature" (Hebrew), *Daat* 17 (Summer 1986), 23–33; and Berger's response, "Concerning Miracles and Nature in the Teachings of the Ramban" (Hebrew), *Daat* 19 (Summer 1987), 169–70.
11. In his commentary to Leviticus, 26:11.
12. For a more elaborate discussion of the Maharal's view on this matter, see A. Kleinberger, *Ha-Maḥshavah ha-Pedagogit shel ha-Maharal mi-Prague* (Jerusalem, 1962), 78–89; and my critique, "The Miracle as Added Dimension in the Philosophy of the Maharal of Prague" (Hebrew), *Daat* 17 (Summer 1986), 81–96.
13. *Gevurot ha-Shem* (London, 1961), 15.
14. This comparison is made both by Kleinberger, op. cit., 89, and by S. Malin in his translation of the Maharal's *Book of Divine Power: Introductions* (Jerusalem, 1985), 57–58 n. 9.
15. *Gevurot ha-Shem*, chap. 64, 295–96.
16. For an explication of this similarity between Kant and Rav Dessler, see my essay, "The Power of Choice in the Thought of Rabbi Dessler" (Hebrew), *Daat* 12 (Winter 1984), 111–26, espec. 114–20.
17. For the sake of completeness, it should be noted that the Maharal also makes use of a similar distinction between a *nes muḥash* (a palpable miracle) and a *nes nistar* that is not *muḥash*, but his use of this terminology is quite different from that of the Ramban. For whereas the Ramban uses the term *nes nistar* to refer to a miracle that on the surface does not violate natural law, but in the long term is at least statistically improbable, the Maharal applies this term to miracles that are so evidently a violation of nature that they cannot be reconciled with it at all, but must be relegated to a higher, "hidden"—or metaphysical—plane, while leaving the normal course of nature completely untampered.
18. E. Dessler, *Mikhtav me-Eliyahu* (London, 1955), I, 186.
19. *Orot ha-Kodesh* II, 385.
20. Ibid., 386.

21. Ibid., 385.
22. See Rav Yoseph Yozel Horowitz, *Madregat ha-Adam* (Jerusalem, 1976), 3–4; Rav Yeruham Levovitz, *Daat, Ḥokhmah, u-Musar* (New York, 1967), 1:1 1–3; and Rav Dessler, *Mikhtav me-Eliyahu* (Bnei Brak, 1964),II, 138–39, 144. The relationship between various kabbalistic notions regarding the nature of Adam's spirituality before sin, the nature of his sin, and the ideal human condition is elaborated upon in Bezalel Safran, "Rabbi Azriel and Nahmanides: Two Views of the Fall of Man," in *Rabbi Moses Nahmanides*, ed. I. Twersky, 75–107.
23. For a sample expression of Rav Kook's view of the significance of these discoveries, see *Orot ha-Kodesh* II, 538–42.
24. *Arpelei Tohar* (Jerusalem, 1983), 1–2. For a strikingly similar analysis, from a psychologist's point of view, of the transformation of key paradigms regarding the relationship of humanity to its environment that our age is undergoing, and the implications of this transformation for our concept of death, see R. J. Lifton, "On Death and the Continuity of Life: A New Paradigm," in *History of Childhood Quarterly: The Journal of Psychology* , 1, no. 4 (Spring 1974): 681–96.
25. See *Orot ha-Kodesh* II, 375, where Rav Kook states: "It is impossible for the soul of life to find its satisfaction in pursuit of practical arrangements, the ordering of society and life-styles, and in political and communal involvement. True, when all these are not functioning properly, the soul is missing some of the means that could aid it in its particular form of perfection, but these do not constitute the soul's resting point and goal." Expressions of Maimonides' even more emphatic rejection of any relationship between physical well-being and the afterlife can be found in his introduction to *Perek Ḥelek* in his *Commentary on the Mishnah*.
26. Ibid., 563.
27. *Arpelei Tohar*, 5.
28. *Olat Reiyah* II (Jerusalem, 1962), 270. See also Z. Yaron, op. cit., 116–119, for a discussion of this passage and of Rav Kook's view of miracles in general.
29. *Orot ha-Kodesh* II, 571, 406.
30. *Orot ha-Kodesh* II, 395, 398, 527.
31. Compare for example Rav Kook's view of activity for the physical betterment of the individual and society (*Arpelei Tohar*, 6–7), with Rav Dessler's utter disdain for rational human endeavor that attributes any importance to nature (*Mikhtav me-Eliyahu* I, 177–97; ibid. [Bnei Brak, 1977], 170–72).
32. For a more detailed, technical exposition of Rav Kook's version of acosmism, see my two-part essay, "The Concept of God in the Thought of Rav Kook" (Hebrew), *Daat* 8 (Summer 1982): 109–28 and *Daat* 9 (Winter, 1982), 39–70.
33. *Orot Ha-Kodesh* II, 529.

34. See Nelson Goodman, *Ways of World-Making* (Indianapolis, 1978).

35. See, for example, Rav Yoseph Bloch's comments on the relationship between rewards of this world and the next in *She'urei Da'at* II (Tel Aviv, 1943), *She'ur* 4, and Rav Hayyim of Volozhin's commentary to the Mishnaic statement, "Kol Yisrael yesh lahem helek la-'olam haba," in *Nefesh ha-Hayyim* (Vilna, 1874), *Sha'ar* I, chap. 12.

36. *Orot ha-Kodesh* II, 384.

PART THREE

Zionism, Messianism, and the State of Israel

The Land of Israel and Historical Dialectics in the Thought of Rav Kook: Zionism and Messianism

Ella Belfer

The perception of history in the covenantal tradition of Judaism[1] is based on the belief in God, in God's presence in history and in man's responsibility in the face of His presence. Flowing from its perception of history, the messianic vision of Judaism is completely grounded in the grace of God within human history, on the one hand, and human accountability before His judgment, on the other. This traditional perception of history and this traditional messianic vision, however, were fundamentally challenged at the end of the nineteenth and beginning of the twentieth century by the rise of Zionism, with its highly untraditional, if not antitraditional, secular-revolutionary approach to history.

Traditional Jewish thought responded to the challenge of this secular-Zionist revolution in four different ways. The first response rejected the entire Zionist venture, seeing it as an act of secular usurpation, as posing an unacceptable—indeed heretical—alternative to the traditional belief in the Messiah.[2] The second response, that articulated, for example, by Rav Yitzhak Breuer,[3] affirmed the national revival and even viewed it in messianic categories. It, combined that affirmation, however, with a fierce struggle over the very soul of this revival and issued a call for a counterrevolution against the secular world in general and secular Jewish nationalism

257

in particular. The third response, taken by religious Zionists who followed the path of Rav Yitzḥak Reines,[4] adopted, from the outset, a deliberately limited nonmessianic activism.[5] This response allowed religious Zionists to affirm political Zionism, precisely because it distinguished between the national-Herzlian solution to the existential plight of diaspora Jewry, which it perceived as a justified emergency measure, and the enduring and lasting belief in the coming of the redeemer, the restoration of the divine presence, the mending of the world, and the end of days. The fact that these religious Zionists did not attach any messianic significance to the emerging Jewish state enabled them to participate in the political process leading to the founding of that state, while maintaining their ongoing loyalty to the halakhic tradition. This response also allowed for the development of "eclectic" outlooks: the views of socialism were adopted and synthesized with traditional religious obligations, and the religious-socialist synthesis was seen as embodying the values of existence, in contrast to the political realm, which, taken by itself, was seen simply as providing the necessary framework for the sheer fact of existence. The fourth response was that of Rav Kook.

In contrast to the first three responses, the response of Rav Kook is unique, inasmuch as it defines Zionism as "atḥalta di-geulah," the beginning of the redemption. Rav Kook neither rejected the secular-national vision nor did he struggle for the soul of the nation. Rather, he adopted this secular-national vision but placed it within (what was for him) the broader context of a dialectical messianic approach. This approach served to negate the secular autonomous significance of the Zionist venture by seeing it as a necessary and integral stage—but, nevertheless, only a stage—in the salvation history of the Jewish people, a history that is, when all is said and done, a tale of exile and redemption. The historical-Zionist actualization of the messianic dynamic, according to Rav Kook, should not be viewed as a secular transformation of the biblical spirit and certainly should not be seen as embodying the spirit of historical normalization, but rather should be looked upon as deriving from a deep and fundamental, if oftentimes unconscious, faith in the covenantal tradition. The "Zionist" aspect of Rav Kook's thought is rooted, then, in the depths of his faith. Therefore, a study of this aspect requires a knowledge of the essentials of the Jewish worldview and of the way in which the outlook of Rav Kook takes on shape within it.

The covenantal tradition is based upon the belief in a dynamic synthesis between concrete life, with all its political elements, and sanctity of the spirit, with all its tenets of faith and *mitzvah* performances, as the goal of this concrete life. The synthesis thus requires a mutual interaction between this worldly reality and transcendent holiness.

The messianic belief, as the longed-for realization of the covenantal tradition, serves as an expression of the unavoidable tension that flares up between the two dimensions of the covenantal tradition, the realistic-historical dimension and the metaphysical-spiritual one. But, precisely because of that tension within the tradition, there are varying traditional conceptions of the messianic era itself, some that stress the national and particularist aspect of the messianic era and others that focus more sharply on its spiritual and universal aspect. Thus, for example, we have the political realism of Maimonides's messianic theory,[6] which emphasizes the Jewish people's liberation from subjection to foreign domination and their reestablishment of a sovereign Jewish polity as the defining characteristics of the messianic era; and, opposing Maimonides' view, we have Abravanel's more spiritual messianic vision,[7] a vision that minimizes the political-territorial aspect of messianism while stressing the spread of the divine law over the whole world, "as waters that cover the sea" (Isa. 11:9), as the central feature of the messianic age.

It should be noted that this debate[8] does not in any way affect the unequivocal centrality of the Jewish people in the eschatological vision of universal salvation. The issue in question rather revolves about the role that earthly existence and national-territorial components play within the framework of human existence in general and Jewish existence in particular, the purpose of that existence being, of course, the worship of God.

Rav Kook's own messianic vision must be viewed within this complex and tensile messianic tradition with its material and spiritual poles. His vision fuses a particularist view of the fate of the people and land with a universalist goal of the salvation of humanity. It is historicist, well anchored in the political processes of history, and, at the same time, aspires toward an all-encompassing spirituality as the ultimate goal of this history.[9] His conception, thus, adopts a maximalist stand with regard to both poles. With respect to the material pole, the return to territoriality, for Rav Kook, requires the emergence of a real, concrete, national-political entity and not some type of amorphous, quasi-national, or quasi-political entity. With respect to the spiritual pole, in Rav Kook's view, cosmic salvation—the ultimate goal of history[10]—involves not only the salvation of the individual soul, but also a real change in history and an essential change in the nature of humanity, and moreover, includes within itself the redemption of both Israel and the entire cosmos.

This maximalist messianic approach, which includes within itself two complete planes of existence—the completely material and the completely spiritual—sets forth a highly dialectical conception of the lawful processes determining the messianic dynamic. The messianic process must begin in the earthly-material dimension, that is, in the revival of the real historical existence of the Jewish people as a people among peoples and a nation among nations. This renewed physical existence, however, is only the *beginning* of redemption. It is not the end of the road but only the first step on a long path. The end of this path will be reached when the Jewish people will fulfill its mission to mend the world and be a light unto the nations. At the same time, however, the historical realization of material existence, though it is only the first step, will, by virtue of its powerful concreteness, give rise to the longing for an ultimate spiritual essence.

Thus, for Rav Kook, the end of this road is potentially present in the first step, or, to reverse the image, the Jewish people's first step on this long path leads ineluctably to their reaching its end. As he states:

> The quality of the nationalism of Israel, per se, expresses itself in the Messiah, the son of Joseph. The ultimate goal, however, is not just to demarcate an isolated national entity, but to [bring about] the yearning to unite all humanity into one family, so that all of them call in the name of the Lord. And although this [ultimate goal] also requires a special center, the intention is not the center, per se, but

the influence the center exerts upon the universal whole. And when the world must integrate nationalism within universalism, there must take place the destruction of those elements which had taken root as a result of a constricted nationalism. Therefore, the Messiah, son of Joseph, is destined to be killed, and the true and lasting kingdom will be that of the Messiah, son of David. And when the yearning for the universal results in the negation of national isolation, then one further step and evil will also be uprooted from the lives of individuals. Thus, the negation of the evil inclination and the killing of the Messiah, son of Joseph, are related one to another. The Sages, therefore, disagree[11] as to the meaning of the verse, "and they will view the one who had been killed" (Zekh. 12:10), whether it refers to the Messiah, son of Joseph, who had been killed or to the evil inclination that had been killed.[12]

This lawful dialectical process, as found in Rav Kook's messianic vision, moves, then, from a stage in which the emphasis is on developing the temporal-historical side of human capabilities, from a stage in which the primary concern is with fashioning the particularist mode of life of the people on its land, to the ultimate stage in which pride of place will be accorded to spirituality and to the unifying universal nature of this spirituality. The basis for the dialectical lawfulness of the messianic process in Rav Kook's thought is to be sought in his understanding of the fundamental principles of Judaism—the covenant and the Messiah—and the link between the two.[13] His understanding of these principles determined, in turn, his affirmation of the harmony between "life" and "sanctity" and his perception of the world as both capable of and requiring rectification.

Existence, from Rav Kook's standpoint, is total existence, where the presence of God and His holiness are the source of the permanent, inner vitality of earthly matter. There is no dichotomy, then, between body and spirit, nor even the negation of the body in the service of spirit, but rather the sanctification of the body, on the one hand, and the negation of the autonomous bodily essence, on the other. Since the whole of existence is suffused with the divine, and "there is nothing apart from the Lord,"[14] it follows that the conceptual autonomy of the phenomenon of life is negated. Material existence devoid of sanctity is, therefore, an impossible assumption. This view of reality espoused by Rav Kook is described by him

as a "monotheistic outlook tending toward a pantheistic explication, but purified of its [pantheism's] dross . . . and [affirming] that
there is nothing apart from the Lord."[15]

The essence of the bond between "life" and "sanctity" is well
expressed in Rav Kook's analysis of the bond between the "divine
idea" and the "national idea":

> The readiness for the divine idea is found, whether overtly or co-
> vertly, whether in a proper or a distorted form, in the hearts of all
> mankind in all its factions, groups, and peoples. It generates different
> religions and different sentiments of faith, different ways of life and
> modes of behavior that, in turn, result in mighty deeds in the lives of
> nations and individuals, in the social order and the political process,
> which, covertly or overtly, weave and fashion mighty, unfathomable
> deeds in man's spirit and his inner essential life. . . . Will, energy,
> art, imagination and intellect, modes of life and all spiritual tenden-
> cies will coalesce and become spirit-and-body. And social or national
> groups are established, and we can discern, if we examine them
> with a perceptive eye, that all the many factors that influence and
> determine their ways of life and modes of existence, all are included
> within man's inner capability for blending the divine idea together
> with the tendency to establish groups found in the national aspect.
> However, when the latter [the national aspect] has succeeded in
> taking possession of the earth, it expands and becomes fortified and
> acquires for itself a complete being . . . and, at times, even seeks to
> detach itself from its basic root, the content of the divine idea. But
> human history shows that all such attempts have failed to material-
> ize. We see that the supreme divine quality in man, even when it is
> at its lowest ebb and consists of an infinitesimal, barely discernible
> point, even then it is only dormant or faint, but it neither dies nor
> expires; and it is this divine quality that endows all the impulses of
> life with an inward power.[16]

Fundamentally, there cannot be any contradiction between life and
the substance of this life. Therefore, natural life cannot contradict
sanctity, for it is sanctity that is the source of life's vitality.[17]

> Sanctity does not contradict the self-love deeply embedded in the
> soul of all living; rather it sets man at such a high level that the more
> he loves himself, the more the good within him extends to exert its
> influence on everything: on one's entire environment, on the entire
> world, on all of existence.[18]

Spiritual purification derives, then, not from man's struggle with
his natural existence. On the contrary, it is only possible as a result

of man's giving expression to his natural existence to the extent that "if there be even one element in the depths of [man's] cognitive and sensitive soul that has not been actualized he is obligated to artfully bring it into the open." [19]

However, this total wholeness of existence does not pertain to the present, but to the future. To be sure, the divine idea pulsates within the historical process—more, it is this idea that propels this very process. Nevertheless, within the historical dynamic—the messianic goal of which is the revelation of the divine totality suffusing all being—there exists a phenomenological division between materiality and divinity, and secular phenomena maintain an apparently autonomous isolated existence. The definition of the world as the image of God is unequivocal, but the way in which the world reflects divinity necessitates a differentiation between two historical stages: between the *potential* spiritual identity that is inherent within history, on the one hand, and the ultimate *actual* spiritual identity that is the supreme messianic expression of this history, on the other.

Alongside the clear affirmation of natural phenomena, in general, and of the national phenomenon, in particular, as the human-communal expression of nature, and alongside the inclusion of all humanity under the protective and pervasive canopy of the holy spirit, there exists, in Rav Kook's thought, a clear distinction between present historical reality, in which the division between the material and spiritual persists and the vital force of the divine spirit is latent and concealed within life, and the goal of history, where all being will be exalted to the rank of divine spirit and this spirit will be fully and completely revealed.

> The distinctions between the sacred and the secular are [to be found] in the entire cosmos. . . . The profound cognition and awareness of these distinctions are a source that bears much spiritual fruit. However, after this [cognition and awareness], one comprehends with a clear understanding that all these [distinctions] are transient matters, and that the elevation of all [being] toward sanctity and harmony and nondifferentiation and refinement is the eternal idea that always dwells in all noble spirits, while the careful effort to make distinctions is an ephemeral matter that arises from temporal life. [20]

There exist, in effect, two dialectical systems regarding the synthesis between "life" and "sanctity" in Rav Kook's view of the cosmos. First, there is the permanent dialectic that abrogates the immanent essences of physical phenomenon by negating the very possibility of life devoid of metaphysical spiritual sanctity. This is owing to the fundamental absence of any secular immanence in life's being. In the very marrow of existence there cannot be any differentiation between the secular and the sacred. For the essence of existence, deep down, is a total being imbued with the omnipotent, all-vivifying, and all-sanctifying presence of the Creator.

Yet, alongside this *permanent* dialectic, there is also the *dynamic* dialectic of the messianic process. In order for the unity of spiritual-material being to reveal itself, to emerge from potentiality to actuality, from essence to phenomenon, history must pass through stages of the consolidation and fortification of phenomena that, at first glance, are material. Thus, there are stages in history where one must focus upon and strengthen material expressions to the point of fashioning them into independent entities that exist, or so it seems, by virtue of an immanent material-historical essence, the very same essence negated by the permanent dialectic! Only when material, human existence flourishes to the extent that it clashes violently with metaphysical-spiritual values will the yearned-for inversion follow; out of the all-natural, all-material expressions of existence, its all-spiritual truth will arise.

At a deeper level, this process of fortifying the material dimension does not contradict the fundamental principle of the unity of the world and the sanctifying presence of the Creator who dwells therein. On the contrary, since the source of life, at its root, is divine, the more material existence acquires substantiality and concreteness, the more vitality it possesses, the more powerfully it will, paradoxically,[21] reflect the force of the sustaining and vivifying divine spirit concealed within it. Hence, only the complete revelation of the material will precipitate the ultimate revelation of the spiritual light and actualize the union of the physical and spiritual in a world of divine sanctity. This reverse dynamic of the historical process—from the material to the divine—is, thus, a process that allows for—nay, demands—the complete expression of all the apparently contrasting and conflicting aspects of the sacred, divine unity, so that these aspects may ultimately be harmonized and synthesized in the organic wholeness of that unity.

Both facets of the existential synthesis between body and spirit—that represented by the permanent dialectic and that represented by the dynamic dialectic—reserve a central role for the Jewish people. In effect, Rav Kook's vision of the Jewish people serves as a *third* dialectical system, a system that operates as a bridge to the fulfillment and as a key to the understanding of the other two dialectical systems. Jewish existence, according to the covenantal tradition, must bear witness to the presence of divine holiness in history; it must incorporate the unity of the dialectical contrasts between divinity and history, worldly nature and heavenly sanctity, into its faith and mode of life. The Jewish people constitutes a messianic model[22] of the unity of life through focusing on the holiness to be found in the very heart of our premessianic reality, though, as already mentioned, in that premessianic reality the distinction between secular phenomenon and sacred essence must be upheld. The universal future of humanity already resides within the actual being of the Jewish people owing to the very nature of that people. The Jewish people may be classified as a particular communal entity like all communal entities, as one particular people and nation in a world of peoples and nations. Yet the essence of the Jewish people lies in goals that transcend the concrete boundaries of material existence and the historical limitations of national particularism. More, for Rav Kook, the national-material particularism of the Jewish people, in all its specificity and distinctiveness, already contains within itself the universal society. The concrete materiality of the Jewish people, then, serves to express universal ideals.

> Whatever pertains to [the people of] Israel and its essence is not restricted within a limited, particular circle but is centered within a specific circle, and, from that center, influences the entire circumference. . . . The quality of universalism always fills the hearts of all noble spirits, and they feel choked if they are fenced in and circumscribed within their own national circle. But that people which possesses complete universality in the depths of its soul—"The nobles of all nations have gathered [and are incorporated within] the people of the God of Abraham" (Ps. 47:10)—always requires [of its members] deeds that clearly engrave the character [of this people] deep within itself and which deeds [precisely, thereby] become imbued with a multitude of lofty universal ideals. . . . Restriction in deed and

expansion in spirit jointly constitute the primary core of the nature of [the people of] Israel; it is, at one and the same time, "a people which dwelleth alone" (Num. 23:9) and "a light unto the nations" (Isa. 42:6).[23]

Moreover, this very blend of "restriction in deed" and "expansion in spirit," which characterizes the Jewish essence, is itself achieved via a dialectical historical process. The Jewish people fulfills its universal goals by anchoring itself in political-territorial particularism. The spirituality that lies at the heart of Judaism finds its expression precisely in the unique bond between the people and its land. As the concrete particularity of the Jewish people gains in strength, the (universal) essence of this particularity comes to the fore. Thus, universal spirituality—as uniquely characterizing the Jewish world—requires the existence of a physical substrate.

> The people of Israel can engage in independent creativity, in thought, in life, and in deed, only in the Land of Israel. Conversely, in everything the people of Israel accomplishes in the Land of Israel, the universal form becomes absorbed within the unique and individual form specific to this people, and this constitutes a great blessing for Israel and the world.[24]

Through the Jewish polity anchoring itself in the sheer physicality of the Land of Israel, the universal spirituality of that polity will come to the fore. And precisely in this manner—in this dialectical emergence of the spiritual from out of the very heart of the political—the Jewish people serves both to exemplify and proleptically anticipate the universal human goal. The Jewish people may thus be viewed as a "microcosm" containing within itself the entire general teleological development of history to the point where the "divine idea" reveals itself from out of the core of concrete existence and by means of the complete expression of the "national idea." It is true that, for Rav Kook, "the state" is not an ultimate purpose of human existence, but despite this caveat, Rav Kook's philosophy contains an exceptionally positive evaluation of a Jewish state that serves, at the outset, to express the ideal messianic goals of the human spirit.

> The state does not constitute man's ultimate felicity. This [however] pertains to an ordinary state that does not achieve a value higher than that of any large collective, above which the multitude of ideas,

which are the glory of human life, hover but do not touch. This is not the case with a state that is fundamentally ideal, the very essence of which is engraved with the supreme ideal content, which, in truth, constitutes the ultimate felicity of the individual. This state, indeed, ranks highest on the ladder of felicity; and this state is our state, the State of Israel, the base of the throne of God in the world. For its desire is that God be one and His Name be one; and that, indeed, is the ultimate felicity.[25]

The "divine idea" at the heart of Judaism is thus intimately bound up with the national existence of the Jewish people.

The highest perfection is that the body be strong and properly developed and the soul be healthy, strong, and perfected, and, with its mighty force, direct all of the strong and powerful forces of the body toward [attaining] the goal [set] by right and pure reason, namely, [the performance] of God's will in His world. Similarly, God has particularly provided the people of Israel with two forces. The first force is the force that parallels the force maintaining the human body. It is a force that strives to [bring about] the good of the nation and its perfection in its material aspect; and this [material condition] constitutes the proper base for all of the great and holy ideals that distinguish Israel, that it be a unique and holy people in the land and a light unto the nations. The other force is the force for the perfection of spirituality itself.[26]

Thus, because of the interdependence between "body" and "spirit," because of the fundamental dialectical bond between "earthly" and "heavenly," there is paradoxically an inverse relationship between the universal idea of the Jewish people, on the one hand, and the "universal" manner of the Jewish existence in the exile, on the other, an exilic existence that, by its very nature, lacks the particularity of Jewish territoriality.

This leads to the unequivocal negation of the exile, a negation that flows not only from the love of Zion, but also, and primarily, from the longing for the divine presence originating from Zion.[27] And the divine presence resides only in Zion, that is, the presence of the "divine idea" in the world—which is the universal message of the Jewish people—only finds its expression through the strength and vitality of its "national idea," as that "national idea" takes root and flourishes in the land of Israel.

However, because the divine idea, after the exile of the people and the destruction of the temple, lacked a firm place in the expanse of the national idea of Israel, it ascended during the period of exile above the limits of any particular nation toward the lofty heights of yearning for moral justice, of theoretical science and pure reason, and of exalted and abstract knowledge. From there it emitted a few rays of light, the qualitative majority of which penetrated the tents of Jacob by means of remnants of ancient lights, of the heritage of the Torah, and of the residue of the influence of prophecy and the divine spirit. And these scattered lights will, here and there, spread out among the select few, in every people and nation, who seek God and are diligent in the performance of truth and justice. In this way, the vision of the mission of Israel fundamentally triumphed over all of Israel's conquerors. In the end, it purified millions of hearts, influenced peoples and kingdoms with a new spirit, and dispelled much of the evil of pagan man.

But this is not sufficient. The scant influence of a weak and faint morality, devoid of any lofty status in the life of peoples and states, unable to make its influence felt in all its glory and majesty upon its own national idea—of what value is it? The crude shadows that give rise to evil and defilement accompany the scattered lights of the divine idea when it wanders among the nations. And the rupture existing between it and the national idea, which is the cause of all the tumult and confusion in the social and political world, can be mended only in their natural place of convergence—in [the people of] Israel, in its complete and total revival in its land, when the kingdom of God will regain its original strength.[28]

But how did Rav Kook's theoretical position affect his stance toward the practical issues of his day? We would suggest that Rav Kook's attitude to the Zionist venture fundamentally reflected and, indeed, was determined by his all-encompassing historical view of the dialectical interconnectedness between the "national idea" and the "divine idea" in human history in general and Jewish history in particular. The revival of Jewish materialism, which found its expression in the renewed colonization of the Land of Israel, was seen by Rav Kook, from the vantage point of his theoretical perspective, as the stage of the coalescence, consolidation, and, thereby, the strengthening of the national idea. This stage constitutes a necessary phase in the historical process leading to the ultimate redemption. Political Zionism, for him, was the "Messiah, son of Joseph" who would bring about the redemption of the body, the "Messiah, son of Joseph" who by his heroic life and tragic but necessary death would pave the way for the spiritual kingdom of the "Messiah, son of David."[29]

This dialectical perception of the messianic dynamic served as a basis for Rav Kook's affirmation of the Zionist venture[30] and for the historical legitimization he accorded to the national-secular revolution accompanying that venture. First and foremost, no human revolution is possible unless its force and vitality derive from the divine spirit that resides within it and directs it. As to the secular rebellion accompanying the national revolution, this rebellion will ultimately negate itself with the self-negation of the secular essence underlying the phenomenon of secularization.[31] Yet, at the same time, the *phenomenon* of autonomous-secular nationalism must intensify and gain in strength precisely when humanity stands at the very threshold of universal salvation. The crystallization of the particularist national potentiality is the critical stage in the process of redemption.

If all the above pertains to the global messianic process, how much more so does it hold true for the process of Jewish redemption;[32] for the bond between heavenly and earthly and the mutual interdependence between the two are permanent components of the Jewish essence.[33]

The revolutionary-secular radicalism, accompanying the national revival, is an integral element of the stage of the national strengthening of the Jewish people, for this radicalism is part and parcel of the autonomous material aspect of the historical process, achieving, as it were, full expression. Nevertheless, Rav Kook's affirmation of the Zionist venture does not constitute, on his part, an endorsement of—much less, agreement with—the radical revolutionary break that secularization has introduced into the continuum of Jewish history. Rather, this affirmation is made possible only by Rav Kook's highly dialectical interpretation of the Zionist venture, which interpretation enables him to view it as a critical stage in the messianic process, as that process is conceived and described in the covenantal tradition. Together with his affirmation of the national revival, then, Rav Kook deprives that revival of its revolutionary secular character; by bestowing upon it his blessing, he negates the secular attitude that, on the face of it, must follow from the secular phenomenon.

We find in Rav Kook, then, two contrasting but—so he would argue—complementary attitudes toward "secularism." On the one hand, the *permanent synthesis* between heaven and earth (both as a fundamental feature of cosmic being and as the primary defining essence of the Jewish people) negates entirely, in his view, the very possibility of the existence of a secular-national *essence*. On the other hand, the *dynamic synthesis* of secular and sacred necessitates that, flowing from the special dialectical nature of the historical process, there be an intensification of the national aspect of peoplehood with all its apparently all-too-secular historical manifestations.

An additional factor contributing to the complexity of the return to Zion, as perceived by Rav Kook, is rooted in the unique and absolute value of the land. The Land of Israel is the permanent crossroads where "divine presence" and "territory" meet. For Rav Kook, this crossroads makes manifest, by its very nature, the two sides of the covenantal tradition, as he understood it: history and metahistory. For the covenantal tradition mandates a positive approach to the legitimacy and lawfulness of history[34] and an affirmation of its national-physical-material character, while, at the same time, it demands of one absolute faith in the metahistorical goal and constant anticipation of the light of eternal salvation: "The anticipation of salvation is the preservative force of exilic Judaism, while the Judaism of the Land of Israel is salvation itself."[35]

The return to the Land of Israel relates then to two strata of salvation and takes on a differing significance in the differing contexts constituted by these two strata. At the deepest stratum, the absolute stratum of permanent essences, the return to the land is a return to the permanent crossroads of the earthly-heavenly synthesis. In its metaphysical sanctity and earthly nature, this crossroads embodies the substance and purpose of history and, therefore, constitutes "salvation" as an enduring state of being. At the stratum closer to the surface, the variable stratum of historical dynamics, the return to Zion constitutes the people's necessary entry onto the royal road of national revival, that road which, paradoxically, is the only path that leads to universal salvation.

The return to the land of Israel, then, incorporates within itself both the national-particular revival and the permanent spiritual sanctity latent in the sanctity of the land. It follows that, at the historical level, the return to the land *leads* to salvation, while, at the deepest ontological level, the return, itself, *constitutes* salvation.[36]

Rav Kook summarizes the significance of the return to Zion thus:

> We have started to say something great, both to ourselves and the entire world, and we have not finished yet. We are still in the middle of our speech and we cannot nor do we wish to cease. . . . Only a nation that has finished what it had begun, only a spiritual vision that has expressed all that was latent in it to the entire world, can retire from the historical arena. [However], to begin and not to end, such a thing has never happened.[37]

The existential totality illuminated by the divine light, the centrality of Judaism within this totality, and the centrality of the Land of Israel within Judaism—all these are permanent and enduring, firm and fixed foundations. Yet, for the present, they are concealed deep within the shards of historical reality, within the stages of the historical process. But all that is hidden on this path to redemption is destined to be revealed at journey's end.[38]

Notes

1. See E. E. Urbach, *Ḥazal: Pirkei Emunot Ve-De'ot* (Jerusalem, 1982), 247. See also Moses Nahmanides, "Vikuaḥ ha-Ramban," in *Kitvei ha-Ramban*, ed C. D. Chavel (Jerusalem, 1963), 1: 302–20; Leon Roth, "Ha-Hiddamut la-El ve-Ra'ayon ha-Kedushah in *Ha-Dat ve-'Erkhai ha-Adam* (Jerusalem, 1972), 20–30; Jakob J. Petuchowski, *Ever Since Sinai* (New York, 1961); and Martin Buber, *Moses: The Revelation and the Covenant* (New York, 1958).

2. See, for example, E. Don Yehiya, "Tefissot shel ha-Tziyyonut be-Hagut ha-Yehudit ha-Ortodoxit," in *Ha-Tziyyonut* (1984), 70–72; Y. Peles, "Yaḥasam shel Benei ha-Yishuv ha-Yashan le-Hityashvut be-Eretz Yisrael be-Meah ha-Tesha Esreh," *Tziyyon* 41 (1976): 148–63; and Aviezer Ravitsky, *Ha-Ketz ha-Megulah u-Medinat ha-Yehudim* (Tel Aviv, 1993), esp. 11–110. For particularly forceful expressions of this anti-Zionist position, see Rabbi Joel Teitelbaum, "Ma'amar Shalosh Shevu'ot," in *Va-Yoel Moshe* (New York, 1974), paragraph 20; and Rabbi Amram Blau, "Al Elil ha-Le'umiyyut," in *Om Ani Ḥomah*, part 1 (Jerusalem, 1949), 50–51.

3. See, for example, Rav Yitzḥak Breuer, *Am ha-Torah ha-Meurgan* (Tel Aviv, 1944), 8, 17–18; *Moriah* (Jerusalem, 1944), 210; *Concepts of Judaism*, edited by J. Levinger (Jerusalem, 1974), 82–105; 308–14. For critical analyses of Breuer's highly original and dialectical attitude to secu-

lar Zionism, see Gershom Scholem, "The Politics of Mysticism: Isaac Breuer's *New Kuzari*," in *The Messianic Idea in Judaism* (New York, 1972), 325–344; Pinhas Ha-Kohen Peli, "Yitzḥak Breuer: Torah im Derekh Erez Yisrael," in *Yitzhak Breuer: Iyyunim be-Mishnato*, ed. Rivka Horowitz (Ramat Gan, 1988), 101–25; Eliezer Schweid, "Medinat ha-Torah be-Mishnato shel Yitzhak Breuer," in Horowitz, op. cit., 163–73.

4. On the approach of Rav Reines, see E. Don Yehiya, "Ideologiah ve-Itzuv Mediniyyut be-Tziyyonut ha-Datit: Ha-Ideologiah shel ha-Rav Reines u-Mediniyyut ha-Mizraḥi Taḥat Hanhagoto," *Ha-Ziyyonut* 8 (1983): 103–46; Eliezer Schweid, "Teleologiah Le'umit-Tziyyonit be-Reishitah: Al Mishnato shel ha-Rav Y. Y. Reines," in *Mehkarim be-Kabbalah, be-Filosofiah u-be-Sifrut ha-Musar ve-ha-Hagut li-Kebod Y. Tishbi* (Jerusalem, 1986), 689–720; Michael Nehorai, "Ha-Rav Reines ve-ha-Rav Kook: Shetei Gishot le-Ziyyonut," in *Yovel Orot*, ed. B. Ish-Shalom and S. Rosenberg (Jerusalem, 1985), 209–18. The essay of Nehorai, as the title indicates, sharply contrasts the views of Rav Reines and Rav Kook. Though Nehorai presents the contrast in the form of an ostensibly strictly objective and scholarly study, it is quite clear that he personally strongly prefers the approach of Rav Reines to that of Rav Kook.

5. See, for example, "Derashat ha-Rav Natonek," in Tzvi Zehavi, *Me-he-Ḥatam Sofer Ve-'ad Herzl* (Jerusalem, 1966), 198.

6. Maimonides, "Introduction to *Perek Ḥelek*," in *Commentary on the Mishnah*; *Hilkhot Melakhim*, chaps. 11–12; *Hilkhot Teshuvah*, chap. 9; *Guide of the Perplexed* II, 29, 36; III, 11; *Iggeret Teiman*; and many other places in his writings. For recent scholarly studies of Maimonides' messianism, see Amos Funkenstein, "Maimonides: Political Theory and Realistic Messianism," *Miscellanea Mediaevalia* 11 (1977): 81–103; David Hartman, "Maimonides' Approach to Messianism and Its Contemporary Implications," *Da'at* 2–3 (1978–79): 5–33; Aviezer Ravitsky, "Kefi Koaḥ ha-Adam: Yemot ha-Mashiaḥ be-Mishnat ha-Rambam," in *Meshiḥiyyut ve-Eskatologiyah*, ed. Zvi Baras (Jerusalem, 1984), 191–220; and Joel L. Kraemer, "On Maimonides' Messianic Posture," in *Studies in Medieval Jewish History and Literature*, vol. II, ed. Isadore Twersky (Cambridge, Mass., 1984), 109–42.

7. Abravanel, *Yeshu'ot Meshiḥo*; *Rosh Amanah*, chap. 14. See Leo Strauss, "On Abravanel's Philosophical Tendency and Political Teaching," in *Isaac Abravanel: Six Lectures*, ed. J. B. Trend and H. Loewe (Cambridge, 1937), 95–129.

8. For modern analyses, see, for example, Urbach, *Ḥazal* (above, note 1), 585–623; and Y. Klausner, *Ha-Ra'ayon ha-Meshiḥi be-Yisrael*, 3rd ed. (Tel Aviv, 1950), 30–50. A classic medieval discussion of this issue may be found in Saadya Gaon's *Emunot ve-De'ot*, chap. 8.

9. *Orot ha-Kodesh* (Jerusalem, 1964), III, 367.

10. See E. Goldman, "Tziyyonut Ḥilonit, Te'udat Yisrael, Ve-Takhlit ha-Torah," *Da'at* 11 (Summer 1983): 111–15.
11. Sukkah 52a.
12. *Orot* (Jerusalem, 1961), 160.
13. See, for example, Gerald J. Blidstein, *Ekronot Mediniyyim be-Mishnat ha-Rambam* (Ramat Gan, 1983), 229–31.
14. *Orot ha-Kodesh* (Jerusalem, 1964), II, 396.
15. Ibid., 399. It is worth noting that Rav Kook, in this passage, attributes this view to the "intellectual wing of the new Ḥassidic movement", i.e., Ḥabad Ḥassidism. See the appendix to *Orot ha-Kodesh*, listing Rav Kook's sources, by Rav David ha-Kohen, 606:6; and cf. 606:4 for earlier adumbrations of this view in classical Jewish texts. For analyses of Rav Kook's rootedness in and creative use and development of Ḥasidic sources, see the essays of Lawrence Fine and Norman Lamm in this volume.
16. "Le-Mahalakh ha-Idei'ot be-Yisrael," *Orot*, 102–3.
17. *Eder ha-Yakar* (Jerusalem, 1967), 32.
18. *Orot ha-Kodesh* III, 13.
19. "Ma'amar 'al Shir ha-Shirim," *Ha-Mizraḥ* 6; 352ff., reprinted most recently in *Be-oro: Iyyunim be-Mishnato shel ha-Rav Kook*, ed. Ḥayyim Ḥamiel (Jerusalem, 1986), 511–13; and R. Uzi Kelheim, *Aderet Emunah* (Jerusalem, 1976), 149–61; "The Levels of Love: A Commentary on the Song of Songs," trans. Herbert Weiner, *Commentary* 25 (1958): 333–34; and Daniel Landes, "Aesthetics of Mysticism: Rav Kook's Introduction to Song of Songs," *Gesher* 9 (1984–85): 50–58.
20. *Orot ha-Kodesh* II, 312.
21. For a critical analysis focusing on problematic elements in Rav Kook's dialectical conception of the messianic process, see Harold Fisch, *The Zionist Revolution: A New Perspective* (London, 1978), 63–66. According to Fisch, Rav Kook's negation of evil as a real, concrete essence and his messianic optimism flowing from that negation impair a person's ability to cognize evil, confront it, and struggle against it, whether that evil is present externally in historical events or internally within the structures of one's individual consciousness. Fisch further claims that Rav Kook's worldview cannot account for the profound rupture that has occurred in the history of the Jewish people in modern times as a result of the series of crises that have befallen it, beginning with the emancipation and culminating in the Holocaust during World War II. Rav Kook's dialectical view, for Fisch, then, is a doctrine that does not truly make room for the very profound and real polarities that a successful dialectical analysis must take into account. Rather than acknowledging the polar opposition between good and evil and *then* seeking to overcome it, Rav Kook's analysis, for Fisch, blunts the force and the reality of the pole of evil from the outset.
22. Shlomo Avineri, in his study, *The Making of Modern Zionism: The*

Intellectual Origins of the Jewish State (New York, 1981), 194–95, describes Kook's position thusly: "Rabbi Kook views the redemption of Israel as part of a universal process. . . . The salvation of the Jewish people [is] not merely of particular importance, but [also] a universal restoration *[tikkun 'olam]*. God did indeed choose Israel as His people, but the whole world is His creation, and every human being, Jew and non-Jew alike, was created in His image. Let not the tribulations of the Jews make them so involved with themselves as to forget this universal message." In contrast to this very sharply drawn, almost one-sided, universal message that Avineri extracts from the teachings of Rav Kook, one should note that alongside the humanistic and universal emphases that, indeed, *are* to be found in his teachings, Rav Kook always takes care not to blur the distinction between Israel and the nations. Indeed, at times, he sets forth this distinction in exceptionally sharp—many would argue, overly sharp—terms. Thus, in one passage he states: "The difference between the soul of [the people of] Israel, its essence, its inner longing, its aspirations, its characteristics, and its status, and the soul of all the nations, in all their levels, is greater and deeper than the difference between the soul of man and the soul of an animal, for between the latter two there is only a quantitative difference, whereas between the former two a qualitative difference prevails" (*Orot*, 156).

23. *Orot*, 151, 152.
24. Ibid., 10.
25. Ibid., 160.
26. "Ha-Misped bi-Yerushalayim" (A eulogy for Theodor Herzl), in *Ma'amarei ha-Reiyah* (Jerusalem, 1984), 94. A vocalized version, with annotations and a full commentary, prepared by Eliezer Eliner, can be found in *Be-Oro*, 257–71. The cited passage is on 258.
27. There are many striking resemblances and parallels between these ideas of Rav Kook and the worldview of Judah ha-Levi. See *Kuzari*, parts 2 and 4. For the connection between Rav Kook's doctrine and that of the Maharal, see Fisch, op. cit., 62–63, 176–77; also see the essay of Tamar Ross in the previous section.
28. "Li-Mahalakh ha-Idaei'ot be-Yisroel," 109.
29. *Orot*, 160.
30. This affirmative dialectical approach to the Zionist venture, based on the imagery of the Messiah, son of Joseph, and the Messiah, son of David, is the major theme of Rav Kook's eulogy for Herzl, "Ha-Misped bi-Yerushalayim" (see above, note 26). For Rav Kook, Herzl's heroic life and tragic and untimely death made him the ideal embodiment of the "Messiah, son of Joseph." More broadly speaking, of course, it was the *movement* of secular political Zionism, founded by Herzl, which, as noted in the body of text, filled for Rav Kook the role of the "Messiah, son of Joseph." See H. Peles, "Ha-Hitpathut ha-Dialektit shel ha-

Ra'ayon ha-Tziyyoni," *De'ot* 45 (1986), and Rabbi S. Aviner, "Harigat Mashiaḥ Ben Yosef," *Nekudah* (Tamuz 1980), 10.
31. *Iggerot ha-Re'iyah* (Jerusalem, 1962), II, 186–89 (letter 555).
32. Ibid. (Jerusalem, 1965), III, 155–59 (letter 871).
33. *Ḥazon ha-Geulah* (Jerusalem, 1941), 71.
34. On Rav Kook's perception of history as a progressive process and the parallels between his view and major currents of nineteenth-century thought, and, in particular, on the many close resemblances between his historiosophical views and those of Moses Hess, see E. Goldman, "Tziyyonut Ḥilonit, Te'udat Yisrael, Ve-Takhlit ha-Torah" (above, note 10), 115.
35. *Orot*, 9.
36. "Te'udat Yisrael u-Le'umiyyuto," *Ha-Peles* (1901), 63–64, reprinted in *Otzerot ha-Reiyah*, ed. Moshe Zuriel (Tel Aviv, 1988), 693–733; cf. *Orot ha-Kodesh* (Jerusalem, 1963), I, 155.
37. *Orot*, 136.
38. I wish to thank Lawrence Kaplan for his very helpful observations and bibliographic suggestions.

CHAPTER II

Zion and Jerusalem: The Jewish State in the Thought of Rabbi Abraham Isaac Kook

Jerome I. Gellman

Rabbi Abraham Isaac Kook is widely recognized to have been one of the outstanding rabbinical figures of this century, and the most prominent rabbinical personality to actively support and encourage Zionism and Jewish settlement in Palestine. The rich corpus of his writings returns again and again to the themes of the Land of Israel, the Jewish national revival, and the Zionist movement. Through his writings and by the power of his personality, Rav Kook has emerged as the chief ideologue of religious Zionism. Today major religious Zionist groupings in Israel speak in his name. Most strongly identified with Rav Kook are the Merkaz Harav Yeshiva, which he founded, and Gush Emunim, an activist movement dedicated to the settling and eventual annexation of all territories occupied by Israel in the Six Day War of 1967. Both these groups, whose memberships overlap to a significant degree, are motivated by strongly nationalistic feelings and by a mystical attachment to the Land of Israel. They find the roots of these attitudes in the writings of Rav Kook. Rav Kook was a great lover of the Jewish people and the Land of Israel, and placed important mystical meaning on their reuniting after the dark night of Jewish exile. This aspect of Rav Kook's thought has constituted his strongest influence on the course of events in Israel. It has given an ideological basis to a quasi-religious, nationalistic, perception of Israel's problems and destiny, and has furnished the rationale for right-wing politics among the religious and their close sympathizers.

Thus, it has been concluded on the basis of Rav Kook's ideology that the Jewish state is Messianic in nature, and that its aims are properly subordinated to its Messianic destiny. Followers of Rav Kook have been motivated by a fervor to advance and verify at one and the same time the Messianic meaning of the state.

In the following pages I wish to take a fresh look at Rav Kook's understanding of a Jewish state in our times. My intention is to uncover a side of Rav Kook's thinking that has been largely neglected, though it plays a major role in his thought. It is a side of his thought that stands in stark contrast to the prevailing understanding of him, and stands to be a corrective of the excesses of selective interpretation. There exists in Rav Kook a philosophical point of view different from what has so far influenced the course of events in Israel. It is this I wish to present here.

In the year 1917, Rav Kook proclaimed the formation of a new movement, to be separate from and parallel to the Zionist movement founded by Theodore Herzl.[1] The new movement was to be called "Jerusalem," and was to be composed of two organizational structures: "Histadrut Jerusalem," a governing body of Rabbis, and "Degel Jerusalem," the general membership, to be comprised of religious Jews. In time the movement came to be called by Rav Kook simply "Degel Jerusalem" and succeeded in having branches in England, Switzerland, and the United States, in addition to its branches in Israel. Rav Kook envisioned great historical importance for "Jerusalemism," similar to the historical importance of "Zionism." His conception of "Jerusalemism" and its relationship to Zionism can serve, I believe, as a point of departure for his views on a Jewish state. Because he died in 1935, thirteen years before the founding of the State of Israel, Rav Kook never confronted the reality of a Jewish state and did not define it directly. I propose to extrapolate from his writings on Zion and Jerusalem, Zionism and Jerusalemism, a view on a Jewish state. This material is both a particularly fertile source for conceptual development, and also reveals practical consequences for what it means for a Jew to be a citizen of the State of Israel.

In various public calls and in other writings, Rav Kook made a sharp conceptual distinction between the *concepts* of "Zion" and "Jerusalem."[2] "Zion" denotes the *secular* dimensions of Jewish peoplehood, whereas "Jerusalem" is the principle of *holiness* in the Jewish people, ostensibly the identifiably *religious* expression of Jewish existence. "Zion" is "our worldly power" and is referred to as "our kingdom" or "the expression of our kingdom," and "the representative of the secular side of our national life." As such, Zion pertains to what Rav Kook calls the "external" side of Jewish national identity: statecraft, economics, and social institutions. On occasion Rav Kook goes so far as to exclude from Zion any activity pertaining to the religious life of the Jewish nation.[3]

Although Rav Kook does speak of a "holiness" in Zion, he clearly opposes Zion to Jerusalem, the principle of holiness and religiosity.[4] Jerusalem is "the site of the Temple," and as such is "the holiness itself." This holiness pertains to the interior of Jewish national existence, "to our inner world." The Jerusalem movement is therefore to engage in "holy matters" and to be a counterweight to the Zionist movement: the holy, as opposed to the secular, the profane. It is to provide religious education, rabbinical institutions, and frameworks for the realization of Jewish religious practice in Palestine.

For Rav Kook, existing religious organizations were incapable of providing the concentration of religiosity to be embodied in "Jerusalem."[5] The Mizraḥi organization, a pioneer in religious Zionism, is "compromising" on religious matters, and is in any case an insignificant minority in the Zionist movement. Its efforts are diluted and unfelt in the overwhelmingly secular context. Agudat Yisrael, though more loyal to the stringencies of Jewish law than Mizraḥi, was non-Zionist, and in any case strongly oriented toward Jewish life in Eastern Europe. Therefore, a new organization was needed, founded on adherence to pious religiosity and focused on Jewish life in Palestine.

Rav Kook envisions two separate movements, Zionism and Jerusalemism, one secular, the other holy, acting in mutual cooperation, but each preserving its integrity in the face of the other: "Zion—Thy city, and Jerusalem—Thy Holy Temple."

Already in 1904, Rav Kook wrote of two diseases infecting the body of the Jewish nation.[6] One debilitated the aspect of the holy in the people, and the other weakened the aspect of activism and engagement in the world ("gevurah" in Rav Kook's terminology). Both are diseases of the Exile and are to be cured by a return to the Holy Land. The two movements are apparently Rav Kook's solution to the two diseases. "Jerusalem" is to be the instrument for returning to Judaism the richness and depth of holiness diluted in exile, and "Zion" is to restore the Jewish people to a life of active engagement in the world.

From Rav Kook's writings proclaiming and propagating the new movement, Jerusalem, there emerges a clear attitude on his part as to the primacy of Jerusalem and its eschatological importance. He writes: "The ultimate aim of the holy is not merely a state, but 'the seat of God in Jerusalem,' the seat of glory, the place of the Temple."[7] Rav Kook, playing on the verses of Psalms 137, notes that when the Jews sat on the waters of Babylon and remembered Zion, they proclaimed their longing for Jerusalem, and not for Zion: "If I forget thee, Jerusalem, may my right hand wither."[8]

So Jerusalem, not Zion, is therefore "the highest goal in the ideal of Jewish existence."

These pronouncements of Rav Kook's have been used to justify what I shall call an *instrumentalist* view of a Jewish state. On this view a Jewish state exists for the sake of something beyond it toward which it is a means. In particular, Rav Kook's views have been used to justify a view of a Jewish state as an *instrument* for bringing about a Messianic era. The Messianic era, perceived in theological/religious terms as the culmination of Jewish history in heightened revelations of holiness, is posited as the goal toward which the Jewish state is a means. "Zion" exists for the sake of "Jerusalem," the latter external to and thus beyond the parameters of its (Zion's) own existence. And this instrumentalist view of a Jewish state, of the State of Israel, is invoked repeatedly to justify acts that otherwise would be morally intolerable. The nature of the state itself is subordinated to what is perceived as its true eschatological role, the bringing into being of a holiness beyond.

A closer look at Rav Kook's writings reveals a different turn of thought in which the above relationship between Zion and Jerusalem, and the instrumentalist view of Jewish statehood, are seen to be without foundation. I now turn to such a closer look and will later return to consider the question of the proper understanding of Rav Kook's practical program for the Jerusalem movement that we have already seen.

In a letter written in 1925 to one Rabbi Shmaryahu Menasheh Adler, eight years after the founding of the Jerusalem movement, Rav Kook enunciates a philosophical principle that, as we shall see, was central to his thought.[9] He writes that what is manifested in the world as a lowly holiness is in truth possessed of a very high holiness, whereas that which appears to be of sublime holiness is really low in its quality of holiness. Our experience presents to us an "upside down" world: what appears low is really very high, and what appears high is actually low! Rav Kook justifies this astonishing principle on the grounds that the higher a holiness is, the less it is able to be revealed in our world, its quality and power must be hidden from a world not ready for such sublime holiness. "Their great height does not allow them to reveal their holiness in the world."[10] Because their nature is covered up, the higher holies appear lowly. Their potency is suppressed. On the other hand, the less potent, lower holiness can be openly revealed. The eyes of this world can bear its open manifestation. Thus the lower holies are fully revealed. As a result, the fully revealed lower holiness appears higher than the hidden, repressed higher holiness.

In a daring application of this principle, Rav Kook asserts that the days of the week are in reality possessed of a holiness that exceeds that of the holy Sabbath! And in general, the secular or profane in appearance is in its inner reality holier than the holy in appearance. Elsewhere Rav Kook repeats this general observation: "The holiness in the profane, which has descended to complete nonholiness, is more sublime and holy than the holy in the holy, only it is very hidden."[11]

If Zion is profane, and Jerusalem holy, then it follows that Zion in its inner source is higher than Jerusalem. And this is exactly what Rav Kook concludes in that same letter: "The aspect of Jerusalem, because external, as compared to Zion, in its source, is here below revealed in the power of holiness," and, "Because the aspect of Zion is internal, it is not recognizable in its holiness in this world."[12]

So here is the real truth about Zion and Jerusalem: Zion is really more "internal," higher in holiness; Jerusalem "external" and lower. The appearance of the opposite is only an appearance. Rav Kook's pronouncements as to Jerusalem being the highest end are statements, therefore, only about the appearances, and not about the truth. Jerusalem is lower than Zion.

Elsewhere, Rav Kook affirms this same truth explicitly concerning statehood itself: "The activity of a state . . . belongs to the highest revelations of holiness, and because of its great holiness it cannot shine openly, in a light possessing an open holiness." [13]

In adopting this principle of the "upside-down" world, Rav Kook was influenced by kabbalistic ideas, especially as developed by the founder of the Ḥabad Ḥassidic movement, Rabbi Schneur Zalman of Lyady (1745–1813). Rabbi Schneur Zalman's writings are permeated by the intricate working out of this principle of the upside-down world and its implications.[14] Here I wish to summarize five main points in Rabbi Schneur Zalman's writings, each of which, I will then show, influences Rav Kook's thinking on Zion and Jerusalem. (The richness of Rabbi Schneur Zalman's thought, of course, defies any such simple summation.)

1. The principle itself: what appears low is in reality very high, and what appears high is in reality very low. Several examples will illustrate the principle for Rabbi Schneur Zalman: in the true order of the chain of being, the inanimate holds the highest rank, the vegetative the next highest, then the animal, and lowest is the human; the so-called "animal-soul" of a person, the source of material desire, is of a higher nature than the so-called "divine soul," the source of spiritual aspiration in a person; the performance of the divine commandments, involving physical actualization, is higher in its root than the manifest, but intellectual, study of the Torah; the penitent comes from a higher source of holiness than does the saint who has not sinned; Ishmael is really higher than Isaac, and Esau higher than Jacob in their source; and finally, women (despite appearances) are higher than men in their real essence.

2. In "time to come" the true right-side up order of being will be revealed. The true reality will become manifest reality.

3. The more a thing appears low, and thereby known to be really

of great holiness, the weaker is its own individuality, and the stronger its generalized nature. For example, in the inanimate world there is great uniformity within a natural kind, and little individuality (one stone—of a certain composition, say—is much the same as any other). Humans, in contrast, display emphatic individual differences beyond the commonality of their humanity. This is because humans are of a lower origin than the inanimate.

4. Rabbi Schneur Zalman taught that the potency of the suppressed holiness expresses itself in this world in disguised forms. This accounts, for example, for the great power of the "animal-soul" as opposed to the lesser potency of the "divine soul," and for the immense force inherent in the inanimate. These are sublimated expressions of the power of holiness.

5. Finally, something can gain power for holy purposes from something apparently lower than it, because that thing is really higher! For example, a person can drink water, eat vegetation, and meat, and gain thereby the power to perform the divine commandments, because water, vegetation and animal meat all derive from a source of holiness higher than that of persons. Thus they can form the basis for holy activities.

All of these points influence Rav Kook's thinking on Zion and Jerusalem. We take them point by point:

1. Rav Kook endorses the inverted chain of being of Rabbi Schneur Zalman (exempting the Jewish people from the principle of inversion). Thus, as we have already seen, Zion is from a higher source than is Jerusalem.[15]

2. Rav Kook taught that as Messianic times unfold, the true nature of Zion is revealed. Rav Kook distinguished between two dimensions of the holiness of the Jewish people: "Segulah" (Treasure), the innate, natural holiness of the Jew, hidden deeply inside him, and "Behirah" (Choice), that holiness that accrues to a Jew as a result of an active choice to be holy.[16] Behirah expresses itself in an externally discernible religiosity. Rav Kook writes, "The portion [of holiness] of the Segulah is incommensurably greater and more holy than the portion dependent upon Behirah."[17] I suggest that for Rav Kook, Segulah includes Zion and is a holiness possessed even by secularists who do not manifest a holiness (chosen by them) embodied in a life of traditional piety. This is a deep and hidden

holiness. Beḥirah would then be the holiness of Jerusalem, the holiness made manifest in overt religious practice.[18] The deep hidden holiness is of a higher type than the manifest holiness. Rav Kook adds, "In the era of the 'footsteps of Messiah,' the power of Segulah gains power."[19] At the onset of Messianic times, the hidden holiness begins its self-revealment. And the higher holiness of Zion begins to emerge from beneath its cover. It is well known that Rav Kook believed his times to be the beginning of the Messianic era.[20]

3. The secular Zionists display a degree of a sense of oneness with the fate of the Jewish people, and a degree of self-sacrifice for the good of the nation, that is not found, according to Rav Kook, in the circle of traditional Jewish piety. In the latter, the emphasis is stronger on personal holiness. Also, the secular Zionists display a heightened devotion to universal human aspirations and values. These features of secular Zionism are explainable metaphysically by the high source of Zion, expressed in its greater *generality* and lesser individuality.[21]

4. The Zionist movement has an activism and a power of being largely missing in the religious establishment. Rav Kook calls this "gevurah," here meaning a power of self-affirmation and action. This power is a sublimation of the higher potency of holiness hidden in the depths of Zion. That potency gets revealed in a transformed way.

5. Finally, the apparently higher can "feed off" the apparently lower, because the latter is truly the higher. Thus Jerusalem is "nourished" by Zion, just as the vegetative grows from and is nourished by the inanimate. And thus Jewish statehood can form the basis of religious and spiritual growth. As Rav Kook writes: "There is a holiness that grows from the profane, just as the vegetative grows from the inanimate, and just as the living transforms the vegetative, and ascending life forces are thereby revealed."[22]

The profane nature of Zion is a place wherein holiness can grow, precisely because Zion is in reality from a higher source of holiness. This does *not* mean that Zion exists for the *sake* of Jerusalem. It only means to explain how it can be that Jerusalem *can* be strengthened by Jewish statehood. Indeed, given Rav Kook's overall position, Zion cannot exist for the *sake* of Jerusalem, because a higher degree of holiness simply cannot exist for the sake of a lower degree!

And Zion has a higher degree of holiness in its essence than does Jerusalem.

So we must reach the conclusion from Rav Kook's philosophical understanding that a Jewish state does not exist wholly or mainly as an instrument for religious ends and clerical purposes. Instead, a Jewish state is an end in itself, not in the sense that the very existence of such a state is an end in itself, but in the sense that the purpose of such a state is essentially to make manifest that very holiness immanent within the state itself. A higher holiness simply does not serve a lower one. And Rav Kook writes the following about the Jewish state he envisions: "A state is not the highest happiness of humanity. This can be said about an ordinary state . . . but not about a state that is idealistic in its foundation, that has chiselled onto its being the highest content of the ideal. . . . Such a state is truly the highest on the ladder of happiness. And our state is such a state, the state of Israel, the source of the seat of God in the world." [23]

This should not be taken to imply a worship of the state and its institutions. Rather, it is meant to assert that the holiness of the state does not transcend it. The state and its institutions are a means to an end: an end inherent in themselves. And in the light of this, I suggest that Rav Kook's practical program for the Jerusalem movement, which contravenes the philosophical position, be understood as a tactical program, a transitional practical prescription for bringing into being an ideational reality. Rav Kook has written: "The boundaries of the holy and the boundaries of the profane must be set in all areas of existence, in all forms of life, in the entirety of private life, and in the entirety of public life. Only with the distinction made correctly, with an exact distinction between the holy and the profane, will there arise a unity between them, and the root oneness at their source." [24]

A clear distinction must thus be made between Zion, the profane, and Jerusalem, the holy. A definition of "secular" is to be imposed upon the Zionist movement, and a definition of "religious" upon the Jerusalem movement. But this is not for reasons of the metaphysical adequacy of such definitions. They are not adequate in that regard. The separate and separating definitions are meant to liberate each of them, the holy as well as the profane, from the overbearing influence and domination of the other, thus allowing the profane to reveal from within its own inner workings the true nature of its holiness.[25] The practical, organizational program must thus be considered philosophically subordinate to Rav Kook's vision of a Jewish state.

Now I wish to turn to some implications of our discussion for the way a Jewish state is to be administered and its citizens are to relate to it, in Rav Kook's view. One important consequence is that since the Jewish state in the era of the "footsteps of Messiah" is to be a revelation of a higher holiness than previously manifested, it, the Jewish state, cannot be a mere return to ancient forms of Jewish existence. Rav Kook interprets the Jewish prayer, "Renew our days as of old," not as a supplication to reinstate a Jewish past that was, but rather as expressing the desire that our own days be days of renewal, days of change and novelty, just as in ancient times our days were filled with development and a dynamic process.

In particular, the Jewish state cannot be a return to the moral standards and policies embodied in the Jewish state of old. Higher standards of state-morality must emerge in the new state, revealing a holiness higher than that previously manifested in statehood. For example, Rav Kook writes, "In the matter of wars, it was impossible when all of its neighbors were dangerous wolves, that only Israel not engage in war, for then we would have been destroyed. On the contrary, it was an utmost necessity to impose fear upon the wild nations, even by cruel behavior."[26]

In ancient times the Jewish nation had to act with cruelty and barbarity toward its enemies. This did not reflect a Jewish ideal but was a justified necessity for self-defense. Had the Jews not so acted, they would have invited cruelty and barbarity down upon their own heads. In ancient times such concessions to the moral ideal were justified. And in ancient times, as a result, the great holiness of Jewish state-morality was concealed beneath the exigencies of statecraft. But this state of affairs was interrupted by exile.

The long exile put an end to Jewish political life and to the need for moral concessions in Jewish existence. The exile has provided "a space of rest, suspension of the practical involvement in constant public life, which holds back the more idealistic and pure thoughts from developing and appearing in accordance with their sublime value within the inner character of the treasure of life."[27] In other words, as long as the Jews engaged in political activity, their higher, inner moral political sense could not develop out into history. This was because the demands of statecraft, as then practiced, fell short of the ideal, as, for example, in concessions to pure morality for the purpose of self-defense. Only by disengaging from politics entirely, by going into exile, did the deeper moral sensibilities gain the spiritual space in which to grow, reaching deep down into the inner character of the Jew. The centuries of exile have been centuries of concealed growth: "The desire for political aggrandizement and domination that pollute the purity of the national divine morality, ceased for a long time; this disengagement thus bringing it about for the Jewish people that the divine morality, natural to her, began slowly to return and penetrate into the inner point of her self-hood."[28]

The exile has been a long hibernation, in which higher moral powers have grown and been stored, ready to come alive in the era of Messianic history. And now the time for moral concessions to statecraft and in statecraft has passed! The long years of exile are coming to a close. If barbarity and cruelty could be justified in ancient times, they cannot be condoned or tolerated in a Zion of modern times: a Zion in which a higher holiness is to become manifest: "We abandoned world politics unwillingly, yet with an inner will, until that happy time shall come when it shall be possible to conduct a kingdom without wickedness and barbarity. . . . It is not fitting for Jacob to engage in statecraft at a time when it must be full of blood, at a time that demands the ability to be wicked."[29]

The voice of Jacob must rise above the hands of Esau, whose hands are full of blood. In the above passage Rav Kook is not condemning unjustified barbarity—that he condemns always, both in ancient and modern times. He is condemning barbarity that is justified by the exigencies of the situation, by the needs of the moment. What he *is* declaring is a resounding conviction that a state that must have recourse to justified barbarity is not the state envisioned in his Messianic vision. And he is declaring that such a state is better not to exist. The modern Jewish state is to embody the eschatological hope of revealing in the world that sublime holiness hidden deeply in Zion; a holiness higher even than Jerusalem. The modern-day/Messianic revelation of Zion is to be of a higher order than anything previously revealed within Jewish statehood, and is to bring out into the open the deepest holiness of the Jewish nation.

When speaking at the dedication of a headquarters for the Jewish National Fund in Tel Aviv, Rav Kook praised their work for fulfilling the words of Isaiah: "Open the gates, there shall enter a just nation, that keeps the faith." The gates of the Holy Land are opening to the Jewish people, and the latter, faithful to their covenant, are returning to their homeland, to the Promised Land. This "keeping of the faith," however, is combined with the higher morality of the new Zion, a nation of justice: "When we now return to our land we conquer it not with force and not with the sword, but by peaceful means; and we pay good money for each and every inch of land of our land, even though our rights to the land of our holy country have never expired."[30]

In this passage, Rav Kook expresses an ideology of "not one inch." He is not willing to take one inch of land without paying for it.[31] This even though he believes the Jewish right to the land has not expired. "Keeper of the faith"—the Jews are renewing their ancient tie to the land, their ancient right to the land; "a just nation"—they pay for every inch of it.

Rav Kook praised the Jewish National Fund for its role in the peaceful redemption of the land. The sense of justice, the demands for a higher morality that recognizes the duty to pay for that which is yours, overrides the nationalistic, historical claim to the Land of Israel. Rav Kook added, "We want to fulfill the commandment of love they neighbor as thyself not only with regard to individuals, but also with regard to nations."[32] Most significant is the date of this address, May 1930, less than a year after the Arab uprisings of 1929 in which many Jews were murdered, and in which an entire Jewish community, in Hebron, was massacred. In the face of Arab hatred, Rav Kook called for a higher morality for the new Zion.

This then is a most important element in Rav Kook's conception of Zion and Jerusalem, and hence of a Jewish state. It might be said in reply, though, that Rav Kook's teaching, calling for a higher morality that reveals a higher holiness, is naive and grossly impractical in the difficult political reality of present-day Israel. My purpose in this study has not been to argue the practical adoption of Rav Kook's higher morality in our present political situation. Times are indeed complicated and trying, far more so than Rav Kook ever dreamed. Nonetheless, Rav Kook's conception of a Jewish state is a welcome corrective to the nationalistic excesses and religious fervor that too often sins against morality, sometimes in his name. To be a citizen of a Jewish state is not to be construed simply in terms of loyalty to nationhood or country, but as a dedication to the inner holiness immanent in these ephemeral constructs. My purpose has been to bring before the reader what Rav Kook actually wrote and to urge the rejection of a selective reading of his texts. The issue is not to determine what Rav Kook would have said were he alive today, but to determine the set of values he can be claimed to have cherished for a Jewish state.

Notes

1. See *Iggerot Ha-Ra'ayah* III, 148–51, for the proclamation, which was first published in Yiddish.
2. See ibid. and IV, *passim*, but especially 83–84.
3. Ibid., III, 242.
4. See especially ibid., IV, 32.
5. See ibid., 32–33.
6. In "Jerusalem," appearing in *Ma'aamarei Ha-Ra'ayah*, 298–301.
7. *Iggerot Ha-Ra'ayah* IV, 83.
8. Ibid.
9. Ibid., 217.
10. Ibid.
11. *Orot*, 85.
12. *Iggerot Ha-Ra'ayah* IV, 217.
13. *Arpelei Tohar*, 6–7.
14. The following is a partial list of sources in Rabbi Schneur Zalman's writings where this principle surfaces (listed according to pagination given in Hebrew letters): *Torah Or*, 30, 43–44, 72–73, 93–94; *Likkutei Torah*, Leviticus, 34, 37–38; Numbers, 6, 70, 72–73, 81–82; Deuteronomy, 25–27, 35, 37, 74–76; Song of Songs, 9–11, 14–17.
15. See *Orot Hakodesh* II, 414–15.
16. *Iggerot Ha-Ra'ayah* II, 186–88.
17. Ibid., 187.
18. It should be noted that elsewhere Rav Kook gives a different interpreta-

tion to *Segulah* and *Beḥirah* with regard to Jerusalem and Zion. See "The Treasure of Zion and Jerusalem," in *Ma'aamarei Ha-Ra'ayah*, 81–83.

19. *Iggerot Ha-Ra'ayah* II, 187.
20. See for example, *Orot*, 82 83, 159; *Iggerot Ha-Ra'ayah* II, 188; *Ma'aamarei Ha-Ra'ayah*, 86–88.
21. *Iggerot Ha-Ra'ayah* I, 45.
22. "Ne'edar Ba-kodesh," in *Ma'aamarei Ha-Ra'ayah*, 406.
23. *Orot*, 160.
24. "Ne'edar Ba-kodesh," 407.
25. The overbearing influence of religiosity on the profane, thus retarding the latter's development, is a recurring theme in Rav Kook's writings. See *Orot Hakodesh* I, 145, and *Orot Ha-emunah*, 24, 62.
26. *Iggerot Ha-Ra'ayah* I, 100.
27. "Neḥamat Yisrael," in *Ma'aamarei Ha-Ra'ayah*, 281.
28. Ibid., 283–84.
29. *Orot*, 14.
30. *Ma'aamarei Ha-Ra'ayah*, 252.
31. In the same speech Rav Kook says that "Because we are a righteous nation our conquering will be—*where possible*—only in the way of peace by monetary acquisition" (my emphasis). From the context of the speech it is clear that what is intended is that where it is *not* possible to acquire land by monetary means, it will not be acquired. It is entirely inconsistent with the rest of the speech to think that Rav Kook meant to recommend force where monetary means will fail.
32. *Ma'aamarei Ha-Ra'ayah*, 252.

CHAPTER 12

Zionism As a Return to Mount Sinai in Rabbi Kook's Thought

Warren Zev Harvey

Mount Sinai Is Suspended above Us!

In a sermon written for the holiday of Shavuot, Rabbi Abraham Isaac Ha-Kohen Kook took as his text the famous midrash on Exodus 19:17, "And they stood at the bottom of the mount": "This teaches that the Holy One, blessed be He, overturned the mountain above them like a tub, and said to them: 'If you accept the Torah, all well and good; but if not, your burial shall be there!'" (*Shabbat* 88a). Rabbi Kook's exposition of this text went as follows:

> On this day of the Giving of our Torah [i.e., the holiday of Shavuot]. . . , we must remember that it was not only in free will that we took upon ourselves the yoke of the Torah, but it was done under coercion by our having had the mountain suspended over us like a tub. With the eternal pronouncement, "If you accept the Torah, all well and good; but if not, your burial shall be there!," the Torah was engraved in the depths of our souls.
>
> And now, when we must return to the days of our youth, and the steps of the national revival are heard in their resounding beat, we are returning once again to that solemn situation. Once again we are . . . to receive the Torah under coercion, by having the mountain suspended over us like a tub . . .
>
> For several years, the multitudes of peoples throughout the world have seen that the ensign has been lifted up on the mountains, proclaiming the return of the holy and ancient nation . . . to its Land, the land of wonders. . . Yet barely had the ensign begun to be lifted, when there appeared a sort of weakness in the hands lifting it. . . .

There have arisen among us individuals who see but the vision of their own hearts. . . . There reverberates within our camp the frail voice of idealism and free will, which has lightning and luster, but which will give us only flowers and not fruit . . . , not the living light and the might [*gevurah*] of the soul, and not the thunderous might [*gevurah*] of the radiance of prophecy . . . for which every noble soul, among us and among all humanity, so yearns.

We know that in the end the quality of might [*gevurah*] will prevail, but precisely out of decree and law, and not by virtue of the free ideals . . . ; precisely out of the great and august Necessity, out of the Might [*gevurah*] from on high, out of "the voice of the Lord in power . . . the voice of the Lord which breaketh the cedars" [Psalms 29:4–5] . . . This voice . . . is once again . . . saying to us: If you accept the Torah, all well and good! Only if we accept the Torah, the fountain of life and light, will we have a national revival which is whole and pure, prodigious and awesome. Only if we accept the Torah, and institute it as a Torah of life and as the law of the nation, in the land of our past and our future, in the Land of Israel, will our national revival be firmly based, with strong and powerful roots, with an end and with a hope. . . .

In virtue of . . . having the mountain suspended over us like a tub, we shall receive the Word of the Lord as a law of life and a national constitution in our Land. . . . And we shall become in the eyes of all the nations what we must be by necessity: the great and holy people in the Holy Land, as in days of old, and as in ancient years.[1]

In Rabbi Kook's bold, startling image, modern Zionism is portrayed as a return to Mount Sinai. Today, as in the days of Moses, the people of Israel are being offered the Torah; and today, as then, God has uprooted the mountain and has lifted it up high over our heads like a tub, and once again we are being threatened: "If you accept the Torah, all well and good; but if not, your burial shall be there!"

What other image could make as emphatically clear the momentous and urgent importance that modern Zionism held in Rabbi Kook's eyes? What is at stake, according to him, is the life or death of the Jewish people, and the future of God's Torah. Will the Jewish people today accept the Torah and live, or reject it and die? Rabbi Kook believed with perfect faith that the Jews today, like the children of Israel in the days of Moses, would be compelled by reality to choose life, not death, and that Zionism would augur the revival of the Jewish nation, not its burial.

On one level, Rabbi Kook is making a simple and unremarkable argument, which might be restated as follows. The Jewish people are the Jewish people only by virtue of the Torah (cf. Saadia Gaon, *Beliefs and Opinions* III, 7); if in returning to Zion they were to reject the Torah, they would cease to exist as the Jewish people. Thus, even though the new heterodox Zionist ideologies may be exciting and enticing, they cannot sustain the Jewish people: there is no substitute for the light and the might of the Torah. Those newfangled ideologies, writes Rabbi Kook, offer us "flowers," but no "fruit." This metaphor is borrowed from a well-known line in a poem by Rabbi Judah Halevi: "Do not let Greek wisdom beguile you, which has no fruit but flowers" (from the poem "Devarekha be-Mor 'Over Rekuḥim"). Just as Rabbi Judah Halevi had warned in the twelfth century that Plato or Aristotle can be no substitute for the Torah, so Rabbi Kook in the twentieth century warns that modern heterodox ideologies can be no substitute, either.

However, Rabbi Kook is not merely affirming, with Saadia and Halevi, that the Torah is essential to the Jewish people. He is making the audacious claim that the contemporary return to Zion is no less than a return to Mount Sinai. In his view, the people of Israel today are in a position similar to the one during the days of Moses: leaving Exile, entering the Land of Israel, and being asked and coerced to accept the Torah. Moreover, Rabbi Kook is also making a prediction: overwhelmed by the miraculous reality of the return to Zion, the people will indeed accept the Torah.

In order to understand more fully in what sense Rabbi Kook saw modern Zionism as a return to Mount Sinai, we shall now turn to consider his distinctive views on the Torah and Zion.

The Oral Torah Descended unto the Deep Bottom!

The Torah, according to Rabbi Kook's analysis, is in dire distress owing to the Exile. The crisis of the Torah is explained systematically but concisely in the opening chapter of his little kabbalistic book, *Orot ha-Torah* (Lights of the Torah). Rabbi Kook discusses there the relationship between the Written Torah and the Oral Torah, and the repercussions of the Exile on their relationship. He writes:

The Written Torah we receive through the highest and most expan-
sive channel of our soul. We feel from within it the flare of the beauty
[*tiferet*] of the universal living light of all existence. By means of it
we soar above all logic and intellect. . . . It was not the spirit of the
nation that wrought this great light. The Spirit of God, the Creator of
all, created it. . . .

With the Oral Torah, we descend already to life. We sense that we
are receiving the most high light through the second channel in our
soul, through the channel that approaches the life of deed. We sense
that the spirit of the nation, which is connected as a flame to coal in
the light of the Torah of truth [cf. *Sefer Yetzirah* 1:7], is that which,
by its special nature, has caused the Oral Torah to be created in its
special form. . . .

The nurturing of the Oral Torah is by concealed means from
heaven and by revealed means from earth. The Land of Israel must be
built and all Israel dwelling on it, with everything in order: sanctuary
and kingdom, priesthood and prophecy, judges and officers, and all
their appurtenances. Then, the Oral Torah . . . grows and buds, and
conjoins with the Written Torah. . . . In the Exile, the twins were
separated. The Written Torah disappeared into the heights of its
holiness, and the Oral Torah descended unto the deep bottom, yet it
receives covert nourishment from the light of the Written Torah,
from the aftergrowth of the past that suffices to sustain it in restricted
life. And it is descending and falling with each and every day, until
there will arrive the day, and the living light shall come forth from
the treasure house of eternal redemption, and Israel shall do mightily,
shall be planted in its land, and shall flourish in all the glory of its
ordinances. Then the Oral Torah shall begin to sprout . . . and to rise
upward and upward, and the light of the Written Torah shall once
again shine its rays upon it. . . . And the lovers shall unite in their
bridal habitation.[2]

To be sure, according to common Rabbinic usage, the Written
Torah is the written Law received by Moses on Mount Sinai, and
the Oral Torah is the interpretation of that Law throughout the
ages, which is held to have also been revealed on Mount Sinai.
However, in the kabbalistic symbolism presupposed in this passage,
the Written Torah and the Oral Torah are also identified with
divine *sefirot*: the former with the sixth *sefirah*, the male Tiferet;
the latter with the tenth and lowest *sefirah*, the female Malkhut.
Tiferet and Malkhut are lovers and strive to unite. When the people
of Israel (who are also identified with Malkhut) were driven into
Exile, a breach was caused between the two lovers, which has been

widening ever since. This intradivine breach between Tiferet and Malkhut is manifested in the empirical breach between the Written Torah and the Oral Torah.

With the people of Israel in Exile, without "sanctuary and kingdom, priesthood and prophecy, judges and officers, and all their appurtenances," that is, without national independence, the Torah was not called upon to confront the fundamental political, social, and economic problems of the "life of deed." One might say it was reduced to a merely cultic or ceremonial law, concerned with marriage, divorce, kosher food, and the like.

Untested and unexercised, the Oral Torah was stunted in its growth, and became weak, undernourished; it was forced to subsist minimally on the "aftergrowth," left over from the ancient days of Jewish independence in the Land of Israel. At the same time, the Written Torah was coming to appear exclusively sacramental, irrelevant to workaday affairs. Separated from the Oral Torah, the Written Torah "disappeared into the heights of its holiness"; separated from the Written Torah, the Oral Torah languished and "descended unto the deep bottom." Moreover, the situation is rapidly deteriorating: the Oral Torah is *descending and falling with each and every day*" of Exile, and the breach between it and the Written Torah has become an ever-expanding chasm.

The Torah, according to Rabbi Kook's analysis, is thus in imminent danger, and can be rescued only by the speedy return of the Jewish people to the Land of Israel. Only the reestablishment of Jewish national life in the Land of Israel can make possible the union of the Written Torah and the Oral Torah, Tiferet and Malkhut. Zionism thus gives the Jewish people a precious opportunity to receive the Torah once again in its pristine wholeness: the return to Zion is also a return to Mount Sinai.

While Rabbi Kook's analysis of the Torah and Zion is rooted in the Kabbalah, it also should be understood against the background of contemporaneous Zionist thought.

Aḥad Ha'am,[3] for example, had argued that the Torah reflects the spirit of the Jewish people, and that just as the spirit of the people had become ossified in the Exile, so had the Torah. What was needed, he thought, was a rejuvenation of the spirit of the people, which would involve a rejection of the old Torah. Such a rejuvenation, he held, would require the creation of a Jewish cultural center in the Land of Israel. Rabbi Kook's statement that "it was not the spirit of the nation that wrought this great light" may be taken as a response to Aḥad Ha‘am: the Jewish people did not fashion the Torah, but the Torah fashioned the Jewish people! However, Rabbi Kook's comments about the Oral Torah show a measure of agreement with Aḥad Ha‘am: the spirit of the people has indeed become ossified in the Exile, and this has taken its toll on the Oral Torah, which is closely bound up with the spirit of the people; a rejuvenation of the people is truly necessary, and this can be achieved only by the full revival of Jewish national institutions in the Land of Israel (and not merely by the creation of a cultural center there); however, this rejuvenation will not involve the rejection of the Torah, but rather the rejection of the fragmented and debilitated Torah of Exile in favor of the full-bodied Torah of the Land of Israel; that is, it will involve the acceptance anew of the Torah in its true scope and power.

Rabbi Kook's analysis of the Torah and Zion strikes me as also having an affinity with the radical Zionism of Ber Borochov.[4] For Rabbi Kook, as for Borochov, Zionism was not an *ad hoc* response to the accidents of history, but a deep historic necessity. In Borochov's Marxist system, this necessity was seen as material; in Rabbi Kook's kabbalistic system, it was seen as spiritual. Borochov spoke of the worsening national condition of the Jews, which, for him, had to be understood in terms of economics; Rabbi Kook spoke of the worsening national condition of the Jews, which for him, however, had to be understood in terms of the crisis of the Torah. Borochov described the abnormal situation of the Jews in the Exile in terms of his Parable of the Inverted Pyramid: in a normal nation, the base of the pyramid is wide (the majority work in the primary level of production or in basic industry; e.g., farmers, fishermen, miners, quarriers) and the top is narrow (only a minority are involved in jobs remote from production; e.g., bankers, shopkeepers); however, in the Jewish nation in Exile, the base is narrow, the top wide. Rabbi Kook's description of the Torah in Exile might be similarly illustrated by the Parable of the Inverted Pyramid: in normal circumstances, the base of the Torah is wide (laws concerning the primary necessities of national life; e.g., agriculture, government, civil justice) and the top narrow (laws remote from the primary necessities of national life; e.g., kosher food, personal *rites de passage*); in the Exile, the base is narrow, the top wide. Borochov believed that the revival of the Jewish nation in the Land of Israel and the concomitant overturning of the pyramid were part of a "stychic" process that would be realized regardless of the will of the Jews. Rabbi Kook believed in like manner that the revival of the Jewish nation in the Land of Israel and the reinstitution of the Torah as a law of life were part of a process that would be realized regardless of the will of the Jews, and he described this necessity as God's holding Mount Sinai over our heads.

It is in the light of Rabbi Kook's analysis of the Torah and Zion that one may understand his positive attitude toward many secular Zionist thinkers, including downright rebels like Berdyczewski and Brenner. He thought these thinkers were motivated by a correct perception that the Torah was in crisis, and he further respected them for their sense that what was called for was a return to Zion. Of course, in his view, they seriously erred in that they supposed the return to Zion was to be instead of the Torah, when in fact it was to be for the sake of the Torah. Even so, he was convinced they were on a higher spiritual plane than those ultra-orthodox anti-Zionists who neither perceived the crisis of the Torah nor dreamed of the immediate return to Zion.[5] Rabbi Kook did not doubt that the time was at hand for the revival of the Torah and the Jewish nation in the Land of Israel. Let us now address ourselves briefly to the historical perspective in which he saw Zionism.

The Time of "Zamir" (Singing or Cutting Down) Is Come!

In an important essay, "The War," first published in 1920, Rabbi Kook expressed his thoughts on the significance of the Great War and on its relationship to the anticipated reestablishment of the Jewish nation in the Land of Israel. The naive messianic enthusiasm with which Rabbi Kook interpreted the war was unexceptional at the time and reflected a Hegelian optimism shared by many of his contemporaries, Jews and non-Jews alike. However, Rabbi Kook's comments on the circumstances of the Exile of the Jewish people from the Land of Israel were definitely exceptional. His analysis went as follows:

> When there is a great war in the world, the power of the messiah is aroused. "The time of *zamir* [singing, pruning, cutting down] is come" [Song of Songs 2:12], the *cutting down* of tyrants [cf. Rashi on Exod. 15:2 and Isa. 25:5]. The evil ones are eradicated from the world, and the world is redolent; "and the voice of the turtledove is heard in our land" [Song of Songs 2:12]. . . . When the war is over, the world is renewed with a new Spirit, and the feet of the messiah are manifestly seen. In proportion to the greatness of the war . . . will be the greatness of the anticipation of the footsteps of the messiah. In the present World War, the anticipation is awesome, great, and profound. . . .
>
> We left world politics [after the destruction of the Second Temple] under a compulsion that had in it an inner voluntariness, until there would come a happy time, when it would be possible to conduct a government without wickedness and barbarity. . . . Our soul was disgusted by the dreadful sins that go with political rule in evil times. Now the time has come, it is very near, the world is redolent, and we can already prepare ourselves, for soon it will be possible for us to conduct our own government on the foundations of goodness, wisdom, justice, and the clear divine light. "Jacob sent the purple [i.e., royal] garments to Esau" [*Genesis Rabbah* 75:4 on Gen. 32:4]. "Let my lord [Esau] please pass over before his servant [Jacob]" [Gen. 33:14]. It is not befitting that Jacob occupy himself with statehood at a time that needs be full of blood, at a time that demands a talent for evil. . . . We were dispersed among the nations . . . until "the time of *zamir* is come, and the voice of the turtledove is heard in our land."
>
> Had it not been for the sin of the Golden Calf, the [Canaanite] nations that dwelled in the Land of Israel would have made peace with Israel. . . . For the Name of the Lord . . . would have aroused in them sublime awe. No manner of war would have been conducted. They would have been influenced by ways of peace, as in the days of the messiah. The sin alone caused this to be delayed thousands of years. But now all the factors in the world are joined together to bring the light of the Lord into the world, and the sin of the Golden Calf will be erased entirely, and then all who see [the people of Israel] will recognize that they are "the seed the Lord hath blessed" [Isa. 61:9]. And the world shall be mended by the way of peace and feelings of love, and the pleasantness of the Lord shall be sensed in every heart.[6]

There are two highly suggestive propositions in the foregoing text. First, the biblical war for the conquest of the Land of Israel was a result of the sin of the people of Israel: had the Israelites not been tainted by the sin of the Golden Calf, the Canaanite nations would have been awed by their holiness, and would have welcomed them in peace. Second, the people of Israel went into Exile voluntarily: they did not want political sovereignty in the Land of Israel, if it meant they would be required to do acts of cruelty.

These two propositions evidence Rabbi Kook's deep conviction that the Jewish people must act in accordance with stricter standards of morality and piety than are prevalent among the nations. The two propositions also hint at a common thesis: the reinstitution of Jewish sovereignty in the Land of Israel will be accomplished peacefully. Jews returning to the Land of Israel will no longer be tainted by the sin of the Golden Calf, and if they conduct themselves as a holy people, they will be welcomed in peace by the other inhabitants of the Land, the Arabs. Moreover, the Jews will be interested in regaining sovereignty in the Land only if they are able to do so in peace.

The two propositions clarify further Rabbi Kook's concept of Zionism as a return to Mount Sinai. When in the days of Moses the people of Israel received the Torah at Mount Sinai, they sinned by making the Golden Calf. Zionism takes them back to Mount Sinai and gives them a new chance. This time, Rabbi Kook is confident, the Jews will receive the Torah in holiness, will enter the Land in peace, build it up in peace, and govern it in peace. He could not imagine otherwise.

Postscript

Writing this essay here in Jerusalem almost fifty-five years after Rabbi Kook's death in 1935, and almost forty-two years after the proclamation of the State of Israel in 1948, I cannot help asking myself: *what would Rabbi Kook say today?*

I have little doubt that he would no longer subscribe to the simplistic Hegelian optimism that led him to assign immediate messianic dimensions to what we now call World War I. He would admit, I believe, that his kabbalistic system suffered at certain points from an overdose of Hegel.[7]

Nonetheless, I do not want to suggest that Rabbi Kook should be faulted for his belief that Jewish independence would come about peacefully. No one, not even a great visionary like Rabbi Kook, could have been expected in 1920 to foresee World War II and the Holocaust; and thus he could not have been expected to foresee the traumatic conditions that accompanied the proclamation of Jewish independence and that indelibly transformed the Zionist reality.

Still, I think it is reasonable and important to ask what Rabbi Kook would say about the present-day State of Israel. The question, however, will not admit of an easy answer, for the State is so different from what he had envisioned. After all, the Jews have not accepted the Torah. The State does not function according to the Torah, but according to secular laws; and "sanctuary and kingdom, priesthood and prophecy, judges and officers, and all their appurtenances" have not been reestablished in accordance with the Torah. It is true that the Torah, by the agency of the Chief Rabbinate, is responsible for marriages, divorces, the supervision of kosher food, and the like; but that is merely to say that it is responsible for essentially the same limited areas for which it was responsible in the Exile. Tiferet and Malkhut have certainly not been united in conjugal love. Can it even be said that the breach between them has been narrowed? And what of war? Since its birth, Israel has been in a state of continuous war with its Arab neighbors. Moreover, the rule over one and a half million Arab inhabitants of Judea, Samaria, and the Gaza Strip, who do not accept Israeli sovereignty, and who in recent years have been waging a violent uprising, has forced the Israeli army to use methods that have resulted in hundreds of injuries and deaths. Is not the State of Israel facing the Palestinians in the same situation as Jacob facing Esau? Would Israel, therefore, be required to surrender its rule over those territories it cannot govern in peace? Moreover, why is it that the Arabs have not welcomed us Jews? Must we say that it is because we did not accept the Torah as a living law, a national constitution? Could it be that just as the people of Israel in the time of Moses worshiped the glittering Golden Calf they had fashioned with their own hands, so too we have worshiped the glittering ideologies we have fashioned in our free will? Above all, given that we do have a Jewish state in the Land of Israel, but have not accepted the Torah, what must we do to prevent the mountain from crashing down upon us?

Post-Postscript

As this volume is in press (September 1993), significant agreements have been reached between Israel and the Palestinians. No one knows what will be the results of these agreements. My hope is that when you read this, much of what I wrote in the Postscript concerning Israel and the Arabs will be anachronistic. My prayer is that these agreements will contribute toward realizing Rabbi Kook's vision of peace and the true rejuvenation of the Torah.

Notes

1. *Ma'amarei ha-Rayah* (Jerusalem, 1984), 166–67. The sermon first appeared in the weekly *Ha-Tor* 3, nos. 25–26 (1923), 1–2.
2. *Orot ha-Torah* (Jerusalem, 1985), 9–10 (1st ed., 1940). The text quoted here appears also in *'Arpelei Tohar* (Jerusalem, 1983), 23, 25, and was already included in the pages printed (but not bound) in the aborted original edition (Jaffa, 1914).
3. Most of his writings were translated into English by Leon Simon in three volumes: *Selected Essays* (Philadelphia, 1912), *Ten Essays on Zionism and Judaism* (London, 1922), and *Essays, Letters, Memoirs* (Oxford, 1946).
4. A selection of his writings is available in English: *Nationalism and the Class Struggle* (New York, 1937).
5. See, e.g., Rabbi Kook's essay "Souls of Chaos" (*Ha-Neshamot shel 'Olam ha-Tohu*) in *Abraham Isaac Kook*, trans. Ben-Zion Bokser (New York, 1978), 256–58; originally in *Orot* (Jerusalem, 1950), 121–23.
6. *Orot*, 13–14. The essay first appeared in the shorter *editio princeps* (Jerusalem, 1920). A partial English translation is found in Arthur Hertzberg, *The Zionist Idea* (Philadelphia, 1959), 422–23. The midrash cited from *Genesis Rabbah* construes Genesis 32:4 thusly: "And Jacob took off [vayishlah] the royal garments [mal'akhim (messengers) = melakhim (kings)], (and threw them down) before Esau." The midrash explains: "He took off the purple garments, and threw them down before him. He said to him: 'Two *zarzirim* [wrestlers or starlings] cannot sleep on the same mat.'" In Rabbi Kook's understanding of the midrash, the people of Israel (Jacob) voluntarily relinquished to Rome (Esau) sovereignty over the Land of Israel; cf. *Gittin* 56a-b.
7. However, the Hegelian elements in Rabbi Kook's thought have been strongly emphasized in the theologico-political doctrine of his son, Rabbi Zvi Yehudah Kook. It is this emphasis on the Hegelian elements in Rabbi Kook's thought that has enabled Gush Emunim ideologists to see themselves as loyal to his teachings.

CHAPTER 13

What Would Rav Kook Have to Say about the State of Israel Today?

Tamar Ross

The popular guessing game—"What would so-and-so say if he were alive today?"—is one that often tempts us, but is more often than not quite worthless. Not only is such guesswork highly speculative, but also—to the extent that human beings are attuned to their times—it might very well be that if so and so were alive today he would not be the same person we are thinking of.

I therefore tend to regard the debates that take place in Israel between followers of the Gush Emunim camp and those of the more dovelike Oz ve-Shalom movement as to whether the venerated Rav Kook—whom each of them would like to adopt as their mentor—would or would not hold to an intransigent stance regarding the principle of *Shelemut ha-Aretz* (inviolable completeness of the land) as a dubious exercise. One group bases its contention on the very Judah Halevi-like view of the unique relationship between the Jewish people and the Land of Israel that Rav Kook held, and on the fact that he regarded the struggle for political independence as an effort of ultimately religious value. The opposite group, on the other hand, cites instances of Rav Kook's extreme humanitarianism and tolerance, his expressions of sensitivity for the value of humanity in general as having been created in the image of God, and his conviction that the achievement of statehood envisioned by Jewish Messianism is one that obviates the necessity for the type of barbarism and cruelty entailed by more usual forms of nationalism. For example, Rav Kook confesses a special love for the Jewish people but contends that this love in no way conflicts with a natural spontaneous love for all nations.[1] He also expresses his belief that the Jewish people were forcibly spared involvement in world politics and the struggle for power during their long exile precisely because they were meant to return to national life only when this could be achieved by merciful means.[2] Guesswork is doubly difficult when dealing with Rav Kook, because of the innovative and original way in which his mind worked. Even when one acquires a grasp of the basic underlying principles of his thought, it is not always easy to anticipate the startling applications he might be likely to come up with, which many a time involve paradox and the *Ipkha Mistabbera* (reasoning contrary to the expected).

However, some speculations could be regarded as safer than others, because they refer to issues that have not substantially changed since the lifetime of the person concerned. Regarding the political/religious question of whether or not to return the occupied/liberated territories, one could claim that what facilitated the formulation of Rav Kook's pre-state stance in an ideologically purist vein, uncomplicated by considerations of *realpolitik*, was the fact that he wasn't faced with the growth of Palestinian nationalism, a virile Arab opposition, and the overt involvement of the international superpowers. The issues did not present themselves as *Shelemut ha-Aretz* versus *Shelemut ha-Am*, or as the rival claims of two nations which, subjectively at least, equally regard themselves as oppressed. Therefore, romantic considerations could reign supreme. It is thus a moot point to what extent Rav Kook would nowadays allow a blind faith in the commitment of Providence to the Zionist ideal to "give" in the face of pragmatic or humanistic considerations, and reformulate his nationalist aspirations in the light of previously ignored factors.

But I am less hesitant with regard to another question, and that is: What would Rav Kook have to say regarding the secular nature of the State of Israel today? At first blush, it would seem that here too the situation we confront is not comparable to the one Rav Kook had to contend with. But regarding this question I do believe that Rav Kook's stance at least implicitly is pertinent to present-day conditions as well.

It is well known that a major feature of Rav Kook's thought is his response to the challenge of secularism. At the turn of the century he was witness to a dramatic surge of advancement in technology, the arts and sciences, and the emergence of all sorts of ideological "isms" intended for the betterment of humanity in general. More specifically, this was the period of the intense awakening of Jewish nationalism, and an idealism of a new sort, dedicated to ensuring the physical welfare of the Jewish people, and aspiring to create for them a unique social order predicated upon the ideals of justice, equality, economic independence, an ingathering of the exiles, and freedom from the yoke of foreign nations. There was a tremendous amount of *Mesirut Nefesh* (sacrifice) involved on the part of the young *halutzim* engaged in this task. Rav Kook felt it impossible to ignore this idealism, as it was directed to goals that belonged essentially to the traditional vision of Messianic times.[3] Yet along with the admiration and celebration came perplexity; how could the palpable idealism and high moral quality of these vanguards of the Messiah be tallied with their blatant apostasy? For did not these very *halutzim*, who were willing to fight and die for their people and country, also deny the existence of God and rebel against their Galut forebears in one and the same breath?

Rav Kook's solution to the dilemma, first explicated in one of the earliest articles he wrote after his appointment as regional Rabbi of Jaffa and the surrounding settlements (entitled "Hador"—referring to his generation),[4] was to reinterpret the talmudic statement (in Tractate Sanhedrin 98a) that the Messiah will arrive in a generation that is *kulo ḥayav* or *kulo zakkai* (entirely guilty or entirely innocent) to mean that the generation will not be either ḥayav or *zakkai*, but both at the same time. On the surface, the generation is totally wanting; its professed stance is obviously *ḥutzpa kelappei shemaya* (brazenness toward Heaven). But this is so only because the protagonists of this militantly antireligious view do not recognize that their motives are subconsciously religious ones. It is the discrepancy between their high moral standards, and organized religion as it is popularly conceived and explicated, that forces them to their position. There is a justified dissatisfaction with the sort of religious view that does not take into account the everyday concerns of real life and which regards universal considerations of justice and physical well-being, as well as the creative urge for self-expression and the dynamic concern for *yishuvo shel olam* (settlement of the world) as irrelevant to the Divine, and it is this which breeds the religious rebellion of the young idealists. Viewed from the vantage point of eternity, this rebellion is ultimately *kulo zakkai*, for it is born of an intuitively constructive desire to broaden the horizons of religious understanding and serve as a catalyst for a more satisfactory formulation of what faith in God really means—a knowledge that was previously held by *yehidei-segulah* (rare special individuals) but is now demanded by the masses.[5]

In order to illustrate the problematics entailed by the existence of a positive seedling embedded in secular Zionism, Rav Kook brings the Midrashic example (*Exodus Rabbah* 84) of a bird perched on the statue of the king, whom the hunter dares not attack lest the icon be destroyed.[6] Secular Zionism is perched upon and nourished by genuinely religious values. Therefore, to attack it indiscriminately involves either dislodging it from its kindly base or destroying it along with that base to which it is inextricably attached.

It was Rav Kook's conviction that once the leaders of the professedly religious camp would confront the challenge of secularism, and be forced by this challenge to reformulate their expressions of faith in less narrowly clerical terms, the antireligious trappings of Jewish nationalism would fall away, and its basically religious nature would become evident to all. In the interim, an understanding of its essentially God-oriented yearnings provides the justification for tolerance and cooperation, and even for embracing the secularists and viewing their rebellion as a religious blessing in disguise.

A Renewed Assessment of Rav Kook's Position

Today, forty years after the establishment of the State of Israel, there seems to be a need for a renewed assessment of Rav Kook's position. Ostensibly, the rosy assumptions Rav Kook made regarding the religious potential of secular Jewish nationalism seem to have been completely refuted. For now we are not dealing in the main with the admirable idealism of Hashomer Hatzair youth and the parting words of Trumpeldor: "It is good to die for one's country"; but with the crass materialism of Tel Aviv's Dizengoff Square, and the "Rosh Katan" me-generation of Sabras who resent demands made in the name of national needs on their private lives and careers. Regarding the secularism of this generation, Rav Kook's optimism could conceivably be regarded as naive, to say the least. It would seem that history has proven his faith in the unconscious religious character of avowedly secular Jewish nationalism to be unfounded, and serves merely to confirm the dire predictions of religious anti-Zionists that no good could possibly come of *meḥalelei shabbat be-farhesya* (those who publicly desecrate the Sabbath). What positive value can be eked out of the secular nature of the state today?

However, I believe the Kook ideologist still retains the power to relate to present day secularism as affirmation of the original religious legitimacy of the Zionist ideal. In fact, in one of his more astonishingly prophetic statements, Rav Kook himself seems to be engaging in just such an exercise. In this passage he predicts that there will come a time when "physical calm will descend upon a certain segment of the nation." This will occur when some of the people will imagine that they have already realized their goals to the full, and this misplaced satisfaction will "diminish their soul." But, adds Rav Kook, it is precisely this misplaced self-satisfaction that is required to invoke the necessary spiritual backlash capable of redressing the balance.[7] What the cultural bankruptcy of secular Israeli life comes to confirm in the eyes of the hard-line Kookian is that no valid idea can exist for any protracted length of time without receiving nourishment from its source. If secularism in Israel has been divested of its idealism and moral fervor, and turned decadent and sour, this is merely the logical outcome of estrangement from its religious underpinnings. Jewish nationalism is unlike any other nationalism and cannot survive without the orientation of faith.

There is a lesson here to be learned by the old guard Zionists, and it is this: if Zionism is to continue as a vibrant movement, it must recognize its underlying religious significance. But to take this position one step further, I would imagine Rav Kook's dialectical reasoning undergoing an additional twist, when applied to the latest phenomenon of the *ba'al teshuvah* movement, particularly in its dominantly *ḥaredi* and anti-Zionist version. Rav Kook would surely have been heartened by the intensified interest in observance of *mitzvot*, and interpreted it as an intuitive reaction of the Jewish people against the divorce of religion and State. But he would no doubt have also seen the anti-Zionist character of this revival as yet another regrettable effect of the mistake of divorcing religion from national and universal moral concerns. Here the accusing finger would be pointed not only at the secularists, who failed to recognize the true nature of their position, but also at the leaders of the religious camp, who failed in broadening and developing religious thought beyond its Diaspora-type categories.

The truth is that there is a profound theological background to Rav Kook's position that often gets lost in more popular expositions of his relationship to secularism on a practical level.[8] Rav Kook had a progressive view of history and the development of ideas in general, and religion in particular.[9] Just as mankind advanced from paganism (with the gods portrayed as glorified humans) to monotheism (with God as a transcendent being), so it was destined to move forward to the realization that in actual fact all is Divine, and therefore no human activity insignificant. In fact, Rav Kook believed that most expressions of atheism were merely the rationalization or sublimation of misplaced feelings of jealousy at the paltriness of human affairs in comparison with the perfection of the Almighty, and therefore concluded that the usual version of monotheism was counterproductive to true religious belief.[10] But every intellectual advance from one stage of belief to the next is dependent upon a corresponding advance in moral stature.[11] The return of *Am Yisrael* to *Eretz Yisrael*, and the unconscious impulse to create a society that expresses the Divine in every aspect of life, and not only in the narrowly ritual, which is entailed in this return— these are factors that carry the potential of forcing the theological-development to take place. It is up to the religious thinkers of the generation to explicate the connection and spell out the bridge between historical occurrence and religious import. Once this is accomplished, the Zionist movement will have fulfilled its hidden Messianic role.[12]

Notes

1. *Arpelei Tohar* (Jerusalem, 1983), 31. See also *Orot Ha-kodesh* (Jerusalem, 1938), III, 349.
2. *Orot*, "Ha-Milḥamah" (War), 14, paragraph 3.
3. For a summary of the traditional picture, see Maimonides' introduction to his commentary to *Perek Ḥelek*. For expressions of Rav Kook's difficulty, see his essay "Hador," in *Ikkevei Hatzon*, republished in one volume together with *Eder Hayakar* (Jerusalem, 1985), 107–16.
4. "Hador," 107–16.
5. Rav Kook believed that the ever-narrowing gap between the masses and their spiritual leaders was yet another symptom of pre-Messianic times; see ibid., 110–11. For further illustrations of the narrowing of this gap offered by Rav Kook, see *Orot ha-Kodesh* (Jerusalem, 1964), II, 539–41.
6. *Iggerot ha-Reiyah* (Jerusalem, 1946), II, 171.
7. *Orot*, "Orot ha-Teḥiyah," 84, paragraph 44.
8. For a morc detailed, technical, exposition of Rav Kook's theology, see my article: "Musag ha-Elohut shel ha-Rav Kuk," *Daat* 8 (1981) and 9 (1982).
9. For illustration of how a progressive view of the history of ideas pervades Rav Kook's analysis of the development of religion, read his article "Avodat Elokim" in *Ikkevei Hatzon*.
10. *Orot Hakodesh* II, 397, 399.
11. *Eder Hayakar* (Jerusalem, 1985), 36; *Orot Hakodesh* II, 488–90.
12. It is interesting to note in this connection the late Professor Gershom Scholem's rejection of the attempt to interpret Zionism as a form of Messianism, since Zionism is a transformed and secularized version of the old, traditional ideal. Rav Kook does not really disagree—he merely ascribes a hidden theological motive to the modern secular version. His point would be that this hidden motive is what makes the Zionist movement significant theologically. Hence the present-day crisis could be interpreted, as above, as a product of the impossibility of Jewish nationalism continuing to sustain itself without an acknowledgment of its underlying theological roots.

Bibliography

Robert Carroll

[Editors' note: Robert Carroll compiled the items listed under "Secondary Literature" in 1991; the editors then added a list of primary sources. The editors also added a few references to items in the Secondary Literature.]

Primary Sources

Primary Sources in Hebrew

This heading includes only books that collect Rav Kook's writings or addresses. An exception is the collection of Rav Kook's poetry listed as *Shirat ha-Rav (repr. in Otzerot ha-Reayah)*. Selections from Rav Kook's many contributions to periodicals and other vehicles may be found in *Maamarei ha-Reayah* and in Tzuriel, *Otzerot ha-Reayah*.

To mark the fiftieth year since Rav Kook's passing (1985), the Mosad HaRav Kook in Jerusalem reissued most of Rav Kook's Hebrew writings. Earlier editions of the works included in the 1985 release, and editions of those works produced by other publishers, are not noted below.

Arpelei Tohar, ed. Y. Sheilat. Jerusalem: Ha-Makhon 'al Shem ha-Rav Tzvi Yehudah Kook, 1983.
Be'ar Eliyahu (commentary to Elijah of Vilna's glosses on the laws in *Ḥoshen Mishpat*). Jerusalem: Mosad Harav Kook, 1985.
Da'at Kohen (responsa pertaining to the *Yoreh Deah* section of the *Shulkhan Arukh*). Jerusalem: Mosad HaRav Kook, 1985.
Derashot ha-Reayah le-Yomim Noraim. Jerusalem: Ha-Makhon 'al Shem ha-Rav Tzvi Yehudah Kook, 1992.
Eder ha-Yakar. Jerusalem: Mosad HaRav Kook, 1985.
Ein Ayah (on Talmudic Aggadot). Jerusalem: Ha-Makhon 'al Shem Rav Tzvi Yehudah Kook, 1986.

310   ROBERT CARROLL

Etz Hadar (concerning the laws of *etrog*). Jerusalem: Mosad HaRav Kook, 1985.

Ezrat Kohen (responsa pertaining to the *Even Ha-Ezer* section of the *Shulhan Arukh*). Jerusalem: Mosad HaRav Kook, 1985.

Halakhah Berurah (commentary on parts of the Babylonian Talmud, together with *Birur Halakhah* compiled by students). Jerusalem: Makhon Halakhah Berurah im Berur Halakhah, 1970.

Haskamot ha-Reayah (Rav Kook's approbations of works by others). Jerusalem: Ha-Makhon 'al Shem Rav Tzvi Yehudah Kook, 1988.

Ḥavosh Pe'ar (on laws of phylacteries). Jerusalem: Mosad HaRav Kook, 1985.

Ḥazon ha-Geulah/Ikkevata di-Meshiḥa (writings on redemption). Jerusalem, 1941.

Iggerot ha-Reayah (collected Letters). Vols. 1–3: Jerusalem: Mosad HaRav Kook, 1985. Vol. 4. Jerusalem: Hamakhon 'al Shem ha-Rav Tzvi Yehudah Kook, 1984.

Ikkevei ha-Tzon. Jerusalem: Mosad HaRav Kook, 1985.

Ma'amarei ha-Reayah (various essays and addresses). Jerusalem, 1984.

Mishpat Kohen (responsa pertaining to the *Ḥoshen Mishpat* section of the *Shulkhan Arukh*). Jerusalem: Mosad HaRav Kook, 1985.

Mitzvot Reayah (Halakhic disquisitions). Jerusalem: Mosad HaRav Kook, 1985.

Musar Avikha/Middot ha-Reayah (on ethics). Jerusalem: Mosad HaRav Kook, 1985.

Olat Reiyah (prayerbook and commentary). 2 vols. Jerusalem: Mosad HaRav Kook, 1985.

Oraḥ Mishpat (responsa on the *Oraḥ Ḥayyim* and *Ḥoshen Mishpat* sections of the *Shulkhan Arukh*). Jerusalem: Mosad HaRav Kook, 1985.

Orot. Jerusalem: Mosad HaRav Kook, 1985.

Orot ha-Emunah (essays on faith). Brooklyn: Langsam Associates, 1985.

Orot ha-Kodesh. Vols. 1–3. Jerusalem: Mosad HaRav Kook, 1985; Vol. 4, 1990.

Orot ha-Reayah. Jerusalem: Mosad HaRav Kook, 1985.

Orot ha-Teshuvah (on repentance). Jerusalem: Mosad Ha-Rav Kook, 1985.

Orot ha-Torah. Jerusalem: Mosad HaRav Kook, 1985.

Otzerot Reayah. Ed. M. Tzuriel. Yeshivat Shaalvim, 1988.

Rosh Millin (mystical explanations of Hebrew alphabet, vowels, and cantillation notes). Jerusalem: Mosad HaRav Kook, 1985.

Shabbat ha-Aretz (on laws of the sabbatical year). Jerusalem: Mosad HaRav Kook, 1985.

Shirat ha-Rav (poetry). Ed. A. Haberman. *Sinai* 17, 1 (1945).

Tov Ro'i (on various Talmudic tractates). Ed. B. Teena, B. Elon, et al. Bet-El: Makhon Tov Ro'i, 1988.

Zivḥei Reayah (novellae on tractate *Ḥullin*). Jerusalem: Mosad HaRav Kook, 1985.

Primary Sources in English Translation

Bick, Abraham. *Exponent and Philosopher of Religious Zionism.* New York: Hashomer HaDati of North America, 1942, 32–47.

Bokser, Ben-Zion, ed. and trans. *Abraham Isaac Kook: The Lights of Penitence, Lights of Holiness, The Moral Principles, Essays, Letters, and Poems.* New York: Paulist Press, 1978.

———. *The Essential Writings of Abraham Isaac Kook.* Warwick, New York: Amity House, 1988.

Carmy, Shalom, (ed. and trans.). *Shevivim: Sparks from "The Lights of Holiness.".* New York: Department of Torah Education and Culture, World Zionist Organization, 1987.

Feldman, Tzvi, ed. and trans. *Rav A. Y. Kook: Selected Letters.* Maaleh Adumim: Ma'aliot Publications of Yeshivat Birkat Moshe, 1986.

Hertzberg, Arthur, ed. and trans. *The Zionist Idea.* New York: Doubleday Press, 1959, 416–27.

Jerusalem Organization. *Banner of Jerusalem: An Open Letter by Rabbi Kook.* London, 1919.

Landes, Daniel. "Aesthetics as Mysticism: Rav Kook's Introduction to *Song of Songs.*" *Gesher* 9 (1985): 50–58.

Merowitz, Morton S. "Judaism and the University Address." *Judaism* 19 (Fall 1970): 390–95.

Metzger, Alter Z. *Rabbi Kook's Philosophy of Repentance: A Translation of Orot ha-Teshuvah.* New York: Yeshiva University Press, 1968.

Naor, Bezalel, trans. *Orot.* Northvale, N.J.: Jason Aronson, 1993.

Noveck, Simon. *Contemporary Jewish Thought: A Reader.* Washington, D.C.: Bnai Brith, 1985, 95–124.

Sefer Ha-Yovel li-Keved Ḥaq Yovel ha-Shiv'im shel Peer Nedivei Yisrael, Yisrael Aharon Hari Fishel. "The Institute." Ha-Makhon li Drishat ha-Talmud u-Mishpat ha-Torah 'al Shem Harry Fischel, 1935.

Sokolow, Moshe. "Rav Kook on Shir ha-Shirim: A Study of Aesthetics and Allegory." *Texts and Topics in Jewish Studies* 7. New York: Department of Torah Education and Culture, World Zionist Organization, 1989.

Stitskin, Leon. "The Constant Prayer of the Soul." Introduction to *Olat Reiyah. Tradition* 3, 2 (Spring 1961): 211–16.

Yoshor, Moshe. *Saint and Sage (Hafetz Hayyim).* New York: Bloch Publications, 1937, 267–72.

Secondary Literature

Agus, Jacob B. "Abraham Isaac Kuk." In *Great Jewish Thinkers of the Twentieth Century,* ed. Simon Noveck, 73–96. Washington, D.C. Bnai Brith, 1985.

———. *Banner of Jerusalem.* New York: Bloch Publications, 1946. Reprinted as *High Priest of Rebirth: The Life, Times, and Thought of Abraham Isaac Kuk*. New York: Bloch Publications, 1972.

Amital, Yehuda. "The Significance of Rav Kook's Teaching for Our Generation." In *The World of Rav Kook's Thought*, ed. Ish-Shalom and S. Rosenberg, 423–35.

Ariel, David. "Rav Kook and the Mysticism of Political Renewal." Review of *Abraham Isaac Kook: The Lights of Penitence, The Lights of Holiness, The Moral Principles, Essays, Letters, and Poems*, edited and translated by Ben-Zion Bokser. *Judaism* 30, 2 (1981):250–54.

Arieli, Naḥum. "Aspects of Rav Kook's Practical Approach to Society and Culture." In *The World of Rav Kook's Thought*, ed. B. Ish-Shalom and S. Rosenberg, 156–86.

———. "Ha-Teshuvah be-Mishnato shel ha-Rav Kook." *Hagut* 3 (1979–1980):81–97.

Ashkenazi, Yehuda. "The Use of Kabbalistic Concepts in Rav Kook's Teaching." In *The World of Rav Kook's Thought*, ed. B. Ish-Shalom and S. Rosenberg, 149–55.

Atlan, Henri. "Etat et Religion dans la Pensee Politique du Rav Kook." In *Israel, le Judaisme et l'Europe: Actes du 23e Colloque des Intellectuels Juifs de Langue Française*, ed. Jean Halperin and Georges Levitte, 32–64. Paris, 1984.

Avidor, Shlomo Hakohen. *Hai-ish Neged ha-Zerem*. Jerusalem: Orot, 1962.

Aviḥayil, A. "Eretz Yisrael be-Haguto shel ha-Rav Kook." *Morasha* 10 (1975–76): 105–20

———. "Yisrael ba-Amim 'al pi Torat ha-Rav." In *Matitya*, ed. Aryeh Morgenstern, 191–209. Netanya: Yeshivat Bnei Akiva, 1971.

Aviner, Shlomo Hayim. "Maran ha-Rav Kook ve-Havdalah bein Kodesh le-Ḥol." *HaMaayan* 52, 1 (1981–82): 66–69.

Avineri, Shlomo. *The Making of Modern Zionism*. New York: Basic Books, 1981.

Avineri, Yosi. "Ha-Rav Avraham Yitzḥak ha-Kohen Kook u-Maga'av 'im Anshei Aliyah ha-Sheniyah ba-Shanim 5664–5674." In *Bi-shevilei ha-Teḥiyah*, ed. A. Rubenstein. Ramat Gan: Bar Ilan University, 1982–83.

———. "Meuravuto shel ha-Rav Avraham Yitzḥak haKohen Kook be-Parashat Retzaḥ Orlozorov ve-Hashpa'atah 'al Ma'amado ve-Tadmito." *Ha-Kongress ha-Olami le-Madda'ei ha-Yahadut*. Congress 9, sec. Bet, vol. 2 (1985–86): 133–38.

———. "Relations between Rav Kook and the Second Aliyah Pioneers." *Morasha* 4, 2 (Fall-Winter 1985): 27–34.

Avinoam, A. *Ha-Rav: Educational Program Devoted to the Late Rabbi Kook*. Jerusalem: World Zionist Organization, 1969.

Beery, Yehushua. *Ohev Yisrael bi-Kedushahi: Hagut Ruḥo ve-Siaḥ Levavo shel ha-Rav Avraham Yitzḥak ha-Kohen KuK*. Tel Aviv: Sifrei: Ḥ. Y. K., 1989.

Ben-Nun, Yoel. "Nationalism, Humanity and Knesset Yisrael." *The World of Rav Kook's Thought*, ed. B. Ish-Shalom and S. Rosenberg, 207–54.

Ben-Sasson, Jonah. "Mishnot he-Hagut shel ha-Rav Avraham Yitzhak haKohen Kook ve-ha-Rav Yosef Dov Soloveitchik; ha-Yesodot ha-Metodologiyim: Iyyun Mashveh." In *Be-Oro*, ed. Haim Hamiel, (1985–86): 353–510.

Ben-Shemmai, M. H. "Rav Avraham Yitzhak haKohen Kook: ha-Sofer ha-Mass'ai." *Mabua* 14 (1978–79): 119–41.

Ben-Shlomo, Yosef. "Shelemut ve-Hishtalmut be-Torat ha-Elohut shel ha-Rav Kook." *Iyyun* 33 (1983–84): 289–309.

———. *"Shirat ha-Hayyim": Perakim be-Mishnato shel ha-Rav Kook*. Tel Aviv: Katzin Hinukh Roshi, Galei Tzahal, Misrad haBittahon, 1989.

Bergman, Samuel Hugo. "Death and Immortality in the Teachings of Rabbi Kook." *Judaism* 7, 3 (Summer 1958): 242–47. Reprinted in *Essays on the Thought and Philosophy of Rabbi Kook*, ed. Ezra Gellman, 61–68.

———. "Prayer in the Thought of Rabbi Kook." *Conservative Judaism* 20, 4 (Summer 1966): 29–42.

———. "Rav Kook: All Reality Is in G-d." In *Faith and Reason: An Introduction to Modern Jewish Thought*, ed. S. H. Bergman, trans. A. Jospe, 121–42. New York: Schocken, 1961. Reprinted in *Essays on the Thought and Philosophy of Rabbi Kook*, ed. Ezra Gellman, 76–88.

Berlin, Meyer. "Rabbi Kook: An Appreciation." *New Palestine*, 28 March 1924.

Bernstein, Y. "Le-Oro." In *Ha-Reayah* (1965–66): 34–38.

———. "Mi-piv u-mi-Pi Ketavav." In *Atikei Nehalim*, 68–71. Nehalim. Yeshivat Bnei Akiva, 1974–75.

Bick, Avraham. "Homer ve-Ruah ve-Tikkun ha-Hevra be-Mishnat ha-Rav Kook." *Mibifnim* 33, 1 (1970–71): 107–10.

———. "Iyyunei Tefillah be-Mishnat ha-Rav." *Petahim* 11 (1969–70): 17–19.

———. "Moreh ha-Nevukhim be-Mishnato." *Sinai* 97, 1–6 (1984–85): 91–106.

———. "Netzah ha-Reayah: Perakim mi-Mishnat ha-Rav Avraham Kook 'al ha-Hayyim ve-ha-Mavet." *Peri ha-Aretz* 6 (1982–83): 46–61.

Bokser, Ben-Zion. "A Commentary on Rabbi Kook." Review of *Mishnato shel ha-Rav Kook*, by Zvi Yaron. *Conservative Judaism* 29, 1 (Fall 1974): 72–80.

———. "Hidden Meanings in the Writings of Rabbi Kook." *Proceedings of the American Academy for Jewish Research* 44 (1977): 19–27.

———. "Jewish Universalism: An Aspect of the Thought of ha-Rav Kook." *Judaism* 8 (Summer 1959): 214–20.

———. "The Poetry of R. Kook." *Conservative Judaism* 25, 3 (Spring 1971): 56–64.

———. "R. Kook as a Mystic." *Judaism* 24 (Winter 1975): 117–24.

———. "R. Kook, Builder and Dreamer of Zion." *Conservative Judaism* 19, 2 (Winter 1965): 68–78.

Bokser, Ben-Zion. "Rabbi Kook the Poet." *Conservative Judaism* 25, 3 (Spring 1973): 56–63.

———. "Rav Kook: The Road to Renewal." *Tradition* 13, 3 (1973): 137–53.

———. "The Religious Philosophy of Rabbi Kook." *Judaism* 10 (1970): 396–405. Reprinted in *Essays on the Thought and Philosophy of Rabbi Kook*, ed. Ezra Gellman, 89–100.

Brainin, Reuben. "Rabbi Kook: An Appreciation." *New Palestine*, 28 March 1924.

———. "Rabbi Kook: The Poet of Our Faith." *New Palestine*, 28 March 1924.

Bromberg, A. Y. "Ha-Rav be-Iggerotav." In *Ha-Reayah*, ed. Y. Rafael, 52–58. Jerusalem, (1965–66).

Carmy, Shalom. "Optimism and Freedom in R. Kook's Teaching on Repentance." *Morashah* 4 (Fall-Winter 1985): 22–26. Reprinted in *Essays on the Thought and Philosophy of Rabbi Kook*, ed. Ezra Gellman, 114–20.

———. "Rav Kuk's Theory of Knowledge." *Tradition* 15 (1974): 193–203. Reprinted in *Essays on the Thought and Philosophy of Rabbi Kook*, ed. Ezra Gellman, 101–13.

Cohen, D. "Al ha-Ḥinukh ve-Torat Eretz Yisrael be-Mishnat ha-Rav." *Morasha* 10 (1975–76): 96–104.

———. "Yesod ha-Kelalut." In *Ha-Reayah*, ed. Y. Rafael. Jerusalem, 1965–66, 10–19.

Cohen, S. Y. "Emunat ha-Kodesh." In *Ha-Reayah*, ed. Y. Rafael. Jerusalem, 1965–66, 110–20.

Cohen, Yedidyah. "Mitzvat Hava'at Bikurim ke-Semel le-Ideal ha-Hityashıvut ha-Ḥaklait be-Yisrael." *Shedemot* 71 (1978–79): 61–65.

Cohen, Yeḥezkel. "Ha-Maḥloket bein ha-Rabbanim Kook ve-Uziel zt"l 'al Mattan Zekhut Beḥirah le-Nashim." *Hagut* 5 (1982–83): 83–95.

Dreyfus, Theo. "Signification et Importance de la Terre d'Israel Dans la Pensée du Rav Kook." *Yod* 2, 2 (1977): 41–50.

Efrati, B. "Ha-Politika ha-Yisraelit be-Mishnato." In *HaReayah*, ed. Y. Rafael. Jerusalem, 1965–66, 214–236.

———. "Ha-Rabbanut ve-ha-Miflagot be-Yisrael be-Hashkafat ha-Rav Kook." In *Ha-Reayah*, ed. Y. Rafael. Jerusalem, 1965–66, 59–68.

———. *Ha-sanegoriyah be-Mishnat ha-Rav Kook*. Jerusalem, 1958–59.

Elfenbein, Israel. "Chief Rabbi Kook as I Knew Him." *Jewish Outlook*, June 1944.

Elimelekh, Moshe Giora. "Musag ha-Umah be-Mishnat ha-Rav Kook be-Hashva'ah le-Herzl, Aḥad Ha-am ve-Klatzkin." *Ha-Umah* 66/67 (1981–82): 23–33.

Elkins, Dov Peretz. *Shepherd of Jerusalem: A Biography of R. Abraham Isaac Kook*. New York: Shengold, 1975.

Englander, Lawrence. "Rav Kook's Doctrine of Teshuvah." *Judaism* 34, 2 (1985): 211–20. Reprinted in *Essays on the Thought and Philosophy of Rabbi Kook*, ed. Ezra Gellman, 121–32.

Epstein, I. *Avraham Yizhak Hacohen Kook: His Life and Work*. London: Brit Chalutzim Datiim-Bahad, 1951. Reprinted in *Guardians of Our Heritage*, ed. Leo Jung, 483–509. New York: Bloch Publications, 1958.

Feuchtwanger, O. *Righteous Lives*. New York: Bloch Publications, 1965, 142–45.

Filber, Y. "Beurim u-Mekorot le-Sefer Orot ha-Teshuvah." In *Ha-Reayah*, ed. Y. Rafael. Jerusalem, 1965–66, 121–36.

———. *Eretz ve-Shamayim: Pirkei Midrash be-Yahasei Adam ve-hevrah, Homer ve-Ruah, Hoveh ve-Netzah 'al pi Mishnat ha-Reayah Kook*. Jerusalem: Hamakhon le-heker mishnat ha-Reayah, 1982.

———. "Ha-Hinukh be-Mishnat ha-Rav zt"l." In *Matitya*, ed. Aryeh Morgenstern, 169–90. Netanya: Yeshivat Bnei Akiva, 1971.

Fisch, Harold. *The Zionist Revolution: A New Perspective*. New York: St. Martin's Press, 1978, 59–66.

Fishman, Y. L. haKohen, ed. *Zikkaron le-Nishmat ha-Rav Avraham Yitzhak haKohen Kook li-Melot Eser Shanim li-Petirato*. Jerusalem: Mosad Harav Kook, 1945.

Fried, Yohanan. "Hokhmat ha-Kodesh: Seder Ihud ha-Kelalot ve-ha-Peratot." In *Ha-Reayah*, ed. Y. Rafael. Jerusalem, 1965–66, 206–13.

———. "Iggerot u-Te'udot (mi-Tokh ha-Genizah)." *Sinai* 97, 1–6 (1984–85): 235–43.

Gallant, Batya. "Spirituality and Law in the Letters of Rabbi Abraham Isaac Kook." *Morasha* 4 (Fall-Winter 1985): 27–34. Reprinted in *Essays on the Thought and Philosophy of Rabbi Kook*, ed. Ezra Gellman, 133–44.

Gellman, Ezra, ed. *Essays on the Thought and Philosophy of Rabbi Kook*. Rutherford, N.J.: Fairleigh Dickinson University Press, 1991.

Gellman, Jerome [Yehudah]. "Aesthetics." In *The World of Rav Kook's Thought*, ed. B. Ish-Shalom and S. Rosenberg, 195–206.

———. "Between Rationalism and Mysticism: Review Essay [of Ish-Shalom, *Ha-Rav Kook: Beyn Ratzionalism le-Mystikah*]." *Jewish Action* 51, 3 (Summer 1991): 74–76.

Gershuni, Yehuda. "Derekh ha-Mahshavah shel Rabbenu ha-Gadol. *Sinai* 97, 1–6 (1984): 123–43.

———. "Mishnato shel Geon Yisrael ha-Rav Kook z"l be-Mahshavah ve-Halakhah." *Torah she-Be'al Peh* 27 (1985–86): 24–30.

Gewirtz, Leonard. "Elements in Rav Kook's Legacy." *Tradition* 5 (Fall 1962): 42–57.

———. "From Rav Kook's Vision of Redemption: 'Footsteps of the Messiah.'" In *Jewish Spirituality: Hope and Redemption*. Hoboken, N.J.: Ktav, 1986.

———. "The Writings of Rabbi Kook." In *Jewish Book Annual*. New York: Jewish Book Council of Jewish Welfare Board, 1960.

Glicenstein, Simon. *Mazkir ha-Rav; Kevutzat Maamarei Zikhronot 'al Rav Avraham Yitzhak haKohen Kook zt"l*. Jerusalem, 1972–73.

Goldman, Eliezer. "Rav Kook's Relation to European Thought." In *The World of Rav Kook's Thought*, ed. B. Ish-Shalom and S. Rosenberg, 139–48.

———. "Responses to Modernity in Orthodox Jewish Thought." In *Studies in Contemporary Jewry*, vol. 2, ed. Peter Medding, 52–73. Bloomington: Indiana University Press, 1986.

———. "Tziyonut Ḥilonit, Teʻudat Yisrael ve-Takhlit ha-Torah: Maamarei ha-Rav Kook be-ʻha-Peles' 5661–5664." *Daat* 11 (1982–83): 103–26.

Gruenwald, Itamar. "The Concept of Teshuvah in the Teachings of Maimonides and Rav Kook." In *The World of Rav Kook's Thought*, ed. B. Ish-Shalom and S. Rosenberg, 283–304.

Grundman, Zvi. "'Rosh Millin' be-Eynei Tzayyar." *Mabua* 17 (1981–82): 122–37.

Haberman, A. M., ed. "*Shirat ha-Rav*." *Sinai* 17, 1 (1945): 6–22.

Hadani, Yakov. *Ha-Rav Kook ve-ha-Hityashvut ha-Ḥilonit: Massaʻot u-Magga'im*. Jerusalem: Misrad ha-Ḥinukh ve-haTarbut, ha-Mahlakah le-Tarbut Toranit, (1979–80).

Hadari, Ḥayyim Yeshayahu. *Ha-Teshuvah be-Mishnato shel ha-Rav Avraham Yitzḥak haKohen Kook zt"l*. Jerusalem: Ha-Maḥlakah le-Ḥinukh ve-Tarbut Toraniyim ba-Golah shel Ha-Histadrut Ha-tziyonit Ha-Olamit, 1955.

———. "Mi-Pi ha-Shemuʻah: Torat ha-Beʻal Peh shel ha-Rav." In *Be-Oro*, ed. Ḥaim Ḥamiel, 33–48.

———. "Shenei Kohanim Gedolim (65 Shanah li-Petirat R. Zadok mi-Lublin; 30 Shanah li-Petirat ha-Rav)." In *Ha-Reayah*, ed. Y. Rafael, 154–68. Jerusalem, 1965–66.

Hadari, Yeshaya H. "Ha-Halakhah be-Haguto shel ha-Rav Avraham Yitzḥak haKohen Kook." In *Hagut ve-Halakhah*, ed. Y. Eisner, 57–71. Jerusalem: Misrad ha-Khinukh ve-ha-Tarbut: Ha-Makhlakhah le-Tarbut Toranit, 1967–68.

———, ed. "Mi-shemuʻot ha-Rav Avraham Yitzḥak haKohen." *Barkai* 2 (1984–85): 169–77.

Ḥamiel, Ḥaim, ed. *Be-Oro: Iyyunim be-Mishnato shel ha-Rav Avraham Yitzḥak haKohen Kook zt"l u-be-Darkei Hora'atah*. Jerusalem: Ha-histadrut Ha-tziyonit, 1985–86.

———. "Ha-Rav Avraham Yitzḥak haKohen ʻal ha-Semikhut bein Birkat Kohanim le-Birkhot ha-Torah." In *Be-oro*, ed. Ḥaim Ḥamiel, 73–86.

"Ha-Rav u-Mishnato: Musaf le-Tziyyun 50 Shanah li-petirato shel ha-Rav Avraham Yitzḥak haKohen Kook." *Ha-Tzofeh*, 15 Sept. 1985, 28.

Henschke, David. "What Has Happened to the Lights of Rav Kook?" *Morasha* 4, 2 (Fall-Winter 1985): 2–5.

Herschaft, Reuven. "Selected Works of Rabbi Kook." *Morasha* 4, 2 (Fall-Winter 1985): 35–37.

Hilewitz, Alter. "Le-Beʻayat Daʻat Mukhra'at be-Halakhah ve-Shittat ha-Rav Avraham Yitzḥak haKohen." In *Be-Oro*, ed. Ḥaim Ḥamiel, 121–52.

Hoffman, Joshua. "Rav Kook's Mission to America." *Orot* 1 (1991): 78–99.
"Hoveret Zikkaron le-Rabbenu ha-Gaon Rav Avraham Yitzhak haKohen zt"l" *Or ha-Mizrach* 15, 2 (1965–66): 65–120.
Hutner, Yehoshua. "Ha-Rav Avraham Yitzhak ha-Kohen 'al Pi Toledotav." *Sinai* 97, 1–6 (1984–85): 107–22.
———. "Malakh Hashem Tzevaot." In *Ha-Reayah*, ed. Y. Rafael, 92–101. Jerusalem, 1965–66.
Ish-Shalom, Benjamin. *Ha-Rav Kook: Beyn Ratzionalism le-Mystikah.* Tel Aviv: Am Oved, 1990.
———. "Religion, Repentance, and Personal Freedom." In *The World of Rav Kook's Thought,* ed. B. Ish-Shalom and S. Rosenberg, 373–419.
Ish-Shalom, Binyamin, and Shalom Rosenberg, eds. *The World of Rav Kook's Thought.* N.p.: Avi Chai, 1991.
———, eds. *Yovel Orot: Haguto shel ha-Rav Avraham Yitzhak ha-Kohen Kook Z"l.* Jerusalem: Ha-Histadrut ha-Tzionit ha-Olamit, 1985. [See previous entry for English translation of this book. In this bibliography, the titles and page numbers of individual articles in this collection are those of the English edition. Only those articles whose principal focus is Rav Kook are cited separately in this bibliography.]
Jung, Leo. *Guardians of Our Heritage.* New York: Bloch Publications, 1958, 489–509.
Kahana, Kalman. "Ha-Gaon Rav Avraham Yitzhak Kook ve-ha-Shemitah." *Ha-Ma'ayan* 26, 1 (1985–86): 10–15.
Kalheim, Uzi. "Be-er Meged Yerahim." In *Ha-Reayah*, ed. Rafael, 169–205. Jerusalem, 1965–66.
———. "Hakdamat ha-Rav Avraham Yitzhak haKohen le-Shir haShirim." *Niv ha-Midrashya* (Spring 1970): 101–8.
———. "Hesber Ra'ayoni le-Mattenot Kehunah be-He'arat ha-Rav Avraham Yitzhak haKohen." In *Be-Oro*, Haim Hamiel, 167–71.
Kaplan, Zvi. *Bi-Shepulei Gelimato: Mashehu 'al Maran ha-Rav Avraham Yitzhak haKohen Kook.* Jerusalem: Makhon Peri Haaretz, 1984.
———. "Le-Darko shel ha-Rav Kook be-Halakhah." In *Ha-Reayah*, 69–78, Jerusalem, 1965–66.
Karlinsky, Haim. "Al Tekufat Limmudo shel Maran haGaon Rav Avraham Yitzhak haKohen Kook be-Samargun." *Shanah be-Shanah* (1981–82): 389–98.
———. "Rabbi Kook: Reminiscences and Impressions." *Jewish Horizon*, November 1945.
Klein, Menahem. "Ikkeronot Tefissato ha-Ra'ayonit shel ha-Rav Avraham Yitzhak et ha-Halakhah." In *Be-Oro*, Haim Hamiel, 153–66.
Klonsky, Y. A. "Atzmiyyut ha-Adam." In *Ha-Reayah*, ed. Y. Rafael, 79–84. Jerusalem, 1965–66.
Kook, Zvi Yehuda. *Be'urim le-Orot ha-Teshuvah.* Jerusalem: Ha-Makhon 'al Shem ha-Rav Tzvi Yehudah ha-Kohen Kook zt"l, 1986.

Kook, Zvi Yehuda. "Ha-Torah ha-Goelet." In *Ha-Reayah*, ed. Y. Rafael, 8–9. Jerusalem, 1965–66.

Kula, Amit. "Yesodot le-Ra'ayon Torah ve-Avodah be-Kuzari u-be-Orot." *Bikkurim* 2 (1984–85): 66–81.

Kurzweil, Tzvi. "Ḥazono ha-Ḥinukhi shel ha-Rav Kook." *Kivvunim* 4 (1978–79): 23–32.

————. *The Modern Impulse of Traditional Judaism*. Hoboken, N.J.: Ktav, 1985, 109–16.

————. *Modern Trends in Jewish Education*. New York: T. Yoseloff, 1964.

Lamm, Norman. "The Essence of Rav Kook's Teachings." In *The World of Rav Kook's Thought*, ed. B. Ish-Shalom and S. Rosenberg, 10–12.

————. *Rabbi Kook: Man of Faith and Vision*. New York. Jewish National Fund, 1965.

————. "Rav Hirsch and Rav Kook: Two Views on Limudei Kodesh and Limudei Ḥol." *Gesher* 3, 1 (1966): 30–40. Also published as "Two Versions of 'Synthesis,'" in *The Leo Jung Jubilee Volume*, ed. Menahem M. Kasher, Norman Lamm, and Leonard Rosenfeld, 145–54. New York: Schulsinger Brothers, 1962. Reprinted in Norman Lamm, *Faith and Doubt* (Hoboken, N.J.: Ktav, 1966) and as "In Synthesis" in *Essays on the Thought and Philosophy of Rabbi Kook*, ed. Ezra Gellmann, 145–55.

————. "Torato la-Amitah." In *Yovel Orot*, ed. B. Ish-Shalom and S. Rosenberg, 1985, 19–20.

————. "The Unity Theme and Its Implications for Moderns." *Tradition* 4 (Fall 1961): 44–65. Reprinted in *Essays on the Thought and Philosophy of Rabbi Kook*, ed. Ezra Gellman, 17–36.

Landes, Daniel. "Aesthetics as Mysticism: Rav Kook's Introduction to *Song of Songs*." *Gesher* 9 (1985): 50–58.

————, ed. *Kook and Soloveitchik: Alternative Models for Jewish Education*. Coalition for Alternatives in Jewish Education, 1979.

Lewis, Justin Harvey. *Vision of Redemption: The Educational Philosophy of Rabbi Kook in Historical Perspective*. New Haven, Conn.: Four Quarters, 1979.

Lipshitz, Ḥayyim. "Ha-Ḥinukh be-Mishnat ha-Rav Kook." In *Ha-Reayah*, ed. Y. Rafael, 137–53. Jerusalem, 1965–66.

————, ed. *Hazon Yisrael: Pirkei "Orot" 'al Yisrael u-Teḥiyyato mi-Yesodo shel Maran Avraham Yitzḥak haKohen Kook*. Jerusalem, Ha-Makhon li-Drishat ha-Talmud u-Mishpat ha-Torah 'al Shem Harry Fischel, 1972–73.

————. *Hogim ve-Ḥozim: Maran ha-Rav Avraham Yitzḥak haKohen Kook u-Benei Doro . . . Masot Makhon ha-Rav Avraham Yitzḥak haKohen le-Ḥeker u-le-Hasbarah shel Mishnat ha-Rav Kook*. Jerusalem, 1965.

————. "Kodesh ve-Ḥol be-Mishnato shel ha-Rav Avraham Yitzḥak ha-Kohen Kook." *Bi-Tefutzot ha-Golah* 7, 3 (1965–66): 106–23.

————. "Maḥshevet ha-Ḥinukh be-Mishnat ha-Aḥdut ha-Kolelet shel Maran ha-Rav Avraham Yitzḥak haKohen Kook zt"l." In *Ḥinukh ha-Adam ve-Yi'udo* (1966–67).

Lipshitz, Ḥayyim. "Mishnat ha-Teshuvah (ba-Ḥasidut u-be-Maḥshevet ha-Rav Kook)." *Tzofeh* 5 (1966): 4, 6.

———. *Roeh ha-Orot, Shirat ha-Adam, Shirat ha-Teshuvah: be-Mishnat Maran Avraham Yitzḥak haKohen Kook zt"l.* Jerusalem: Ha-Makhon li-Drishat ha-Talmud u-Mishpat ha-Torah 'al Shem Harry Fischel, 1974–75.

———. "Torat Eretz Yisrael ve-Shabbat ha-Aretz be-Maḥshevet ha-Rav Avraham Yitzḥak HaKohen Kook." *Torah she'Baal Peh* 5 (1965–66): 25–39.

Lipshitz, Ḥayyim, and Zvi Kaplan, eds. *Shivḥei ha-Rav Avraham Yitzḥak haKohen Kook: Devarim she-superu 'al Maran ha-Rav Avraham Yitzḥak ha-Kohen Kook zt"l.* Jerusalem, Ha-Makhon li-Drishat ha-Talmud u-Mishpat ha-Torah 'al Shem Harry Fischel, 1979.

Livnah, Shmuel. "Perakim mi-Torat ha-Musar (Iyyun be-*Orot ha-Kodesh*)." *Sinai* 97, 1–6 (1984–85): 77–90.

Luz, Ehud. "Halakhah va-Aggadah be-Mishnato shel ha-Rav Kook." *AJS Review* 11, 1 (1986): 1–23.

Maimon, Yehudah Leib. *Azkarah le-Nishmat Avraham Yitzḥak haKohen Kook.* Jerusalem, Mosad HaRav Kook, 1936–38.

———. *Ha-Rav Avraham Yitzḥak haKohen Kook.* Jerusalem: Mosad HaRav Kook, 1965.

Mamlak, Gershon. "Abraham Isaac Kook: The Sacred Element in Zionism." *Midstream* 31 (December 1985): 21–26. Reprinted in *Essays on the Thought and Philosophy of Rabbi Kook*, ed. Ezra Gellman, 156–67.

Mirsky, Samuel. "Rabbi Kook: Sage and Visionary." *Jewish Horizon*, October 1945.

Moriel, Yehudah. "Ha-Tefillah be-Mishnato shel ha-Rav Kook." In *Be-Oro*, ed Ḥaim Ḥamiel, 49–64, Jerusalem, 1985–86.

Naor, Bezalel. *Hartzaot ha-Teshuvah: Sidrat Ḥamesh Hartzaot 'al Orot ha-Teshuvah le-Maran Ha-Reayah Kook.* Jerusalem, 1990.

———. "Rav Kook and Emmanuel Levinas on the 'Non-Existence' of God." *Orot* 1 (1991): 1–11.

———. "Rav Kook's Role in the Rebirth of Aggadah." *Orot* 1 (1991): 100–11.

———. "Rosh Millin: Mekorot ve-He'arot." *Sinai* 97, 1–6 (1984–85): 69–76.

———. " 'Zedonot Na'asot ki-Zakhuyot' be-Mishnato shel ha-Rav Kook." *Sinai* 93, 1–2 (1982–83): 78–87.

Navon, Yitzḥak. "The Way of Rav Kook." In *The World of Rav Kook's Thought*, ed. B. Ish-Shalom and S. Rosenberg, 8–9.

Nehorai. Michael Zvi. "Rav Kook's Attitude toward Religious Zionism." *Morasha* 4, 2 (Fall-Winter 1985): 6–10.

———. "Rav Reines and Rav Kook: Two Approaches to Zionism." In *The World of Rav Kook's Thought*, ed. B. Ish-Shalom and S. Rosenberg, 255–67.

———. "Ta'amei ha-Mitzvot be-Mishnat ha-Rav." In *Matitya*, ed. Aryeh Morgenstern, 211–23. Netanya: Yeshivat Benei Akiva, 1971.

Nehorai, Michael Zvi. "Al ha-Iyyun ha-Sikhli ve-al ha-Havaya ha-Elohit etzel R. Yehuda Halevi ve-ha-Rav Kook." *Morasha* 6 (1972–73): 82–88.

――――. "The State of Israel in the Teachings of Rav Kook." *Daat* 2–3 (1978–79): 35–50.

Neriah, Moshe Zvi. "Batei Midrash Beit Avraham be-Polin. (Mi-Yesod Dovekei Maran haGaon Rav Avraham Yitzḥak haKohen Kook zt"l, Ne'emanei Ḥasidut ve-Tziyyon)." *Itturim* (1985–86): 159–81.

――――. *Bi-sedei ha-Reayah: 'Al Demuto ve-Darko ve-Al Neemanei Ruḥo shel Avraham Yitzḥak ha-Kohen Kook.* Kefar Ha-Roeh, 1986–87.

――――. *Celebration of the Soul: The Holidays in the Life and Thought of Rabbi Avraham Yitzchak Kook.* Trans. and adapted by Pesach Jaffe. Jerusalem: Genesis Jerusalem Press and Feldheim, 1992.

――――. "Ha-Rav Avraham Yitzḥak haKohen Kook: Iggeret Hadrakhah le-Ḥaverei Beit Va'ad la-Ḥakhamim Be-Yerushalayim." *Barkai* 2 (1984–85): 217–22.

――――. "Ḥayyei ha-Rav Avraham Yitzḥak haKohen, Tekufat Yafo, Yemei ha-Aliyah ha-Sheniyyah: Pirkei Toldotav shel Maran, Gaon Yisrael ue-Kedushato, ha-Rav Avraham Yitzḥak haKohen Kook zt"l." *Moriah*, Tel Aviv-Yafo, 1983.

――――. "Maran ha-Rav zt"l u-'Benei Akiva." *Sinai* 97, 1–6 (1984–85): 186–96.

――――. *Mo'adei ha-Reiyah: Haggim u-Zemanim be-Haguto u-be-Oraḥ Ḥayyav shel Maran ha-Rav Avraham Yitzḥak Ha-Kohen.* Jerusalem: Moriah, 1980.

――――. "Rav Kook: A Portrait." In *The World of Rav Kook's Thought*, ed. B. Ish-Shalom and S. Rosenberg, 13–15.

――――. "Reiyah va-Ḥazon: 'Al Yaḥasei ha-Kavod Bein ha-Gaon Rav Avraham Yitzḥak haKohen Kook le-vein haGaon Rav Avraham Yeshayahu Karelitz ha-Ḥazon Ish." *Shanah be-Shanah* (1985–86): 191–204.

――――. *Siḥot ha-Rav Avraham Yitzḥak haKohen.* Tel Aviv: Moreshet, 1978–79.

――――. *Tal ha-Rav Avraham Yitzḥak haKohen: Lamed Tet Shenotav ha-Rishonot shel Maran ha-Rav Avraham Yitzḥak haKohen Kook zt"l.* Kefar Ha-Roeh, (1984–85).

――――. "Tefillato shel Maran ha-Rav Kook zt"l." *Shanah be-Shanah* (1981–82): 386–92.

――――. "Ve-Haya ke-Nagen ha-Menagen." *Morasha* 6 (1971–73): 64–67.

――――. *Berurim be-Hilkhot ha-Reayah.* Jerusalem: Bet ha-Rav, 1991–92.

Oyerbach, Rafael. "Ha-Rav Kook ve-Yaḥaso le-Shittat 'Torah im Derekh Eretz' ve-Ishehah." In *Be-Oro*, ed. Ḥaim Ḥamiel, 528–48.

Peles, C. Y. "Ha-Rav Avraham Yitzḥak Kook u-Maavak ha-Poalei ha-Mizraḥi' 'al Zikkato le-Hityashvut." *Morasha* 9 (1974–75): 81–83.

Peli, Pinḥas. "Ha-Rav Kook ke-Ḥelek Min ha-Sifrut ha-Ivrit." *Maariv* 19 October 1984, 27, 29.

Rafael, Shiloh. "Shittat ha-Rav be-Halakhah." *Torah she-be-al Peh* 27 (1985–86): 31–38.

Rafael, Yitzhak. "Ha-Rav Avraham Yitzhak haKohen Kook zt"l 'al ha-Dat ve-ha-Tziyyonut." *Sinai* 97, 1–6 (1984–85): 5–14.

————, ed. *Ha-Reayah: Kovetz Maamarim be-Mishnat ha-Rav Avraham Yitzhak haKohen Kook*. Jerusalem, 1965–66.

————. *Kitvei ha-Gaon Rav Avraham Yitzhak zt"l: Reshimah Bibliografit*. Jerusalem, 1937–38.

————. "Mikhtavei Gedolim le-Rav Avraham Yitzhak haKohen Kook." *Sinai* 80, 3–4 (1976–77): 77–102.

————, ed *Zikhron Reayah*. Jerusalem: Mosad ha-Rav Kook, 1986.

Raffel, Dov. "Erekh ha-Tehiyah." In *Be-Oro*, ed. Haim Hamiel, Jerusalem (1985–86): 292–308.

Ratzhavi, Yehudah. "26 Sheelot le-Yehudei Teiman." *Et-Mul* 5, 5 (31) (1979–80): 6–7.

Ravitzky, Aviezer. "Navi Mul Hevrato be-Mahshavah ha-Yehudit ha-Hadashah: Idea u-Metziut Enoshit be-Haguto shel Ahad haAm, Buber, ve-ha-Rav Kook." *Hevra ve-Historiya* (1979–80): 155–172.

————. "The Prophet Vis-à-Vis His Society: Idea and Social Reality in the Thought of Ahad ha'Am, Martin Buber, and Rabbi Kook." *Forum* 32–33 (1978): 89–103.

Rosen, D. "Kelim le-Orot." In *Ha-Reayah*, 106–109. Jerusalem, 1965–66.

Rosenberg, Shalom "Ha-Rav Avraham Yitzhak haKohen ve-ha-Tanin ha-Ivver: Orot haKodesh u-Mishnato shel Schopenhauer." In *Be-Oro*, ed. Haim Hamiel, 317–52. Jerusalem, 1985–86.

————. "Introduction to the Thought of Rav Kook." In *The World of Rav Kook's Thought*, ed. B. Ish-Shalom and S. Rosenberg, 16–127.

————. "Musag ha-Medinah ba-Yahadut be-Haguto shel ha-Rav Avraham Yitzhak haKohen Kook." *Sekirah Hadashit* 4 (1977): 34–38.

————. "Setirot ve-Dialectica be-Musar ha-Hevrati be-Hagutam shel ha-Rav Avraham Yitzhak haKohen Kook ve-shel ha-Rav A. S. Tameret." *Hevra ve-Historia* (1979–80): 137–54.

————. "Torah u-Madda be-Haguto shel ha-Rav Kook." *Mahalkhim* 8–9 (1974–75): 35–50.

Ross, Tamar. "Mekomah shel Torat ha-Tzimtzum ha-Lurianit be-Shittot ha-Rav Kook." In *Mehkarim be-Hagut Yehudit*, ed. M. Idel and S. O. Miller-Wilensky, 159–72. Jerusalem: Magnes Press, 1989.

————. "Musag ha-Elohut shel ha-Rav Kook." *Daat* 8 (1981–82): 109–28, 9 (1983): 39–70.

Rotenstreich, Nathan. "Harmony and Return." In *Jewish Philosophy in Modern Times: From Mendelssohn to Rosenzweig*, 219–238. New York: Holt, Rinehart and Winston, 1968. Reprinted in *Essays on the Thought and Philosophy of Rabbi Kook*, ed. Ezra Gellman, 168–86.

Schochetman, Eliav. "Al Shittat ha-Limud shel ha-Talmud be-Ikkevot Hazono shel ha-Rav Avraham Yitzḥak haKohen." In *Be-Oro*, ed. Ḥaim Ḥamiel, 87–120.

Schreiber, M. "Ha-Teshuvah be-Mishnatam shel ha-Rav Kook ve-shel Martin Buber." *HaDoar* 49 (1969–70): 619.

———. "Rav Kook and Martin Buber on Teshuvah." *CCAR Journal* 16, 3 (1969): 31–35.

Schwartz, Dov. "Ha-Zikah shel Shmuel Hugo Bergmann le-Mishnat ha-Rav." *Sinai* 97, 1–6 (1984–85): 225–34.

Schweid, Eliezer. *Ha-Yahadut ve-Ha-Tarbut ha-Ḥilonit*. Jerusalem: a-kibbutz ha-Meuḥad, 1981, 110–42.

———. *Ha-Yehudi ha-Boded ve-ha-Yahadut*. Tel Aviv: Am Oved, 1974, 178–92.

———. "Two Neo-Orthodox Responses to Secularization, Part II." *Immanuel* 20 (1986): 107–17.

Shafran, Y. "Darko ha-Ḥinukhit shel ha-Rav Avraham Yitzḥak haKohen Kook le-Or Iggerotav." *Bitzaron* 62 (1970–71): 86–93.

Shaharya, S. "Mishnato shel Eved le-Am Kadosh." *Ha-Doar* 53 (1973–74): 421–23.

Shapiro, Avraham. "Bein Shlomo Tzemaḥ ve-A. D. Gordon le-ha-Rav Avraham Yitzḥak haKohen Kook." *Shedemot* 69 (1978–79): 31–37.

Shapiro, David. "The World Outlook of Rabbi Kook." In *Samuel Mirsky Memorial Volume*, ed. Gersion Appel, 75–100. New York: Yeshiva University Press, 1970. Reprinted in *Essays on the Thought and Philosophy of Rabbi Kook*, ed. Ezra Gellman, 187–210.

Sharvit, Yosef. "Ha-Rav Kook u-Me'oraot 5689." *Sinai* 97, 1–6 (1984–85): 153–85.

Shatz, Rivka. "Emdat ha-Rav Kook bi-Sheelat ha-Teḥika ha-Datit bi-Shenat 1920." *Kivvunim* 33, (1986–87): 101–4.

———. "Reishit ha-Massa Neged ha-Rav Kook." *Molad* 6 (1973–74): 251–62.

———. "Utopia and Messianism in the Thought of Rabbi Kook." *Forum* 32–33 (1978): 78–88.

Shaviv, Yehuda. "Ḥataei Bereishit be-Mishnato shel ha-Rav Avraham Yitzḥak haKohen." In *Be-Oro*, ed. Ḥaim Ḥamiel, 19–32.

———. "Ha-Teshuvah ve-ha-Sifrut be-Mishnat ha-Rav Kook." *Mabu'a* 9 (1971–72): 185–95.

Shermer, Oded. "Hora'ah Contextualit shel Hagut ha-Rav Avraham Yitzḥak haKohen be-Shiurei Historiah." in *Be-Oro*, ed. Ḥaim Ḥamiel, 551–72.

Shragai, Shlomo Zalman. "Ha-Am ve-ha-Aretz be-Aspekloriyah shel Maran ha-Rav zt"l." *Sinai* 97, 1–6 (1984–85): 197–214.

———. "Ha-Kabbalah ve-ha-Ḥasidut be-Mishnat ha-Rav Avraham Yitzḥak haKohen Kook zt"l." *Sinai* 97, 1–6 (1984–85): 144–52.

———. "Ha-Rav Avraham Yitzḥak haKohen Kook zt"l 'al Hashavat Mekom Mikdashenu le-Am Yisrael." *Sinai* 85, 5–6 (1978–79): 193–98.

Shurin, A. B. *Keshet Gibborim*. Jerusalem: Mosad Ha-Rav Kook, 1964.

Singer, Zvi [Yaron]. "Ha-sovlanut be-Mishnato shel ha-Rav Kook." *Molad* 1 (1967–68): 665–86.

———. "The Philosophy of Rabbi Kook." *Ariel* 18 (1967): 5–18.

Skulsky, Shlomo. *Yehudim Mefursamim be-Torah be-Madda be-Mediniyut u-be-Ummanut.* Tel Aviv: S. Zimson, 1954, 257–63.

Soleh, M. Z. "Haguto shel ha-Rav Kook: le-Yom Petirato." *Amudim* 418 (1979–80): 409–11.

———. "Ha-Hashkafah ha-Monoteistit be-Mishnat ha-Rav Kook." In *Ha-Reayah*, ed. Y. Rafael, 85–91. Jerusalem, 1965–66.

Sperber, S. "Hemshekh ha-Dorot be-Mishnato." In *Ha-Reayah*, ed. Y. Rafael, 39–46. Jerusalem, 1965–66.

———. *Ma'amarot.* Jerusalem: Mosad ha-Rav Kook, 1978.

Steinsaltz, A. "Ha-Ba'ayatiyut be-'Orot haKodesh.'" In *Ha-Reayah*, ed. Y. Rafael, 102–5. Jerusalem, 1965–66.

Strassburg, Sarah. "Atzmiut ha-Adam etzel A. D. Gordon ve-ha-Rav Avraham Yitzḥak ha-Kohen Kook." *Daat* 12 (1983–84): 91–97.

"Symposium: Professor Rivka Schatz-Uffenheimer, Rabbi Menahem Fruman, Dr. Aviezer Ravitsky, Professor Shalom Rosenberg, Professor Nathan Rotenstreich." In *The World of Rav Kook's Thought*, ed. B. Ish-Shalom and S. Rosenberg, 443–88.

Tal, Shlomo. "Al ha-Tefillah: Hagut mi-Tokh Olat Reiyah." In *Be-Oro*, ed. Ḥaim Ḥamiel, 65–72.

Tamar, David. "Al ha-Rav Avraham Yitzḥak haKohen Kook be-'Alei Tamar.'" *Sinai* 7, 1–6 (1984–85): 215–24.

———. "Bein ha-Meshorer (H. N. Bialik) la-Rav (Avraham Yitzḥak haKohen Kook)." *Yediot Aḥaronot* 12 July 1985, 20.

———. "Ḥad Badoro: 120 Shanah le-Huladto shel ha-Rav Kook ve-50 Shanah le-Petirato." *Aviad* (1985–86): 399–405.

———. "Ha-Rav Kook u-Parashat Orlozorov." *Yediot Aḥaronot*, 16 August 1985, 21.

———. "Ha-Sofer ve-ha-Rav: Agnon ve-ha-Rav Kook." *Haaretz* 1 March 1985, 18.

———. "Iggeret lo Yedu'ah shel ha-Rav Kook bi-Shevaḥ Gevurat ha-Guf." *Yediot Aḥaronot*, (19 August 1977, 3–4.

———. "Rabbenu." In *Ha-Reayah*, ed. Y. Rafael, 47–51. Jerusalem, 1965–66.

Urbach, Ephraim. "The Uniqueness of Rav Kook." In *The World of Rav Kook's Thought*, ed. B. Ish-Shalom and S. Rosenberg, 131–38.

Ushpizai, Moshe Ben-zion haLevi. *Iyyunim ba-Sefer "Orot" le-Maran ha-Gaon Rav Avraham Yitzḥak haKohen Kook.* Ramat Gan: Otzar haTalmud, 1978–79.

Volk, Y. "Ne-um 'she-Lo be-Ito' o Ne-um 'be-Terem Et'?" *Ha-Universitah* 17, 2 (1971–72): 48–52.

Weiner, Herbert. "On the Mystery of Eating: Thoughts Suggested by the Writings of Rav Abraham Isaac Kook." *Oesterreicher* (1981): 329–38.

Weiner, Herbert. "Rav Kook's Path to Peace within Israel." *Commentary* 17, 3 (March 1954): 251–63.

———. "The View from the Root Above." In *9 and a Half Mystics: The Kabbala Today*, 291–326. New York: Macmillan, 1969.

Winer, Gershon. *The Founding Fathers of Israel*. New York: Bloch Publications, 1971, 225–238.

———. "Religious Nationalism of Rav Kook: On His Twenty-fifth Yahrzeit." *The Reconstructionist*, 24 March 1961, 17–21. Reprinted in *Essays on the Thought and Philosophy of Rabbi Kook*, ed. Ezra Gellman, 211–18.

Yaron, Zvi [Singer]. "The Concept of Tolerance in the Writings of Rav Kook." *Niv Ha-midrashia* 8 (1969): 8–37. Reprinted in *Essays on the Thought and Philosophy of Rabbi Kook*, ed. Ezra Gellman, 219–50.

———. "Kodesh ve-Ḥol be-Mishnato shel ha-Rav Kook." *Molad* 5 (1972–73): 155–68.

———. *Mishnato shel ha-Rav Kook*. Jerusalem, ha-Mahlakah le-Ḥinukh u-le-Tarbut Toraniyim ba-Golah, ha-Histadrut ha-Tziyonit ha-Olamit, 1974.

———. "Mystika ve-Sekhel be-Mishnato shel ha-Rav Kook." *Mabua* 9 (1971–72): 196–205.

———. *The Philosophy of Rabbi Kook*, English version by Avner Tomaschoff. Jerusalem: Department for Torah Education and Culture in the Diaspora of the World Zionist Organization, 1991.

———. "The Philosophy of Rav Avraham Yitzḥak Kook." *Jewish Life* 3, 1 (1978): 57–69.

———. "Rabbi Kook: Judaism and Modernity." *Shefa Quarterly* 1 (1977): 7–16.

Yosef, Gavriel. "Shivat Zion be-Haguto shel ha-Rav A. Y. Kook." *Gazit* 17–18 (1983–84): 393–408.

Zavieli, Binyamin. "Ha-Rav Avraham Yitzḥak haKohen Kook ve-Yahaso le-Sifrut u-le-Umanut." In *Be-Oro*, ed. Ḥaim Ḥamiel, 518–27.

Zevin, S. Y. *Ishim ve-Shittot*. Tel Aviv: Beitan ha-Sefer, 1958.

———. "Shabbat ha-Aretz." In *Ha-Reayah*, ed. Y. Rafael, 20–29. Jerusalem, 1965–66.

Zoref, E. "Ha-Rambam, ha-Maharal, ve-ha-Rav Kook: 'Al Nes Pakh ha-Shemen." *Sedeh Ḥemed* 15 (1971–72): 155–57.

———. "Ha-Tefillah ve-ha-Adam be-Mishnat ha-Rav Kook." *Maḥanayim* 109 (1966–67): 71–74.

———. *Ḥayyei ha-Rav Kook*. Jerusalem: Hotza'at ha-Sefarim ha-Aretz-Yisraelit, 1947.

Zuckerman, Yehoshua. "Art." In *The World of Rav Kook's Thought*, ed. B. Ish-Shalom and S. Rosenberg, 187–94.

Zuriel, Moshe. "Ha-Kodesh, ha-Nistar, ve-ha-Aggadah be-Haguto shel ha-Rav Avraham Yitzḥak haKohen." In *Be-Oro*, ed. Ḥaim Ḥamiel, 172–256. Jerusalem, 1985–86.

Index of Names, Terms, and Topics

In entries for proper names, we generally have followed common spellings rather than strictly adhering to the transliteration rules followed elsewhere in this book. We have omitted all honorifics from these entries.

Individual passages from Rav Kook's works appear in a separate index. Entries for works by Rav Kook in the present index identify only those pages on which a work is referred to without specific texts being cited from that work.

Index of Passages from
Rav Kook's Writings

There is no standard edition of the works of Rav Kook and no standard way of referring to his works. The editions of his works upon which this index is based are the ones referred to in the bibliography. When page numbers are given in parentheses under the entry *Arpelei Tohar*, these refer to the 1914 edition, which Benjamin Ish-Shalom uses in his article. *Tehumin* refers to Volume 1 (1980) of the Annual. Mishnat ha-Rav refers to a book about Rav Kook by Rabbi Moshe Z. Neriyah (Tel Aviv, 1980).

Arpelei Tohar

1 (1) [Ki-shem]: 187
1–2 (1) [He-Ḥutzpah]: 189, 246
2–5 (2–3) [Ha-Kedushah]: 182, 186, 187
5 [Ki-she-Yitaleh]: 248, 250
5 (4) [He-Hasharot]: 183
6–7 (5) [Tikkun]: 182, 52 n. 31, 281
8–9 (7) [Kakh]: 185
9 (7) [Ha-'Et]: 183–84
12–13 (9) [Ki-she-ha-Teshukah]: 185–86
15 (11) [Li-Feamim]: 200 n. 21
17 (12) [Ha-Kedushah]: 204 n. 71
18 (13) [Ha-Maḥashavah]: 197, 229 n. 19, 224
18 (13) [Yeshnam]: 201 n. 32
19 (14) [Ha-Instinct]: 185
22 (17) [Li-ha-Rambam]: 203 n. 60

23 [Torah:Bi-Torah]: 293–94
25 [Yenikat]: 293–94, 299
26–27 (19) [Kol]: 201 n. 28
27 (19) [Ki-Shem]: 195
28 (20) [Ha-Sigim]: 201 n. 35
31 [Anil]: 302
32 [Mekor]: 201 n. 31
34 (24) [Kol]: 184–85
42 (29) [Be-o]: 204 n.71
45 (32) [Le-'umat]: 187
46 (32–33) [Ki-she-ha-Haskalah]: 193–96
47 (33) [Eini]: 187
67–68 (47) [Mi-Tokh]: 188
86–87 (60) [Mekubalim]: 191, 201 n. 35
105 [Emunah]: 205, 210